THE BIGGEST MINING VILLAGE IN THE WORLD

A Social History of Ashington

by
Mike Kirkup

SANDHILL
PRESS

Twenty four hours a day
the winding gear keeps churning away;
up and down, round and round,
grinding the miners into the ground;
deep in the bowels of the earth,
where men eat coal, but never eat dirt;
in Ashington...
biggest mining village in the world.
(Extract from 'Wor Jackie' Musical by Mike Kirkup)

Dedicated to my parents, Lizzie and Jack Kirkup, who did as much as anyone
in formulating the history of Ashington.

ACKNOWLEDGEMENTS

The author would like to thank the many people who gave interviews and loaned personal photographs in the course of his research, all of whom are named in the text.

Cartoons are taken from the Ashington Colliery Magazine 1922-40 and from the Ashington Advertiser, courtesy *Ron.*

Many of the photographs were taken by old-timers such as Alf Jensen, Johnny Briggs, Pentland, Cud Stephenson, Jackie Laws, and Bob Johnson; more recently, photos are included from Mrs A Horn, Jack Wallace, Bill Harrison, Reuben Daglish, Brian Wade, and the scrapbooks of Ashington YMCA, Mrs W Barron, Mrs J Hindmarsh, Mrs G Davies, Mrs J Leithead, Mrs S Lyons, Mrs M Davies, Ross Miles, Jimmy Hill, Jim Slaughter, Bob Scott, T Hogg, Fred Bennett, Joyce Tinkler, and Jack Mather. (with apologies for any omissions)

Other photographs supplied by Newcastle Evening Chronicle and Journal, Wansbeck Council, and archives of Woodhorn Colliery Museum.

Thanks to the staff at Ashington, Bedlington and Blyth Libraries, and to Northumberland County Records Office, for access to old records and newspapers, also to Ashington Lions for contribution of old posters.

Calligraphy by Edna Ralph.

Front cover - Ashington Miners Banner at Woodhorn Colliery Museum
Back cover - Bobby Charlton at former Hirst North School, courtesy British Gas.

First published in Great Britain in 1993.
Sandhill Press Ltd.,
17 Castle Street,
Warkworth, Morpeth,
Northumberland, NE65 0UW

Designed by Sandhill Press, set in Times 10point.

© Mike Kirkup

ISBN 0 946098 30 1

Printed by Martins the Printers Ltd.
Berwick upon Tweed

CONTENTS

Anglo-Saxon origins, first schools and churches, getting down to business, Sheepwash Bridge collapses, Fifth Row's bleezin', Low Market Clubland, Talbots and Kirkups, the Duke of Portland, Ashington grows then goes to War, Hospital opens its doors, 1916 an eventful year, United Bus Company, Methodist Central Hall, the Laski letters, Lynemouth - a new model village, Fred Reed- poet, Hirst Park Modern, the Main Street in 1927, Ashington Institute, Ashington Mining School: the original NORCAT, town 'Going to the Dogs', medical men, dentists, another World War, local paper chronicles the War Years, the Italian connection, post-war emancipation of women, the year of '47, the year of '64, demise of the railways and Ashington newspaper, Ashington Grammar School goes comprehensive in 1974, pitmatic twang, town loses 'cloth-cap image' in the Seventies together with pit heaps, the Eighties and beyond with Sir John Hall.

Musicians, dancers, painters, Wallaw Pictures, Princess Ballroom mystery blaze, Ashington Operatic Society and Thespians, singers and more musicians, TV Top Town, 1957 Variety Cavalcade, Ashington photographers, Millican and Nesbitt, Ashington YMCA, Leek Shows, football, Milburns and Charltons, rugby, cricket, motoring, tennis, hockey, athletics, boxing, netball, cycling, billiards and snooker, professional running.

Jonathan Priestman and the Ashington Coal Company, children in mines, early living conditions, population and housing boom, working class pioneers, explosion at Woodhorn Pit, pitch 'n' toss, the 1926 General Strike, a public schoolboy's 1936 view, Mines & Rescue Brigade, the coal-leaders, the 1944 Bevin Boys, pits nationalised in 1947, a personal view, the colliery tankeys, Lynemouth Colliery fire, drop in manpower, pit heaps to go, the age of 'press-button' pits, Linton and Woodhorn collieries close, 1984 Miners' Strike, Ashington pit closes (1988) and entire colliery is demolished (1991).

Woodhorn Memorial. 1923.

Aſhington (t), which was one of the manours of the barony of Bothall, and now belongs to George Sandiford Crow, Esq. It ſtands on an eminence, well ſheltered with tall foreſt-trees; a fine view from it of the ſea, alſo of Seaton-Delaval, and Bebſide, through the openings of the plantations; the grounds ſloping regularly to a bank of oaks by the river Wansbeck, freeſtone rocks conſpicuos through them, under which is a fine graſs-area of a mile in length by the river, which for all that ſpace forms a moſt beautiful ſerpentine canal, a bank of oaks on the oppoſite ſide. On the weſt ſide of a ſtreamlet, called the Den-Burn, by a grindſtone-quarry, the river Wansbeck makes a flexure, where is a beautiful ſlope, now in tillage, ſhaded by ſpreading oaks and other timber on all ſides but to the ſouth, the river making another flexure a little to the weſt of it, croſſed by Shipwaſh-bridge, in ſight; a boat in it for a ſalmon-fiſhery. Mr. Crow's extent of ground by the river from within a ſmall fields lenght of the bridge, or the rectory-glebe, weſt, to the Stakeford, eaſt, is about a mile and a half, meaſured; thus beautifully chequered with wood, rock, and river-ſcenery; a foot-walk by the river the whole length.

"History of Northumberland - J. Wallis. 1769."

PROLOGUE

In the beginning was the Word, and the word was *Coal*. The Industrial Revolution shaped both the landscape of the North East and the lifestyle of its inhabitants. Prior to this, Geordie prosperity was reaped from the fertile fields that surrounded the tiny hamlets of Northumberland and Durham. Communities tended to be fragmented with workers huddled together for security into small pockets of agricultural feudalism under the jurisdiction of the Lord of the Manor.

But by the mid-19th century wealth was being measured *under* the ground in vigorous black seams, for where there was coal there was power. Not only power to fuel the forward thinking of George Stephenson and James Watt, but that other kind of power which degrades and corrupts, benefitting the privileged few at the inevitable expense and degredation of the masses.

Such was the background to *the biggest mining village in the world*, at one time servicing a network of collieries employing 9,000 men. A town whose national recognition only came about in the 1930s when a group of local men formed the now famous Ashington Group of painters; twenty years later the whole world knew of the pit community which spawned local legend Wor Jackie Milburn and later his illustrious footballing relatives the Charlton brothers, Jack and Bobby. But sandwiched between the bread and butter names of Milburn and Charlton is the red meat of the town: hard-working local folk equally deserving of accolade and recognition. In 1938, the managing director of the Ashington Coal Company, Ridley Warham, expressed the view that "Ashington has *always* been a home of surprises and we have long since ceased to marvel at anything." Strangers often ask: "How did a grimy little pit town become the hotbed of so much talent?" And looking at the long, impressive list of men and women who have emerged from the colliery rows to stride the glittering streets of excellence, the question is not an easy one to answer.

Today, Ashington is typical of dozens of similar mining towns scattered around the North East. The pits have closed one by one until only nearby Ellington Colliery waves the British Coal flag from its winding gear. Where once there was hustle and bustle as hundreds of miners enacted the ritual changeover of shifts at the Bothal, Duke and Carl shafts, small groups of men are now swept together against roadside railings on the corner of the garish main street. Once this had been the *Grand Corner*, as popular then as today, with the one major difference being that now, to these men, *work* is an archaic four-letter word. The eyelids may have blinked away the last remnants of coal dust, but the eyes still find difficulty in focussing on what lies ahead.

Using personal memories, archive records, and the reminiscences of many local people, I have tried to give a rare insight into the coal industry to the general public, many of whom will be learning for the first time of the conditions under which their fellow human beings lived and worked. I invite the reader to participate in the evolution of coal and a particular coal town, Ashington, comparing both as they stand today, barely marking time, in this the Year of Our Lord: Nineteen Hundred and Ninety Three.

FROM AESCEN-DENU TO ASHINGTON

"Travellers in the buses approaching Ashington will see spread out before them an untidy, sprawling town, flat and uninspiring, without character or beauty, notable chiefly for its architectural monotony." The Wansbeck Annual by Isaac H Binns, 1905.

Lying sixteen miles north of Newcastle, Ashington's strength was always destined to lie, not in historical buildings or scenic beauty, but in its people; men and women who worked long and hard in a glorious effort to put Ashington on the map. Yet the first village rarely interested cartographers; it was sparsely populated, consisting of a farm and four cottages on the site of the present Ashington Farm.

But the area's history goes back much further than that. True, the name *'Ashington'*, as it is spelled today, did not exist until 300 years ago. However, there is reference to an Essende as early as 1170. This was probably derived from Aesc, a Saxon invader who sailed his ship from Northern Germany, found himself at the mouth of the River Wansbeck, navigated as far upriver as was possible, then settled in a fertile valley near the river bank. As the Anglo Saxon for valley is 'denu' (dene), the first settlement became known as Aescen-denu, meaning *'the valley of Aesc'* or his sons. Another possible derivation of the name was that Aescen-denu meant *'valley of the Ash trees'* of which there are many in the area.

Hodgson, in his *History of Northumberland*, noted that the first recorded mention of Essende found in 1170 was inscribed upon a pipe roll. A pipe roll being the roll of the exchequer containing the pipes or annual accounts of the sheriffs and other officials.

In 1294, Sir Ralph d'Essenden gave to his son John and wife Isabella "the manor of Essenden." John eventually conveyed the title to Robert de Coventre whose daughter, Margaret, carried it by marriage to Robert de Fenwick.

In the same year, Robert Bertram, Baron of Bothal, at the Assizes in Newcastle, established his ancient right to take felons and hang them within his manor. The execution ground was close to the boundaries separating the parishes of Bothal and Woodhorn, and was known as Gallows House Close, later renamed Gallows Hill. (The field is a few hundred metres north of Portland Park, down what was once known as Piggs Moor Road).

The same Bertram gave to Hugh de Morwick, his brother in law, "Lands and services in Essindene by the old dyke which stretches between the tillage lands of Langhurst (Longhirst) and Hebre to the wastell, extending eastward, and to the whole plain as far as the place where Baln-we-sic (Wansbeck?) goes out of the wood up to the boundaries between Langhurst and Hulcham (Ulgham), and again as between Langhurst and Peggesworthe (Pegswood), and also between Langhurst and Bothal, as the fisherway goes to the east, except the culture which was called Threpfurlongs (Three Fields) which was then the lord's demesne land of Bothal."

From Stowes Chronicle, 1598, comes the news that "On the 13th of June, about VI of the clock at Shepewash there happened a tempest of lightning and thunder, after the which of a sodanie, came a great shower of haile, amongst ye which were stones of divers shapes."

Either side of Ashington were two hamlets with far more of a cultural heritage. Overlooking the river Wansbeck, Bothal Castle can be traced back to the 14th century, while St Mary's, which nourished the souls of Woodhorn Village parishioners, is the oldest church in Northumberland.

In 1821, Bothal Parish, which was known as the East Division of the Castle Ward, contained within its boundaries: Ashington, Bothal Demesne, Pegswood, Longhirst, Old Moor and Shipwash. The census of that year shows that 258 persons lived within the parish, with the majority (92) working in agriculture.

The other main industry of the locality, Ashington Quarry, was being worked in the early 19th century. Roland Bibby in his book *Bothal Observed* noted that it was one of the only quarries which could provide stones suitable for the new bridge which was about to be built to ford the river Wansbeck at Morpeth. Opened in 1831 to carry the Great North Road, this was destined to be called the Telford Bridge.

The Quarry was situated at Ship Wash (the furthest point to which keel boats could safely navigate) and let to a Mr Pattinson of North Shields at a rent of £20 per year. Pattinson finally recognised that the river Wansbeck was not navigable beyond a point where the present Sheepwash Bridge now stands, and he abandoned the scheme altogether.

The Reverend John Wallis in his 1763 *History of Northumberland* makes reference to a well within Ship Wash Woods, commemorated to the name of St Margaret:

About a quarter of a mile east of the grindstone quarry, under a bank of oaks and other trees, close to a hedge, is a sacred fountain, called St Margarter's Well, pleasant and soft to the taste, many of the small fresh water buccinae at the bottom; the north side faced with stone, natural and semi-circular, coated with moss, and a thin crust of earth in which the primrose and meadowsweet have taken root, emitting their pleasant odours round it in their season of flowering.

Another place destined to become part of Ashington was Hirst. Formerly Hurst - also called North Hurst - it derived its name from 'hurst' meaning wood. Part of the Hurst was in Bothal Parish, the remainder being in Woodhorn Parish. The first recorded mention of Hurst is in the *'Memoirs of the Missionary Priests of the Roman Church'* when it was observed that "George Errington, gent, born at Hurst, Northumberland, was put to death at York on the 29th November, 1536, for trying to convert a Protestant."

At the east end of what is now Woodhorn Road, stood a farmhouse with fortified battlements and a small tower. This became known as Hirst Castle, standing at the head of the now familiar Castle Terrace. Stone dykes surrounded the building as protection against cattle raiders and other ne'er-do-wells. Rumours that an underground escape passage led all the way to Bothal Castle were never verified. But there were several sightings of a miser named Jobson who lived next door, and was "given to wearing a long black and white plaid which streamed out in the wind when he walked."

It was, of course, the coal lying directly *under* the open fields sweeping down to the North Sea which proved to be the catalyst that had speculators scouring the Ashington countryside like prospectors in the Klondyke. But it was the search for gold of a different colour that spurred two Morpeth men, William Dickinson and Robert Short, to lease a strip of land near Stakeford.

Their first bore hole sunk at Pity Me, near Black Close, in February, 1842, proved abortive, and the two entrepreneurs were granted a second lease. But their first failure had cost them dearly, and they had to bring in fresh money from Messrs Wright, Turner, Lee, and Henderson.

A shaft was sunk in 1849 about one thousand metres to the north of their initial probing. A colliery was established named after the royalty holder, the wealthy Duke of Portland. The *Portland West Hartley Colliery* was sited on land close to the west end of Ellington roadends, becoming forever known as the *Fell-em-Doon* pit. The quaintly named Fell-'em-Doon is included in a comprehensive 1815 list of unusual Northumberland place names and on a map of 1825. A popular theory for the name's derivation was that a plantation had to be felled to make way for the new houses in High Market, and that trees were removed by workers being urged on by the villagers with cries of *'howay lads, fell-'em-doon'*. But since the colliery wasn't begun until 40 years after that map was drawn, perhaps a more realistic explanation is that the name originated as Felham-denu, meaning the *'valley of Felham'*, though who or what Felham was still remains a mystery.

Still lacking sufficient funding, the original group of speculators brought in two experts: Harrison and Carr, to work and manage the colliery with an option to buy shares. Both men took advantage of the offer, but by 1856 the shares were taken over by a businessman called Large, first name Carl, hence the later-named 'Carl' pit. In 1867 Jonathan Priestman and William Milburn became major shareholders.

FIRST SCHOOLS AND CHURCHES

As Ashington was still in the parish of Bothal in 1873, there was little discussion in finding a name for the town's first purpose-built educational establishment. The original 'Bothal' school can be dated back to 1725 when the Earl of Oxford, then owner of the estate which included Bothal Village, decreed that a school should be erected. The Archdeacon of Northumberland noted in 1727:

The present Lord Oxford hath built a school-house and a house for the master, at his own charge, near the churchyard. The Rev Mr Stafford, rector there, by will, the last year, bequeathed eighty pounds to be put out in interest by the Archdeacon of Northumberland, the interest thereof to go to the master of the said school for teaching eight scholars yearly. The sum is paid into my hands of the executors, 1737.

Gleaned by Roland Bibby from Bothal Church manuscripts are some of the Rules for the school which were still in operation in 1848 under teacher George Gallon:

The usual hours of schooling to be from 8am to Noon, and from 1 pm to 5 pm, except when darkness renders an early dismissal necessary.
The first hour in the morning to be devoted to religious instruction.
The Master is recommended to study the lesson beforehand, so as to be prepared with his principal questions.
Those children who may be capable, to be taught to sing, in a correct and pleasing manner, all chants, anthems, etc., which are sung in the Parish Church.
Spelling to be taught chiefly by dictation, writing out, and writing from memory.
Writing to be executed with much care and cleanliness.
Mrs Gallon to take charge of the whole school when her husband is called away to perform his duties as parish clerk.
Children who break windows to pay for the damage.

In response to Forster's Education Act which stipulated that all children should be given an elementary education, the Ashington Coal Company set aside a sum of money for the building of a new school in the High Market area of town. As education then was under the umbrella of the National Society, the name given to the new building was 'The Bothal National School'. The first entry in the school's log book was made by headmaster, S Latham:

1873, December 1st. Opened this school by admitting Scholars, and addressing the parents upon the duty and responsibility resting upon them with reference to the education of their children...and dismissed them...in consequence of delay of National Society's parcel of apparatus and books.

Not a very auspicious start for the new school to be declared open with one breath and dismissed the next through lack of basic equipment. This latter was corrected on December 8th, when Latham noted:

Went to Newcastle on Saturday, and traced the parcel of books from National Society to its delaying point.

Because the children were considered to be so backward, the Christmas holiday that first year was curtailed to only one day. The early curriculum consisted of: "Lessons in dictation, reading, handwriting, arithmetic and mental, colour and form object lessons, sewing, knitting, and musical drill."

The emphasis on music was substantiated by an account of the Infants School Concert which took place on Friday December 4th, 1897, declaring: "The Second Annual Concert was in every way (except the noise) a success."

Poor attendance was blamed as one of the main reasons for pupils' abysmal results in examinations. A fine of five shillings was imposed on parents who deliberately kept their children away from school. Some of the entries observed:

14-11-1879 Dr Cunningham visited the school today and informed me that miners' children had the fever.

22-3-1880 Closed the school for three weeks owing to measles.

20-5-1896 Very wet morning. 37% of children absent.

2-9-1898   The attendance has dropped very much today especially among the girls - the Flower Show is to be held tomorrow.

The problems of financing the school, with pupils having to pay a penny a week for their own tuition, were further compounded by the government's *payment by results* philosophy: if the pupils failed the State-set exams then money could be withheld. It was natural then that lessons tended to be learnt by rote so that answers could be chanted into the ears of visiting schools' inspectors. The three 'Rs' were drummed into children; handwriting had all to be of the same style, pens held at identical angles, and knuckles were rapped if this didn't happen.

Some of the earliest reports were damning. The first in 1875 noted that: "The children passed a bad examination." With similar condemnations in the next three years, the 1878 report hinted that government grants might be witheld if there was no improvement: "This grant is allowed with great hesitation, and after taking into consideration the peculiar difficulties of the school during the year."

The average attendance in those early days was 132. To control and teach that number, the headmaster had only a staff of one pupil-teacher and a monitor. Little wonder that Latham felt under stress when he wrote: "The school is very noisy, high in numbers and almost beyond my power from limited assistance."

By 1879 the school roll had risen to 296 pupils, and a new room was added for infants. Through other piecemeal additions, the school of 1890 consisted of six rooms, but a year later the school population, reflecting the boom in migrants to the town, had been boosted to a colossal 1,100.

Expenditure on salaries in 1887 was £939-9s-8d, and for books £126-11s-2d. By 1894 salary expenditure had risen to £1601-19s-5d, money spent on books dropped to £124-15s-6d.

By additions to the staff who drilled the unwilling pupils in set examination questions, the Bothal School began to get things right, at least as far as the HMIs were concerned. A favourable report in 1898, stated: *The School continues to be conducted in a very methodical and efficient manner. The lessons are exceedingly well illustrated, and the children's progress is very creditable.*

Some of the children who were singled out for praise that year included: Christina Wylie, 3 Six Houses; Harriet Bell, 1 Old Colliery; James Tilley, 10 x 9th Row; and John Craigs, The Store. The latter two boys went on to play a significant role in the development of the town, both as professional businessmen and councillors.

Fourteen-year-old pupil teachers taken on in the year 1893 included Maggie Johnson, Agnes McLachlan and Olive Bickford, their salaries ranging from £6-10s-0d to £10.

Ashington's first official teaching establishment was far from being a model school. What windows there were in classrooms were placed high upon the walls so that children would not be distracted by what was going on in the town; a meagre light was provided by oil lamps, and by the end of the day a grey gloom descended upon the class, causing an entry to be made in the log book: "Singing is now taken as the last lesson each afternoon as it is now too dark for anything else." Another discomfort was the cold. Successive headteachers complained of "badly burning fires". In 1884, a December log entry complained: "There is not one fire burning in the school today. The children and the teachers are benumbed with the cold."

Miss Elizabeth Joisce became a teacher at the Bothal School on October 1st, 1920. By then the school had been split between the sexes, with John Gray operating as head of the Boys, while Miss M Dixon was in charge of the Girls. Miss Joisce wrote in the school's 1973 centenary booklet:

I simply could not wait to get rid of the domination by the Boys School, and to establish the Girls as a separate entity. One thing that irked me was that a boy rang a bell for the whole school, and that our clocks were set at ten minutes slow by Greenwich Mean Time.

This strange time-keeping came about because the Coal Company decreed that their buzzers should always be set at ten minutes slow to accommodate men travelling by rail, and the school was compelled to follow suit.

Even though opened for the best part of 40 years when she arrived, the primitive conditions had only marginally improved. On her first day, as Miss Joisce was shown into a very long room separated only by a flimsy curtain, her heart "dropped with a thud." A community of mice had established themselves in the rookie teacher's cupboard. They were partial to the children's exercise books, nibbling away at the frayed edges. She ordered that mouse traps be brought in, and there was a squeal of delight each time one went off, accompanied by a string of eager voices chorusing: "Please, Miss, it's my turn to take the mouse out."

Corporal punishment played a significant part in enforcing school discipline. One day a girl called Lena Ward gave the new teacher a parcel saying that it was "a present." Inside was a leather taws with the school mistress' initials, EJ, cut in the top. The girl's father was a saddler at the Colliery - this was his way of saying: "Use it with my blessing." It was a parental attitude that was far removed from the line in the 1979 protest song: *"Hey, teacher, leave that kid alone."*

Miss Joisce found that the girls had been mechanically coached into practically every movement they made in the class. On the command 'Stand', they went through a complicated drill of "Turning, and putting the right hand on the desk behind; swinging both legs over the seat to the other side; then standing up, facing the front. On the command 'Sit', they performed the whole thing in reverse."

'Pen-drills' were practised until the children achieved a uniformity of intricate motions with their hands. Teachers were instructed that a line of copper-plate writing had to appear twice a week on the blackboard so that the class could laboriously copy it into their books. Children were never told the meaning of what they were copying. It was teaching without substance, not education, but a meaningless exercise in obedience.

Like all new entrants into the teacher profession, eager to change the system, Miss Joisce set about placing her own individual stamp on the girls:

I got the desks moved and piled up on top of each other, so that we had a small space cleared. On this minute square my class learned to do Country Dancing, one set at a time while I sang the tune. At this small taste of freedom and the unusual, my class was thrilled, but such innovations were not really approved by Authority.

Driven on by this small success, she thought that some form of sporting activity would get her pupils out of the gloomy classroom, and so the game of Netball was introduced. Initially played on the broken cement of the playground in ordinary footwear, she found that the greatest hazard was the ball ending up in one of the earth closet toilets which were only a few feet away from one of the goalposts. If a ball did end up in the disgusting mire, a giggling girl would tie a handkerchief over her nose, and leap in to retrieve it.

Miss Joisce called her girls' endeavour: The Ashington Spirit! "The children never gave up," she said, "it was an Ashington characteristic." This fine teacher later became Head of PE at the Hirst East Girls School, afterwards taking the headship of the new Wansbeck School which opened in 1932.

ASHINGTON RISES TO PARISH STATUS

With its tremendous growth in population and self esteem, it was thought seemly that Ashington should have its own place of worship and not have to rely on the church at Bothal village.

In March 1885, a meeting of parishioners was called by the Reverend W E Ellis, Rector of Bothal, who explained a scheme for the erection of a church at Ashington, which, it was proposed, should become a new and separate parish. The Duke of Portland had promised two acres of land on which to build the church, and a gift of five hundred pounds towards its cost. Ashington Coal company pledged a further three hundred pounds.

It was thought that the church would cater for about 300 souls and cost a little over one thousand pounds. Reverend Ellis said that if it was necessary to enlarge it to accommodate more people then double that sum would be needed. A building committee was set up at this meeting with the Reverend J Lightfoot as secretary.

Work on the church began in February 1886 to the design of W S Hicks of Newcastle; the first section of nave and chancel were completed in January 1887. It was then that it was named The Church of the Holy Sepulchre, after a church which once existed at Sheepwash. It was consecrated by the Bishop of Newcastle in June, 1887. The building was of stone in an early English and Norman style, consisting of chancel, nave of five bays, north and south aisle, and a western belfry containing one bell. An Altar Cross presented to the church on Easter Sunday, 1887, by the Reverend G L Butcher, was called the Ruby Cross.

In May, 1889, the Reverend J Lightfoot, formerly Curate of Bothal, was inducted by the Bishop of Newcastle as the first Vicar of Ashington. Up until the year 1892 the church had cost £2,806 and could accommodate 700 people. One of its most popular early custodians was the Reverend Sammy Davison who arrived in 1905 from Durham University. He was often spotted on the main street of Ashington, wearing his distinctive hat and, likely as not, riding his bicycle. He was a very keen oarsman and was patron and coach to a successful local rowing club for many years.

Parishioners at North Seaton Colliery in the 19th century had attended a small church dedicated to St Laurence, commonly known as 'The Tin Church'. On November 11th, 1897, came the consecration of the present St John's Church at Seaton Hirst, and the old building was later used to house pit ponies during one of the colliery strikes. By May, 1905, the parish of Seaton Hirst was formed and finally divided from the old Woodhorn Parish. In 1891, the population of the area covered by the church was 57, but by 1903 this figure had risen to over 9,000. Welshman, the Reverend Robert Owen Owen, took charge after crossing the river by Wheatley's Ferry from Cambois where he had been living. In a 1949 Church booklet, the Reverend J E Gordon Cartlidge who had joined Owen Owen shortly after the church was consecrated, wrote:

It is difficult to realise the arduous task of those early days - poor roads - ash footpaths - little lighting - pools of water all over the place where the ashes were worn down or washed away - open ashpits - earth closets - no Picture Palaces - only two hotels - many workingmen's clubs - no public park - no buses, and yet there was an amazing friendliness and cheery smile wherever we went.
It was a grand life, the work was constructive, we were creating something - the spiritual and cultural life of a new community - and we were trying to keep it Christian against tremendous odds. There were difficulties enough, but there were golden opportunities and we seized them. My work for four years at Seaton Hirst must ever remain the greatest impression in my long ministry.

ST GEORGE'S PRESBYTERIAN CHURCH

Presbyterianism in this area can be traced back to 1647 when the Reverend John Thompson BA, described as "a diligent preacher" took over the rectory at Bottel (Bothal). Thompson, later to live at Pegswurth (Pegswood), was "cast out of the Parsonage of Bottel" after which he "preacht to the plain country people." This happened during the Restoration period when he took an oath of loyalty to the Crown. Thompson was eventually "taken in the Bishopric and imprisoned in the common gaol at Durham for his non-conformity; the imprisonment brought him into a dropsy of which he died." He was still very well thought of in spite of some of his views: "He was a man of learning, a man of peace and an excellent preacher."

David Wise of Ashington has collated the following comprehensive information concerning the rise of Presbyterianism in this locality. He writes:

Following the Revolution of 1688 and the Accession of William III and Mary II, dissent from Episcoplianism in England and Presbyterianism in Scotland was permitted. In these more tolerant times, Presbyterian churches were established in Morpeth (1693) and Widdrington (1765). Since no presbyterian church existed in the parish of Bothal (which included Ashington) it was to these congregations that parisioners must have adhered.

Presbyterianism definitely took root, for in 1736, Bishop Chandler visited the parish and made the following note 'Families 107 - 10 Presb., one Papist'.

With the development of collieries in the district, Scots and Borderers settled in Ashington and the numbers of Presbyterians in the area grew. Initially, the adherents attended Newbiggin Presbyterian church, founded in 1861. Ralph Richardson, Session Clerk at Newbiggin, helped to start a Sunday School in the 'old Band Room' at the end of the Fourth Row. In 1886 the congregation moved to the Recreation Hall and then the Store Hall.

Young probationers acted as missioners for short periods, the first being the Reverend William Weatherstone. Hard work and fund-raising efforts resulted in the foundation of a church erected on a site opposite the Seventh Row which later became a garage. This first Ashington Presbyterian Church cost £400 to build. The Reverend Henry King was minister at this time.

On February 1st, 1898, Ashington became a sanctioned charge, and the Reverend Thomas Wardrop MA was appointed as the first minister at a salary of £160 per annum. Progress was such that it was decided to build a large church and hall. The old church was sold to the Salvation Army, and services were briefly held again in the Store Hall. The final cost of the new church built in 1899 was £1,800.

On the 24th January, 1917, during the ministry of the Reverend Robert Robertson BA BD, the congregation unanimously resolved to dedicate the church to St George. Twenty-five young men of the congregation lost their lives during the Great War, and a memorial tablet was placed in the aisle.

The church was a strong one and Scout and Guide Groups were formed in the 1930s. The 3rd Ashington St George's Scout Troop wore tartan scarves. In 1937 the old crossing spire, about fifteen feet high, came down in a snowstorm and was not replaced due to a shortage of funds.

During the second war, a forces canteen operated in the church hall, and the minister, the Reverend William Cutler BA (1935-44) acted as chaplain to a Scottish unit in the area, including the Black Watch and the 10th Royal Scots Fusiliers, who paraded to church headed by their pipe-band. A lectern was given in 1947 dedicated to the memory of Lt W L Carr DLI, killed in active service in 1944.

In 1972, the Presbyterian Church of England and Congregational Church in England and Wales united to form the United Reform Church. Discouraged by falling attendances - the Manse was sold in 1983 for £35,000 - and the difficulty of calling a minister, the congregation voted to form a Local Ecumenical Project, based at St George's, with the Station Road Methodist Church. The first lady minister in the history of the church was the Reverend Mrs V A Reed, BA, ordained in August, 1991.

SALVATION ARMY

A staunch and long-time member, George Elliott, former painter and ex-lecturer, has poignant memories of his involvement with the Corps. It was he who talked me through the history of the Salvation Army in Ashington. Ashington Salvationist appeared in 1899, using a church opposite the Seventh Row, but George was a member of the Hirst Corps which operated strictly within its own boundaries. This first entry in the Hirst log book shows that it started on September 27th, 1924:

Opened as a society this day Lt. Col. Brown, assisted by Adj. Whittaker, Newbiggin and Alnwick officers. Ashington and Newbiggin bands were also present. Officers in charge Capt. Harlow and Lts. Perrochet and Richards. After a short service the key was turned by John Ritson JP of North Seaton. There was a very successful tea held in the Co-operative Hall, Hawthorn Road.

A year later, Lt. Lee joined the Hirst Corps, she was destined to become the wife of one of the SA's most memorable leaders, General Coutts. Their first hall, little more than a wooden shack, was in Milburn Road. It was noted by their log keeper on November 13th, 1924 that although 225 Almanacks were sold *"I should think 300 could be easily disposed of."*

A newspaper cutting for March, 1925, shows that Adj. Booth, daughter of the founder General Booth, paid a visit to the Milburn Road Hut where a public tea was held at 3.45pm. VIPs present included local MP G.H.Warne and Miss Irene Ward who was later to become Labour MP for Tynemouth, and a Dame of the British Empire. The scribe observed that "The accommodation was scarely sufficient and people were being turned away. I should try for the Central Hall (opened the year before) as it seats 1,110."

On July 14th, 1925, a children's outing was arranged to Longhirst Hall, but it rained incessantly and, according to the writer "They were compelled to return at tea-time as there was no shelter. That ought to be considered in future." In September, 1925, the Hirst Corps celebrated its first birthday by uniting with the bands of Ashington, Bedlington and Newbiggin for a Massed Festival at the Central Hall which was lent free of charge.

In July, 1926, it was noted that *"Owing to the strike we could not take the children away. I had a Field Day with them in a field owned by Mr. Gray. We had an enjoyable time."*

December, 1926, *"We worked a good few streets three nights before Christmas, commencing at 7pm until 9pm. Started at Garden City and finished in Rosalind Street. On New Year's Eve we ended up in Elder Square, raising £5.7s.6d."*

January, 1927: *"Self Denial Effort; this was a great struggle owing to the strike and coal depression. Target fixed was £70, and with a big struggle we raised £51.10s.0d."*

December 26th, 1927: *"On Boxing Day gave a dinner to 1,500 poor children in the Princess Ballroom. The farm at Ashington Colliery gave half a ton of potatoes and half a ton of swedes; W. Burgess of the White Shop Butchers very kindly gave large weights of meat; Mr Scott, Police Superintendant, donated five pounds for same; and Walter Lawson of Wallaw Pictures gave six pounds for puddings. Each child had a toy and an orange."*

Cottage Meetings were held on October 3rd, 1934, at the following houses:

Mrs Picton, 17 South Villas   Mrs J Turnbull, Laburnun Terrace

Mrs Evans, Pont Street   Mrs Purdy, Elder Square

Mrs Charlton, 17 Rosalind Street

Leaders of the Hirst Corps changed at regular intervals, averaging between one and two years. Captain Liptrott took over in May 1940, full of enthusiasm, writing *"Throughout the weekend we felt the power of God in our midst. Believing for great things at Hirst."*

He had, however, become somewhat disillusioned three months later when he observed: *"Commenced by faith to repair hall and paint it. The Brothers worked hard. We managed to pull off the old roofing and put a new felt on, also tar the whole building. The hall was in a shocking state, a disgrace to all, a nightmare."*

That particular nightmare came to an abrupt end on January 21st, 1944, when Captain Liptrott noted: *"The hall has been destroyed by fire. A great loss. The Saturday night meeting was held in the 7th Avenue church...the meeting on Sunday was held in the Hawthorn Road Methodist Church."*

Just over five hundred pounds was realised from their Insurance Fire Claim, and over the next decade the Hirst Corps used many venues including Thwaites Chapel, and the Co-operative Hall on Milburn Road. They eventually merged with the Corps from East Villas which was formed in 1934, changing their name to the Ashington Central Corps. On June 27th, 1951, a log entry states *"Local Officer meeting to discuss the possibilities of the Corps buying Sycamore Street Methodist Church. Locals and COs went to look at these buildings and it was felt that it be the very suite of buildings for our Army activities in the district. The cost of these buildings meets with our cash and will enable us to have a suite of buildings of our own."*

More than 40 years later, the Ashington Central Corps of the Salvation Army is still carrying out its good deeds from that same building, presently (1992) under the leadership of Capt. Squirrell.

ADVENT OF ROMAN CATHOLICS

The Catholic population of Ashington in 1890 was neglible, made up mostly of Irish navvies brought in to build the roads knotted loosely around the sprawling town. Without a church of their own, they travelled to either Bedlington or Morpeth to be baptised, hear Mass, get married, and to be buried. A group of like-minded men which included: Edward Hennessey, James Ellingworth, John McDonald, Patrick Davitt, Michael Kelly, and J Broderick, met in the old Recreation Hall. Their quest: to find a priest, then build a church and a school. They arranged to meet William Sample, agent to the Duke of Portland, based at Bothal Castle, with a view to obtaining a site on which to build a church. Having made out a very strong case, the delegation were asked by Sample why they had not brought a parish priest with them.

Once the circumstances were explained to him, Sample said that he would be willing to enter into further discussions if they could arrange for a priest who was willing to take on the Ashington parish to accompany them to the next meeting. Fr Placid O'Hear was sent to Morpeth in 1892 with the brief of establishing a Mission for the Ashington Catholics. His first priority was to find a place in which to say Mass. One building they looked at was a very old noncomformist chapel which was on the market. It was judged to be unsuitable. Fr S W Fossato, the original priest sent to organise the parish, wrote:

The only other place was a large public house called the Portland Arms, a building which had not been long opened. There was what I considered a grand public hall for the use of the miners' gatherings, especially on Saturday nights. I interviewed the manager, and we agreed I might have the use of the hall on Sunday mornings if I could find someone on the spot to clean and prepare the place on the previous Saturday night. At this point my drives to Ashington were broken off by eight weeks of Arctic weather, with depth of snow which made me a prisoner at Morpeth. When the snow disappeared so did I, to Cleator Moor, leaving the parish in the capable hands of Fr O'Hear.

O'Hear cleared the first hurdle when the Co-operative Store Hall was booked. Every Saturday night it was used for dancing, and every Sunday morning a couple of the faithful had to make the place respectable. John Broderick noted:

We had to sweep the floor, move out all the benches from round the room into their proper places, light a fire, and fix up the altar on the small stage which was used for concerts.
When Fr. O'Hear applied for the hall, another group was using it on Sunday mornings for a religious ceremony, but they totalled only about six souls, so the manager offered them a smaller room on the same landing, and let the hall to us; then the fun began.
The other party thought they had been badly used, and appealed to the committee to have the Catholics removed. However, things were finally settled in our favour, and the small party occupied the room across the landing, singing vigorously all the morning and disturbing our congregation.

Another obstacle to overcome was that of hearing Confessions. These had to be heard on Sunday mornings before Mass, but there were so many that they were transferred to the house of John Bell (destined to become the first manager of St Aidan's school) on a Saturday night.

The question of building a school arose, and Fr O'Hear organised bazaars, sales of work, and teas, with very profitable results. On one occasion, hearing that a very influential man was coming to open a bazaar, the priest arranged for him to be picked up by cab from Morpeth Station. It was taken for granted that a very handsome cheque would ensue, but this turned out to be wishful thinking as the gentleman left without once putting his hand into his pocket.

One fruitful source of income was the 'sixpenny tea'. The tea was provided by each woman in her own house, and the others, who were her guests, each paid sixpence. Even if a lady did not attend she was still liable to pay her dues. The proceeds were used to buy materials to make garments for sale in the bazaar.

The men contributed, too. They knew that the new priest had to be supported, and it was decided to pay one shilling to the priest and tuppence towards the building fund, each fortnight. These donations were 'kept off the wages check' at the colliery.

By 1893 the Catholics of Ashington had grown to about two hundred and fifty, and were fast becoming an important body. They sought help from the parish priest at Bedlington who brought some of the children of his parish to Ashington to give a performance of a cantata to help swell funds. Dances, concerts, and lotteries were run. The pressing need was to obtain money - fast.

Fr O'Hear began negotiations for the building of a school, his philosophy being that if the child was caught quickly enough then the parents would automatically follow. The first problem of finding a site had already been overcome by Sample, on behalf of the Duke, making available an acre of land next to what became the Miners' Theatre. Raising the money was more difficult. The priest went cap in hand to his Bishop. But the money was not given immediately as it was thought that the congregation was too small to be able to pay the interest and support the mission.

Eventually, in the middle of 1893, money was made available, and the building contract was given to a Mr McCann, an Irishman. The Catholics' first milestone had been reached, progress had been made, and soon they would have a place of their own at last.

The foundation stone of St Aidan's School was laid on Saturday, September 22nd, 1894. The ceremony began at 3 pm with the Ashington Duke Pit Brass Band playing a selection of music. Fr O'Hear escorted the Mayor and Mayoress of Newcastle on to a platform erected around the spot where the stone was to be placed. The united choirs of Ashington, Morpeth and Blyth, took up their positions beside the band, and all was ready for the clergy and attendants to march in procession to the platform. They were: The Very Reverend Prior O'Neill, OSB, of St Edmund's, Douai; the Very Reverend Benedict Tickell, OP; Fr Burchall, Cowpen; Fr Mackinlay, OSB, Blyth; and Fr Bamford, OSB.

Fr O'Hear presented the Mayoress with a silver trowel on which was inscribed: 'Presented to the Mayoress of Newcastle, Mrs Stephen Quinn, on laying the foundation stone of new Catholic Schools at Ashington, 22nd September, 1894'. A bottle containing coins of the realm, copies of newpapers of that date, and an official document was deposited in a cavity. The Mayoress with her new trowel, spread the mortar, the stone was lowered into position, and, with a "dainty wooden mallet," tapped each of the four corners, and declared it "duly laid."

On February 18th, 1895, the school was opened when the Head Mistress Miss E Thompson and her assistant teachers Miss M Thompson - they were sisters - and Miss M McCarthy, arrived to find 66 children waiting to be received; by the end of the week the number had risen to 110, many of whom were non-Catholics. The Thompson sisters had to travel by train from Morpeth each morning. It was reported in the church magazine:

Their journey from Hirst station to the school was along a country lane with a hedge-row at each side and no footpath. The new school was the first building on the left from the station. The houses in the Seventh Row were the first buildings on the right. The road leading to the school (Park Road) was entered through a gate and was in a very ploughed-up condition.

The original school consisted of one very long narrow room, undivided by partitions. At the north end was "a big gallery for infants," but this was soon removed to the south end, as the infants were thought to require more light. The school was furnished with long desks, "having movable tops to form seats suitable for church purposes," as the school was transformed into a church on Sundays. There was very little but the bare necessities to begin with, no pictures and very little apparatus. But the parents rallied around to make the place look a little more lived in - one woman sent a cage of white mice, while others provided pictures and plants.

In order to help pay off the debt on the school, the children performed a 'cantata' every year. The first took place in the Portland Hotel; and after the Miners' Theatre was built the management there kindly gave the school one night annually for the children's performance. This continued until curtailed by war in 1914.

KATHLEEN NEWTON'S parents were typical of the Catholic newcomers to Ashington at the beginning of the 20th century. Her father was a butcher by trade, but soon began work as a cutterman down the pit. Born in 1904, Kathleen remembers:

We lived at Ellington first when I was very small. Visits to Ashington for shopping were always made on the pit tankey. The seats were filthy and we had to carry a newspaper to sit on for each visit.

The nearest Catholic school was at Ashington so the family moved to a house in Woodhorn Road. The two Miss Thompsons, Elizabeth and Margaret, ran the school, Lizzie being head of the big school while Margaret looked after the infants. We were all taught in the main building beside the church.

I didn't gain a scholarship from there, but I boarded out at St Anthony's in Durham until I was eighteen. It was there I passed my certificate and became a pupil teacher back at St Aidan's in Ashington when I was eighteen.

I felt very isolated on my first day, and was very glad when Hannah Bell, about twelve years older than me, took me under her wing. She was a local, but Dolly Bell - no relation - originally came from Manchester. The one thing which brightened up my day was that I was able to wear my hair up for the very first time. I thought I looked very grown up.

My impression of the children was that there was great poverty in the town. Many children came to school barefoot and were sent home through no fault of their own. There were very few books - I only had a scratchy slate in my own schooldays - but the children in my class had to take very good care of any we did have.

To give us some more room, the Infants took over the Hut next to the churchyard. I thought it was a bit harsh on the people who used it, scouts etc, but still welcomed the extra space. Hannah Bell was put in charge of the Infants, and when both the Thompson sisters left, Mr McGough took over as head at the big school. Maisie White, later Mazzolini, came and took over the scholarship class, that's when we began to get a lot of children into Grammar School.

There was no such thing as a staff meeting. In the early days Lizzie Thompson just brought us a piece of paper and said: "This is what we're doing." We had a timetable to get through, but if the teacher before you hadn't covered the syllabus you spent most of your time getting the children to catch up. We didn't even have a kettle to make ourselves a cup of tea at the beginning. Later on we did manage to get one, but the only break was at playtime when the children had to have that long walk up to the big school playground.

My first wage was two guineas, and even that was brought around in cash by the priest. All the children paid a penny a week into the School Fund, and we teachers had to pay as well.

I worked as a teacher at St Aidans for 40 years and retired in 1964. I've had a lovely life, travelled the world, seen and done everything that I wanted without any unfulfilled ambitions. I am very content.

THE 'NORTH' SCHOOL

Another of Ashington's oldest surviving teachers is Miss **VIDA SAMPLE**. She says with a twinkle in her eye:

I go back to the beginning of the century, but I never tell anyone how old I am!

I was born at number 9 Chestnut Street when there was hardly any houses from there until you came to the Hirst Castle. And on the other side of Woodhorn Road were only two large houses built for Dr Trotter and Dr Goldie. No other building existed until you reached Woodhorn Colliery where there were ten houses, built for colliery officials, one of whom was my father who was the foreman blacksmith.

Woodhorn Colliery where we eventually settled was a long way off any of the schools in Ashington. But when it came time for me to begin school I went to the North. It was a long walk with no houses except for the Hirst Castle on that side of the road. We - my sister Rhoda and I, Hilda Mawson, and Cissie Easton - then turned into Hawthorn Road and along the Second Avenue to the school. One day the road from the Castle was absolutely flooded, and after we came home for dinner - which we had to do every day - we couldn't get back for the afternoon session. We wore little pinafore dresses, and if they got wet there was nowhere in school to dry clothes, although they did have big hot-water pipes.

The North then was a senior and junior school, with the girls segregated from the boys. Junior girls and boys were downstairs, and senior boys and girls upstairs; the infants in another building were mixed, and the playgrounds were all fenced off. The teacher in charge upstairs was Miss Heslop, but when I started in the infants the headteacher was Miss Baxter. Head of juniors was a Welsh lady called Miss Williams. She often attended St John's Church at Seaton Hirst, and her marvellous voice was like a whole choir singing. One of her favourite songs which she taught us was 'Killarney'. She got me to write a letter while I was in Standard I to someone who lived in Manchester whom she knew. My mother and father helped me out, describing everything about the school so that I could write it down.

As children we were taught everything including printing; we had writing books and we were taught how to join up our printed letters. We moved up through the classes until reaching Standard IV, and that's when we went upstairs. Mrs Grice was in charge of that class. It must have been 1913 because Hirst East had just opened, and our class was transferred along to the new school, which was much easier for me, being closer to home. Miss Heslop who had been head at the North got the headship at the East, and Miss Wiseman got the head's job at the North school.

The East was absolutely modern. It was a single storey building with better toilets - still outside - but much better, and they had a Cookery centre. The caretaker at the East, whose house adjoined the centre, was a Mr Stephenson, the father of photographer, Cuthbert Stephenson, and grandfather of Trevor, now a doctor at Newbiggin.

I think I taught longer than anyone else in Ashington - forty-five years! We had a good party that day when I left at the Queen's Head in Morpeth. I got a letter from the director of education, saying that he was so sorry that I never got a headship. But I'd never applied! I'd had one after another telling me that I should apply for this post or that post, even HMIs. I was asked if I would apply for Cissie Joisce's post in charge of PE at Hirst Park when she left. I was asked to put in for the headship of the South School, too.

There were so many highlights in my teaching career. We were busy with so many different things. I took folk dancing a lot with my girls. I entered them for the North of England Tournament which was held at Newcastle's City Hall, and we used to win. And then Keep Fit came along after that. If someone was absent somewhere, I would be asked; "Will you take my class?" Miss Alexander, PE advisor at County Hall, would ring and say; "Will you save my life and take a class at Amble?" What she hadn't told me what it was a whole session, not just one class. But I had a great time in teaching ... a lovely time.

A 1928 timetable for the Ashington New Hirst Council School (the North) gives a breakdown of time spent on each subject. Top of the list with 270 minutes was Arithmetic, then in descending order came Reading (240), Composition (140), and Religious Instruction (125). Bottom of the league was Physical Education with 60 minutes per week.

THE 'SOUTH' SCHOOL

Ashington New Hirst South Council School took its first intake of pupils on 12th October, 1908. It was then split into three: a Boys' school with 450 pupils under the headship of Mr Harrison Clough; a Girls' school with 351 pupils led by Miss Isabella Mathewson (as a 14-year-old she had been a pupil/teacher at Bothal School in 1893); and a Mixed Infants & Junior of 171 boys and 152 girls whose teachers included Isabella Burgess and Jessie Sproat. Christina Haynes was appointed head on June 1st, 1912.

Only six months after opening, the school had to be closed for three weeks because of a measles epidemic. Some other revealing items, collated from an early log book by ex-pupil Colin Wanless, show how schools were directly affected by what was happening in the community in those days:

22/5/1911	Closed this afternoon. A circus is visiting the town.
2/2/1912	Very stormy morning. Teachers and pupils arrived with wet feet. So did not mark register - sent children home.
12/2/1913	School closed at 12 am to allow children to see aeroplane.
28/8/1913	School closed at 2.05 pm, owing to official opening of New East School.
31/10/1916	School closed. The premises have been requisitioned by the Military.
4/6/1917	We resume occupation of South School
25/1/1918	A very poor attendance again. The necessity for children to seek and stand waiting for food supplies.
3/7/1918	Almost half the school (514) absent through Spanish Influenza.
26/8/1918	Class V has 84 children under one teacher.
30/6/1919	The men have laid the Pit idle till Wednesday. The 'Mob' tried to shut the school.
31/8/1921	Mr Clough terminated his duties as Headmaster.

THE 'EAST' SCHOOL

An article in the October edition of *The Building News* in 1913, commented on the opening of the new Ashington Hirst East School:

The school was officially opened by Sir Francis Blake, chairman of Northumberland Education Committee. The buildings form an interesting example of the quadrangle principle, and are the first of its kind to be built in the North of England. It provides accommodation for 700 mixed and 362 infant children, and occupies a site of almost two acres. A feature of the arrangement is the shape of the classrooms, which have been designed so that the distance between the window walls and the walls opposite has been reduced to 21 ft, thus insuring considerably more light to the back rows of desks than is afforded in the earlier type of classrooms.
The hall is easily accessible from both departments, and has cross ventilation as well as lighting. The necessary teachers' rooms are provided with lavatory and WC accommodation adjoining each room, but the conveniences are separate from their compartments.
The buildings have been erected with red pressed facing bricks and covered with Westmorland green slates. The school was designed by, and carried out, under the supervision of Mr G Topham Forrest. Mr J P Bell of Newbiggin acted as clerk of works.

As a tribute to the work done by the Education chairman, Sir Francis Blake, all Northumberland schools later competed in soccer for the 'Blake' Cup, and it was fitting that the name of Hirst East figured more prominently than any other among the list of winners.

THE TOWN GETS DOWN TO BUSINESS

One of the first businesses to appear in Ashington was that of newsagent, John Wilkinson. Indeed, the original shop still stands, displaying above its door: *Established in 1895.* Alderman John Wilkinson came to the village in the late 1880s and set up in Market Place, now known as High Market. He built a shop which was the first in the village, apart from the old Post Office. Curious passers-by scorned John's efforts as he laboured erecting his home and shop, saying that he would make "nowt but trouble for himself." Despite the ridicule, John's shop opened and his first day's takings from selling newspapers was three shillings and sevenpence halfpenny (less than 20p).

Once the area was seen to lure customers, other establishments sprang up making Market Place the centre of attraction for the shoppers from Pegswood, Ellington, Guide Post and North Seaton. It was North Seaton which decreed that its first branch bank, outside of its own village, should be built at High Market. The first depositor? who else but John Wilkinson.

Another firm link with the present was forged when John Craigs, father of the late William N Craigs, solicitor, was appointed general manager of the Ashington Pit Co-operative Society, while James Drysdale held a similar position with the Old Pit Co-op. A later amalgamation produced the present Ashington Co-operative Society, now based in Woodhorn Road.

Listed as surgeons were Alex Duncanson of 24 First Row and A Leitch who lived at 3 Sixth Row. A chemist, George Thomas Marshal, was housed at 29 Ninth Row, and the village's first cobbler was Hugh Singer of 14 Fifth Row. Residents obtained their meat supply from a lady butcher, Mrs Ellen Dickinson of Glebe Cottage, and only one local bobby was needed - big John Marshall who began his duties on August 1st, 1890, salary £80 plus boots - to see law and order prevail in a community which by the end of the 19th century had swelled to some four thousand people, most of whom worked at the colliery.

Up until 1896, Ashington's civic affairs were controlled by Morpeth Rural Council. It had been obvious for a long time that a new and more effective local administration was required to keep pace with the rapid expansion which was taking place.

Ashington Urban District Council came into being when almost fifty candidates (reduced to thirty because of mis-spellings) fought for fifteen seats in 1896. Successful candidates included: William Bland, Keeker, 424 votes; John Wilkinson, stationer, 420; William Wilson, draper, 420; Joseph English, miner, 292; William Charlton, engineer, 272; E O Southern, colliery manager, 267; J Bell, engineer, 213; and C Young, master shifter, 210. The first chairman elected was E O Southern.

Once installed, the new councillors realised what a task lay before them. Primitive sanitation in the form of long lines of open middens laid the village wide open to the ravages of epidemics; water was available only from stand-pipes in the backstreets; the dull straight lines of colliery rows were unpaved and unlit; social amenities were non-existent.

But the councillors most acute problem was in finding a base in which to tackle the many issues which presented themselves. The inaugural meeting of the new council was held in the Bothal School, and the first item on the agenda was the vexed question of a more acceptable meeting place. The suggestion that the council should share premises at the proposed new police buildings was met with icy silence before someone voiced the opinion that such a move would not be 'respectable' for an urban district council.

The council had still not resolved their dilemma three years later, causing it to be noted that the AUDC had 'the horse out at lodgings'. Indeed, the council *had* bought a water cart but had no accommodation for it. A temporary home was found for the council - and the cart - on a sub-tenancy basis in one of the bank branches on the north side of Station Road.

A number of paid officials were appointed by the council including a medical officer at £40 a year; one man who took on the responsibilities of inspector, highways surveyor, and inspector of dairies, received a salary of £100; Clerk to the Council received £60; and for the dreaded job of collecting rates, a man was paid £30.

At their second meeting the council debated the format of a seal for the local authorities headed paper. It was quickly decided that the seal should incorporate a picture of the Duke Pit heapstead, but much argument ensued over the inscription *'Labour Conquers All'*, not because of its content, but whether or not the wording should be in Latin or plain English. The village's classical scholars won the day, and the words *'Labor Omnia Vincit'* provided an umbrella over the pit's winding gear, the seal still being used to this day.

One of the council's first good deals was the purchase of the Portland Recreational Field, now the familiar, Peoples Park. Prior to that they had paid an annual rent of thirty shillings an acre. When the transfer of ownership was completed a magnificent arch was erected for the opening ceremony when the previous owner, the Duke of Portland, donated an ornate bandstand to the town. Many trees were planted for the occasion at the west end of the park, and the small wooded area became known as the Plantation.

By 1911 the Council had moved nearer to the railway station by taking possession of the new council offices. The stone-faced structure was heightened in 1937 by the addition to the original two storeys of more offices, a council chamber, and a clock tower.

The abstemious coal owner Jonathan Priestman died in 1889, and it is surely no coincidence that the town's first two public houses, the Portland Hotel and the Grand Hotel, were both opened within six years of his demise. They were quickly followed by one of the first of 22 workingmens' club to sell beer in Ashington, built in 1902. This was the Ashington and District, known better as the West End club. The previous tenants had used the premises as the town's first Council Offices. Even earlier records show that it been a bank and a barber shop run by schoolmaster, George Hay.

The West End continued in the converted premises until after the first war when it was used as a barracks for troops, then it was extensively reconstructed into the building which now stands today.

Much of the cultural activity of the miners was carried out at the Mechanics Institute, and a Literary and Debating Society was founded in 1899. It lasted for over thirty years, destined to become the seed from which grew the town's famous Pitmen Painters Goup. Initial objects of the society were 'to promote the moral, mental and social improvement of the members thereof'.

Ashington and district, in the year of 1892, suffered a particularly bad winter. One victim of floodwater was the Sheepwash Bridge. A local paper reported:

It was as a result of floods following frosts that the old bridge at Sheepwash was broken by the turbulent waters of the the swollen Wansbeck.
The bridge was narrow and stood on four arches, with refuge niches for pedestrians to use when horse-drawn traffic was passing over. It partially collapsed when the weir above it was breached by the flood waters as they plunged and roared violently into the sea. There were places in Bothal Woods where the waters rose to a height of ten feet, and right on to the sea the river banks were submerged for days afterwards.
The river invaded the Angler's Arms at Sheepwash, and even in late July of the same year the footpath through Bothal Woods was practically impassable because of river mud and standing water.

Another local disaster happened in the following year. It seems that a group of Ashington football supporters were returning from a match at Widdrington by horse-drawn brake when they spotted a glare in the sky above the colliery rows adjacent to Ashington pit.

At first they imagined that it was just the pit heap which often glowed bright red. But as they approached the village it was obvious that some houses were on fire in the Fifth Row. The incident became known as: 'the Fifth Row's bleezin'.

The fire had started at number 14, occupied by a Mrs Elliott, who was incapacitated and confined to bed. A neighbour, Mrs Cole, a kindly lady given to administering the sick, had visited the invalid only ten minutes earlier. When she left, Mrs Elliott was asleep. Mrs Cole, grandmother to Edna Ralph (nee Henderson) was of the opinion that the fire had begun either by a spark from the fire igniting the paper ceiling, or that an oil lamp which hung from the ceiling had caused the paper to flare because of the heat.

Whatever the cause, near neighbours were soon packing their belongings and stacking them outside in the relative safety of their gardens. Mrs Elliott was brought out of the house unscathed, but such was the inadequacy of the amateur fire brigade of the day, half a dozen houses were completely gutted. Eventually, the demolition of a house in the path of the blaze effectively halted the conflagration.

LOW MARKET CLUBLAND

The number of workingmen's clubs which once thrived in Ashington varies between 22 and 23 depending on whether or not you recognise the British Legion as being a *bone fide* affiliated club. What is not in question is that there were five premises used for selling liquor crowded into the Low Market (Woodhorn Road) part of town.

First was the *Hirst East End*, opened in 1907, next to the Co-op, in the premises once used by Moses Sixsmith, a general dealer. Some of the founder members decided to open for refreshments the day before the official opening was due to take place, and it cost three men a nominal fine when they appeared in court.

Next door to the East End until 1910 was the Hirst Post Office, but with minimal alterations to the bare walls and concrete passages, this building was destined to become the *Northern Club*.

For some reason the thirsty miners allowed a shop to remain between the Northern and their next watering place, the *Linton and Woodhorn*. This club was really an offshoot of the *Grand Street Club*, but so many men were using this establishment that it was thought necessary to build an annexe. As the name would suggest, most of the clientele were drawn from those two collieries. On a cold day the miners could warm their fish and chips on an old fashioned kitchen range standing behind the central pillar in the main bar.

The Premier was another club which was still being used as a grocery shop in 1910. A round coke oven stood in the middle of the bar and the furniture had seen better days on steamships and breakers' yards. In 1920 the club expanded into the drapers shop next door.

Only spitting distance along the road, the *Indus* was opened in 1913, taking over the boozer once known as the *Shamrock, Thistle and Rose Club*. If you were looking for an Irishman or a fight then this was the place to come. The club was rebuilt in 1924, but the General Strike was responsible for a crisis in the club's finances as they were unable to pay the interest charges on a £3,500 loan. It took until 1939 for the members to drink sufficient beer to settle the debt.

Way down at the bottom of Woodhorn Road was a house built for a Dr R W Goldie in 1894. This was converted into the *Universal Club* in 1909. It was originally named the *Royal*, probably because the date coincided with the coronation of King George V.

One link with the early days of clubmania in Ashington is **HARRY DAVISON** who was born in 1902 at West Cramlington. His father, Walter, worked at the local pit, but in his spare time took portraits in a greenhouse which he had converted into a studio. Walter, after marrying a farm girl, moved to Ashington to work at Woodhorn Colliery. Very keen to get into the licensing trade, Walter served his apprenticeship waiting on and serving behind the bar of the *White Elephant*. He later became steward of the old Northern Club in Low Market while his brother, George, took over next door at the Hirst East End Club. Harry remembers:

It was my father who began the quoit throwing at the back of the Northern, and in the big strike he organised a soup kitchen. I used to go into the club as a laddie to cadge a penny for some sweets, and the stour of baccy smoke used to hit you as you went through the door. My father died of lung cancer at 56 years of age, and I'm sure it was the smoking that did it.

I left the North School at thirteen, but I'd already been working as a lather boy for a barber who had a shop opposite the council chambers. I had to use a bristly shaving brush to put the lather on the men's chins, and when the barber tapped on the floor I moved to the next customer so that he could come in with the cut-throat razor. My wages for that - and I worked till nine o'clock at night six days a week - was two shillings and ninepence. Threepence of that used to go straight away on sweets and entrance to the pictures for me and my brother at the old Wallaw. That was my pocket money all blown in one go, and mother got the other half a crown.

We had a big family of three boys and four girls - a brother and sister born either side of me were deaf and dumb - and you had to be fed on the cheap in those days. I got sick of seeing this big cast iron pot simmering away every day on the fire bars: mutton broth! One day I saw the empty eye-socket of a sheep floating around on the surface - that put me off broth for life.

We lived at 114 Hawthorn Road in those days, opposite where Jack Allen had opened his beer shop. Our house was the first to have a flush toilet in the whole street. It was done privately by a workman my father knew. I helped him to dig up the backyard to lay the pipes.

I enjoyed going to Paddy's Market down the Lonnen as a lad; they sold reject china and barrels full of grapes packed in cork granules. There was a huge fella there who called himself Doctor Bernard, but he was a quack really. He sold John Bull's Cough Mixture from a massive motor car. He stood on the broad running board and shouted for custom, and if it was slow in coming he used to pull people's teeth out for free while they waited.

Blooms Auction Mart was on the go then as well. In between selling periods it was held in a big tent - various local artists would show off their talent. My father carried me on his shoulders to the opening of the Pavilion Theatre, that was when we lived in Severn Street which later became Sycamore. It was there that I saw my first nude act, but it wasn't intentional! At the end of a pantomime, Buttons went to collect a bouquet from the conductor, bent down to pick up the flowers and split his pants from top to (literally) bottom.

I worked at Brough's the grocers when I left school; it was on the corner, opposite the Grand Hotel. We did long hours then for not much money. I used to clean up and take groceries out on a hand trolley. You can still see the place on the side wall where the horse and cart was loaded up with groceries. Sometimes the delivery men would be out till ten o'clock at night, going up as far as Broomhill. The manager was a hard-faced fella with a little tash; he looked just the part of a gaffer, but one day he was caught pinching and got the sack.

A policeman stood on the Grand Corner - though there was hardly any traffic and he used to watch out for us kids riding bikes without lights. In those days we used a carbide lamp similar to those used down the pit. He would stop you, and you would say: "The lamps's just gone out", and he would feel the top of the lamp and say: "It couldn't have done - the things clay cold."

TALBOTs AND KIRKUPs

My mother's family, the Talbots, arrived in Ashington via Old Benwell, Lemington, and Bells Close, all in the west end of Newcastle. Michael Talbot, my gandfather, was born in 1866 and married an Irish girl, Ann Cain, who came across to England with her family from Bally Mull, in County Mayo. Ann, twenty years of age when married, followed the fashion of all Irish Catholics at the time and gave birth at two-yearly intervals until she had produced 12 children - nine boys and three girls, including my mother, Lizzie.

Old Mick, as the father became known, worked at the Montagu Pit while living at Benson's Buildings in Lemington, but decided to move the family to Ashington in 1907. It was a good decision, for not long afterwards there was a pit disaster at Montagu, causing the deaths of 30 men.

The entire family moved into a four-roomed colliery house at 95 Sycamore Street. Mick went to work at Woodhorn, as did all the sons once they had reached the age of thirteen and left St Aidan's school.

At the outset of the first world war, three of the boys, Michael, William and James, enlisted in the army to ease the cramped conditions at home. None of them returned. Michael was killed in France after only three months; James was caught up in a gas attack and was invalided out to a Middlesex hospital; and William was badly injured by shrapnel, spending many months in a hospital at Stratford upon Avon. In the course of time, William and James met, courted, and married Nellie and Alice respectively, and set up homes near London.

At the age of fifty, old Mick, having sired nine sons, decided that his working days were over and quit his job at the colliery. But tenancy of a colliery house was only guaranteed if at least *two* workers lived there, and three of the sons, Jack, Jacob and Frank, married and left home. Manny and Dick were left, but only Dick was in work. The Talbot family were not now legitimate tenants.

My mother remembered:

We never knew anything until my mother, Ann, who was out in the back street daddin' pit clays on the wall, saw some workmen over the road tidying up an upstair's flat. She asked a neighbour if she knew who was moving in and was told that it was for a family who were being evicted. And she still never twigged that it was for us. They put us out the very next day and we shifted the furniture just across the back lane into 102 Poplar Street.

The name of KIRKUP is one of only a dozen to appear on the 1861 census for Woodhorn. John Kirkup, listed as 'shepherd', was my great grandfather. Woodhorn Village then consisted of a church, manor, farm, a scattering of cottages, and a wide expanse of green fields running down to the sea at Newbiggin. Like the Talbots, it was the Kirkup's tied cottage which was put in jeopardy by the breadwinner.

John Kirkup decided that he had had enough of farm labouring and took himself off for a walk one day to North Seaton where a colliery had been in operation since 1859. He asked for, and was given, employment. Overjoyed, he rushed back home and told the rest of the farm workforce how much he would be making by working down below. It was far in excess of what could be earned working the land, and rustic heads began to shake.

On finding out that one of his workers was inciting the rest to down tools and leave, the owner of the farm threatened to evict the entire Kirkup family. Matters were sorted amicably, but eldest son, John, my grandfather, eventually got himself a job as a miner when Woodhorn colliery was opened in 1894.

He married Agnes Cassidy, an Irish girl, then living in Morpeth. Their first colliery house was at 183 Clyde Street, and when children began arriving they moved down a couple of blocks into 289 Chestnut Street. My father was the oldest of four sons, Jack, Laurence, Sidney, and Denis; an equal number of girls, Margaret, Dorothy, Edith, and Mary, made up the Kirkup family.

My father, like the rest of his family and the Talbots, went to St Aidan's R C School. He managed to pass what was then known as the *Scholarship*, but lack of money coming into the family coffers prevented him from taking up a place in higher education. He loved the outdoors, and as a youth worked on a farm in Moorhouse Lane. But, like the rest of my male relations, he found it difficult to stay out of the pits. Shortage of money inevitably outweighed all other considerations, and he went down Woodhorn Colliery, the same pit as his father.

THE DUKE OF PORTLAND

William Bentinck, the Duke of Portland, was the owner of much of the land under which Ashington's coal was being mined. He had two children: a daughter and son who reached his 21st birthday on March 16th, 1914.

To commemorate the occasion, a silver medallion was struck and given to all the children of the area at their Sports Day. On one side was an engraving of the Duke and Duchess, and on the other was the inscription: *William, Arthur, Henry, Marquis of Titchfield*.

The Duke held an 'Open Day', and at the entrance to the Castle grounds an arch was built showing the dates 1889-1914 and the words: *'Welcome To Bothal'*.

ASHINGTON KEEPS GROWING

Before the first world war there was a distinct split in the town. Ashington and Hirst were two completely separate places, physically bisected by the Railway Station Bridge. The men to the west of the railway line invariably worked at Ashington Colliery, and those residing on the east travelled to Woodhorn or Linton pits. Indeed, the two latter pits merged into one when a new headquarters was found for them in the Linton & Woodhorn Miners' Hall. The same name was given to a social club in Woodhorn Road. And at the *top-end* of the town, when Ellington Colliery was opened in 1913, the men living in *high* Ashington became associated with the new pit and a private drinking club - *the Ashington & Ellington* - was formed, catering for the two sets of miners.

Ashington and Hirst were now bursting at the seams as private building overtook that of the Coal Company. Each part was now a self-contained community, catering for the many and varied needs of its inhabitants.

In May 1914, Ashington Urban District Council presented the following figures showing the number of houses and buildings in Ashington and Hirst, to a House of Lords Committee:

Houses owned by Ashington Coal Company	2527
Houses owned by other private owners	2714
Shops with houses attached	173
Shops	74

Churches	15
Clubs	17
Schools	5
Theatres and Picture Halls	5
Institutes	3
Co-operative Stores	8
Farms	2
Hotels	3
Railway Stations	2
Council Premises, including Hospital	4
Post Office	1
Banks	3
Public Halls	5
Police Station	1
Factory	1
	5563

Brothers **SYDNEY & RICHARD OXNARD**, two Newcastle-based builders, came to Ashington looking for work. They found it in plenty. Ashington Coal Company could not cope with the ever-increasing influx of workers, and it was just the right time for private entrepreneurs to step in.

At first the brothers concentrated on the Hirst, and built houses in Castle Terrace and Queen Street. When these were completed they moved to the land next to the railway station, and started on Cresswell Terrace, Council Road, and part of Station Road.

Syd Oxnard built the end house in Council Road for his wife and family - three girls, Ivy, Doris, Winnie, and one boy, Norman. But his wife found out that the adjacent land contained a limeyard, and at the gable end of the street was a stable, so she refused, and the Oxnards moved into the second-end house, number 33. Cinema magnate, Walter Lawson, a colliery electrician, lived at number 22, and his sister lived next door.

Syd Oxnard's daughter, Winnie, who still lives in the same house, remembers:

As children we would often play next to the railway platform where the miners got aboard the tankey for Linton and Ellington. Father would tip the guard and he'd let us travel in a carriage with plush seats - the others had hard wooden benches, and were only used by miners in pit clothes.
The tally men (credit collectors) came on the train from Newcastle every Friday afternoon to collect their 'tick'. And even before the train stopped you would see them jumping off and scurrying in all sorts of directions, hoping that they would be the lucky ones to get paid that day.
Father helped to build the Pavilion Theatre, and me and my sister used to take his bait down to him every day. He had an argument one day with the Council surveyor, Osborne Blyth, about the pit heap which seemed to be right on our doorstep. Mother would get up very early, before seven o'clock, to brush and clean the doorstep as well as the brasses - because father had a brass nameplate on the wall. But with all the fumes coming from the heap the whole place was coloured purple in a couple of hours. Father complained to the council official, telling him to get rid of the heap which smouldered into flame every so often. Mr Blyth told him: "Better to shift your house, because that pit heap is here to stay!"

When the first war broke out, the Oxnards had their own building business, but Syd decided to enlist, and joined the army as a driver.

THE TOWN GOES TO WAR

For the 5th Battalion of the Northumberland Fusiliers which contained many Ashington men, New Year's Day, 1915, was seen in at a camp near Seaton Delaval. An unnamed writer in the St George's Gazette noted:

At the time of the Christmas vacation we were still at Blyth and spent really quite a festive season here, although the night trench work continued uninterruptedly. As a coast defence unit, no leave was granted and ranks combined to spend as enjoyable a time as possible. Services were conducted in the little chapel at Cambois by the Rev C Smith, Battalion Chaplain, and the rest of the morning was spent in football and other games.
Christmas dinner, thanks to the generosity of the officers and their friends, was a mixture of goose, pork, vegetables, plum pudding, dessert with beer and mineral waters.
The most important event of the month has been the change to four company organisations. The following are confidently expected to form strong combinations: A Company (Morpeth) and H Company (Berwick), No. 1 Company; B Company (Ashington) and D Company (Alnwick), No. 2 Company.

Four months later these particular army units were engaged in some of the bloodiest battles of the war. The writer continued in his diary:

April 20th - Left Cambois, our coastal defence station, after farewell address by Col R Scott. Second line battalion sent their band and gave us a hearty send off from Blyth.

April 21st - Crossed from Folkstone to Boulogne. Left in the evening by train for Cassel.

April 22nd - Marched to Winnezeele. Billeted in farms.

April 23rd - Marched to ......, a stiff march, and remained overnight.

April 24th - Marched in evening through Ypres, which was being heavily shelled and in flames. A few losses.

April 25th - Pressed on but were ordered to retire owing to lack of support. Had some 50 casualties. Officers wounded: Capt Flint, Second-Lieutenants Donkin and Adams.

April 26th - After gas attack on Canadians, Northumberland Brigade ordered to attack St Julien. A brilliant advance under terrific shell and machine gun fire ended in Germans evacuating the village. Losses were heavy, 11 officers and over 400 other ranks.

My uncle, Michael Talbot, lost his life in that battle - he was one of over 700 local men who were killed in the so called Great War. A week before he died, Michael sat down in the dug-out and scribbled a message to his mother, my grandmother, thanking her for sending him some cigarettes. He ended his pencilled note by writing: "*The German dogs are at it again.*"

A young second lieutenant was injured in the same battle that killed my uncle. His name was **WILLIAM CRAIGS**. William was brought back to England, and eventually to Alnwick where he recuperated from his wounds. Good officers were scarce at the front, and after a few months he was back again, promoted to captain. Further bravery earned him a Military Cross in 1917.

That young officer was to become better known to the people of Ashington as W N Craigs, solicitor, son of John Craigs who played such a prominent role when the town was barely managing to stand up for itself. William Craigs' skills as a letting agent placed him as much in demand as Jack Rodway's flat bogie whenever a family decided to move house.

Born in 1891, William lived in his father's house, Station Villa, now the Community Initiative Centre, standing next to Ashington Library. He attended Bothal School and was then educated at Barnard Castle, later studying law at Queens' College, Cambridge, where he coxed the college rowing team.

He was already a member of the Territorial Army when the first war began. Said his son, Michael: *"He never talked about the war, but I know he took a full Company into battle and came out with only 20 men."*

W N Craigs continued working right up to his death in 1976. He served on many committees including two terms as President of Ashington Rotary Club, holding the same position with the Newcastle Law Society and the Ashington branch of the British Legion.

HUGH CAIRNS, born in 1896, a pupil at the Bothal School, was Ashington's only Victoria Cross holder.

Hugh emigrated to Canada when he was fourteen. With the Canadian army, he went to fight with the Allies in France in 1916. He was involved two years later in taking an enemy machine gun post single handedly. Not content with that act of bravery, he repeated his one-man attack further down the line, capturing 18 Germans in one onslaught and no less than 50 on another occasion.

Attempting to take out another enemy outpost in which he captured 60 Germans, he was mortally wounded. A monument to this brave Ashington hero stands in the Canadian town of Saskatoon, and a street is named after him in Valenciennes.

Another local man whose life is commemorated elsewhere is **EDWARD SLAUGHTER**, son of a Norfolk horseman who moved to the North East in the 1890s. Mr Slaughter Snr became head horsekeeper for the Duke of Northumberland, before moving to Pegswood and finally Ashington.

Son Edward was given the name *Dick* because of his *'Devil Dick'* carefree attitude to life. Typically, the young lad lied about his age and joined the army at seventeen. But after a very short time at the front in France, he was blinded by an enemy shell.

Dick lived until he was in his eighties with a lifetime of memories to keep him company, but probably his greatest moment was when the management at that great seat of learning, Eton College, commissioned his bust to be sculpted, displayed, and dedicated to 'All those killed, wounded, and suffering, as a result of the First World War.' He was yet one more Ashington man who, undoubtedly, showed the courage to 'face and overcome disability'.

ASHINGTON HOSPITAL OPENS ITS DOORS

Ashington Hospital had its roots in the suffering and hardships of the miners of the town. In the 19th century, if an accident occurred down the pit, the victim was brought home and left to the care and limited skill of family and neighbours.

The men paid into the *Ashington Fatal Accident Fund*, making money available to pay capable women to assist in nursing injured miners. One step further forward was the formation of the *Nursing Association*, again supported by regular contributions from the men. In 1910, this latter group decided that more medical services were needed in the town, and plans were laid for the building of a hospital.

Delays in decision making meant that it was 1913 before the foundation stone was laid. James Noble, writing in the Ashington Advertiser at the age of eighty-two, recollected:

The idea came to us when a group met one Sunday morning. We felt that Ashington needed a hospital and that something should be done about it. A planner called George Beattie from Wallsend, offered his services free, and each colliery in the district sent men daily to help where they could. Eventually the day came to open the Hospital and we were all there. Mr Ebby Edwards was there to make a speech, but he said the honour should go to George Beattie. I said all we now needed was a doctor. We got one, built him a house, and fixed his salary.

The hospital had cost £15,000 by 1914, but because of the war it was not completed until a year later, when it was given over to the military, free of charge. During hostilities a total of 2,860 servicemen were treated.

But, two years into the war, the hospital staff had the heartbreaking task of dealing with fatalities much nearer home when a gas explosion claimed 13 lives at Woodhorn Pit.

AN EVENTFUL YEAR - 1916

The following sundry items are based on information from the Ashington Post of 1916:

The question of poor pay for teachers was placed under consideration by the Northumberland Education Committee. Mr Gilbertson, Hirst, said: *"Teachers in Ashington are starving on less than £1 a week. And remember, the pound is only worth half of what it was pre-war."*

Baden Powell, in his rank of Lt. General, visited the area, and there was a big turn out of scouts and sea corps when he went down to Newbiggin. He made a number of presentations to individuals and scout troops on the Moor where a very large crowd had gathered.

In a time when all the working class males were being forced into either the pits or the army, the news that three heads of department at Bedlington Co-operative Society had been given exemption, must surely not have gone unnoticed. A Tribunal was told that the three departments: funeral, furnishing and jewellery, did business in excess of £100,000. Only a month earlier a similar Tribunal had turned down an appeal for exemption from a woman who said her 28-year-old son helped her in the family business. Having being told by the woman that her son had a bad foot, chairman of the Tribunal, Colonel Jobling said: *"The military will soon put that right."*

An appeal tribunal with Colonel R Kidd presiding, was told that a shop assistant from the Meadow Dairy, Ashington, had appealed for exemption on conscientious grounds. Having heard the applicant say he was a spiritualist, the chairman asked: *"Have you communicated with spirits?"* On being told that the answer was *"no"*, the appeal was dismissed.

With the war now in its third year of senseless loss of local men, societies such as the *Ashington and District Distinguished Service Recognition Society* had emerged. Corporal W Fairless, holder of the DCM, was presented with a gold watch and chain. This brave man had volunteered for a mission which had already claimed the lives of five of his friends. He carried half a hundredweight of guncotton across no-man's-land, fixed it to a house occupied by enemy snipers, and returned safely through the fierce glare of searchlights.

Nearer home, at the billets in Cowpen to be precise, a Corporal Laufear was cleaning his rifle which went off accidentally; the bullet shot through an open window and pierced Elizabeth McShane in the leg. It was reported that the poor woman suffered more from shock than from the actual wound.

In another incident, this time at Seaton Hirst, a young soldier just home on leave, began to take a hand grenade to pieces, having previously told his mother and grannie that it was harmless. It was thought unlikely that he would live after it exploded.

An aggrieved Ashington man, Bill Glendinning of Rosalind Street, complained to the press that an invention of his had not been given full recognition, saying: *"I think it only fair just to claim what is my due. I am the only man in the world originating the ideas concerning aerial navigation, and these ideas are now working out. I am sorry to say I never got one penny for my labour, other people getting the benefit."*

The Miners' Picnic was discontinued during the war, but the Northumberland Miners Association were determined to have a parade, as was the local Federation for they had commissioned a new banner to represent the lodges of the Ashington group of collieries. The miners' demonstration at the Peoples Park was judged to be a great success when the new banner was unfurled on July 31st, 1916. The picture on one side of the banner was *"a plea for the nationalisation of the mines, and on the other for unity among all sections of the working classes."* A demonstration the same day at Blyth called for the old-age pension to be increased from five shillings to seven shillings and sixpence.

A local journalist noticed some horseplay by young lads taking beasts to the Ashington Co-operative slaughter house, and wrote: *"Our district is acquiring an unsavoury reputation in the respect of treatment of animals. It has become almost a weekly occurrence to see disgraceful scenes in connection with tired out beasts. Some of the drivers thought it great fun to get astride the poor animals - some no bigger than dogs - and ride them like ponies."*

It was noted that juvenile crime in the area was on the increase, and that a number of offences had occurred by boys *"beyond the control of their parents."* It was advocated that: *"local JPs adopt punishment to offenders that will be at once a corrective of a radical kind,"* probably the first *"short sharp shock."*

Only a month later it was reported: *"Spare the rod and spoil the child is evidently the motto guiding parents in regard to the upbringing of their children. The result is seen in the number of cases in the area. If magistrates would only remember that part of the equipment of every police station is a birch, and would order it to be applied, there would quickly be a falling off of cases."*

A new ambulance was presented to the local Volunteer Aid Detachment by the miners of the Ashington group of collieries. Costing £550, it was formally presented in front of the recently-opened Ashington Infirmary.

A new school was opened at North Seaton, built by T Hedley and Sons of Blyth. Costing £4,900, the *"splendidly equipped"* building was expected to fill *"a long felt need"*. Seating accommodation for pupils numbered 392 in eight classrooms (almost 50 per class). Two staff rooms and a large hall were also provided.

In front of a large crowd, a new bowling green was opened at the Hirst Park in August by Mr Walter Wilson, chairman of the urban district council.

UNITED BUS COMPANY

The first buses which operated in the area came on the scene around 1900. To begin with they were used only as *feeders* from the various railway stations. Regular bus services started when the first world war ended, and many of the war surplus vehicles used for transporting troops were converted so that they could carry paying passengers.

One of the first railway-owned firms to have a bus route around the Ashington area was that of *Amos, Proud and Co* of Choppington. Hal Amos later sold the business and went to work for United as a driver. Jack W Nesbit of Ashington ran the Linton buses from a garage near the 'top' store, selling the concern to *Wansbeck Motor Services* in 1941; *County Motors of Stakeford*, owned by the Gordon brothers, ran long distance routes between England and Scotland, services between Newcastle and Whitley Bay, and catered for the Ashington to Newcastle route; W & J Robson, operating under the title *Eastern Motor Services*, ran a service between Ashington and Amble; G Morton ran buses between Ashington and Newbiggin; a pioneering coach company, *Orange Brothers*, operated between Edinburgh and London, but picked up at Ashington en route; the *District Motor Services*, running between Lynemouth and Ashington had no fewer than five partners, three of whom were Gordon brothers.

In time, most of the small companies were swallowed up by the Lowestoft-based *United* in the years following the 1930 Traffic Act. The familiar livery of United was first spotted on Ashington's roads in 1920. But the firm had been in existence since 1912 when it began operations simultaneously in Sussex and Durham. In 1919 the company purchased a number of War Department ambulances and converted them into passenger vehicles at their bodyworks depot in Lowestoft. It was then they moved into Northumberland. Initially, there was no terminus as we know it today in Ashington, and the buses picked up passengers from bus stops dotted along the main street. United built a garage in 1920 and in 1936 eventually opened a depot on the site of Hirst Farm.

Said Ashington Depot Superintendant Tom Taylor, who became an Inspector in 1973 after 20 years service: *"Most of the problems in the early days came about because of the suspension on the poor roads; then, of course, initially, the buses could not travel faster than 12 mph, and a 600 mile round trip to London was an ordeal. But some of the engines on those buses would have run forever - not like nowadays."*

THE ASHINGTON METHODIST CENTRAL HALL

The Reverend W S Weddell was the first to bring to the notice of the Methodist public the need for a new building to house the expanding population. The first Methodist meetings had been held in the Band Room: two back-to-back houses in the Long Row knocked into one for the purpose.

This building filled an important place in the life of the early community, catering, not only for the band, but, on a Sunday evening, for the Established Church service at 5 pm, and the Wesleyan service an hour later.

As the Hirst developed, the Ashington Society of Methodists commenced cottage services in the house of Mr James Curtis in Sycamore Street. From there, after a brief period at the Store Hall, they moved into permanent accommodation at the Hirst School Chapel in 1898.

The foundation stones for the Wesleyan Central Hall in Woodhorn Road were laid on March 21st, 1923. The principal stone on the south-east corner was laid by Mr T Errel, in the name of all past workers, and other stones were laid by Mr Cuthbert Bainbridge, on behalf of the Coalfields Commission, the Rev. J T Wardle Stafford, on behalf of the chapel committee, and Mr Francis Priestman, on behalf of the Ashington Coal Company who had donated £500 to the cost of the new building.

The plans for the chapel, which was by far the most ornate building in Ashington, were drawn up by Messrs Brocklehurst of Manchester, at a cost of £18,000. The contract was secured by Mr Joseph Walker, and the first sods were cut on January 27th, 1923 by Mr W Gray; Master Harry French, on behalf of his grandfather, Mr W H Thwaites, then lying ill; and Master Cecil Patton, on behalf of his grandmother, who was then the oldest member of the Hirst Society.

The opening ceremony for the new Wesleyan Central Hall took place at 2.15 pm on Wednesday, May 21st, 1924, when the sermon was taken by Mrs Ridley Warham, wife of the Managing Director of the Ashington Coal Company. The Dedicatory Service was performed by the Rev. T Naylor, and the first concert was held on Wednesday, June 18th, with the Orotario 'Elijah', being sung by the Newbiggin Co-operative Choir, under their conductor J Normanton Barron.

THE BIRTH OF LYNEMOUTH VILLAGE

In 1924 work began on erecting 200 new houses at Lynemouth in readiness for the new pit opening. As at Ashington, imagination and flair in the naming of the streets and roads was limited, and someone decided to stick to the simple letters of the alphabet: first came Albion Terrace, followed by Boland Road, Chester Square etc. No two street names began with the same letter.

Children of the workers who were building the village and sinking the shafts attended a school at Ellington. It was a dreadful mish mash of wooden huts, and children and teachers alike could hardly wait to see the last of it. Here is an account of its last few weeks, as seen through the eyes of the headmaster G T Herron:

The end draws nigh. There will not be any mourners. Extremes of heat and cold; wading through a sea of mud from hut to hut; admitting, always admitting newcomers, and finding places for them; cutting up old desks to fit odd places; removing checks on windows to allow greater space for the admission of fresh air - then later replacing them to keep out rain or snow; yet, withal, everyone cheerful and bright through it all has been our record.

A new Admission Register was opened a year past Easter. There are 525 names on it now. Over the last twenty months, the names of nineteen members of the teaching staff appear, some temporary some supply. Difficulties in obtaining lodgings, difficulties of travelling, difficulties everywhere. Yet everyone has worked loyally and well.

As I write, the children have their rooms in the huts decorated for a Christmas Party. They have soon settled into a happy family. A Merry Christmas to them all! But the end draws nigh. There will not be any mourners.

Although the entire coalfield owned by the Ashington Coal Company was at a standstill throughout most of 1926, work was almost completed in building the new *model village* of Lynemouth to house the workers of nearby Ellington colliery and the future workforce of the new Lynemouth Colliery.

This letter appeared in *Kiddies Korner*, a page devoted to children's comments in the Colliery Magazine.

38 Dalton Avenue
Lynemouth.
24/2/1926

Dear Editor,
There is one thing that is missing that would be very nice here at Lynemouth, and that is a Gym, the same as I read about at Hirst and Ashington.
Of course we can enjoy ourselves in the summer. We live so near the sea and there are some high sand banks that are lovely for playing on, although the high tides this winter have undermined them for quite a long way along the beach.
I am ten years old and attend the Ellington T.C. School, but I expect the new Lynemouth School to be opened about Easter, then it will be much nicer than going to Ellington when it is bad weather, although I am head of the class and like my teacher.

Yours Truly,
AMANDA McSORLEY

A month later, the progress of the new town was being reviewed by Capt Ledgerwood in the Colliery Magazine:

We are pleased to mark an improvement of our town band on their recent perambulation of the streets. It is a big undertaking to run a new band. Ready-made players are not picked up anywhere, and there is a tremendous amount of drudgery requiring much patience on the part of everyone connected with a young band. When the band first made its appearance a few months ago some of us felt proud of our own band as if it had been the famous St Hilda's. There are instruments available for any players who are as yet unattached.
Lynemouth has at different times been the subject of much favourable criticism and speculation. Having an ideal situation geographically, every effort is being made to create a town second to none in its design and in the amenities provided.
The various types of houses erected are the realized dreams of our political idealists of half a century or more - ideal homes set in a town designed to aid progress towards better ideals, a healthier race. True, our town is as yet in the making, and there is still in places that unfinished state which is at times akin to the unbeautiful. But even the loveliest of pictures in an unfinished state seems but an ugly mess. However, it does not require the trained eye of an artist to discern the beauty of the design in the mind of the creative artist.
Just so with this new town of ours. At first glance in places it appears plain, almost to ugliness, but to the discerning eye there is that promise of a beauty rarely met in industrial centres. Broad sweeping roads, wide footpaths, open spaces and gardens, hedges and shrubberies, avenues of trees - how lovely Lynemouth should be in the years to come.
How fortunate we ought to feel in having handed into our guardianship a place of such promise. Shall we in years to come look back and regret our failure to take care of it?
Sometimes we wonder on this. On a recent Saturday night, beautiful young trees growing along one of our main roads were deliberately and wantonly destroyed. We do not suggest this was the work of any inhabitant of Lynemouth. The evidence available indicates otherwise. But our own people, however isolated the case may be, are responsible for peeling bark off the trees. Although the whole of this destruction cannot have

happened unobserved there has never been any one case of wilful damage reported.

Come then, people of Lynemouth, if not for your own sakes at least for the good of the generations of the future, strive to make the most of the opportunity that has been placed in your hands to create not only lovely surroundings but an altogether beautiful environment, a clean healthy town, a cleaner and healthier portion of the human race.

In a new town of such mushroom growth, populated by migrants from a score or so of other villages or towns, there can be no set tradition. And so we are anxious that although the inhabitants of Lynemouth may have seemed to have nothing in common to commence with they will weld themselves into a body with one common ideal, the welfare of their own town and all associated with it.

A great deal of speculation is going on as to the probable date of the opening of the new Institute. The industrial stoppage has delayed things so much that it will probably not be opened until the autumn. Without doubt it is one of the finest buildings of its kind in the north of England. The word 'Institute' appears to me to be the wrong term to apply to it.

We are so used to Institutes being a matter of four brick walls divided up to cater for billiards and reading. Welfare Club would be a far better term. The Welfare Superintendent announced that the furnishings alone were to cost between £1,300 and £1,400. So you can see that it is going to be no mean place.

However beautiful a building may be provided, it will not achieve its purpose unless the right spirit pervades it. The policy of the Club must be largely determined by those using it.

If you see houses and gardens well cared for, it is the people inside who are responsible. If, on the other hand, you see slums, it is equally the people who live there who have made them.

Our Institute will be what we, who use it, make it.

During the crisis Lynemouth has been very quiet. Gardening has been the chief occupation of everyone. A rather nice feature has been the dance or two held on the sward down in the Dene, to music provided by the world's greatest Dance Bands, the Savoy Orpheans, etc., via the humble gramophone. A very pleasant way of spending idle moments.

In order to raise funds for the relieving of any distress, an entertainment committee has been got together. Already one Community Singing Concert has been held, conducted by Tom Rickaby. There is no doubt of the beneficial effect of a hearty sing along to banish the care and worry for a few moments. How well we can remember the YMCA singsongs during the war, with two or three hundred fellows as happy in bondship of music as if they had been reared under the one roof.

On May 18th, (1926) another concert was held in connection with the Relief Fund. The following artistes contributed to the programme: Mrs F Stimpson, Miss G Foster, Miss E Downie, Mr C S Main, Mr J Baldson, Mr W York and Mr T Rickaby.

With the strike now in its third month, Captain Ledgerwood's tone became more sombre:

The gloom and depression inevitably attendant on such a period as we are passing through at present is beginning to bear witness of its presence among us. The happy carefree expressions have vanished. Instead, everyone is thoughtful almost to despair. All thoughtful with a sincere hope that a lasting settlement will soon be obtained. All wishing for a return to normal conditions.

Despite it all though, there is in our community a feeling of goodwill. This has evidenced itself again and again since the commencement of the strike and it augers well for the Lynemouth of the future. No matter how any one section of the community may strive to gain over any other, the ultimate gain can only be a reflection of the state of prosperity of the whole.

For some time the majority of our schoolchildren have been receiving a good sound meal at school. A kitchen was organised by a committee representative of all interests. They are sound honest-to-goodness workers. They have been foraging, collecting, cooking and serving, and right well have they done it. Something like 320 children have been provided with a wholesome nourishing two-course dinner every day, which they receive and consume at their places in school.

We cannot pass on without complimenting Mr William Bates, of Ellington, the master cook, on his organisation in the cookhouse itself, and the class of food he provides. There has been a lot of hard work done, but it has been for the children.

The Entertainments Committee in conjunction with the Kitchen Fund has done good work in providing concerts and a dance every week. Full House has been the rule, testifying to the popularity of good clean entertainment. Our Town Band provided a delightful evening in our Dene. They were to have repeated their performance but the fickleness of Dame Nature caused its abandonment.

But by August the weather and the Captain's outlook upon the situation turned decidedly brighter:

The glorious weather has brought in its train many visitors to Lynemouth. The char-a-banc proprietors are beginning to include the town in their itinerary. The prolonged holiday most people are having, engenders the picnic spirit. Sea bathing is very popular with the young folk of both sexes.

But don't be too venturesome on our particular little bit of coast. Experienced swimmers consider Lynemouth not a good place for novices. One evening a young lady resident in Ariel Street, Ashington, was rescued from drowning by three of our Lynemouth Estate workmen, Messrs Allsop, Salkeld, and Hogg. The lady got into difficulties and Allsop had to enter the sea fully clothed to get her in time. After about twenty minutes first aid they resuscitated the lady.

Our town band is not in too good a position financially. The strike hit us rather hard and left us without any source of income. Sometimes three times a week the band has rendered programmes of music either in the Dene or on the Sports Field. They certainly have helped to brighten the place up.

They have obviously had a good effect on our younger inhabitants, for Lynemouth has been singularly free from trouble of any kind. However, the annual Children's Gala has been postponed for a few weeks in the hope that we will shortly get back to normal conditions. In any case there will be a gala, so the bairns need not worry over it unduly.

With the strike over, the Captain had good reason to feel pleased when the movies eventually arrived in town in April, 1927:

At long last! Lynemouth, upholding its reputation as a model town, now boasts its own Cinema and Dance Hall. No more walking to Ashington is necessary in order to see the pictures - they are here, on our own doorstep.

The Welfare Hall with its pictures and dances, and concerts, and gymnasium, will prove a great blessing to Lynemouth. And since only the best films are to be exhibited, they need not be afraid to bring their visitors.

It looks as though Lynemouth is going to be more popular than ever this summer, if we can take as a guide the number of vistors here on Easter Monday. And why not? Is not Lynemouth well worth coming to look at, with everything bright and clean, games in plenty, a wonderful stretch of sand, a beautiful Dene, rich in wild flowers, with a pretty burn rippling through it, and now a Cinema and a Dance Hall. How many places can boast such a list of advantages?

With a change of reporter came a change in outlook. March 1928 saw R P Watson writing copy for the Magazine:

Although Lynemouth is a model place, and everything is clean, or looks clean, we have one or two things to get rid of. One is the emptying of ash-bins into open carts, at any time of the day, and regardless of whatever or whoever may be in close proximity.

The writer passed one of these carts as the men were about to empty a bin. Did they stop? Did they look round to see if they would cover anyone or anything with dust and ashes? If they had, they might have seen an ice-cream cart and wafer biscuits etc., being simply smothered in dirt. Could not this emptying business be done in the early hours of the morning, leaving the streets clean for the many traders who bring food to the doors?

Sadly we have to report that Mr Ralph Saint, well known to all in this district, and especially at Linton, died on Friday, January 20th, 1928, at the age of seventy-two. Mr Saint retired only three years ago, after having worked 30 years at Linton Colliery. He started work first, however, at North Seaton Colliery as a trapper boy, at the age of ten. At fourteen he was boiler fireman at Cambois Colliery, and afterwards he came to Linton, during the sinking operations, as engineman. On the 13th July, 1896, he was in charge of the winding engine which raised the first tub of coal to bank at Linton. The total weight of coal drawn to bank on that day was 28 tons. All sympathise with those who mourn his death.

The snow we had recently reminded some of how very near we are to being isolated in Lynemouth. When the buses began to run a skeleton service we began there and then to lose touch with the outside world.

But the Postal Authorities are not content with the snow. According to their new arrangements, a letter posted at Ashington before 9 am will not arrive until 9 am the next day; and we see the postman go away with the last collection at about 4.30 pm in the afternoon; and we still cannot send a telegram! We are very nearly isolated.

One thing the recent stoppage has done is to produce vocal talent hitherto undreamt of. The propensity of the lads as vocalists and instrumentalists leave one wondering. And boxing too! We have some really good fellows at the game, Dan Robson, of course, 'daddies them all'.

A pleasing litle ceremony was performed by Mr A. E. Holliday, the Manager of Ellington Colliery, on Saturday, June 14th, 1928, when he declared open the new Bowling Green at the Welfare Ground. Lynemouth is peculiarly fortunate as it happens to be the only Welfare centre in the Ashington group which contains provisions for this class of sport.

Over sixty of the residents have joined the Bowling Club so there is every reason to suggest that the Lynemouth venture will be a success. Mr Halliday congratulated the Club upon obtaining the services of such a seasoned bowler as Mr T Freeman as their Chairman, ably assisted by Mr J Coulson. The visitors at the first match were the Hirst Club, and the enjoyment of the afternoon was considerably enhanced by the presence of the Lynemouth and Ellington Silver Band, whose performance was very much appreciated.

To emphasise the importance of the welfare work being done in the area by the Ashington Coal Company, a visit was arranged for the Duke of York, destined to become King George VI. It was noted in the Magazine:

His Royal Highness who is President of the Industrial Welfare Society, paid a flying visit to Ashington on Monday, July 16th, 1928. On his arrival at 10.30 am the Directors and Officials were presented, after which he signed the visitor's book. A tour was then made of the Screens, the Ashington Recreation Ground, the Continuation School, the Hirst Welfare Ground, Ellington Pithead Baths, and the new model town of Lynemouth.

Graced by the presence of Royalty, Lynemouth had come of age.

FRED REED - ASHINGTON POET

The town produced a number of men who combined pitwork with literature, and perhaps the best known exponent in the world of serious verse was Fred Reed.

In 1928, Fred, still working down the pit, had a book of sonnets published, entitled *An Undine Overture*. He later won the Sir Arthur Markham award, which was given annually to a 'labouring miner'. The slim volume went on sale, priced at one shilling, printed by Wilkinson's of High Market. Fred was obviously experimenting with the sonnet form at that time, and much of his more acclaimed work came later when he put the Northumbrian dialect to work with such effect.

Here is a sample taken from this, his first book, and inspired by the sea at Newbiggin:

> *Lo! as I slumber, roaming into night*
> *My weary soul doth hearken to the Sea;*
> *There shall it sip some vigour of its might,*
> *There shall its thoughts be tinged with majesty;*
> *There shall the muffled symphony of waves*
> *Sweep through its caverns with a cleansing roar.*

A few years later when writer Alan Robson, moved on from the Ashington Colliery Magazine to become a reporter with the Shields Gazette, Fred came out of the pit and joined the Welfare Staff on the writing team which published the Magazine.

(As a postcript: I was fortunate enough to win the same award as Fred, sixty years later, for a one-act play based on local legend, Jackie Milburn.)

HIRST PARK SCHOOL

The Hirst Central School (later Hirst Park Modern) opened in 1928 catering for boys and girls between the ages of 11 and 14. Leading the Girls School was Miss Gordon while Mr C Hemmingway was Head of Boys.

The *Park* was modern in every way, even to the extent of having flush toilets. From the beginning a great emphasis was placed on school pride and discipline; children wore uniforms, which up till then had been used solely by the Grammar Schools.

It was natural that much of the education had a leaning towards the practical with adequate workshops and domestic science rooms in the building. **MILDRED WATSON** joined the teaching staff of the girls' school in 1936 as a 20-year-old.

Mildred was brought up in Morpeth, going to Morpeth Council School and then the High School. She then went to Sunderland Teacher Training College for two years, and straight from there to teach at Hirst Park, appointed for Physical Training and English, but after a couple of years moving on to History and Music. She recalls:

It was a big school and the classes were streamed; my first class was a 'C' group. I was very glad going into the Staff Room to find people who had been at Morpeth High School with me, so I knew I had somebody to go to for help. On the first day, I had a timetable, but nobody told me that I was supposed to take my own Scripture lesson first. I waited and waited for the bell to go, but it never did. I went next door and asked Hazel Pollard why, and she explained that I should be teaching Scripture - I had no idea!

Miss Auty was Headmistress then and Miss Joisce had all the 'A' forms for PE. We had a hall, a library, heating you could regulate, much better than you can today, although the classrooms were built around a grassed courtyard with open arches to corridors, making it very draughty. These were filled in much later and what a difference that made to warmth. We took children from the South and North Schools. There was a variety of talent, but we had some very good children. The 11+ exam was taken in the Junior School, and we got some children who had very near misses with the exam - some had a chip on their shoulder. But they blossomed out, and maybe I shouldn't say it, but they received just as good an education as they would have had at grammar school.

My first year at school was hard and hectic. Because of my subjects, I had to take part in four school competitions with outside adjudicators, namely PE, folk dancing, verse speaking and play productions. For the latter, my mother and neighbours made lots of costumes out of curtains etc.

Netball took place in the schoolyard; the field at Hirst Park was full of ashes and rubbish. When I was doing Local History I took classes to meetings in the Council Chambers, and once the chairman said the girls could ask a question if they wanted. To my amazement, one girl stood up and said that the school couldn't play

Rounders on the field because of all the glass, and please could they do something about it. And they did! They came very shortly afterwards and levelled it.

There was a school canteen in the field in the early days. It was a building just below the school with a cook in a kitchen at one end, while at the other were some fine oak tables and chairs. We fed about fifty children each day - and that was long before school dinners were introduced - for twopence ha'penny a day. They were very necessary because times were hard.

The school closed at the outbreak of the second world war, in September, 1939, and we remained closed for about six weeks. It became an Air Raid Precaution post. The staff had to fill sandbags! I got an SOS to go up to an Amble school to do some teaching, and that was a nasty journey, travelling to Ashington from Morpeth and then catching a bus to Amble. Luckily I was only there a few days when I received word that I had to come back to the Park - they were re-opening.

The History syllabus came up through the ages. We always tried to get up to the present day because that was missed out of a lot of syllabuses. There were two kitchens for Domestic Science, a Needlework Room, an Art Room, and classes went to each kitchen for either half a day or a whole day while Needlework and Art shared classes. We made our own schemes of work, passed by the head. The occasional boy who wanted to be a chef came to us for cookery lessons. During the war we had 'American' and 'Russian' weeks. Concerts were arranged by CAMDIN, (an organisation set up to promote the Arts in Northumberland) and Hirst Park Girls took part together with Bothal and East schools. Later the Music and Drama Association was formed, and for years the Central Hall was packed when they performed. Children filled the upstairs while guests sat downstairs. Christmas Carols were sung massed and individually with guest conductors. We formed a Guide Company for the girls, and there were many trips abroad for the children.

The first opera we did was Hiawatha in 1953. Sheila Armstrong was only eleven when she came into prominence with her first part in 1954 as Hansel; Dorothy Hall was Gretel; and Joyce Williams played the witch. We repeated that show a few years after, and Irene Middlemiss took the part of Hansel. There were lots of play productions, including French plays, and also dancing displays organised by Mrs Ingram.

But we had lots of good girls, many of whom still keep in touch, they're grandmothers now. A lot of our girls did well. Elizabeth Steel became a sister at the Freeman Hospital, some became midwives, lots became nurses, some took degrees, others started their own business.

I enjoyed the 40 years that I spent at Hirst Park.

Hewer (who has not had a tub for half a shift):
   "Heor! Is't Sunday morn oot theor?"

Bill (during heated argument) : "Aa'll bet ye
   ma pay."
Geordie: "Nivvor mind about yor pay; Aa'll
   bet ye a bob."

THE 'MAIN STREET' IN 1927

After a dreadful year of poverty in the town which saw many businesses close to shutting up shop, Station Road, or the *Main Street* as it was called, settled down to provide the people for miles around with one of the best retail complexes in Northumberland. The following list of business premises was taken from Kelly's Directory of 1927:

1	BROUGHS LTD., grocer		GRAND HOTEL
3	ORIENTAL BAZAAR, (J. Gibson prop)	2-6	RUSSELL COOK, drapers
5	PRUDENTIAL ASSURANCE	8	ARMSTRONG, Maggie, confectioner
5a	DOWSING, Miss L., sh/hand teacher	10	MARCHETTI, Guiseppe, refreshments
7	MIDLAND BANK	12	AISTON, John, ladies outfitter
9	BARCLAYS BANK	14	WILKINSON, Arth, stationers
11	DAVISONS, mantle warehouse	16	WOOLWORTHS
11a	WHITE, Hry, piano teacher	18	HARWOOD, Jas, draper
13	MAIN, John, cycle maker	20	DUNN, F. & Sons, bootmakers
15	SELIG, Myers, money lender	22	COSTELLOE, John, pawnbroker
15a	GLOBE, bootmaker	24	MAYPOLE DAIRY, grocers
17	PUBLIC BENEFIT BOOT CO.	24a	DICKINSON, Jas, photographer
19	SNOW's, George, ladies outfitter	26	ARROWSMITH, George, men's outfitter
21	MILLERS, bakers	28	HOME & COLONIAL stores
23	MACDONALD's, John, drapers	30	BOOTS CASH CHEMISTS
25	GALLEY, Harry, bootmaker	32	BURTON, Montague, tailors
25a	HETHERINGTON, Jas, dentist	34	GALE, George, butcher
27	MARSHALLS, furniture	36	LIPTONS, grocers
29	DAVISONS, mantles	36a	BURNS, Rbt, jeweller
31	WISEMAN, Eleanor, milliner	38	DOCHERTY, Wm, tobacconist
33	STEWARTS CLOTHIERS, tailors	40a	DOCHERTY, Wm, tobacconist
35	RIGBY, John, ironmonger	42a	GRAY, Robert, auctioneer
37	JOHNSON BROS, dyers	42-48	BLACKLOCK, Rbt, draper, bootmaker
37a	MOSSMAN, Mgt, Voses depot	50	HUNTERS THE TEAMEN, grocers
37b	MILLER, Fred. dentist	52	TYLER, A, bootmakers
39	BURGESS, Wm, butcher	54	PORTLAND PRINTING WORKS
39a	CARTER, Wm, dentist		
41	MARCHETTI, Alfredo, conftr		
43-45	BUFFALO CINEMA		
47	WALTEN, Jes, furniture		
49	BRITISH BAZAARS		
51	SHEARER, LW, auto engineer		

WINNIE OXNARD had first-hand knowledge of two of Ashington's biggest shops: Blacklock's and Snow's. She said:

I went to the Bothal School then began work at Blacklock's on Station Road. It was the tallest shop in Ashington, with a basement and four floors. On the flat roof was a ballroom and a tea-garden with waitress service. They had mannequin parades, whist drives and a Tea-dance every Saturday afternoon.

Both my sisters were working there when I started. The eldest was on Display, dressing the window; the second left to go to Snow's. You were trained in every department then.

But Robert Blacklock, who lived at The Haven, in Newbiggin, made the shop too posh for Ashington. It wasn't the kind of place miners' wives felt comfortable in. They thought it was making too much money, the way the shop always sold the best clothes. But Blacklock's did have better merchandise than anyone else in town.

Father helped to cover the upper front of the building with the white marmola exterior. When it was finished it was a lovely store. Russell Cook's was nice, though not half as classy as Blacklock's. But they kept wages very low - I was only getting five shillings at fourteen, which hardly kept me going in stockings. The shop had an overhead pulley system for sending money up to the cashier, and I was forever putting a hole in the sleeve of my frock through yanking away at the lever. It wasn't all cash transactions, there were quite a few ticket-agents, such as Joe Embleton - not the bookie - who moved into Dunkeld on High Market; another was Hunter, Dowson and Keeble, a mother and two daughters. Vouchers then were usually for about five pounds.

Robert Blacklock always said "Missee do this, Missee do that." We worked from 9 am to 6 pm weekdays, except Wednesday when we finished at one o'clock; every other Friday we stayed open till 8 pm and on Saturdays it was a nine o'clock finish.

But they mustn't have been making a profit, and went into liquidation; a Bishop Auckland firm took them over: Doggarts, who were Quakers. Many of the staff were finished, but some, including me, were kept on. I must have been lucky for jobs were hard to get in those days.

But I didn't stay long after that and followed my sister, Doris, across the road to Snow's. George Snow was a lovely man to work for. Initially, he had been a buyer for Dormand Stewart, but had bought this shop in Station Road from two sisters who, by sheer coincidence, were called 'Snow' as well, but were no relation. One of them later married Aitcheson, the stationmaster's son.

George knew exactly what the customers wanted. He would walk down the main street and see silk stockings on sale at McDonald's for one shilling a pair, and hurry into his own shop and tell me to mark ours down to elevenpence ha'penny. He sold cheaply, but turned his stock over very fast, basing his prices on small profits - quick returns, and it worked. We sold everything there; I can remember selling motley-coloured Long Johns at one shilling a pair, and as the sizes went up so you added thrupence to the price. Every member of staff was trained to be a buyer.

He was great with his staff, and gave me the position of buyer. I knew all our suppliers by numbers. George would ask: "Who did you get that price from?" and I would say: "Number 17." Then he might ask if I couldn't have got a better deal from Number 3. I once won a tanner off him that way, when he queried a price. The staff were well looked after. He knew how to keep us happy and there would be boxes of chocolates or strawberries if we were asked to work late or maybe miss a lunchbreak. I lived nearby so came home for my lunch. He was the only man in the shop until 1946 when his son, Denis, came out of the army.

Shortly after that George became ill and Denis took over the running of the shop. I must have been getting about three pounds ten shillings a week by then, which was still a poor wage. As shop assistants, we worked on a commission and were able to buy clothes at a good discount: cost price plus five per cent.

One day, I went to a Newcastle warehouse on business, and I was told by the owner that Norman Howard, of Farnon's department store in Nun Street, was looking for a new buyer. He asked me if I would be interested in going for an interview. I said that it had never occurred to me to leave my Ashington job. But after having an interview, I was offered the job, and I said I would take it. Coming back home on the bus I thought to myself: "What have I done?"

When Denis Snow found out he offered me more money, but I told him a forced raise was no good. My first wage at Farnon's was over seven pounds, and with a 12-journey bus pass costing only seven shillings and sixpence, I was a lot better off.

After I had been working at Farnon's for a while, Mr Howard said that what he needed was a duplicate Miss Oxnard, and would I ask my sister, Doris, still working at Snow's, if she would join me, and she did. Ivy had left by then - she had married a policeman before the second war broke out.

There's never been shops like Blacklock's, Snow's or Russell Cook's in Ashington since they closed. You knew that you were buying quality then, but now, well...it's not the same.

As for the pit heaps...do you know, as soon as they got rid of that huge pile of ash it became ever so draughty here in Council Road - they had acted as a wind-break, you see. I never thought I'd miss them.

JIMMY MAIN, the youngest of a family of ten, was born in the flat above Paddy Mullin's shop in Station Road in 1917. His father was a tin miner in Cornwall who came to the north east with his four brothers in the 1890s. They were among a number of Cornishmen brought in by the Coal Company to break a strike, and Jimmy's father, whose real name was John Tremayne, decided that his surname was too obviously Cornish and changed it to Main.

John Tremayne met and married a Cambois lass, Mary Jane Frazer, while working at Ashington pit. But his heart wasn't really in mining at all - he had a clever pair of hands and began to repair bikes, initially working in his own backyard in Clyde Street, before taking over the back premises of a shop in Station Road.

In 1918, a year after Jimmy was born, John severed his ties with the pit and bought a shop at 13 Station Road. Main's Cycles sold all the popular makes such as BSA, Raleigh and Enfield, but these were all standard size machines which didn't cater for the small or large person. Jimmy Main remembers:

The family began making their own bikes custom-built to suit orders. They used to stove-enamel them using an acetylene burner in the back yard. I even made a bike myself when I was very young. It was to carry me and three of my mates to Bothal School - one on the crossbar, one on the handlebars, me on the seat, and I fixed a couple of steps either side for the fourth who was sometimes Jack McLauchlan or Bob Hogg.

I didn't do all that much schooling in my last year as the headmaster, John Gray, used to send me for all the messages on my bike. I was a bit of a tearaway at school, and the day I left Mr Gray showed me a leather tawse which was in tatters. "Jimmy", he said, "that was brand-new the day you started - now look at it!"

The day after I left school I began work in the garage at 102 Station Road. Initially, this place had been a fish and chip shop which my father had converted from a private dwelling. My two sisters, Mary and Kate, looked after that business. After a while, the place was renovated again and surfaced this time as a garage. We repaired and sold cars, motor bikes and cycles. I was there till the second war began when I joined the RAF. I decided to enlist rather than waiting to be called up and maybe risk having to go into the Navy - I'm a real bad sailor.

When I was demobbed we bought a draper's shop called Hope Herriotts at number 1 Laburnum Terrace. During the war, the shop and backyard had been used by the army as a depot. We converted it and stayed there until retiring in 1980. As soon as we packed up, seven different cycle shops opened in Ashington.

The bikes we made were cheaper than the brand names. We used to charge four pounds nineteen shillings and sixpence, and an extra five bob if you wanted a three-speed gear attachment. We even ran our own Hire Purchase scheme, risking the bad payers. Somewhere along the way we acquired another letter in our name, and the cycles were stamped Maine with an 'e'.

Jimmy Main has been a member of the Rotary Club for over forty years and is a past president. Like many others, he was taught a musical instrument as a boy - a fiddle - by Bill Henderson at the Harmonic Hall. Jimmy was one of several Round Tablers who organised regular fancy dress parties. One particular night at the Harmonic Hall, he surprised and terrified the audience with a display of knife-throwing, using a wooden netty door for a backdrop and a trembling Tabler for a target.

"ASHINGTON'S NOT SEE BAAD"

By 1928, Ashington folks had settled into a routine: they had social amenities including many halls for entertainment, and a modern main street in which to do their shopping. Obviously well satisfied with his lot, Will Cain, in the 1928 Colliery Magazine, wrote the following, entitling his piece: *Ashington's Not See Baad*:

When ye taak aboot Ashington ye waant te think o' waat it used to be, and then be very thankful ye waarn't born twenty or thorty yeors syunnor. Nee shops, nee pictor haals, nowt atween the Grand and the Portland - whey, cheps hed nowt to dee but git drunk, an' the dee tell me, though Aa nivvor seed it, that on New Yeor's Eve they carried men yem in coal boagies.

Aye, that's aad Ashington, but just luk at it the day. Waat d'ye think o' the railins an' the pavement alaang Sivinth Raa front, eh? Waat d'ye think o' the skyscrapers Blacklock's and McDonald's? Darsay they wud myek any Yankees feel duzzy. Then there's Woolworth's. If a toon hes a Woolworth's, it kind o' classy, ye knaa. Then there's the Fire Brigade. Waat odds if there's nee wetter when they git ti the fire, they aalways look bonnie i' those uniforms. An' the Footbaal team! Aa divvent waant nee arguments, so Aa'll say nowt abbot it, but it's a gud groond they hev.

An' then luk at the pictor haals! The Wallaw for the folks wi brains, ye knaa, a quarter o' chocolates for the wife an' a pipe o' baccy for the chep, an' there they sit. The Buff for the tother kind - in at the fowerpenny end, and oranges an' monkey nuts for the wife an' a packet of Woodbines for the chep. Then the Miners - that's where ye gaan when yor wife wants aal th' oficials' wives to see hor new hat that's as gud as theors any day (so she says). Nee toon can beat Ashington for pictor haals. (A'ave missed the Piv oot, but ye knaa wat kind o' folks gans theor!) Ashington hes nee Boxing Stadium, proper like, but they built the Cooncil Chambers insteed, an' Aa think it's ivvory other Thorsday neet the meet. An' so Aa cud gan on showin' ye that Ashington's not haaf se baad as people myek oot! Nee toon's like it. So fetch yor sooth-country folk, an' Aa'll taak te them. An' if they divvent like it, Aa'll just hev to tell them waat a graand bus sarvice we hev, so's they can easy git oot on't.

ASHINGTON INSTITUTE

The official opening of Ashington Miners' Welfare Institute took place on a sunny Saturday, November 15th, 1930. Like the one opened earlier at Lynemouth, this was more than just one more building for miners and veterans to meet and have a game of billiards. Standing in one of the most pleasant spots in Ashington, tucked away into a corner of Peoples Park, the 'Top Tute', as it became known, catered for a wide variety of tastes. It was opened by Manny Shinwell, a Member of Parliament and Secretary for Mines: a man genuinely interested in the miners' social welfare. He formally unlocked the door, climbed the stairs and went out on to the balcony to address a large crowd.

A variety of exhibition games were played. Two bowling champions from Scotland gave a display of indoor bowls; the Billiard Room was opened with an exhibition match between J Barrass, Pitmen's Champion of Northumberland and J Simpson of Ashington receiving 70 points out of 300. Mrs J Nicholson played a varied selection on the piano in the Ladies' Room, and tea was provided by the directors of Ashington Coal Company in the Portland Hotel after the opening. A whist drive was held in the evening.

The Welfare building was voted the best in the North. On the ground floor was a reading and writing room; a library; secretary's office; a hobbies room equipped with power-driven lathes and work benches; a photographic dark room; and a six-table billiard room. Upstairs was a games room which incorporated skittles, carpet bowls, darts, table tennis, bagatelle, and rope quoits; a lecture room opening on to a veranda; a games room for draughts, chess, dominoes; and a ladies' room used as a private sitting and work room. An outdoor bowling green was planned as well as provision for a putting green and three hard tennis courts and a swimming pool. Charges for miners were one penny a week, plus the same to the guarantee fund. The general public paid three shillings and sixpence a quarter. Aged miners were allowed free use of the building.

Temporary repairs to Sheepwash Bridge. 1894.

Hirst Castle. 1890.

Ashington Railway Station. c.1910.

Station Road. c.1910.

Council Chambers. c.1910.

Memorial at Harmonic Hall. c.1910.

Grand Hotel. c. 1910.

Miners Hall and Theatre. c. 1910.

Low Market and Woodhorn Road. c. 1910.

J. Main's shop in Laburnum Terrace. c. 1956.

Kathleen Newton's Class of 1950. St. Aidan's R.C. Infant School.

Hirst East Boys School. 1950.

Cllr. J. Devon receives cheque for overseas aid for Senegal. 1986. Hawthorn First School.

Pity Me isolation ambulance. c. 1926.

Ashington Hospital League of Friends present a blind. c. 1950.
(left to right) Mr. Wright, secretary, Mr. Scott, president, Matron Olive Tanner, and founder members Mrs. Eva Stimpson, Mrs. Scott and Mrs. Winifred Barron.

ASHINGTON MINING SCHOOL

On 30th July, 1931, John Murray, was appointed Headmaster of the new Ashington Welfare Educational Institute, in Darnley Road, with a salary of £510.

It was the Education Committee who decided on this rather long-winded title for what later became known simply as the 'Mining School'. The Director of Education stated that the Central Committee for the Miners Welfare Fund would bear the cost of the building and provide equipment which amounted to £11,158.

At the inaugural meeting of the governors, chaired by Fred L Booth, and including Alderman John Craigs, Captain William N Craigs, and the Reverend Sammy Davison, it was decided to offer Murray the headship because: *"He has successfully conducted the Day Continuation School for ten years."*

A meeting of the sub-committee took place to consider applications for caretaker on 13th October. Thirteen applicants plus their wives were asked to attend two interviews. The candidates included two miners, one fireman, a baths attendant, a loco driver, and eight unemployed men.

Wilfred Richell was the lucky man who was selected, collecting £2 a week for his wages plus twelve shillings rent allowance for his house at number 7 Duke Street, with the proviso that he moved nearer the Institute when a house became available.

From the outset, the take up of student places was very disappointing and only 95 students enrolled for the first year's Day Classes.

The governors were asked to set £124 aside for crazy paving to lay on the two quadrangles so that *"physical exercises can take place."* The Headmaster reported that the grounds adjoining the school had been trenched by eight men who were to use the land as allotments. He said: *"The men have agreed to relinquish the land on demand without any compensation."* It was recommended that 15-20 shrubs and trees be planted at the front of the school.

With the school opened for over two years it was noted by the governors: *"We deplore the fact that in such a large mining community so few lads are willing to take advantage of the facilities provided."*

But there was little wonder that places were not being taken up. The subjects which were being taught, mainly Mining and Engineering, were narrow in scope and aimed solely at examinations. The same regime who had controlled the old school had moved into the new premises, and were patently lacking in innovation and drive.

The problem was highlighted in 1935 with the visit of two of His Majesty's Inspectors of Education. HMIs Stelfox and Lawton were critical of the syllabus for its lack of breadth, saying that, with regard to the subjects of Maths and Science: *"the interests of students appear not to have been consulted."* They also criticised the headmaster for his lack of *"vision, energy and resources."*

Leaping to the school's defence, Captain Craigs said:

With regard to the syllabus, let it be borne in mind that the Youth who attend this school are not the intellectual cream of the District. The criticism of the Headmaster is not justified - he has done everything asked of him.

If any serious alterations were made to the present curriculum it may be the case that the Ashington Coal Company would withdraw its very substantial financial assistance from the School.

This thinly-veiled threat referred to the prime role that the Coal Company played in financing the first Day Continuation School when it opened in 1919, which included in its constitution that the establishment *"Should further the education of selected lads who had only an Elementary School education."* With no signs of any type of further education in sight, it was the ACC, holder of the purse strings, who were confident that educationists would not dare to force 'modern' ideas upon what they obviously regarded as 'their' school.

Following on from the HMI's critisism, appeals were made to all the collieries in the Ashington area, asking them to send more students. It was also reported that the syllabus of Maths and Science had been revised to make them: *"a little less ambitious."*

49

With the outbreak of war in 1939, instructions were issued to all schools to the effect that Ashington was a 'neutral' area and that no evacuation of children or reception of children from other areas would take place.

On the 12th February, 1941, it was decided to adopt the name *Ashington Mining School*.

An Air Training Corps was established in Ashington with its Headquarters at the Mining School under the leadership of Mr Donald Hindson. A Youth Group was also based at the school, organising many field trips to Stannington and Belford.

John Murray, then sixty years old, resigned his post with effect from 31st December, 1941. It was decided to offer the headship to Robert Hay, with a salary up to a maximum of £610. Mr Hay accepted, and also took on the position of Adjutant with the ATC. After barely twelve months, and meeting twice a week, the membership of this organisation had risen to one hundred and fifty. As the war dragged on it lost many of its members to the Royal Air Force.

The immediacy of the war was obviously being felt in Ashington when it was reported in the governors' minute book on the 18th June, 1941, that tenders had been accepted from G Arrowsmith Ltd for the supply of blackout material; other items bought that day included a roll of linoleum purchased from Ashington Co-operative Society, priced at six pounds seventeen shillings and sixpence, which included 'laying'.

In June, 1944, Robert Hay took up an appointment as a Schools' Inspector, and Charles Pulford, of Cannock in Staffordshire, was appointed Principal. Because it was a wartime appointment, Pulford's contract was only on a temporary basis.

When the 1944 Education Act was passed it became necessary for the school to change its title once again, and it adopted the name: *Ashington County College and Mining School*.

With the added responsibility of new courses starting up - Bakery and Confection drew in 30 students, Motor Engineering another 45 - Pulford saw his salary rise to £725 in 1945.

The nationalisation of the coal industry on the 1st January, 1947, resulted in the absorption of the Ashington Coal Company by the National Coal Board. Their ties with the school were severed by a letter from the Education Committee on the 14th April, noting that: "We are very grateful to the ACC for the role they have played in Education in the Ashington area."

At the same time a new *County Plan* for education had been drawn up based on three points:

1 A Technical School for boys and girls be built at Ashington as part of the extension of the Mining School as a Technical College.
2 A County College for boys to be established at Ashington for Day Students only.
3 The existing Mining School to be remodelled as a Technical College with departments for Industrial Art, and Design and Crafts.

The buildings for all the above were to be "...provided on the existing site plus additional areas of approximately 17 acres and 18 acres to the south and south-west of the present site."

After the war, servicemen began to drift back to Ashington and the Mining School flourished. A Student's Association arranged Common Room facilities; football and cricket teams competed in local leagues; an annual College Ball proved a big success.

But amid the euphoria there was an undercurrent of tension among the overworked staff. It spilled over on 9th November, 1949, when a dispute arose between a teacher, Mr Dos Santos, and the Deputy Principal, Mr Clerehugh. The former was not happy with an extra chore which he had been ordered to do: check day-release pitmen's time cards.

A fracas took place in the staffroom which culminated in Dos Santos ripping off Clerehugh's tie. More was to follow, for when the pair were summoned to the Head's office to explain their conduct, Dos Santos said he had nothing to hide and that he would inform the police. He attempted to pick up the receiver on the Head's desk, but was restrained by the other two.

Pulford ordered him to put the phone down, and Dos Santos alleged later that both the Head and his Deputy assaulted him. It was all very unsavoury and resulted in the temporary suspension from duty of Dos Santos who terminated his employment a couple of months later.

Going into the 1950s, the student population of the school rose to over 1000, straining both accommodation and administration. As a short-term remedy it was resolved that:

a) a modern typewriter be installed,
b) that a telephone be connected to the staffroom, and
c) that night class overspill was to be housed at the Bothal School.

On the 7th February, 1951, the governors resorted to desperate measures in order to` ease the space problem by bringing in three wooden huts which had stood derelict at Cresswell since the end of the war. Each had a pot-bellied stove in the centre, and one caused the rafters in the roof to overheat to such an extent that the Ashington Fire Brigade had to be called in to deal with a classroom blaze.

Word came through from the Education Committee that a Principal was to be appointed to take up his duties at the new Technical College with effect from 1st April, 1955. However, it was envisaged that it would be September, 1956, before the new building was ready. The move could not come soon enough for the harrassed teachers, some of whom were doing 60-hours excess class teaching every week.

In the run-up to the changeover it was announced that Charles Pulford would take over the running of the new Technical College.

On 14th May, 1957, the governors of the Mining School handed over the administration to the County Technical College, as the new establishment was to be known. Captain William Craigs, who had been a founder member since its origin in 1931, said: *"I have enjoyed the work and am proud to have been associated with the Mining School. I hope the Technical College will meet with the same success."*

On 9th February, 1960, the name of the new building on the site of Wembley Field was again changed, this time to the *Northumberland County Technical College.* It was soon catering for students from all over the county, and Halls of Residence were built in 1963 to accommodate the commuters.

Charles Pulford retired in May, 1965, and his place as Principal was taken by Alan Davies, former Principal of a College of Further Education at Aberdare, Glamorgan. Future custodians were to include Brian Hardcastle and Roy Beasley. Willie Mills, Falkirk-born sportsman and former vice principal at Grantham College, now has charge of *Northumberland College*, happily relieved of its trendy acronym NORCAT, which has almost tripled in size since its inception.

ASHINGTON GOES TO THE DOGS

Many Ashington hands were thrown up in horror in 1936 when the town acquired a Greyhound Stadium at Portland Park, headquarters of the local football team. Up until then the miners had enjoyed a Sunday morning session of whippet racing where bets were struck with opposing owners and the odd Flash Harry who considered himself expert enough to make a book on each race.

The Ashington Colliery Magazine, which had always strongly condemned any form of gambling or drinking, waded into the miners each month exhorting them to see the error of their ways.

Methodist ministers continued to harangue the pitmen gamblers of the community. None more so than the visiting Reverend Percy S Carden who, on hearing that the United Bus Company had been refused an application to put on duplicate buses to get people to the local dog track, had this to say:

What are the things in Ashington I most admire? I admire the wide streets and well-kept gardens; I admire the cleanliness and homeliness of the houses in the colliery rows; I admire the splendid schools and the people who staff them; I admire the doctors who can be seen at all hours of the day and night assiduously carrying on their ministry of the healing; I admire the quiet efficiency of our Ashington undertaker and the reverent way in which neighbours show respect in the hour of death; I admire the men I meet coming home from the pits, begrimed though they be, and always think of them as men to whom we owe a debt which we can never pay, for it is one of my fundamental beliefs that a miner should be as well paid and as well housed as a lawyer, a schoolmaster, or a parson; I admire the fine work done in our hospital, where doctors, sisters and nurses, scorn delights and live laborious days; and I admire the good work done by our public servants and councillors.

But I loathe the Greyhound Racing Track, with its hideous Totalisator, its crowd of simple greedy fools who prey and are preyed upon by the Gambling Vampire who always gets the blood of the children; I loath the clubs if they be simply drinking clubs, rather than the houses of fellowship and good comradeship they were intended to be by their best-intentioned founders; but I admire the Picture Halls and the variety of shows they present - shows which are often well worth seeing, though naturally not always so; I admire the Central Hall with its fine imposing front and wonder why the people of Ashington do not appreciate it more; and the churches which in the main are not so well attended as one could desire - and many other things. I also admire the decision of the Northern Area Traffic Commissioner to prevent henceforth the duplication of buses on routes used mainly by people who in more senses than one are 'Going to the Dogs'.

MEDICAL MEN

Dr J J HOBBS came to this area from Newcastle in 1940 to take up his first medical position as junior house surgeon to Dr Bonar at Ashington Hospital. He remembers:

There were only three wards then, two for men, one for women, and each with 24 beds. But very often, because of lack of space, we had to have a number of beds running up the centre of each ward.

Andrew Bonar, the Superintendent, was a marvellous man. He did almost everything from gynaecology to complicated abdominal surgery, as well as dealing with all the traumatic stuff we got from accidents at the pit. My accident call-outs down the pit were often a bit of a non-event. They were usually for men who had been trapped by falls of stone, but by the time I got there the poor fellow would have been freed and I would meet him being stretchered out. On my first venture underground I ruined a perfectly good suit, claimed for its cleaning from the Ashington Coal Company, but received a brusque refusal by return of post. After that I made sure that I was supplied with overalls and a hard hat.

I was on stand-by at the hospital for the major accident which happened when the plane crashed in the colliery rows in 1940. Several people were severely burnt. It's amazing how wartime seems to give an impetus for new ideas in medicine. Then it was thought necessary to treat severe burns immediately; now, of course, you treat the patient for shock first. We had lots of fatal cases of TB - it was called consumption then - but the introduction of the drug, streptomycin, has made tuberculosis a rare disease. In those days it was recommended that TB patients be moved out on to the balcony for the fresh air, even in winter; the only result was that they not only died, but died in great discomfort. Another medical fallacy in the treatment of high blood pressure, was to refuse to feed the patient on any red meat.

We were desperately short-handed. The hospital boilerman named Biggins was supposedly just there to keep the fires stoked up with coke, but he performed many other duties. He was the hospital porter; occasionally took X-rays; he put plasters on broken limbs then took them off again; he even stitched up the dead body after a post mortem!

There was also at that time the Pity Me Infectious Diseases Hospital, built on what is now Nursery Park estate at North Seaton. This was usually full of young children, often two dozen or more, suffering from Diphtheria. This was a serious problem, and it was the first childhood disease to be controlled by immunisation.

After about six months at the hospital I returned to Newcastle, but came back in 1941 to take over the practice of Dr Bruce at 174 Station Road. He was a grand old man, working right up till he died at the age of eighty five, still cycling around the town on his visits to patients. Because of his age it was a relatively small practice: about three hundred. It took some time for a new doctor to be accepted into the mining community, and a newcomer was in trouble if he gave an old lady a bottle of green medicine when she had been used to pink. Families then paid sixpence a fortnight into the Public Medical Service, a kind of early NHS. The miners were on what was called the 'Lloyd George' which gave them free medical attention and prescriptions. Doctors were paid on the number of people they had on their list. Other practices in Ashington then included Dr Noble (father of John), MacLean, Macfarlane, Spence, and Andrew Irvine at Lintonville. I moved down to Laburnum Terrace and took Bill Beattie as a partner.

My wife and I began to get involved with the Central Hall choir in the 1950s under Normanton Barron, and enjoyed the Celebrity Concerts very much. I was also president of the Ashington YMCA at the time the new building was opened by the Princess Royal in 1960. In 1966, together with Dr Beattie, I moved into the Lintonville Medical Group with Alan Barr, and the Irvines, Andrew and his son Donald. I was there till I retired in 1976.

ERIC BIRD's father, Stanley, arrived in Ashington from his home town of Penrith, riding on a motorbike with the Army Dental Corps - this was prior to 1920. One of the first dentists to set up practice in the area, Stanley met and married Sadie Fail, a local shop owner and, she says, related to the sheep-stealing Fails from the village of Pegswood. Eric was born in 1925 and his brother, Ivor, four years later. Eric remembers:

Young girls in those days had all their teeth extracted as a 21st birthday present from their parents. A father once brought twin girls into the Dental Hospital in Newcastle in 1943 when I was a student, and ordered that we remove all their teeth, but we chased him. It was criminal the way people wanted to get rid of perfectly good teeth just so they 'wouldn't have to bother with them later on'. When my father first set up practice in North Seaton Road there were very few other dentists in Ashington: Arnold Cawthorne, who combined a chemist's shop with a dental practice in the back room, was one, and Fred Miller another.

I went to Morpeth Grammar School and played a lot of rugby and cricket. My parents had a bungalow at Cresswell - a sort of second home - and it was there that I took up an interest in birds. In those days, long before the formation of Cresswell Pond, what are rare birds today were abundant - corncrakes breeding on the coastal fields. My mother bred budgies and small foreign finches. One lady asked her if she could breed her a Scotch budgie, one with a Scottish accent when it said 'Pretty Joey', and she was serious! I also loved music, and tried to play tenor saxophone in the band at the Princess Ballroom before it burned down.

Eric's wife, Lena, remembers that night vividly. Her family were living just behind Ashington Co-op, in Viewlands, and they all went out into the garden to see the flames leaping up into the sky. Eric continued:

It was a shame. The Rink, as it was called, was owned by Alf Shepherd, and had a very big orchestra with about a dozen musicians. Much later, a group of Rotarians, of which I was a member, started up the 6-Club in the cellar of the old Grand Hotel. We used to have a 'do' every Saturday night with dances and fancy dress competitions.

I qualified as a dentist in 1948, and did two years in the RAF with a commission of Pilot Officer and later Flight Lieutenant. At one station, a group of Canadians had gone home and left a stack of musical instruments behind. Alan Hollins was there at the time, he played drums, so we started our own band.

My brother Ivor was a very good athlete, and we both played rugby for Ashington. He became a professional runner and almost persuaded me to take up the sport. We were training with Jackie Milburn at the Rec, and this old fella was watching me run. He said to Ivor: "Hey, Ivah, I wouldna' run him ower hard - he doesn't luk varry strong."

It was all fixed up for me to run at Peoples Park the next day in a professional foot handicap. Ivor had entered me with the nom de plume of Z Zombie of Ashington. Typical! But I never turned out. It would have affected my amateur status, and I had a rugby trial for the county lined up. Later, Ivor was reinstated as an amateur.

I began to take photographs of birds around the 1960s, and captured them on old 8mm cine. I have had photographs published in various magazines; in 1992 one of my photos is going into the Photography Year Book. Although I'm retired now, I'm often asked to give slide shows and talks. I was made an Associate of the Royal Photographic Society - I'm proud of that.

THE SECOND WORLD WAR

In 1939 I went to my first school: the South. It was pure expediency on my mother's part because we were living at the time in Monkseaton Terrace, only a couple of hundred yards away from the huge red-brick building. I can remember nothing of the few months spent there.

Being a strict Catholic, my mother decided to move nearer to the RC school so that I would be brought up *in the faith*. We shifted on Jack Rodway's flat trolley to the second block of Poplar Street, to live in an upstairs flat above the Berkelys. Grandfather Talbot went too. My grandmother Ann, wearied with continuous childbearing, had died at the age of sixty, a year before I was born. It was to be the first of many moves that our family made, always at my mother's instigation, and *always*, it seemed, because of me and my particular circumstances.

In spite of Britain's austerity, the war years of 1939-45 seemed to bring the people of Ashington even closer together. Basic commodities such as bread and eggs were scarce, and the worst blow for the children was the complete lack of ice cream. Ration books appeared for almost everything from sweets to suits, and the jubilant cry: "There's tabs at the Store!" sent scores of pinny-clad housewives scurrying up the main street to join the long queues already forming at the Co-op.

Queues became a way of life, stretching from most of the grocers, bakers and butchers shops. Women would tag on at the end, clutching small children and large wicker baskets, sometimes not even knowing what they were waiting for.

In preparation for serious food shortages throughout Britain, domestic pets were destroyed in large numbers; only six months into the war there were reports of a plague of rats and mice, and a plea went out to stop the slaughter of cats in an attempt to keep the vermin under control and out of the local bakeries and butchers' shops.

As fears of large-scale bombing passed away in 1941, Ashingtonians were not alone in suffering privation as the war moved into the sea, and the *Battle of the Atlantic* saw food supplies dwindle to practically nothing. The weekly ration of certain basic foods amounted to little more than what had previously only served one person. Now a whole family had to exist on a shilling's worth of meat (about half a pound); one ounce of cheese; four ounces of bacon or ham; eight ounces of sugar; two ounces of tea; eight ounces of fats (including no more than two ounces of butter); and two ounces of jam or marmalade.

Women had to *register* at a particular shop, and under-the-counter dealings became commonplace.

The Ministry of Food provided recipes for all manner of strange substitute dishes: *Woolton Pie* (vegetables and potatoes); lentil roast; and carrot cake. One of my favourite dishes was dried egg: a yellow powdery substance which made up into savoury pancakes. Later we were issued with servicemen's surplus rations, and I remember marvelling at scraping cheese out of a tin.

The very young children were deprived without even knowing it. Never having had the choice of grapes or bananas, peaches or nectarines, I thought that the gooseberries and strawberries grown on our allotment were the only fruit which existed - apart from an orange and an apple which miraculously appeared in my father's pit stocking, hung at the bottom of my bed, on Christmas mornings. Chocolates and sweets were strictly rationed on a points system. An 'E' coupon enabled you to guzzle a quarter pound of sweets, while a 'D' only got you two ounces, or a small bar of chocolate. With materials also scarce, toys were usually made of wood: forts, guns, tops and whips. There were no footballs, and us lads had to make do with kicking pieces of felt material stitched into a round shape and stuffed with clippings left over from a proggy mat. But there was always a tin can lying in the gutter to kick and chase on the way to school.

On other days we played *Penky Folla* up Station Road. This was played with marbles or penkers (ball-bearings) and the object was to hit your opponent's marble which then became your own. The trouble with winning was that the victor had to sit through an entire day's schooling with a pocketful of rattling glass marbles, invariably dropping one at a time through the small hole which worked its way into every young boy's trouser pocket.

After-school games normally meant using a small ball in some way or another. For *Hot Rice* you needed a bat as well, held in front of the body like a shield to ward off other lads's shies at you; *Cannon* was contested with one person building four pieces of wood upon a tin can while the rest of the group ran to the nearest lamp post and back; a similar game was *Tinny*, only this time everyone had their own can; *Itchy Dabba* was another favourite, being a form of Hopscotch; *Mount the Cuddy* was an hilarious romp consisting of two or three lads forming a hump against the netty wall while others jumped on their backs. Girls were allowed to join in with the lads in their games, but only the most boisterous ever bothered.

Fish and chip suppers were a luxury for the well-off, and many shops vied for customers - at one time 27 fish-fryers opened nightly in the backstreets of Ashington. Most folk proved loyal to one shop whether it be Renzo Cosimini's opposite the Mortimer Club, Meg Dawson's in First Avenue or Bailey's on Hawthorn Road. The gable ends of most Ashington streets, housed these fish and chip emporiums - some you might even *sit in* and you could always hear someone saying that Mrs So-and-So's fish was the best in town. A fish and a pennorth during the war cost about a tanner, and that was for a very generous helping, crowded with a pile of scrampshuns, small crinkly pieces of batter.

Air raid warnings often came in the middle of the night. When the sound of the siren blared out - it was situated on the top of the police station - my mother would lift me out of bed and carry me downstairs to the flat below. Our neighbours - the Lynch's - had converted some space below the stairs where we huddled until the *all-clear* went. For some reason this was looked upon as the safest place in the house. Many people crouched under specially bought steel dining room tables, while others, my father among them, said that if they *had* to die they would prefer it to be in their own beds.

There cannot have been many towns in Britain that went through the second war without at least one story of personal tragedy, and Ashington was no exception. The date was June 6th, 1940; the time 1.45 am. The following is an amalgamation of information given by Jim Slaughter, who witnessed the disaster, and H Ling of the Royal Air Force in a letter to Colin Wanless.

Jim's father, Ernie, coming home from nightshift, noticed a plane circling continuously over the town. He disturbed his wife who awoke and went into a bedroom where her four sons lay fast asleep. As she approached the small upstairs' window a huge black shape loomed down on her, roaring like some demented flying monster. She ducked and the object passed just over her head.

Now the lads were all wide awake and frightened out of their wits. A terrific crashing noise sent the boys dashing to the back window just in time to see an aircraft turn a house in the next street into a flaming inferno. Within seconds a mass of people crowded the colliery row already lit up like a bonfire. They helped as best they could with stirrup pumps and buckets of water. But someone spotted, silhouetted in the blazing sky, first one parachute then another, and as the two figures plummeted to the ground, thoughts of a German invasion leapt to bewildered minds, and children were rushed indoors.

One parachute was caught up in a tree in Long Row; the other floated down to the level crossing at the end of the Cross Row. Angry miners waited for the airman, whom they believed was a German, to land. As if sensing their antagonism, a voice drifted down to earth: *"I am British."*

Someone alive to the danger of explosions asked the stranger if there were any bombs on board. *"No,"* the flyer confirmed, *"but there is a lot of ammunition."*

The voice was that of Pilot Officer Westlake who had been flying the aircraft, a Bristol Beaufort bomber of 22 Squadron, Coastal Command, based at RAF North Coates. Conjecture was that Westlake had ditched the plane in what he had mistakenly thought to be the North Sea. Seemingly the pilot's error could have occurred because Ashington's ranks of serried colliery rows when viewed from the air in moonlight look uncannily like waves upon the sea.

The other parachutist, and only other survivor, was Sgt Twitchen. It was later confirmed that two air gunners, Sgt Harris and Sgt O'Flaherty, were both dead on the aircraft before it crashed, killed by enemy fire during their mission near Flushing.

It wasn't until daylight that the full impact of the damage could be assessed. One engine had demolished the downstairs of number 77 Fifth Row killing the two parents of the Cox family instantly. A daughter, Gladys, jumped from an upstair's window to escape the flames but died in Ashington Hospital the next day from horrific burns; son William was reached some time after the impact, and suffered serious burns to his arm.

According to Tom Boutland's diary, there were an incredible 237 air raid alerts over Ashington. Bombs and land mines were dropped, but luckily without loss to human life.

Perhaps the most spectacular aerial attack to take place over Ashingtonian heads occurred around noon on Thursday, August 15th, 1940. Jim Slaughter was working on bank at Ashington Colliery. He remembers:

It was a beautiful summer's day when the siren went. Most of the men headed for the shelters in the Timber Yard. Essential workers stayed by their posts until a second Emergency Warning was given. Now there was a real scramble for safety. After a short time some of us ventured out of the shelter and watched scores of tiny dots trailing white vapour across the sky.

It transpired that over 130 German aircraft had left Stavanger in Norway bound for the north-east airfields of Dishforth and Usworth. Their brief was to flatten these fields then give an almighty pasting to Newcastle, Sunderland and Middlesbrough. Each of the 72 Heinkel bombers which made up the first wave, carried 3,000 lbs of bombs. They were escorted by over 30 twin-engined Messerschmitt fighters.

But ahead of the main thrust, 20 Heinkels were supposed to act as a diversion, drawing out the north-east based British fighters. However, a bungling navigator in the lead plane of the main group took the 130 aircraft along the *same* route as the diversionary planes. There was no element of surprise as the radar camp at Anstruther had already reported a major strike by the enemy. RAF Acklington quickly scrambled 12 Spitfires; they were soon joined by reinforcements from 72 Squadron, plus 12 Hurricanes of 605 Squadron based at Drem near Edinburgh; number 79 Squadron's Hurricanes at Acklington were also placed under readiness.

The Hurricanes of 605 Squadron engaged the enemy in an area stretching from Blyth to Amble, giving some bewildered Ashington folk a breathtaking display of aerial warfare right above their heads. By now the sky was full of planes and the 12 Spitfires from Catterick merely added to the confusion.

At least nine enemy bombers were shot down, two Heinkels crashed into the sea at Cresswell, and the crews were plucked from their dinghy by an astonished fisherman from Amble. Coastal anti-aircraft fire was said to have accounted for shooting down at least one other plane. The German fighters turned tail at 12.40 pm, leaving 12 of their aircraft in the North Sea. Extravagant claims of losses on both sides were made, but a realistic assessment released later said that the Germans lost 21 planes while the British lost only one, a Hurricane of 605 Squadron. The raid had achieved nothing, and only a few civilians of Seaham in County Durham suffered, while 20 houses were damaged in Sunderland. The folks of Ashington crawled out of their shelters and continued as though nothing had happened, most of them blissfully unaware of the part they had just played in the 1940 Battle of Britain.

Retired teacher, George Davison, recalled another near miss:

An air raid took place on Tuesday April 15th, 1941. A German bomber dropped two land mines with parachutes attached. One landed in Sheepwash and exploded with a deafening bang which shook all the windows in our house, some three quarters of a mile away. The second bomb landed amongst some trees and remained suspended by the parachute cords which had become entangled in the branches. Three days later, at about 4 pm, a bomb disposal squad detonated the bomb, but failed to give any prior warning. The resultant bang did nothing to calm the nerves of the residents still trying to get over the shock of the first bang.

Perhaps the biggest shock to the local pitmen's system was registered when a bomb fell at Woodhorn Colliery, shattering the steam fan. It was common knowledge that enemy bombers used the huge 180 ft Woodhorn chimney as a landmark to veer inland from the North Sea. Fortunately, no-one was injured.

LOCAL JOURNALISM

Credit for publishing Ashington's first newspaper goes to the Wilkinson family for putting the *'Ashington and Hirst Press'* into the houses of local people as early as 1900. Initially, the four-page broadsheet carried no advertising of any kind.

October 8th, 1909, saw the paper providing full front-page coverage to an address given at a meeting of the Institute of Mining Engineers in Newcastle. The main thrust of the piece was devoted to the sinking of a mine shaft at *The Carrs* in Newbiggin.

Letters to the editor were not of the sniping, snide kind one reads nowadays. This particular edition contained two reasoned arguments; the first entitled 'Symbolism in the Church of England', and the second 'The High Church Controversy', written by Joseph John Hills of Newbiggin, and J Gordon Cartlidge, respectively.

The paper reported the opening of the original Morpeth Cottage Hospital by Mr Blencowe Cookson, describing it as: "*A substantially built house, having on three sides fine open views of the Wansbeck Valley, standing at the foot of the Dogger Bank on the Mitford Road.*" Sporting enthusiasts were well catered for, with lengthy descriptions of local football matches, racing pigeons, and leek shows.

The *Ashington and Hirst Press* continued to be printed by the Wilkinsons, until changing its name in the 1930s to the *Ashington Post*. It was subsequently taken over and absorbed into the *Blyth News*.

E N DAVISON's name appeared at the bottom of the *Ashington & District Advertiser* and practically every local dance or lottery ticket, greyhound or football poster for nearly forty years.

Edward Norman Davison originally lived in the small village of Snitter, quite close to Rothbury. On leaving school there, he served a seven-year apprenticeship with a local printer. After coming out of his time, and anxious to start up on his own, he attempted to buy premises in Bedlington. When this deal fell through he came to Ashington in 1932 and carried on for some time printing in the backyard of his rented house at 27 Poplar Street.

But the authorities clamped down on this little cottage printing industry, and the Davisons moved first to Woodhorn Road before converting the butcher's shop at the old Equitable Stores on 2nd Avenue. His widow, Bridget, remembers that it was Walter Lawson who stood as their guarantor at the bank, and that they leased the place from W N Craigs. Indeed, it was Craigs, the solicitor, who was instrumental in building the Davison's next, and most well-known printing works, behind Ashington YMCA in 1936.

The Ashington Advertiser was the town's first free newspaper, financed solely by advertising space. Michael Wilkinson, son of the man who had the first post office in High Market, was publishing the *Ashington and Hirst Press* and, for a while, the two were in direct competition.

However, according to Norman Davison Jnr:

There was no competition at all, because our papers were delivered quickly and efficiently by good Catholic lads who ran the others off their feet.

Because of a paper shortage, and owing to wartime restrictions, the 1940 copies of the paper were no more than A3-size folded in half. The front page was almost completely taken up with an illustrated advertisement from F R Little, an electrical goods dealer in North Seaton Road, while optician, S Aaron, pleaded with the: 'Many thousands suffering from eye strain caused through Black-Out Darkness' to have their eyes tested at 37A Station Road.

The front inside page was mainly left over to advertising Ashington's five cinemas: *Pinocchio* was showing at the Wallaw, in the week commencing 28th October, 1940, prices: Adults: Stalls 7d. Circle 10d. Child: Stalls 4d. Circle 6d. On the opposite page was the programme of Ashington Dog Stadium where the best dog at the time was *Cosa Maite*, a record-breaking animal who on New Year's Day, 1941, was set to give the following hefty starts: *Larry Lynx* 4 yds; *Pay Packet* 8 yds; *Cosa Disseac* 16 yds; and *Louisianna* 18 yds. Secretary at Portland Park then was Bobby Williams, and J Ulliott was manager.

In the same edition, Ashington Football Club had an interesting team out which included English international, Stan Mortenson. The team due to play Consett was chosen from: Tapken, Hindmarsh, Bell, McLain, Briggs, Daglish, Dobson, Thompson, Farrington, McIntosh, Mortenson, Thornton and Hays.

A regular advert was placed by two domestic agents: Mrs Hill of the 5th Row, and Mrs H Richardson of 89 the 8th Row. These were the two ladies responsible for sending many a young local lass (or lad) into service for well-to-do families around England before and after the war. Another weekly advert was placed by Robert Gray, Rigby & Co, who held Auction Sales on Saturdays and Mondays, with Bobby Gray as auctioneer. After the war he was helped by a young Louis Johnson who, in the first instance, was a general dogsbody, but is now holding auctions in his own right in Morpeth.

Notices of concerts were commonplace, including: 'A Weekly Concert for Soldiers', every Monday evening at the *Middle Market Club,* pianist Mr Ralph Reay; the *Hirst Progressive Social Club* ran concerts: 'To provide Xmas Gifts to members and members' sons serving in His Majesty's Forces', artistes appearing on December 12th, 1940, included: Madam Poxton, Peter Riggs, O'Keefe the comedian; Chairman Temp Atkinson, and piano, Mrs G Thompson. The *Comrades Club* and the *Fell-Em-Doon* ran Sunday Night Go-as-you-Please shows with a two pound prize, featuring Tommy Camsell and Ralph Reay, respectively, on piano.

Bringing the war right into the backyards of Ashington was an advert in the October 25th, 1940, edition from Ashington Industrial Co-op:

Hirst Furnishing Department
WE HAVE FOR SALE
Metal Air Raid Shelters
Tested and Approved
FROM £22-18s-0d

A poignant wartime reminder of the suffering on the home front was camouflaged under the heading Accommodation Wanted: *'Two furnished rooms (near to Central Hall) for soldier's wife and three children (urgent)'*.

The war affected the printing trade more than most and the Ashington Advertiser ceased publication at the back end of 1941 for the duration. Davison Snr was called up as a sapper in the Royal Engineers, and another partner, Billy Davison, (no relation) went into the Navy, while Charles Marshall was conscripted into the Royal Artillery. Bridget Davison and her three young sons carried on as best they could, still printing lottery and dance tickets as well as the dog programmes which she had to have done at Morpeth.

With war costs escalating, towns were being encouraged to donate funds. A War Weapons Week was held in May, 1941, and a target of £100,000 for Ashington and Newbiggin was beaten by over £50,000. No specific weapons were earmarked, but the general aim was summed up in the slogan: Blast Hitler. Author, J B Priestley, was invited to give a talk at a gathering in an effort to swell the fund.

Ashington motorists were warned to be on their guard concerning black market petrol coupons which were said to be circulating the area. Uniformed patrol men were authorised to stop any motorist and ask the reason for his presence in the district. Suspect coupons were destroyed immediately. It was decided to register women born in 1919 and 1920 for war work. Mothers of families were exempt as were wives of servicemen. Wages for agricultural workers were fixed at ninepence (4p) an hour for those over eighteen.

In June, 1941, a journalist for the Blyth News reported:

A small poorly dressed woman approached me as I was waiting for a bus. She asked if I would go into a shop and buy her a packet of cigarettes for her husband. I had to refuse as I knew very few women are served with cigarettes nowadays, and certainly never in a shop where they are unknown.

The scarcity of fruit had Ashington Cllr Hugh Reilly complaining:

That steps be taken to ensure impartial allocation to retail fruiterers in Ashington. People are getting oranges who have never had oranges before. I hope the medical officer will see that fair play is done.

A week later, it was reported that a lady butcher had been fined for selling rabbits at a price above the going rate of tenpence a pound. She was charging one shilling and twopence for skinned rabbit, and was fined £4 plus costs.

Many Ashington miners' wives cheered when they heard that the Northumberland Miners Association had decided to make Thursday a payday rather than Friday. One miner's lady commented: "*With shops closing early and limited stocks going so quickly, a Thursday payday will give us a chance to do our weekend shopping before the last minute.*"

In mid-1941 a new training scheme for young Ashington miners was launched, thought to be the first to be tried in this country. Based on a Dutch idea, it was readily adopted by the Ashington Coal Company, already with a record of consideration for its employees. Men who were given the task of overseeing the young lads on an underground training face in the Plessey Seam of the Duke Pit, included Joseph Docherty, Cud Pringle, Jack Kirkup, Jack Crook, and Tommy Patterson.

A timely pat on the back to the Ashington Group of Painters was given by Lady Ridley when she opened an exhibition of their work at the Laing Art Gallery, Newcastle, in June, 1941. She invited the artists to visit her at Blagdon Hall. James Brownrigg accepted on behalf of the Group.

The vexed question of sport on Sunday was solved by Ashington Council passing, by fourteen votes to six, that: "Sunday games should be allowed in the Veterans Hut at Hirst Park." Prior to this, the man in charge of the Park had been struck by an old man while trying to take away his dominoes.

It was July, 1941, when I was seven years old and living in Poplar Street that a Saturday morning visit to the Hipp almost got me killed. When the pictures came out my friends walked home but, being lazy, I caught the bus at the White Elephant. The nearest stop for me was at the Piv corner. I got off the single decker bus, saw that a lot of people were waiting to get on, and decided to run across the road in *front* of the bus.

Unfortunately, I hadn't seen a wagon - a three tonner belonging to Anderson's the greengrocers - overtaking the stationary bus. It hit me square on, ran right over the top of me, and for a few seconds I was out cold. I regained consciousness to find the driver bent over me; as I looked up I could see the oily underbelly of the wagon - I was lying in the middle of Milburn Road underneath a three-ton truck!

The man asked me if I could move. I tried to get up, but my right hand was still lodged *under* the back wheel. When the driver realised this he jumped back into his cab and pulled the wagon forward a couple of feet. By then a crowd of onlookers hustled around for a better view of the small boy with the squashed and bleeding hand.

The driver - I never knew his name - asked me who I was and where I lived. I looked up at the sea of blurred faces, recognised my cousin, Kay Scott, and pointed towards her. "*She'll tell you,*" I whispered, before passing out once again.

My next recollection is of being stretchered on a trolley along the corridor of what I later learnt was Ashington Hospital. Kay must have done her job because my mother was beside me. A figure in white, later identified as Dr Bonar, loomed over me and placed a piece of black gauze against my mouth. Ether.

I screamed for him to stop. *"You're choking us,"* I yelled, again and again, before the anaesthetic began to take effect.

I awoke the next morning, head bruised, an aching hand swathed in bandages, and lying among crisp white sheets in a strange bed. The chap next to me smiled and said: *"I hope you don't make as much noise awake as you do when you're sleeping, young'un, cos you've been screaming blue murder all night."*

The first of January in the year 1944 arrived in Ashington on a washday-blues Monday. Folks didn't know it, but the end of war was still 18 months away, and even if they had been told, few would have believed it. Pessimism and optimism had merged into one, as reflected in the speech of Alderman William Cookson at a safety awards ceremony to LNER motor drivers at the Grand Hotel:

I envisage a time when the ordinary man, enjoying holidays with pay, will own a cheap car in which he can take his family into the country. I wonder whether Ashington's antiquated system of arterial roads can carry with safety the increased volume of traffic which will ensue after the exceptional developments which can be expected in the motor industry after the war.

Entertainment that evening was provided by the Ashington Alpha String Quartet. Making their first public appearance, the group consisted of Bill Henderson and Tom Chambers (violin), F S Houghton (viola), and R G Webster (violoncelo).

Sport, like most things was rationed, and Ashington football club still kept their promise of the previous year *not* to play in the North Eastern League until cessation of hostilities. Not so patriotic, the Ashington Greyhound Racing Company held a dog meeting at Portland Park every Saturday afternoon. Winner of the first race of the year was evergreen favourite *KTM*, with *Dashing Corporal* coming in a close second; at the famous New Year's Day Powderhall meeting, locals Ossie Sword and R J Hale both won heats; and Tom O'Keefe, the Lynemouth-born boxer, defeated Seaman Davis of Chatham on points over ten rounds.

Attention was drawn once more to the vexed problem of the town's pit heaps. It was already recognised that they presented a serious health problem to the town. Further reinforcement was provided by the Northumberland Association of Urban Councils, which reported on March 10th: *"The new process of delivering refuse on to the Ashington heaps increases the height thereof, with the result that light and breathing space is being depleted. This, coupled with the smoke and fumes, is bound to have a detrimental effect on the health of the community."*

Ashington Colliery had just introduced an aerial ropeway system to carry its waste to the sprawling heap. Gangs of small boys gathered to watch, fascinated, as tiny cable-car buckets transported their unwanted cargo to the top of the festering black slope. Often, the heaps flared into life as the contents were strewn from above. It became a leisure-time activity for the children as the giant mountain turned into an escalating Everest on their own doorstep.

One piece of bad news came on February 24th, 1944, when it was announced that mineworkers in East Northumberland were to have their wages 'made-up' to the 'Porter award minimum', formulated by a government committee looking into the question of miners' pay. The new ruling meant that underground workers were guaranteed a minimum of £5 a week, while their surface colleagues would be paid £4.10s.0d. The pits then worked an 11 day fortnight. But the scheme was closely linked to combat persistent and wilful absenteeism - anyone who lost a shift risked losing a considerable amount of money. Not only that, anyone absenting himself from work without a very good reason was liable to be fined and sacked. It was looked upon as a serious dereliction of duty, akin to cowardice in the face of the enemy. Fining one man ten shillings, Magistrate William Reavly, asked witheringly: *"Do you want our soldiers to fight with their bare hands?"*

On March 6th, Cllr John Brotherton likened Ashington's allotment holders to: *"Everybody's Cinderellas."* This was because two more sites of gardens were being lost; the first because of a new extension to the Darnley Road Mining School and the second to make way for 120 houses at the end of Woodhorn Rd., destined to become Woodhorn Villas.

At an exhibition of children's art on March 9th, 1944, H M Spink, Director of Education said, *"Ashington is one of the liveliest communities in the county, in the widest sense of the word."* The school children's display was combined with the work of the Ashington Art Group, its excellence prompting Cll Hugh Reilly to comment: *"Although Ashington could never be made into a health resort, much good is done by providing local people with the opportunity to view such beautiful works of art. What the town needs now is a good public library."*

At Ashington Magistrates Court on March 13th, 1944, W N Craigs, while prosecuting an Ashington miner for stealing another man's tokens from a coal tub, said: *"The practice introduced last year of placing tokens on the outside rather than the inside of tubs, opens the way for dishonesty."* The man was accused of obtaining one shilling and tuppence to which he was not entitled. He was fined £5 plus costs.

The Ashington Sea Cadets Corps celebrated its first birthday with a Parents' Day at the Princess Ballroom whose owner, Cllr Alf Shepherd, was chairman of the management committee of the corps. Mr Shepherd presented the cadets with six sets of drums, while bugles, donated by James Chrisp and other Ashington businessmen, were accepted by commanding officer Lt D Sutherland.

The Sea Cadet presentation proved to be one of the last functions held at the ill-fated Princess Ballroom. Less than a month later, the luxurious dancehall was burned to the ground on 'all-the-fours': the 4th day of the 4th month, '44.

One fine Saturday in the summer of '44, ten thousand people crammed into Peoples Park to see the many delightful exhibits at the Ashington and District Agricultural Show. The only unhappy people that day were a group of ladies from the Temperance Society who had strongly objected to the granting of a liquor licence, allowing beer to be served from inside a tent.

Professional Foot Handicaps got under way in July, and two Newcastle United forwards, Charlie Woolett and Jack Milburn, entered the £40 80-yds handicap at Croft Park, Blyth. Neither footballer managed to trouble the judge, whereas *four* Ashington runners: N Norman, N Pentland, N Cliff, and W Johns (boy), all won their heats. N Cliff, real name Norman Campbell, went on to win the final from the odds-on favourite, Jackson. The following week another Ashington sprinter, Nichol Dalkin, running as J Nichol, won the Blyth final.

Ashington folk were well used to queuing as the war dragged on into its sixth year, but it was waiting of a different sort which was queried by Ashington councillors following complaints that the cinema queues at the Regal were getting out of hand. It was suggested that the management bring back the system of booking seats in advance which had worked so well in the past. A councillor remarked: *"No Ashington housewife wants to spend all day working in the kitchen, then, just when she should be putting her feet up, be asked to spend up to an hour standing in this time-wasting exercise."*

The penultimate year of the war ended as it had begun, with a greyhound meeting at Portland Park. The last race of 1944 was won by scratch dog *Comet* (nickname *Sharkey)* from *Glentworth Captain*, running off a massive 18 yards.

THE ITALIAN CONNECTION

The Italian connection with Ashington is mainly due to the wanderings of Alfredo Marchetti. He was born in the mountains of Tuscany in the little village of Sommocolonia (High Colony), near the city of Lucca. One of nine children, he left home to seek his fortune in the wide open states of mid-west America in 1904.

Peddling plaster of paris statuettes in a basket, the 14-year-old boy who spoke little English trudged the streets of Chicago and Detroit for nearly three years. Feeling homesick, he returned to Italy. Soon afterwards, someone suggested that he try his luck in one of the booming coal towns of north-east England.

Alfredo began selling fruit at 41 Station Road, next to the Buffalo cinema, in 1911, but it was in the making of ice cream that he was to become better known. In the basement below the shop, using ice-packed hand-filled freezers - no advanced technology then - he made his first helping of delicious ice cream.

Alfredo's brother, Guiseppe, also opened up a confectioners at 10 Station Road, while another brother, Giovanni, stayed at 39 Station Road, but left after a couple of years. Alfredo was married in 1918 to a sweet Italian girl, Amelia Rossi, whom he had met on a previous visit while she was working in a hotel restaurant near the railway station at Lucca.

Alfredo changed the name of his shop to the *Station Temperance Bar*. Many of the workingmen's clubs had opened, selling Federation Ale from their own brewery, but the shrewd business-minded Italian knew that there was still a need for a place where the *women* of the town could congregate. He brought in an American Soda Fountain which he had seen working so well in the States. It proved very successful and he was able to employ three other Italians who came from the same part of Tuscany: Giovanni Rossi, Renato (Sammy) Badiali, and Christopher Arrighi.

In the course of time all three men left to start up on their own. Rossi, who served in the Italian army in the first war, took a shop next to the Pavilion Theatre; Arrighi ended up at Guide Post via Carlisle; and Renato Badiali was offered half of Alfredo's shop to ease the payments of the high rates being charged during the depression years of the late 1920s.

Other Italians followed from the Sommocolonia/Barga area, and immediately took shops. Lorenzo Cosimini had a fish shop opposite the Mortimer Club; his brother Harry owned a similar business in the 7th Avenue; and Peter Mazzolini opened *The Miners Temperance Bar* quite near the Miners' Theatre. They were all astute moves, deliberately placing the shops where a ready market was available.

Two of Ashington's major billiard saloons in the periods before and after the second war were managed by Italians: the large room above Shepherds (now Joplings) run by Coia and Rossi, and the Harmonic Hall (now a car salesroom) leased to Tonieri and Marchi in 1946.

The Pieronis were another family to come from the same village as Alfredo and open up yet another ice cream shop in Ashington's Station Road. Bobby Pieroni and his sister Norma occupied a number of premises before eventually settling in the shop opposite the council chambers.

Other Italians who came to the town in the early days but didn't stay were Gallone and Notarianni, both from the Naples area, as was Fella who began a bus service in the early 1930s from Ashington to parts of remote north Northumberland. One who did stay, but by the seaside at Newbiggin, was Bertorelli who had once lived in a village near Genoa. A daughter, Gioconda, played piano with great expertise at many concert halls all over England before retiring to the fishing village as a teacher of pianoforte.

When the second war broke out, because Italians were thought to be a 'security risk', some of the older men were interned in a prisoner of war camp on the Isle of Man. One such man was Jimmy Padreddi, then living at Cresswell, who had been appointed as a part-time coastguard before Italy entered the war on the side of the Germans. This ludicrous situation was quickly resolved, and the Italian prisoners, who also included Rossi and Badiali, were allowed to return to Ashington.

The Latins spoke a halting staccato type of English which often seemed brusque to the Ashingtonian ear. Giovanni Rossi appeared quite frightening to a small child when he banged his fist down on the counter and demanded: *"Next! Hey, you boy, what you want?"* What was amazing, however, was the way the Italians brought a new meaning to the word 'enterprise' and to the concept of self-help. The typical Ashington miner couldn't wait to get his eight-hour shift done so that he could relax in whatever way he chose; but he was bemused by the Italians' capacity for working way beyond what local traders would term 'shop-hours'. The newcomers became almost a self-contained family within the pit community, bonded together by race, religion, and hard work.

The premises occupied by the Italians became much more than humble shops. Ashington's *Refreshment Rooms*, as one owner called his place, were the forerunner of the 1960s coffee bars. Meticulously clean, many had separate cubicles for couples to sit in private, while large pews accommodated up to ten people. Tables with wrought iron legs and marble tops, gave an air of elegance to each establishment, belying the grimy surroundings in which they stood. Each became a meeting place for courting couples who had nowhere else to go, making teenage socialising that much easier.

Alfredo Marchetti died in 1947, but even before then second generation Italians had begun to open up more shops. Peter Mazzolini's son, Louis, after being invalided out of the army during the second world war, took over from his father; Johnny Bacci moved into the fish shop once run by Louis next to the Store Arcade; an Arrighi girl married Ralph McGregor and provided the people of the Hirst in Milburn Road with a much-needed ice cream shop; Vince Marchetti set up a confectioner's business at the top of Poplar Street while his sister, Nancy, took over Alfredo's Temperance Bar; another Italian man Ottavio Nardini, who had tried his luck first in Scotland, began trading at the bottom of Milburn Road; Amos Gonnella owned a fish shop at the 'top' Store corner, later to become Cuthbertson's; a Bertorelli brother started the Lido Cafe, next to Jas Walten's on the Station Bridge; Luciano Sassetti began trading in Alexandra Road; the Badiali sons, Louis, John, and Harry, after moving out of their Buffalo Cafe, took over the shop near the *Excelsior Club*, once owned by the Mazzolinis.

The town now had nearly as many ice cream shops as clubs, and the children of Ashington were spoiled for choice when the war ended and vital ingredients ceased to be rationed.

But that was far from the end of the Italian influence. Johnny Bacci, who had begun operating at Bedlington station, was later followed into the fish shop next to the Co-op on Woodhorn road by the Bimbi family, now famous for their fish and chip shops all over Tyneside and Durham City. An Italian girl, Adelaide Pavani, who had worked for Mark Reay in Newcastle, met and married John Tait, a Haltwhistle miner. They bought an ice cream factory in Choppington from Italian, Dominic Colonel, which had closed down in 1926. The Taits re-opened it three years later and began trading from shops in 3 Laburnum Terrace, once owned by Clemente Notarianni; in Newbiggin Road, and another on Bedlington bank. The Tait business carries on today, while Ashington's sole surviving shop with pure Italian origins is Mario's Cafe, using the *Temperance Bar* premises bought eighty years ago. The present proprietor boasts the same name as his grandfather, the original owner: Alfredo Marchetti.

POST-WAR EMANCIPATION OF WOMEN

Ashington was always a rough, tough mining town where men were men and women were ... yes, they *were* content to take a back seat in the very early days, to bear and rear sons to take their places down the pit, and to bring up girls to be servile and well-equipped with culinary skills. But the second war changed all that. Women found themselves needed for other tasks beyond childbearing, and the era of emancipation began.

Ashington Business and Professional Women's Club was founded in 1945. It was soon attracting attention from all sides of the community. One of the most outspoken members was Mrs **EVA STIMPSON** whose husband Vic owned a bakery in Woodhorn Road. As the Club's secretary in 1948, she wrote the following open letter to the people of Ashington:

There are quite a number of keen-minded spirited women in our town, but up to the present time they have usually been content to labour in the background, and carry out those tasks allotted to the female such as voluntary work in the social and public health service.

There are still some amongst us who will suggest that a woman's place is in the home with her family, but it should be stressed that woman's concern for her family necessitates her interest in local government, and national affairs, as much as her interest in home-making. She must be prepared to accept outside responsibilities, and women's organisations should aim to train individuals to accept public office as readily as men.

Marriage does not mean the sinking of one personality in another, but should tend to develop both personalities to mutual advantage. Man generally is still a little jealous of women's intrusion into public life and of repeated proofs of her ability, but woman herself is her own severest critic, she needs to dispel that feeling of inferiority which is so apparent when she is asked to compete with man on equal footing.

During the Club's AGM in September, 1949, Mrs Stimpson was elected Honorary President, following on from Mrs Jean Richardson. The latter had stung would-be male councillors by winning a seat as a *Rent and Ratepayer* candidate at an earlier council election. Other women on the Committee included: Miss J Morris, Miss T Clarkson, Mrs E W Graham, Mrs E Harrison, Mrs S Cook, Mrs Cookson, Miss Haggerty, Miss B Macfarlane, Mrs H Deitz, Miss A Stimpson, Miss Rogerson, and Mrs T W Furness.

The B & P ladies were not the only active female group in Ashington. Various Women's Guilds sprouted up all around the town depending upon their location. The Co-operative Society's Women's Guild met regularly, as did the *Tuesday Afternoon Club* who adopted the Great Ormond Street Children's Hospital, sending many donations of cash to help sick youngsters.

More and more women of Ashington were *coming out*, and now it wasn't just the vociferous Women's Temperance League that was making its voice heard.

MARY PRESTON is typical of the Ashington women who eventually threw off the fetters which chained them to the kitchen sink. Now aged over sixty, Mary is an accomplished artist and writer, besides winning numerous friends and prizes for her innovative knitting. She writes:

My first job had been at Stimpson's the bakers in Woodhorn Road. Eva Stimpson came to our house one day and passed me scrubbing the doorstep with a donkey stone. After she had talked to my mother, Eva came out of the house, tapped me on the shoulder, and said: "Come this way, Mary, I've got a job for you to do." I was fourteen, but I felt so new-fangled at having a 'real' job, and this was just my first day after leaving school.
I tried to better myself by going to shorthand and typing lessons with Mrs Tomlinson at her house - that cost one shilling and sixpence a time.
Hours worked then at Stimpson's were from 7 am till 4 pm, with a half day off on Saturdays. But sometimes it was after nine o'clock when I got home. It was 1942, and we supplied troops in the nearby camps at Boulmer, Acklington and Cresswell. Schools and local clubs were also used for billeting soldiers, and we catered for them as well. Customers queued at special times for any surplus we had. They had to have 'bread units' in order to be supplied, and we would have a laugh while they sang 'It had to B U', which was a hit song of the day. Ingredients became scarce, and the flour we were getting was almost brown. We were sent all kinds of 'substitutes' such as liquid paraffin and dried eggs, and one day a huge tin of petroleum jelly arrived. With that the cakes and pastry were a complete disaster. Afterwards, we just used it to grease the tins.
If someone had a birthday, christening, or some other kind of celebration, and they wanted to make a cake, they had to bring in ingredients from their own rations. Mrs Stimpson sometimes bought the staff a bar of chocolate, but we still had to produce our own sweet coupons. She took good care of us, and after her husband died she became President of the League of Hospital Friends, and received an honour for doing so much good work.

The Isolation Hospital for infectious diseases, situated at the aptly named Pity Me region of North Seaton, was never a popular place with the sick *or* the well, even as late as the 1940s. Mary recalls her experiences there as a seventeen year old:

I was feeling ill, and my throat seemed to be closing as I lay on a hard bed. My leg was numb from being jabbed by an outsize needle. A slim nurse asked an orderly for assistance to place two blocks under my feet. The orderly put down her long-handled mop with its swivel head, and helped to tilt the bed so that my head was in a lower position. I had diphtheria.
I was then working as an order-girl for Broughs the grocers, and the local Health Authority were making enquiries into the contacts I may have had. I learned later that they had come to the conclusion that I had become infected through handling money and order-bills in Pegswood where the disease was rife.
A girl of about twelve lay in the bed opposite. "So you've got it as well," she shouted. "So has our Jean and Jack, but they are allowed out, they are only carriers."
A trolley stopped at the next bed to mine. The patient was a four year old girl, too ill to be taken to the

children's ward. She looked so helpless, gurgling and gasping as though for life's breath itself.
Dusk came, heavy rain clattered on the corrugated roof, and I eventually fell asleep. The next thing I knew
was the curtains being drawn to let in the new day. I remembered the little girl and glanced over, but the bed
was empty.

PEGGY MAXWELL's mother was Mary Jane Henderson whose family lived in *The Ducket* at Cresswell.
As a young girl, Mary Jane went to Ellington school, and each time Lady Cresswell went by, she joined the
rest of the school sitting on the wall to wave an acknowledgement to her Ladyship.

Peggy's father, Jack Maxwell, came from a mining family, and gained a county cap playing soccer for
Northumberland in 1908. Not long after he started work at the pit, an injury from a fall of stone left him with
a permanent curvature of the back. Jack became a bookmaker, operating around the colliery rows until one of
his runners cheated him, depriving him of all his capital. He became a checkweighman at Linton pit and was
also Union Treasurer.

The Maxwell children were Peggy, Jim, Alan and Heather. Peggy first learned to clog dance under
the tuition of old Dick Ferrell, a world clog dancing champion, in the back-kitchen of his sister's house in
Newbiggin. Dick had fashioned a piece of wooden board one foot square, and charged sixpence a lesson to
the young hoofers. It was while Peggy attended the Park School that she developed an aptitude for
gymnastics, building her slim shape into that of an athlete, which proved a valuable asset later in her career.
But she remembers that her first job was driving a horse and cart for the Newbiggin Co-operative Bakery:

I had a disaster on one of my very first runs. It was a delivery to a small cafe in Newbiggin called Downie's.
I was backing the cart up to the door when I heard this shattering of glass. And when I went around to see
what was wrong I discovered that I'd backed the cart into the cafe's plate-glass window - there were trifles all
over the place!
When I was sixteen I decided to begin my own class, teaching youngsters how to dance. I placed an advert in
the Ashington paper, put postcards in various shop windows, and by these methods, plus word of mouth, I was
able to hire St John's Parish Hall, behind the White Elephant. The classes were very large - I wouldn't turn
out for less than twenty. Mothers would bring their girls (and boys) and sit around on long benches while I
put the children through their paces. Molly Metcalfe was doing something similar, and she operated from a
building on Station Bridge.
I choreographed for a couple of concert parties: the Co-optomists and the Thespians. When I was eighteen, I
read that there was to be an audition for the Hilda Baker Show, at Blyth. In those days she had her own show
which she produced herself; Danny La Rue got his first big chance through her. An Ashington lad called Bob
Hart was singing with her, too.

It was then that Michael Mooney, Peggy's future husband, entered stage right. He remembers:

I'd come across from Ireland like a lot of other lads as a navvy - a term for navigator - building roads and
suchlike. I had just finished helping to build an Ordnance factory in Nottinghamshire when the whole gang
was moved up to Eshott to build an aerodrome. I had digs in Ashington, went to the Princess Ballroom one
night, and met Peggy there. After that we went around together, and when Peggy went on tour we kept in
touch.

Peggy's dancing feet must have impressed at her audition because she landed a chorus part. After a
couple of years on the road, Hilda Baker took her to one side and said that if she wanted to get any further
than the chorus line that now was the time to branch out. Then, Hilda was paying her chorus girls three
pounds ten shillings, and that was for six nights a week plus three matinees; on Sundays the troupe travelled
to their next venue.

Peggy left that show, next stop, the Garrick Theatre in London. She then went on to work with

Ramsbottom and Enoch and Me, officially called *Happidrome*, on the Isle of Man. By now she was responsible for choreographing entire shows. Towards the tail end of the war, she became part of an ENSA show touring Germany. At one base she was leaving just as Louis Stoddart's son, Brian, a gifted pianist, was moving in.

Wartime Germany was rife with black market goods, and Michael kept Peggy well supplied with parcels of coffee which she was able to swap for "practically anything". ENSA members were also given an alcohol allowance, and as a non-drinker, she was able to exchange those at the going rate. She continued:

After the war, through me being a member of the Variety Artists Federation, I began to get work in British films. In 1946, I was an officer Wren in 'Piccadilly Incident', with Anna Neagle and Michael Wilding; in 'Hungry Hill', a Margaret Lockwood film which also starred Jean Simmons, I choreographed an Irish reel; and I fell down a flight of stairs as Sally Gray's stand-in during 'Green for Danger', in fact I fell down those stairs a few times - I was getting ten pounds a fall! Alastair Sim and Trevor Howard were in that picture, too.

Michael Mooney married Peggy in 1947, and for a while she put her feet up and relaxed. But, as boredom set in, she took up her dancing classes again with renewed vigour. Soon she was giving tuition at half a dozen separate venues: Morpeth, Blyth, Acklington aerodrome, Ashington YMCA, and a Scout's hut down Lintonville. An old 1949 poster shows her advertising for the Arcade Hall: *The Peggy Maxwell School of Dancing, for Tap, Ballet, Acrobatic and Speciality, with Joe Riches on the Piano. Price one shilling and sixpence.* She went on:

It was a hectic routine, sometimes doing two classes a day, and I loved it. But I was too much of a perfectionist. I set myself very high targets, and if the dancers failed to reach them then I became very frustrated. It was when I was asked to put on a pantomime at St Georges hospital, in Morpeth, that I finally told myself that I'd had enough. After the show, Dr Irwin, having paid the fees and expenses said, jokingly, that it would be cheaper if I worked there full-time. So I did! It turned out that I spent 18 years there as an occupational therapist doing social and musical movement with the patients. And now...well, I still go to St Aidan's Centre on a Tuesday afternoon for the sequence dancing, but it's purely for pleasure.

The ever-changing moral values imposed upon Ashington's female population over the years, according to one of Ashington's favourite mums, **CISSIE CHARLTON,** have not been for the better. She stresses:

Call me Victorian if you like, but I think when we were young we were far better off for not knowing the facts of life. I went to the South School where you were segregated, lasses from lads, and I used to hate to play netball. You had to wear this short gymslip and showed all your knickers when you jumped up to catch the ball. My brothers would sit on the wall and watch us lasses playing in the schoolyard, and the whistles and jeers that would come out of them whenever you jumped up made me blush. In fact I begged my mother to keep them away.
I was born in 1912 and was brought up with four brothers, but I still never knew anything about the facts of life. When my mother was carrying our Stan in 1926, she would point at her belly and say: "Watch it, lass, cos this is what'll happen to you if you're not careful." I didn't really know what she was on about. She made me cart our Stan all over in his pushchair cos she knew I couldn't get into much bother when he was around.
I went away to place (service) when I was fourteen, still green as grass. For the first two years I was at a big house in Watford then I went to Harrow. My mother was fretting with me being so far away, so my brother, Jack, fixed it for me to go to Leeds where him, Jimmy and George were playing professional football.
It wasn't so bad there. I worked for a Mr Longstaffe who bought and sold all sorts of things from the markets. His missus liked a bet on the horses and if she knew I had a few minutes to spare she would send me to the local newsagent - who was a bookie's runner - with a bet. There was no uniform to wear there either.

I came home some weekends and got pally with an Ashington lad, Joe Bennett, who I'd met at the dance. We got engaged, but while I was away he knocked around with someone else, and later he broke off with me. I went out with a lad from Leeds who I met at the swimming baths while I was there, but nothing ever came of it. A great pal of mine got herself into trouble with a married man and she had his bairn. Oh, it was a great scandal in those days to get pregnant outside of marriage. Folks called her all sorts of things, but I knew she was a canny lass.

I came back home and got a job at Fred Oliver's pork butcher's shop. I got ten shillings for a 7-day week, sometimes working till very late at night scrubbing the pans for the next morning - he was a hard man, and hated paydays.

With money in our pockets, me and my sister, Esther, used to be dance crazy. We would go all over the place for a dance. Jimmy Padretti had a hut near the sands at Cresswell, and me and Esther would walk there and back, and never think a thing about it. Dances were held at North Seaton Institute, often starting at midnight and going right through till five in the morning. My father was very strict and he would order my mother not to leave the door open, but to light a candle in the wash-house for us. Me and Esther were always worried in case he carried out his threat, but mother was always there waiting to let us in.

Men were to be feared in those days, and the stories of wife-beating were commonplace. My husband Bob was never like that though. We met at the Princess Ballroom and were married in a matter of months. After that we danced all our lives. The ceremony was held at Morpeth Registry and after everything was paid for we had thirteen shillings to live on for a week. Luckily, my aunt had a grocer's shop, and she arranged for us to pay in arrears which saved our bacon.

Our family lived then in 18 Laburnum Terrace. The United Bus Company had a shop on the corner and the workers there used our toilet. They owned the upstairs flat, and when that became vacant, mother blackmailed them, saying that if Bob and me didn't get it then they would have to start looking for another toilet.

Mother was horrified when I had our Bobby just a couple of years after Jack, she didn't think that was a decent enough time. I asked her how to stop having children and her only advice was: "Get off at North Seaton before ye arrive at Ashington." The next one, Gordon, didn't arrive for another six years, and mother enquired: "Are ye wrang again, wor Cissie?". I thought I would get into bother again when I said "Yes," but she just said that if I waited another six years then that would be soon enough.

I might be old-fashioned, but I think life was better when sex was never mentioned. And there was no such thing as divorce for the likes of us. If you did make a mistake in your choice of man you just stuck it out for the sake of the bairns. Me and Bob were going through a bad patch and I said to him: "I'm leaving you the minute wor Tommy is fifteen." Come the day of his 15th birthday, Bob says to me: "Well, are you not leaving then?" "No", I told him, "you've mellowed since then."

I had to have a breast removed when I was forty, and that was something else you never talked about. They were saying prayers for me at St Andrew's, I was so poorly. Tommy was too young to get into the hospital to see me, and he was crying his eyes out at the end of the corridor. I told Bob to bring him around to the outside window so that I could tell him I was all right. He cheered up after that.

A short time ago me and our Jack were appearing on Irish television, and we were asked about our most embarrassing moment as a family. Now, Jack is like me, he's honest about everything, and he looked at me and said: "Should I tell them, Ma?" And I knew what he meant, but just told him to go ahead.

He told the story of how he'd come home after my operation and heard the washing machine making this terrible clanking and grinding noise. Husband Bob, couldn't knock two nails together, so he couldn't fix it. Jack said he would take the washing to the launderette which he did, bunging everything into the washer. Imagine his feelings when this washer began to make exactly the same noise. A crowd of lady onlookers came to view the scene, and there was my bra with one cup made of metal wires bashing itself against the window of the machine every time it rotated.

When Jack had finished relating this story to the studio audience they were in stitches and the interviewer was in kinks. They love Jack over there cos he's so down to earth, just like me.

THE YEAR OF '47

My new bike got me into trouble with the law in 1947.

Even though I only lived a couple of hundred yards away in Pont Street, I always cycled to Priestman's Institute. Chucking out time was ten o'clock, and North Seaton Road was as black as pitch one night when I came out. I jumped aboard the bike which had not been fitted with lights, and headed down towards the *Mortimer Club*. But I hadn't seen the policeman, Sgt Neilson, coming the other way.

He spotted me and shouted: "Stop!" It was, of course, an offence to ride on the public highway without lights. I put my head down and pedalled furiously past him, reckoning that my robust thirteen-year-old legs would soon put distance between me and the ageing bobby. That was a mistake!

Neilson did a *wheely* in a 360 degree turn and was after me like a shot. I took a left turn into Poplar Street to lead him away from my house. I had seen Roy Rogers do that at the Piv. His brakes screeched as he banked his handlebars and gave chase, some 20 yards behind. At the top of Poplar, I turned left again at the public urinals next to the *Grand Hotel*, and whizzed down the back alley. And all the while he was there, shouting for me to stop, and all the while a blind panic told me to keep going.

Ten minutes later, with this hilarious Keystone Cop's chase now into its tenth backstreet lap, I decided that this dogged policeman was not about to give up, so I jumped from my bike and stood stock still. Neilson, puffing and blowing, asked me my name, and proceeded to give me the mother-and-father of a telling off, but he left it at that.

A couple of weeks after this escapade, Sgt Neilson was giving a talk on Road Safety as part of a *Cyclists' Week*. He may have had *me* in mind when he said:

There are the old and the infirm who have crossed the Grand Corner from Arrowsmiths to Shepherds some thousands of times. They are now in danger from increased traffic and those irresponsible youths who have forgotten all that teachers taught them in safety first.

The amiable bobby then went on to describe an incident when a pony attached to the front of a flat cart came across Lintonville Terrace, apparently out of control. Traffic was halted and one bus had to turn into North Seaton Road; as it did so the pony trotted across the Grand Corner. *"Had it hit the back of the bus,"* stated Neilson, *"it would have swung back and gone through a nearby shop window."* Raymond Hicks, of 26 St Andrew's Terrace, eventually halted the runaway.

Thirty-nine girls from the Hirst Park school took part that week in a three and a half miles cycling test through the town. Despite very windy conditions, all finished the course.

Cllr A Rogers, presenting awards said: *"I think the parents will be glad to know that the children are capable of being out on their cycles."* The following girls received certificates: Minnie Burrel, Cynthia Wilkinson, Bernadene Reed, June Kay, Rena Ryce, Dorothy Turnbull, Nancy Foster, Sheila White, Ruth Brenard, Mary Brooks, Jean White, Joan Camsell.

The *Ashington & District Advertiser* started up again after the war. It was then that the three Davison boys, Norman, Tony and Terry, began to get more actively involved in the family business. Terry remembers:

I was still at school when I began delivering the papers. I did all the top colliery rows and most of the streets around Park Road. It was all part of my apprenticeship. In 1945 we had very basic equipment and had to have the paper typeset in Newcastle. I would wait at Ashington railway station to collect the type in heavy boxes from the train, then rush over to get it printed.

The immediate post-war years saw the paper flourish. Alan Robson who had cut his journalistic teeth on the Ashington Colliery Magazine and later the South Shields Gazette, was taken on as a working partner. He began to write astute, often caustic, editorials, as well as doing a tongue-in-cheek column under the *nom de plume* 'Fell 'Em Doon'.

By 1947, the *Advertiser*, although having the same dimensions, contained *eight* pages, and had an average circulation of 7,000. The front page was still dominated by adverts, but now the in-vogue shops were Laburnum Stores, offering *'Utility Furniture'* on attractive hire purchase terms, and the House of Arrowsmith, with *'Styles as Modern as the Hour'*.

New advertisers in 1947 included: *Snow's (We can keep any garment you select until the New Coupon issue on March 1st)*; *Proudlock's* for *'Your Daily Bread'*; *The Silver Library, 'The only library in the district with a constant supply of the latest editions'*; and *Billy Burns, Bookmakers*, of 93 Station Road, with a full list of runners for the 1947 Lincoln Handicap.

On the sporting page it was reported that *"At least one local club is sure to contest the final of the Northern Alliance Challenge Cup as Ashington Reserves are due to meet Newbiggin C W in the semi-final."* As if to show that matches in the bad winter of 1947 were not all postponed, a reporter noted:

There is a fifty-fifty chance of play at Portland Park on Saturday, February 22nd, 1947, for the Northumberland Senior Cup 'derby' tie between Ashington and Blyth Spartans.
The Hirst end of the pitch is clear of snow but the west side is covered by a depth of four inches. The bulk of the snow is expected to be cleared away by Saturday, although enough will be left to cover the hard turf underneath.
The Colliers team will be chosen from: Pattison, Grundy, Brown, Guthrie, Richardson, Clough, Dodd, James, Fenwick, Poxon, Brown, and Homer.

Larry Bell's Boys Club, due to play away at Pegswood the same day, fielded: Pearcy, Bell, (capt.), Nixon, Evans, Neilson, Woof, Thompson, Nichol, Leslie, Randall, and Prior.

Elsewhere, the staff of Wallaw Pictures Ltd had held *"A Staff Dance in the Arcade Hall when over 300 guests danced to the music of Joe Gray and his Arcadians, the MC being Mr J Allan. Guests included Mr and Mrs W Lawson, and managers of the various cinemas in the Wallaw chain: Mr and Mrs L Stoddart, Mr and Mrs A Willgoose, Newbiggin, Mr and Mrs J Allan, Mr and Mrs Robinson, and Mr Blain, Morpeth."*

That edition also carried this letter of appreciation from the secretary of the Brighouse and Rastrick Band - who had played the week before at the Central Hall - to conductor and organist, Normanton Barron:

Dear Mr Barron

The members of our band ask me to say how pleased they were with all the arrangements, the tea and supper provided by Mr and Mrs R Gray, and the friendly welcome we received on the occasion of our visit to the Central Hall.

We were delighted with the very fine audience, and it was a pleasure to play to such an appreciative though critical public.

Yours, E J Roberts (secretary)

At the end of 1947, it was reported that a Jazz Jamboree had taken place at the Arcade Hall on Friday 5th December, in aid of the Musicians Benevolent Fund, which had attracted over 500 dancers. A list of local affiliated Musicians Union bands which operated in the area was given, and included:

Harry Hogarth and his band;	Arcadians Dance Orchestra;
Dalkin's Rhythm Boys;	Jack Summers and his band;
Steve Howard and his band;	Gilbert Grieves and his band;
George Mason and his band;	Tommy Allison and his band;
R Barron and his Boys;	Dave Grieves and his band;

J T De-von and his Music;	Johnny Stenhouse and his band;
Kelly's Accordian Band;	B J Humble and his band;
O H Tyler and Chrisp's band;	Tommy Bell and his Rhythm Boys;
The Billy Milburn Quartet;	Merry Mixers Dance Orchestra.

Earlier in the year, two local musicians had been very well received at the Newcastle City Hall:

"Tommy Camsell, deputy at Woodhorn Colliery, was an outstanding artiste in the big Miners' Broadcast Show. He walked on to the platform before a vast audience and gave a magnificent interpretation of his own pianoforte composition 'Happy Fingers'. Another local entertainer who did well was Billy (Buck) Milburn, accordionist. The concert was the first to be held under the auspices of the National Coal Board."

Another concert covered in that edition was headed: *'Hospital Show by Ashington Entertainers'*:

An excellent non-stop variety entertainment was given for patients of Wooley Sanitorium by members of the Ashington Thespian Operatic Society last week. Artistes were: Tommy Allison and his band (Jim Hunt, Alan Armstrong, Hector Imrie, Harry Gordon), Edna Hudspeth, Olive Weddell, Stan Pearson, Billy Robinson, Dave Parker, J W Straker, Archie Summers and John Hodgson.

The Ashington Greyhound Stadium continued to pack in local punters. Dogs to note were given as: Buckler, Full Fashion, Breakaway, and Bill Bracken. As well as the greyhounds at Portland Park, the *Advertiser* was now beginning to list the runners at Gateshead Stadium. The Universal Travel Agency, based at 21 Maple Street, became sole agents for tickets to outside tracks, operating buses every Saturday evening from the Grand Corner for an all-in price of four shillings and thrupence.

It was noted that: *"An automatic telephone exchange is to be installed in Ashington, taking the first calls at noon on December 17th, 1947. This means that Lynemouth calls, which up until now have been linked with the Ashington Exchange, are transferred to Morpeth."*

The Communist Party was very active in Ashington after the war, and had made several attempts to gain seats in local elections. There was much concern shown by Tom Holliday, secretary of the Woodhorn Miners, at a meeting of Ashington Labour Party in February, 1948, when he was reported as saying:

In my opinion it is not the intention of the Communists in the Urban Council Elections to become councillors, but their object is to prevent Labour candidates from becoming councillors. At a national level the Communist aim seems to be to bring down the Labour Government. It is they who have split our local union over the question of longer hours to help the country in a time of crisis.

While preparing this book, I had access to the St Aidan's RC school log book kept by headmaster, Michael McGough. It was like trespassing into another human being's mind and heart. Before reading it, forty years had distanced me from a man I thought I knew so well. My attitude towards him had been hostile. But from his brief daily notes, I can now see how dedicated he was to that particular school - it was his whole life.

Typical of him was this reflection concerning the raising of the school leaving age to fifteen. The entry is dated July 23rd, 1948:

School closes today at 4 pm for the mid-summer vacation. The Extra Year class had a breaking-up party, and agreed that they had had a very happy year. There were tears at parting, a very unusual occurrence in my experience. In spite of the many and great difficulties - chiefly through my having two classes during the greater part of the year, and occasionally three, and so not being able to give them full attention - they have developed a grand spirit of comradeship and self-reliance, and whilst I was doubtful at first of the merits of raising the school leaving age, I must admit that the results have surprised me.

From reading the headmaster's notes, it would appear to me that teachers absented themselves from school, just as much as they appear to do today. Mr J Rutherford, my teacher, was once away from school for three months, and it usually fell upon McGough to look after non-supervised classes. One entry stated that he was controlling 86 children per day.

Michael McGough's last entry in the log was on July 27th 1951, when he stated in simple non-emotive terms what must have been for him a very sad occasion:

School closes today for the mid-summer holidays. The present headmaster, Mr M McGough, retires from this post today, and from teaching.

Mr McGough died a few years later, horribly burned to death in a house fire at his home in Park Road. Pat Grimes, who with Annie Abbott formed a husband and wife teaching team at St Aidan's in the early 1940s, remembers the headmaster:

He was in many ways a very good head, although to us younger teachers, a little old fashioned. In those days, a good head, according to the Local Authority, was one who kept the running costs of the school as low as possible. Discipline with Michael was rather strict, but he was always honest and straight, and always worked for the best interests of the children. I remember the day of his funeral, being in church and listening to a burst of playtime noise coming from the school playground - a most appropriate accompaniment for a dedicated teacher on his last day above ground.

ASHINGTON SWINGS INTO THE SIXTIES

Business was brisk in the Ashington Council Chamber during the first quarter of 1964.

There was some dismay expressed by councillors that the closure of Ashington's railway passenger service had *not* occurred on the 6th January as hoped. Plans were already well advanced to use the goods yard as part of a new shopping precinct on the Station Bridge, and it was no secret that the Council wished to use the extra space to widen the footpath.

The railway station in Ashington dated back to 1878, six years after a line had been laid to Newbiggin. Then called Hirst Station, and re-named in 1889, it formed a vital link in the chain of Blyth and Tyne Railways. When the Ashington Coal Company began to spread its net to the outlying villages such as Linton and Ellington, the trains, or pit tankeys, transported miners in open-sided carriages to their place of work. But it was in providing an opportunity for leisure that the railway station became important. The area's comprehensive rail network meant that seaside resorts and major shopping centres such as Newcastle became immediately accessible.

On summer Sundays, hundreds of miners and their families crowded the two narrow platforms - eastbound for Newbiggin, westbound for Whitley Bay, changing at Newsham. A ticket to ride behind the steam-puffing engine led the way to an adventure, a thrill a minute journey, providing a talking point to lighten the drudgery of the working week that lay ahead. The fares were kept to a minimum, and as late as 1950 a thrupenny diddler was sufficient to spill boisterous children upon the beach at Newbiggin like so many grains of silver sand.

The last train to Ashington from Newcastle's Manors North station left a full 20 minutes after the last bus from the Haymarket. This was a boon for anyone who had been to one of the city's theatres or perhaps dancing the night away on the magnificent polished floor of the Oxford Galleries. The train was packed with late-night revellers, good humoured in spite of the hard seats and lack of intoxicating drinks served at the Oxford. A rapport existed between perfect strangers, fellow travellers, with thoughts of trouble-making and vandalism lying many stops away down the line.

But Dr Beeching's axe, provided by the Conservative government in the name of progress, severed the Ashington artery, and, like dozens of others, the little station stood shabby and derelict for a number of years, destined, as were many of Ashington's historical landmarks, to become a concrete car-park.

It was announced on the 14th February, 1964, that the East Villas housing estate was to undergo a massive facelift over the next two years at a cost of £40,000. The estate, one of the first to be built by the council after the first world war, had become very run down and acquired the derogatory name of *Chinkytoon*.

One-armed bandits were the subject of debate the following week. Ashington Cricket Club had asked for permission to install a gaming machine, much to the disgust of Alderman George Duddridge who claimed: *"The club is being greedy. These machines are daylight robbery. If I had my way I'd take a hammer to every one I see."* Looking at things a little more objectively, Cllr Larry Lavelle said: *"If the club is paying for it and using it for the benefit of the members, then let 'em have it."* The application was deferred, but was subsequently turned down a month later.

On 21st February it was reported that an end was in sight to the problem of poor communication around Ashington. A five-year road plan was approved that would eventually see a new spine road bridging the river Wansbeck.

A plan to build 216 more council houses on Moorhouse Lane was passed, as was a new rate increase of one shilling which brought the charge up to eleven shillings and sixpence in the pound. Rents to be charged for the new estate ranged from two pounds three shillings and sevenpence for a 3-bedroom, centrally heated house, to one pound for a flat. It was also agreed to put up the rents of nearly two thousand other council properties by one fifth.

As Ashington housing estates encroached ever nearer upon their fishermen friends on the coast, a merger between Ashington and Newbiggin with others was *"fast approaching,"* according to a council spokesman. Another improvement scheme was scheduled for the west end of town with the proposed demolition of the Long and Cross Rows. This was to be the first step in a massive redevelopment of Ashington's *top-end*.

Yet another new project broached in this busy period was the plan for a new library building. The original had been housed at Station Villa, once the home of Alderman John Craigs, but according to head librarian, Peggy Kilbourn: *"Ashington readers now borrow 200,000 books a year. We have 20,000 books in the library read by our 6705 members. We need the extra space."*

The County Council hoped to build a new library on the same site at a cost of £28,000. There was also a plan to build a brand-new library at the east end of the town. When word reached local councillors that the present library was to be rebuilt with only *one* storey, they were adamant that they would not accept a *"pea on a drum"* affair, especially in view of the 6-storey technical college and 3-storey council flats at Alexandra Court.

It was announced that the proposed old folks' home in the Library Park would not be opened until the autumn. The name was to be Essendene, once the ancient name for Ashington. Residents would be asked to pay two pounds fourteen shillings and sixpence towards their keep.

A report in the Ashington Advertiser of March 6th declared:

NEW SCHOOL CHANGES RIGHT OF WAY

In order to make a satisfactory layout to the new Roman Catholic school's playing fields, on the school site east of 6th Avenue, the County Council are seeking authorisation to divert a right of way which crosses the proposed layout. The school is to be known as St Benedict's.

The Advertiser also went on to say that the County Education Committee hoped to provide *two* swimming pools at the Technical College with a view to swimming being taught there. Authorisation was given for a new laboratory at Hirst East School.

Yet another headline in the local paper announced:

COUNCILLORS WILL NOT PADDLE IN WANSBECK

Alderman Duddrige was referring to the pollution of the lower reaches of the river and the danger of contamination when he said: . *"Everyone knows it is a dirty river."* Cllr George Holland replied: *"I blame it all on Bedlington Council for indiscriminate tipping."*

Thirty acres of land at Black Close Bank were set aside by the council on Jubilee Industrial Estate *"primarily for female labour."* Two months later an advert appeared for Hepworth's asking for women to apply for jobs at *"our brand-new, ultra-modern factory."*

On May 1st, the Council approved planning permission for a 5-storey NCB headquarters to be built next to the new fire station opposite Bothal Terrace. Following amalgamation, Ashington Colliery had ceased to be part of the No. 3 Area of the Northern Division.

In the May Council elections, Ashington had a smaller than ever turnout at the polls. Only twenty-five per cent voted at the Hirst where J Brotherton, Labour, topped the poll with 1464 votes; and thirty per cent turned up in the Ashington Ward to make Arthur Gallagher top Labour man with 1570 votes. The Liberals, making their second attempt to break the Labour stranglehold, failed to gain a seat, but vowed: *"We will be back next time."*

More affluent than at any time in the town's history, Ashington's residents demanded more and more amenities. A taxi rank was established on the piece of ground next to the Grand Hotel. Two enterprising young men, John Richardson and Charles Grint, took advantage of a TV Western to start a new taxi business, calling themselves *'Paladin'*; their catchphrase motto was *Have Car - Will Travel.*

One of the more bizarre suggestions at that time came from Tom Dawson of Ashington's Chamber of Commerce. He advocated that *"Ashington's slagheaps be transformed into dry-ski slopes and become a tourist attraction."* The idea might not have been so crazy given that Woodhorn Colliery is now pulling in the crowds as a *Museum*, and who would have forecast that in 1964?

Another *first* for Ashington occurred that year when the local Magistrates Court had its first *woman* prosecutor, Police Inspector Joan Hunt, who was introduced by Inspector J W Mackintosh. She was warmly welcomed by the magistrates, if not by her first 'customer', who was fined twenty pounds when pleading guilty to speeding.

The Swinging Sixties caught Ashington up in its frenetic lifestyle. The long hair as worn by men was highlighted by G W Raffell, local official of the Hairdressers' Federation, in 1964, when he said: *"Ashington men get their hair cut far cheaper than anywhere in the country - two shillings and thrupence. I think it only reasonable that those youths with longer hair should pay more to have it cut off."*

In May of that year the town got itself a genuine nightclub for the first time. Ronnie Harrison, former centre-forward for the Colliers, took over the lease at the Harmonic Hall. The opening night cabaret featured Tyne Tees songstress Ethna Campbell.

Post-war, with the *Ashington Advertiser* doing so well, covetous eyes from across the water at the *Blyth News* group saw what was happening and they put in a bid for the paper's title. The bid was refused but always lay on the table.

In 1966 E N Davison died, leaving what looked like a very prosperous business in the hands of his sons. Plans were put down to move to new premises at the Ellington Road ends. The lads were told that a government grant was available and that it was a mere formality for them to receive it.

Terry Davison recalls:

I was the only one who was against the move. It was costing a great deal of money, not only to move premises, but also for the new technology which was to be installed. But it wasn't just the capital costs - revenue was falling off.

Foss Proudlock, then retired from the NCB, was hired to *"keep an eye on the new machines."* He says:

They had a marvellous American machine, but it kept eating up the paper. In the end a chap came over from the States to have a look at it. I had to carry the printed paper from one room to another, and it was heavy, so I says "why don't you run a conveyor to carry the paper?" They told me to go ahead and fix it up, which I did, getting most of the material such as conveyor belting and rollers which had been thrown away at the pit. But they still had problems.

The great cultural changes which were taking place throughout Britain were being reflected in Ashington. The greyhound stadium had been closed down - Davison's lost that lucrative contract; the football team was in the doldrums - Davison's sold fewer match programmes; the workingmen's clubs moved upmarket, stopped selling lottery tickets, and plumped instead for bingo - that contract went elsewhere; only two cinemas still functioned - less advertising was needed; formal dances gave way to discos - again, less posters and tickets were needed, less printing was called for.

It was the time of a renewed Liberal onslaught upon the Labour stronghold of Ashington Council. Tony Davison's entry into the political arena under Liberal colours was badly timed in a strictly business sense, and staunch Labour-supporting customers were lost.

But the planned expansion still went ahead and Davison's new printing works were opened in November 1968 with a wave of euphoric publicity in their own newspaper:

The Advertiser and the firm of E N Davison (Ashington) Limited, are now settled into new premises at the town's West End, near Ellington Terrace. Our main office is equipped to cope with even more business - modern machines are being installed, and when the extra employment we have taken on gets settled in, Ashington will have a newspaper worthy of its size and potential.

After only two years, acknowledging the fact that they were *not* to receive the government grant and with the high cost of paper and spiralling wages eating into their already depleted resources, the printing firm of E N Davison was placed in the hands of the Receiver and was liquidated in 1970.

ASHINGTON GRAMMAR SCHOOL

With the building of the Northumberland County Technical College already completed, Ashington moved further into the educational big league in 1960, when the inaugural meeting took place of the Governors for the newly-built Ashington Grammar School, sited next to Peoples Park.

Up until then, if an Ashington child had been bright enough, or lucky enough, to pass the Grammar School entrance exam at the age of eleven, it meant going to a school out of the district. King Edward VI Grammar School at Morpeth was looked upon as the best in the immediate vicinity, while Bedlington Grammar School nearly always came second on a proud parent's list. For Catholics, the nearest Grammar School was two bus-rides away at St Cuthbert's at the top of Denton Bank in Newcastle.

On Monday May 2nd, 1960, the governors of Ashington Grammar School, under the chairmanship of J R Tilley OBE, and with guidance from the new headmaster, George Chapman, decided to make the first five appointments of teaching staff. These were:

Ron Edwardson	Physical Education, Head of Dept
Jean Talbot	Physical Education
Jennifer Neave	Domestic Science
Robert Cessford	Art
Alan Epsley	Metalwork, Head of Dept

A couple of weeks later, Hazel Richardson was appointed Head of Maths, Heather Potts, from Bothal, got the job as clerical assistant to the Head, and J Cullingworth became the school's first caretaker.

The Grammar School opened its doors to the first pupils on Monday 5th September, 1960. Three hundred and twenty children enrolled: 148 boys and 175 girls. The fourteen teachers comprised six men and eight women.

It should have been a smooth start, but right from the outset it was obvious that the building was not ready. Many rooms were either incomplete or unusable. These included two changing rooms, five laboratories, the metalwork room, the art room, and the gymnasium. To add to the debacle, a considerable amount of fittings and items of furniture were missing, and there wasn't a classroom in the place with a fitted blackboard.

By the 17th October, many of the faults had been rectified, and the governors congratulated Mr Chapman *"on the work done to get the school in such good working order in so short a time."*

The building was officially opened on 15th February, 1961, by Alderman Brotherton. And when the school entered its second year, seven new members of staff had been appointed, including Peter Thompson, teacher of physics and maths, to cope with another intake of an additional 150 pupils.

With the school population rising so dramatically, extra dinner ladies were recruited. These included: Mrs Smith, Mrs Alderson, Mrs Edgar, Mrs Duddridge, Mrs Christie, Miss Gray, Mrs Strougton, Mrs Scott, and Mrs Rutter.

By the autumn of 1962, it was obvious that more space was needed, and arrangements were made to occupy part of the old Mining School in Darnley Road. Numbers on the school roll now totalled 613, and seven more teachers were appointed, including Jim Beal as Head of Maths.

It was in this year that the first children took GCE 'O' levels. The entire Fifth Year of 33 pupils obtained 5.1 passes per candidate with 27 gaining Distinctions.

In February 1963, on the resignation of Miss Potts, Edna Ralph was appointed as a full-time clerical assistant to George Chapman. In September that year, with 720 pupils to accommodate, the whole of the Mining School buildings were taken over.

I obtained my teacher's certificate of education in July, 1973. After spending my probationary year at Heaton School, I went to teach Commerce and Office Practice at what had been Ashington Grammar School, but was now Ashington High School.

Comprehensive Education arrived in Ashington in September 1974. The town's Grammar School in Green Lane - the smart part of town - opened its doors to reluctant 15 and 16-year-olds from the Bothal and Hirst Park Secondary Modern schools. The school (headmaster then Gordon Lister) grew overnight from a population of 300 pupils and 30 staff to 1200 pupils with 90 teachers.

It was a traumatic time for the old regime. Some established teachers, bitterly opposed to the new system, merely donned blinkers, along with academic gowns, and carried on teaching as though nothing had happened. New members of staff included some who had taught at the local secondary schools. They too were unhappy at being dragged away from a comfortable niche at a good secondary school, and being forced to take on an unfamiliar role in alien surroundings.

Additional accommodation for the pupils was provided by the use of half a dozen portakabins hastily erected on site, and by opening the doors of the old Mining School in Darnley Road as an annexe.

The whole concept of a comprehensive approach to education whereby pupils had the same opportunity to progress barely surfaced in the initial years. Hirst Park and Bothal School children were completely segregated from the more academic pupils who had passed the 11+ examination. There was no integration either educationally or socially among the youngsters, with each group, secondary and grammar, ignoring the others' existence. The atmosphere was only marginally better in the staff room. The opportunities which had existed for promotion disappeared with the hiving off of 'scale' posts to established grammar school teachers in the year prior to amalgamation.

The ex-Grammar School teachers were not prepared for the shock of trying to cope with burly fifth-formers from the secondary schools. They had to rely heavily on the new teachers who had had some experience, and many of them shook their heads asking what to do next. After six months it was decided that what was needed to bring the staff together was some kind of drama production involving as many teachers as possible.

I had begun to write a play while at teacher training college in Newcastle two years earlier. The stimulus had come from a visit to Ashington YMCA to see one of Charlie Mills' productions. The audience, packed to the doors, seemed to fall about laughing at the very mention of a familiar landmark or any local celebrity, usually a councillor. I decided that I would write a play using the same formula exploited so successfully by Charlie over the years. At this point, my play was only three parts finished. I had included a couple of monologues within the script, but when I showed these to Derek Hobbs, Head of Music at the school, he asked if he could put them to music. And so was born the partnership of *Kirkup and Hobbs*.

I decided to call the piece *'Song of the Coal'*. It contained a dozen songs, scored by Derek for a small brass band. The show was premiered as part of the 1975 Ashington Festival. So great was the demand for tickets that we had to bring it back about a month later for a further three nights. Some of the songs were featured on a Tyne Tees Television show called *'What Fettle'*, and I was later asked to adapt it for BBC Radio Newcastle.

The whole project *did* seem to have some kind of unifying effect on the staff. As an ex-pitman, I even arranged a visit for the entire cast to tour the underground workings of Woodhorn Colliery. Those who did not get the chance to make fools of themselves on stage, mucked in making scenery, props etc, or helped with all the paraphernalia which goes into any stage production.

Even as rehearsals of SOTC were taking place, Derek and I were scribbling away on a new piece. He wanted to do a large-scale production involving as many pupils as possible for a Christmas showing. He also had a dozen melodies in his head which only needed lyrics to shape them into songs. We finished writing *'The Greatest Show on Earth'* during the 1975 summer holidays and began rehearsing when the new term got under way.

The comprehensive system was now one-year old. Hirst High School, newly built on the North Seaton Estate, celebrated its first birthday with its second intake of 13-year-olds from Newbiggin Secondary Modern and Hirst East schools.

The Christmas show was a massive project involving over one hundred children and a dozen members of staff. Chemistry teacher, Peter Thompson, and English specialist, Pat Haggerty, were mad enough to jointly direct the play which, by curtain-up time, contained 22 songs. A press release from PR man, Roger Scott, drew a reporter from the *Times Educational Supplement* who reviewed the production as *"the best school play I have seen for years."*

Probably what gave me even more pleasure than the kind words of printed praise, was the way the pupils joined forces and became a single unit for the first time. Ashington High School was up and running.

JOHN EARL joined us at Ashington High School as an English teacher in 1975. Always interested in local dialects, he remembers:

It was my second job as a teacher of English; my first was at an independent day school on Tyneside where I was earnestly asked by a parent whether I would stop his son and heir speaking Geordie. If I had been able, as a newly-arrived southerner, to work out the difference between Geordie and the usual strange argot spoken by all teenagers, then I might have tried to comply with this strange request.
No such problem confronted me in Ashington. Here was an adventure into language as well as a completely different community, even though only a few miles up the coast. Particularly noticeable from the start to a schoolteacher wading through registers was the large number of old border names: Bells, Cessfords, Kerrs, Armstrongs. Ashington folk seemed a world apart.
The language did, too. I had only just got an 'ear' for Tyneside dialect - I did not realise there was more than

one kind of Geordie to adjust to! *Ashington dialect seemed brutal, gutteral, clotted with glottal stops and full of strange ejaculations like 'How! Ye!' shouted at full volume, or muttered references to 'that wifie', referring to a woman. I remember a class of slow learners who entertained me considerably with their skills in dialect, an area where they were anything but slow. I learnt what 'hotching' was, a particularly expressive word for 'to smell'; 'hockling', as in "How, sor, he's hockled on me book," was a word to avoid if possible, meaning 'spitting', but somehow conjuring up a whole new sense image that left the ordinary 'spit' far behind. The verb 'to nack' amused me considerably, being used on every possible occasion, as also was 'wick', as in "Ee, sor, this is wick," meaning everything from 'difficult' to 'mindbendingly boring'.*

One character sticks in my mind. He was from Linton, built like a barn door, and like many of the pupils who had been forced to stay on an extra year with ROSLA, resented every minute of it. His speciality was sitting behind some miserable weed (in relative terms, since most brick walls were less well built than this lad) and persecuting the life out of him. One day I got fed up with this and told him to go and see the deputy headmaster (or 'heedmaster' as he was called in Ashington). I will never forget the sight of him standing furious, filling the door frame and yelling "I'll nack ye for this!" I did not need a translation.

The whole problem was that there was an exciting world out there that pupils had already entered with their language - an adult world of fear and comradeship down the mines. We teachers were just keeping them away from the jobs they wanted to go to, like 'pit yacker', a wonderful name meaning simply a lad who did odd jobs on the surface, but somehow conveying status by its very sound. A hard 'k' sound was common to many of these unfavoured words, and it sounded like digging, to an outsider, at least a mine perhaps, or barriers? Before very long, however, you realised that here was an outward toughness that disguised a very deep warmth, and that once you had learnt something about Ashington by living with it and understanding the language you were accepted. But nobody was about to make it easy for you by translating, and rightly so.

I finally went to my Sweet's Anglo Saxon Primer *for a translation, and there found many of the words still spoken in Ashington; 'wife' is Anglo Saxon for 'woman', 'na' for 'no', 'mooth' retains the Anglo Saxon pronunciation, if not the spelling of 'mouth', and so on.*

I later met Fred Reed, the pitman poet, who was one of the last to understand the linguistic possiblities of this dialect that was fast disappearing even as he was shaping and caring for it in his poems. Some of the old words like 'lowse' that even teachers used, meaning 'leaving work', come direct from the pit, and whereas they will probably survive even now that the pits have all gone, I cannot help feeling that the language will lose a great deal of its vigour. Whatever does happen, I am proud to have known something of the old Ashington when the words, like the coal, came up from the pit and burnt in the fires of experience.

THE SEVENTIES

ANNE CHADWICK, Irish by birth, came to Ashington in 1970 to take up a position as schoolteacher. Now a member of the Wansbeck Writers Group, she gives her impressions of arriving in the town:

In Manchester our furniture was loaded on to the van. There seemed to be an awful cargo of possessions now being set adrift, bound for Northumberland. Time for one last look back from the heights of Stalybridge at the sprawling smoke-screened city, iron grey under the steely sky of a cold Saturday morning, three days before Christmas.

Our train chugged up the slope of the Pennines with its sheep black with soot, over the top and down the other side. On and on to Newcastle and its elegant Central Station, to walk through streets festooned with Christmas cheer and shops bright with expensive goodwill.

There was still a bus to catch and the road to Ashington to be traversed. It seemed a long way through unfamiliar places - Gosforth, Wideopen, Bedlington, and then into the country of strange rows of terraced houses and conical pit-heaps, smouldering under the huge wheels of the winding gear. Choppington, the air acrid, little houses puffing smoke from each chimney, like rows of miniature dragons.

At last, Ashington, long and low, its one street a backbone, head to the river, tail to the sea. The Grand Hotel was large with an air of having seen better days, the shops were small: it was like stepping backwards to within touching distance of Dickens and Mr Polly.

One shop had an open fireplace, coal spluttered, brightening the merchandise with scarlet flames; in the drapers, chairs, tall-backed and round bottomed, were set up for the convenience of the valued customer. Purchases were made in cash and transported on a magic overhead railway to a mysterious den, wherein the maiden checked and counted, and from whence she dispatched the change, carefully wrapped in the receipt, inside a tiny brass box.

The indoor market smelled of birdseed and leather and stiff cheap cotton. A sweet shop sold sweetmeats, unwrapped, sticky, broken into small pieces, all at very favourable prices. Evidence of Christmas was meagre - little had been done to decorate the long street - it seemed that no-one was in a hurry to be lavish with hard-earned cash. The cold hard north wind tunnelled along the main street, straight off the German ocean, sending shoppers quickly in and out of doors. They seemed drably dressed, intent on their own affairs, pleasant, yet incurious.

It was not a Christmas I enjoyed. This place where I had come to work owed me nothing. I had to set to and make my own place in its society of worth and endeavour.

In September, 1972, Ashington Council appointed Jack Ramsay, a Public Relations man who had the brief of smartening up the 'cloth-cap' image of the town.

Said Jack Charlton, then living in, and playing for, Leeds:

If anyone is to blame it's me and our kid. We've both had more to do with it than anybody. And Jackie Milburn, of course. You could call it pride. We've never been afraid to be seen against a background of back-to-back houses where we grew up and played as schoolkids. That is where me and our kid were born and bred. And we've never been ashamed of it.

Ashington's a great little town, developing along the right lines. If the Public Relations man pushes the industry, and says that the people are the the best and amongst the hardest-working in the world, then he could do a good job.

Mr Ramsay, on a salary of £2,500, replied sharply:

There's more to Ashington than the birthplace of footballers. Everyone already knows that Ashington's people are the salt of the earth - you don't have to push the people.

But Cissie Charlton, Jack's mother, wasn't convinced:

That cloth cap image is going to take a lot of getting rid of. In the south they think we eat each other up here. They only show the bad parts of the town.

A Newcastle Journal reporter decided to investigate the town. He wrote:

My first view, by moonlight, a man leading his whippets for a walk. Second view, a fish and chip shop now called a 'barbeque'; and a Chinese takeaway.

The long main street seemed almost deserted. At one of the two remaining cinemas they were showing 'Never Give An Inch'. There was one taxi on the rank. Driver, David Richardson, observed: "This town is changing but it's going to take a long time to alter its image."

I headed for the Conchy (strangers call it the Constitutional Club) and at the bar stood next to Ray Robinson, club chairman and ex-councillor. He told me: "The town is changing tremendously. I'd be really sorry to see the cloth cap image go entirely. It's part of the warmth and friendly side. As for removing the pit heaps, well,

they were put there by blood, tears, toil and sweat. Perhaps they should remain as monuments to the miners."
Up at the Central Club, there were only eight women crowded into a concert room among 250 men. The floor
show that night was billed as 'Scarlett O'Hara - exotic dancer'. Before the war it was unheard of for women
to be members of a club. Said Dickie Jarvis, club secretary: "The town's a hell of a lot better to live in than
when I was a boy; roads weren't made up, and middens ran down the streets. The town's changed from the
ridiculous to the sublime."

Three months after taking office, Ashington's PR man came up with a new logo for all the Council's correspondence. It was in the shape of a large letter 'A', topped with a circle which gave it the look of pit winding gear.

On the 18th January, 1973, it was decided that the *Grand Hotel* was to be demolished. One of only three public houses in the area, the atmospheric *Grand* with its sawdust-strewn bar room floor was to make way for a supermarket and lock-up shops. Drinkers were still to be catered for with the massive cellar below the hotel being converted into an underground alehouse. Later events were to show that the pub's distinctive clientele were driven away by the introduction of a modern 'beer 'n' bite' image, their places taken by youngsters barely above the legal drinking age.

Efforts were to be made to preserve some of the hotel's beautiful stained-glass windows depicting the coats of arms of Northumberland families. But one feature destined to be lost forever was a 20 ft by 12 ft painting on the staircase wall. It was the work of a pre-war signwriter who liked his brown ale but couldn't afford to pay for it in cash. The hotel bore a date-stone showing 1894, but it was said that it had functioned at an earlier date as the *Hirst Hotel*. It also housed what was thought to be the town's oldest public clock. Said Ralph Douglas, publican at the time: *"When this place was built there were no radios or crystal sets, and everyone in Ashington relied on this clock for the right time."*

Also in 1973, final details of a half million pound project to link the two halves of Ashington town centre were announced. It was said that the town had an 'over-the-bridge' syndrome, and retailers in that area were always complaining that shoppers turned around at the railway line, ignoring the numerous shops and businesses 'over the bridge'.

The Evening Chronicle reported:

Preliminary work has started on an ambitious scheme to build a shopping area partly on the bridge and partly
on stilts spanning the railway line. Two old buildings in Station Yard car park have already been demolished
as part of the preparation work, and later this month agreements will be signed by Ashington Council; London
and Northern Properties Ltd, the developers; Amos Hinton and Sons Ltd, who are leasing a supermarket in the
development; and F P A Finnegan Ltd, the builders.

It was envisaged that the two-acre site would incorporate a supermarket, five shops, 7,500 sq ft of office accommodation, and a large pedestrian-only square, with walkways to the town's library. Cllr Arthur Gallagher, chairman of the Planning and Development Committee, said:

The new development will provide a welcome fillip to shopping amenities in Station Road which already
attract shoppers from a very wide area in Northumberland. More than that, it will eradicate for all time the
psychological barrier of the old Station Yard which has resulted in the vast majority of people shopping either
on the West or East ends of the road, but hardly ever on its entire length.

Three months after the contract was signed, John Oliver, Chairman of the Council, took the wheel of an earthmoving machine to shift the first lot of soil in the project that was estimated to cost £300,000.

Sir John Hall talked of the time when, as a laddie in the 1940s, his mother had brought him from their home in North Seaton to Ashington to do the shopping:

It was always on a Saturday afternoon. She would meet her friends at the Grand Corner - everyone did the same. And it would be: "Oh, look, there's Mary So-and-so, she's expectin' again." "Aye, and her man's just left her." The main street was the Coronation Street of Ashington. It was wonderful hearing the gossip. Then there were the shops which never seemed to change: Arrowsmith's, Donkin's, Keith Cazaly's, Chrisp's. People don't believe me when I tell them that the Metro Centre was built around this philosophy. Nothing ever changes. The Metro Centre is Ashington's main street with a roof on! And Metroland is the Spanish City at Whitley Bay.

On Thursday, February 22nd, 1973, art critic and Research Fellow, William Feaver, addressing the Friends of the Laing Art Gallery in Newcastle, said of the Ashington Group of Painters:

The Group is outstanding for its commitment, and for the very high quality of work, especially that of four or five painters. Founded in 1932, it is probably the longest standing art club in active existence today.

In May, 1973, Ashington competed against Blyth in a preliminary round of the BBC TV's *'It's a Knockout'* competition. Organisers whittled down the 150 applications to a squad of twenty, with Alan Mole, Ashington Grammar School sports master, as the leader.

Having disposed of neighbours Blyth, the team were then drawn away at Blankenberge, in Belgium. This caused great excitement in the town, especially in the Council Chambers. Ashington's appearance on Eurovision was looked upon as a wonderful chance to promote the town.

There was talk of a newspaper written in French and German being distributed by the Ashington contingent when they arrived in Belgium. Said Cllr Dick Sanderson:

When we go to Belgium in August we will have a unique opportunity to really spread the word that Ashington and our own particular area of Northumberland is attractive and has a potential worth looking at - we don't intend to waste this chance.

Team captain, Mole, commented optimistically: "We are going to Belgium to *win*." Sadly, not for lack of effort, Ashington failed to progress any further in the competition.

The first phase of Ashington's £400,000 marina project was officially opened in July, 1973, by Mr Geoffrey Rippon, the Environment Minister. Mr Rippon boarded a boat at Black Close to sail up the Wansbeck from Stakeford to Ashington. At the end of the cruise the minister was greeted by Cllr Dick Sanderson, and cut a tape across one of the new country walks along the river bank, observing: *"Very soon, Ashington will be transformed."*

Ten years later, on October 11th, 1983, the town of Ashington was voted: *"The worst for dirty air pollution in Northumberland,"* by the same Department of the Environment. The Riverside Park scheme was one of the most ambitious ever attempted by an urban district council, and it was thought it would eventually have a boating lagoon, overnight caravan park, picnic areas, and an hotel with a ballroom built on stilts over the river. A weir across the river would create one and a half miles of safe boating water.

Yet another high profile project set sail in 1973: Ashington's first custom-built sports centre. Newly-appointed manager, Bob Brind, reported:

My major aim is to develop this complex for the benefit of everybody. I want to build up a sound social community here. I hope that there will be a nucleus of clubs affiliated to the complex and that major spectator events will come to Ashington. Who knows, Ashington may become the sports centre for the North East.

The sports hall, was part of a multi-million pound investment in recreational activities in the town. It was being built to incorporate the Ashington Welfare Institute and the Swimming Baths which had just been renovated at a cost of £20,000 having been closed for a year due to shortage of coal during the miners' 'winter of discontent'. The Baths were very popular, with 3,000 people using them every week. The centre was officially opened on June 26th, 1975, by Sir James Bowman.

On September 14th, 1978, it was announced that the BBC'S *'Roots of England'* documentary series was to feature local favourite Sammy Scott. A BBC TV spokesman remarked: *"By comparison with the rest of the series, peoples' roots in Ashington are obviously shallow, but they do have roots."*

THE EIGHTIES...AND BEYOND

If the 1970s was the time for rejuvenation, for building a new future for the town and giving it a fresh image, the 1980s became a decade of destruction of much of the town's past. Many were to say that the heart was torn out of the town as familiar landmarks disappeared one by one.

On March 25th, 1980, Peter Richardson, won an appeal to instal eight gaming machines at the Prize Bingo hall in North Seaton Road. It had been Jack Richardson who had taken over three of the area's cinemas in the early 1960s and turned them into profitable gambling casinos. Two years after Mr Richardson's successful appeal, Ashington's sole surviving cinema, the Wallaw, just over the road from the bingo hall, closed its doors on August 2nd, 1982, re-opening later as part of the Noble Amusements empire. The last film to be shown in Ashington was the musical, *'Annie'*, which featured the hit song *'Tomorrow'*. Ashington had to wait for over 2,000 tomorrows before seeing their next public filmshow, courtesy Paul Maddison and his new Picture House which opened in 1990 in the buildings once occupied by Ashington's first Co-operative store in High Market.

Cllr Scott and retired mechanical engineer Raymond Sewell, president of the Ashington branch of the British Legion, were present on October 28th, 1983, at the installation of a new War Memorial, sited in the Library Park. Designed by Gene Healy, pupil at Hirst High School, the modernistic sculpture symbolises three trench-coated British soldiers. Gene's original drawing was translated by sculptor Colin Rose of Widdrington. Himself an ex-serviceman, Cllr Scott said: *"We felt that the present memorial in the ground of Ashington's Cricket Club was not a fitting site to honour the memories of those men and women of Ashington who gave their lives."*

The Memorial incorporates four bronze tablets on which are inscribed the names of those Ashingtonians who fell in the first world war. Initially, these had formed part of a Memorial in the old Ashington Infirmary, but had been transferred to the new cricket club pavilion when it was built in 1960. A tree for every local man who fell during the second war (148) was planted around the Langwell Crescent ground at the same time.

A tragedy for the vast army of Central Hall concert-goers came on July 17th, 1989, with the news that the building which had played host to some of the best singers and musicians in the world was to be demolished. The Hall, whose original sponsor was J Arthur Rank, had given the community of humble pitmen their first taste of classical music in 1924. Ashington's Mr Music, long-serving organist and conductor, J Normanton Barron, responsible for organising almost two hundred Celebrity Concerts in the Central Hall, had died in February, 1977. Leader of the Council, John McCormack, on breaking the news of the demolition said: *"The Central Hall should be replaced with a building which has a similar degree of equal architectural merit."*

Another devastating blow to the town came in October, 1991, when Alcan announced that it was to cut its workforce in half, resulting in over 300 men losing their jobs. The giant aluminium smelter had been seen as the town's saviour when it arrived in 1968. The decision to make over 100 miners from Ellington (Alcan's sole supplier) redundant only weeks after the Canadian firm's decision to rationalise had, according to British Coal: *"Nothing at all to do with the Alcan situation."*

Ten years of my life went under the bulldozer when Duke Street Coal Depot, together with the rest of Ashington Colliery, was razed to the ground in November, 1991, to make way for a new Business Park which it was hoped would attract new investors. And Ashington's year ended as it had begun with the controversial news that County Councillors had agreed to extend an experimental pedestrianisation scheme for Station Road, with a view to making it permanent. Traffic had been banned from the main shopping area since January 1990.

Sir John Hall, talking to me about the changes which have come about in the town over the past few years, said:

If Ashington appeared never to have changed, it was because it had a static business when the pits were going strong, and there was no need to change. Had they looked ahead they would have seen that there should have been changes long before the pits started to close. Ashington never had a lot of private housing. Whether they were wanting to keep political control I don't know. But all the new housing was based at Stakeford, that was where I bought my first house, on Leeches Estate. That was the first mass exodus; the houses were sold up overnight with people queuing up to buy. The whole area was static for a long time and change was forced upon them in the end. You have got to know where you are going, and unless you have strong leadership you will fall behind until change is forced upon you.

Business success all stems from good leadership. You have to have a strong man at the top with a plan. At Wynyard we have a 15-year plan. Ashington seems to have grown up piecemeal - a little piece added here and another piece there. I think that Ashington as a town should be telling the world about its successes. If they stand up and moan that the area has twenty per cent unemployment, that will do no good at all. Businessmen don't want to hear about a town's failures, they need to be told of all the good points.

The town has done well with its Industrial Estates, Riverside Park, and other leisure amenities like the Colliery Museum, but there is still a lot to do if they want to prosper even more. At Wynyard we intend to spend a million pounds on marketing all that this huge estate has to offer. We are in direct competition with Ashington, attempting to bring new enterprise to this part of the M1/A19 which I believe is ripe for investment. Ashington is on the tip of this branch of investment potential in the North East, and it must work all that much harder if it is to succeed.

I know it won't make the Council popular with the poll-tax payers, but they have to say: "We know that road needs resurfacing, and we are aware that building needs repairing, but we are not going to do it this year; we are going to spend the money on publicising the town, looking to the long-term prosperity that such a move will bring."

I think Ashington and the district around it spawned so much talent because there was a great deal of commitment by the individuals concerned. There weren't just the footballers, there were artists, musicians, singers. Lots of gifted people. And the thing they had in common was a burning desire to succeed in spite of their environment. You could liken it to the hungry fighter who wanted to get on at any cost. Every generation throws up its own crop of talent. There are still opportunities for Ashington people to attain a high degree of excellence - probably far more now than ever. But they must have the kind of will power and dedication that served the Ashingtonians of the past so well. For Jackie Milburn there was only the pits or football; he had no other choice. There was once a saying that if you shouted down any pitshaft in Ashington for a centre-forward to play for Newcastle United you would get half-a-dozen coming up. I wish we could do that today!

Hospital and Infirmary. 1915.

Methodist's Church Hall, artists impression. 1924.

Station Road, looking east. 1932.

Station Road End, Hirst. 1920.

Woodhorn Memorial at Hirst Park. Erected 1923.

Meadow Dairy. 1952.

Station Road looking east. 1972.

A HOTBED OF TALENT

ASHINGTON'S MR MUSIC

The Barron family arrived in Newbiggin by the Sea on November 11th, 1918. John Garnett Barron, had been a colliery clerk dealing with wages and compensation at Copely Colliery, Durham. An accomplished musician himself, John had always encouraged his son Normanton to play the organ, and had sent him for special tuition under Dr Jacob George when the family lived at Barnard Castle. Once settled at Newbiggin, father and son soon put the tiny fishing village on the musical map by forming the Newbiggin Co-operative Orchestral Society and the Newbiggin Symphony Orchestra, as well as finding time to run the Newbiggin Wesleyan Choir. Normanton was by now receiving further tuition from William Ellis of Newcastle Cathedral.

Normanton Barron had begun his working life in a clothiers shop: Parkinson's of Barnard Castle. Upon arriving in Newbiggin he obtained employment in the Men's Department at Arrowsmiths, a large department store which dominated the shopping area around the Grand Corner for many years.

On the death of George Arrowsmith in 1931, Normanton was made secretary and general manager of the newly-formed G Arrowsmith Ltd., a post he held until the business closed in 1975.

By 1930, the name of J Normanton Baron was drawing people from all over the area, causing a leading national daily newspaper to comment:

Compared with a decade ago, that small but beginning to get fashionable watering-place, Newbiggin-by-the-Sea, with its fine stretch of sands and broad prom on which resident and visitor can loll and watch the sad sea waves, is a revelation of what progressive humans can accomplish. Time was when Newbiggin was, well, just...Newbiggin! But she has blossomed forth and taken on a hue which inevitably will lead to brighter and bigger business in the fishing village which was formerly a harbour.
The world and his wife - on wheels of divers diameters and on 'Shank's Nag' have made Newbiggin their Mecca. The town's Military Band, under that stickler for tunes, Mr Normanton Barron, are making days to be remembered of holidays by the sea which freshens jaded nerves. Newbiggin might well be proud of this gifted musician whose desire is, by uplift in music, to cater for the masses in what is good in mind, body, and soul. Carry on little seaside resort amid giant coalfields, and reward shall be yours in the dawn of brighter and yet happier times.

But by 1931, Normanton was looking for fresh challenges, and he found them in the pleasingly aesthetic Central Hall in Ashington, where he had conducted his own orchestra and choir on many occasions. He resigned from his post at Newbiggin, but continued to live in the village. On May 4th, 1932, in appreciation of his services to Newbiggin, he received a gold watch which bore the inscription: 'Presented to Mr J. Normanton Barron by the choir, congregation and opera section of the Newbiggin Wesleyan Chapel, in appreciation of his services as organist, 1918-31'.

The main motivation for the move came from Normanton's passionate love affair with church organs. The Central Hall had recently installed a magnificent £2,000 organ which up till then had been housed at the Miners' Theatre. It was undoubtedly the finest of its kind for miles around and, together with the marvellous accoustics inside the building, the Central Hall became a regular venue for some of the most talented singers and musicians in the world. A new minister, the Reverend Stanley Parker arrived at the Central Hall about the same time as J Normanton Barron. He gave his organist the order: "Fill the place at all times." And between them they managed to swell the 1100-seater hall to almost unmanagable proportions.

This article appeared in the Newcastle North Mail in 1932:

The combined attraction of harvest festival celebration and the recently appointed minister's promised sermon on: 'Can we save the English Sunday?' attracted an immense congregation of people to the Ashington

Wesleyan Central Hall on Sunday evening. The ordinary seating accommodation was quickly occupied and all manner of 'emergency' seats were hurriedly installed down the aisles for those who had made the mistake of arriving at the usual time. Some people sat in the outer hall but many were turned away. At least two people fainted before the service started. It is estimated that nearly 1,400 people were present.

A feature of this impressive service was the electrically illuminated cross which stood out prominently beneath the pulpit when the hall lights were extinguished. Mr Parker delivered a slashing attack on all desecrations of the Sabbath with special reference to Sunday boxing. "Sunday boxing," he said, "had finance for its only object, and the promoters, in order to fill their pockets, were promoting Sunday boxing shows which were held to satiate the baser instincts and are an abomination."

The Rev Parker certainly pulled no punches himself as he followed that particular sermon with others such as: 'If I were eighteen again'; 'If Christ came to Ashington'; and 'Broken Hedges & Biting Serpents'. On April 17th, 1934, the Ashington Central Hall played host to 'The Spiritual Jubilee Singers': five black Americans from Chicago, singing "exquisitely rendered Negro Spirituals." This was seen as something quite extraordinary at the time, but so successful were the group at filling the Hall, that they were immediately invited back.

In 1938 Normanton married Winifred Garvie. Four others closely connected with the Central Hall Choir were wed around the same time, and the three couples were presented with wedding gifts after one Monday evening choir practice. Mr and Mrs Barron received a mirror; Mr and Mrs L Gray received the same; and Mr and Mrs Robert Wedderburn received a chair.

Like the children of Hamelin, Mr Barron's former Orchestral Society from Newbiggin followed him to the Central Hall. As the Ashington and Newbiggin Orchestral Society, they performed programmes in bandstands and halls in aid of various charities and its own funds. But with the outset of yet another war in 1939, the orchestra took on the added responsibility of providing entertainment at military bases between Tweed and Tyne. Their line-up in 1942 was described by 'Wansbeck' writing in the Advertiser:

VIOLIN - GEORGE VARDY a member since 1930 and leader of the first violins. Commenced playing at the age of eight under John Gardner. Played in Ashington and Blyth cinemas in the days of silent films. Member of Royal Artillery Orchestra during first war and played in France and Germany.

VIOLIN - GEORGE F MULLIN began taking lessons when nine years old and was playing in an orchestra two years later. For many years toured the music halls as 'Sylvesto' the tramp, in which role he appeared at Ashington Pavilion theatre in 1917.

CELLIST - NELLIE YOUNG (nee Wedderburn) commenced playing at fourteen under tuition of Mr Tingle. Played at Birmingham Kingsway cinema and Berwick Playhouse.

FLAUTIST - TOM YOUNG husband of above, began his musical studies under Dave Lowery. Played solo flute in Blyth Artillery Band. Member since 1927.

FLAUTIST - GEORGE M CANNEL standing 6ft 3in, born and brought up in army. Played the fife in military band when fourteen. Performed at Balmbras Newcastle.

CELLIST - TOM GARGETT taught by his father whose family have been violinists for generations. Played solo at Central Hall when works of Mozart, Handel, Mendelssohn and Gounod were given.

HORN - ARTHUR BRUNSKILL a member of RAMC Depot Military Band (Aldershot). Cousin of Tom Gargett, the pair played as part of the original 'Seven Savoneas' the first musicians to bring saxophones to the north.

OBOE - JOHN BAULKS solo oboeist for Ashington Operatic Society when they produced light operas before the second world war. With present orchestra since 1931.

CLARINET - TOM AKENHEAD commenced playing in 1911 under Mr Gleed, Newcastle Empire. Played professionally in all Ashington cinemas. Was solo clarinetist for Dodge Motor Company in Cleveland, Ohio. Leader of Princess Ballroom Band in its early days.

BASS - DAVID DEVON been playing the bass since days when he had to stand on a lemonade box to reach.

Played professionally at all Ashington theatres, also at Empress, Horden, and Alhambra, Glasgow. From a musical family with six playing brothers, President of Ashington Musicians' Union for 14 years.

BASSOON - ALF LYONS has been playing for 30 years. Joined the Volunteer Band of Morpeth at age of seventeen, playing clarinet. Played in 4th Northumberland Military Band and Blyth Amateur Orchestra.

TROMBONE - JOE BELL a member of orchestra since 1934. Taught by Bill Pitchford who was the orchestra's first trombonist in 1924. Joe is now member of HM Forces (1942).

CELLIST - CHARLES CROFT received lessons from early age with George Mathewson at Tyne Theatre. Played at all Ashington cinemas.

VIOLIN - BILL HENDERSON first had lessons from Henry Mitchell in whose orchestra he played at Avenue Opera House, Sunderland, in 1896. As a teacher, Bill has been responsible for over 200 violinists in the district. A member of the Harmonic Military Band, and for 16 years conductor of Ashington Co-operative Orchestra. Served in Home Defence in first war. Played in the 'Old Wallaw' in days of silent pictures, and at 67, claimed to be "the oldest violinist in active service."

BASS - ROBERT TAIT played in orchestra in USA and took up the double bass when in the army during first war. Before bus transport was available, travelled from Ellington to Newbiggin rehearsal by pedal cycle with the bass fiddle on his back. The orchestra's oldest member, played since 1924, he always gives encouragement to youngsters.

VIOLINIST - BOB WEDDERBURN joined a violin class of 50 pupils when he was thirteen. Commenced musical studies in earnest under John Baulks, father of present oboe player. Later taught by Bill Henderson.

VIOLINIST - ROBERT WRIGHT began playing an instrument when only six. Taught by Mr Thompson, music master of Smart's College.

VIOLINIST - ROBERT GELSON at 17 was given lessons by James Mark and then by Herman McLeod of Newcastle. A member since 1936.

VIOLINIST - MRS CLARK playing since her 12th birthday, and her first lesson was in a Bournemouth music school.

VIOLINIST - EILEEN WADE received tuition from Mrs Swan of Alnwick. Both her and Mrs Clark are masseuses at Ashington Hospital.

VIOLINIST - MISS M S GREGORY at the age of nine was a pupil of Paul Vogler, then of Bill Henderson. Played solo at age of twelve. Entered many competitions at Wansbeck Music Festival.

VIOLINIST - GEORGE BROWNRIGG pupil of Paul Vogler at Bothal School when ten, then of Bill Henderson before joining his Harmonic Orchestral Society. In 1927 emigrated to Australia where he played in orchestras and dancebands. Returned to become member of Ashington Art Group.

VIOLINIST - SAM LEADER began playing at eight under John Purvis. Began orchestral work under Bill Henderson and his Co-operative Orchestra. Started playing the cornet but later decided that violin was his instrument.

VIOLINIST - WILLIAM BLAND another of Bill Henderson's many pupils, and a member of the Co-op Orchestra for 14 years.

CLARINET - MILES BARRON brother of Normanton and long-serving member of the orchestra, he was given his first lesson by Robert Turnbull. In RAF in 1942.

VIOLINIST - F S HOUGHTON incurred parental disapproval by joining a brass band in 1898. Played with bands and orchestras in Lancashire, Yorkshire and Durham before coming to Ashington to take up position as stationmaster at local railway station. Owns a collection of antique musical instruments which in 1942 were on display in Laing Art Gallery.

DRUMMER - HARRY GORDON member of the orchestra since 1928, always at rehearsals 20 minutes before they commenced. Self-taught, he has played in all the South Shields and Ashington theatres professionally. Plays the most intricate movements with a smile, and his novelty drum solos are a special feature of the orchestra's troop concerts. He also plays for Princess Ballroom Band.

TRUMPET - ARCHIE LOCKER commenced learning his instrument when aged ten under the guidance of his father who was a member of the North Seaton Colliery Band. Archie served his time with the Ashington

Central Hall Band under Sammy Bond. As a boy he sang with his two brothers, Jack and Jimmy, as the 'Locker Trio'.

TROMBONE - BOB BLACKBURN was taught by Bill Pitchford, the orchestra's first trombonist. Also a member of Newbiggin Colliery Band, after serving his apprenticeship with the Newbiggin Salvation Army Band.

VIOLINIST - ROBERT SHEPHERD one of the 1924 founder members. Awarded a Military Cross in 1914-18 war and served three years in second war.

TRUMPET - JAMES SHEPHERD brother of Bob, and another founder member. *(Namesake of internationally acclaimed cornet player who often returns to Ashington and district to entertain his many fans)*

VIOLA - J LESLIE BROWNRIGG in 1915 began learning violin under Paul Vogler. He later had tuition from Bill Henderson, and transferred his affections from viola to violin. Another member of Ashington Art Group.

VIOLINIST - MATT CLARK joined the orchestra in 1930. Taught by Bill Henderson and A Tait. Had varied experience with operatic, cinema and dance work.

TROMBONE - REGINALD FORD received his early training in army bands. Served with the 5th Battalion Royal Fusiliers, but was transferred to the 1st Battalion where he saw service in 1919 in Ireland and India as a band corporal. Played in the first post-war torchlight tattoo at Aldershot. Also a member of Morpeth British Legion Orchestra.

VIOLINIST - JOHN GREENER a noted boy violinist at ten, he played in all the Ashington and Blyth cinemas professionally until the advent of talkies. During the first war he was in the Royal Artilliery Theatre at Woolwich and was leader of the 84th Entertainments Orchestra which played to troops in France.

TROMBONE - BILL PITCHFORD played trombone in the orchestra's first concert. Commenced playing clarinet in the Amble and Radcliffe Band. Played in several army bands during first war, was wounded and discharged. Has travelled with revues, musical comedy and operatic groups around the British Isles.

VIOLINIST - SID NIXON has a varied experience in orchestral work and was secretary for many years.

TRUMPET - THOMAS NICHOLL played in most of the northern brass bands before joining this orchestra.

CLARINET - ROBERT TUNRNBULL began playing in 1889 at age 17 in the Broomhill Mission Band. He went to Lemington where there wasn't an orchestra so he helped to form one. In 1907 he joined the Wallsend Military Band, and came to Ashington five years later to play in the Harmonic Military Band and Orchestra. Played for many years in places of entertainment in Ashington such as grand opera, variety and cinema orchestras.

GUITARIST - LESLIE ASHMAN plays the violin, guitar and sings. Was taught the violin at age 11 and the guitar at 13. A member of the Central Hall Choir, he won first prize in the open baritone section of the North of England Musical Tournament of 1929. His straight solos and Hillbilly songs with guitar accompaniment are a feature of the orchestra's troop concerts. Also comperes the programme with a lively personality.

SOPRANO - THELMA GIBSON has been travelling with the orchestra since the first troop concert, and is a member of the Central Hall Choir.

GEORGE BROWN AND BILLY BAILES perform a very important non-playing function, attending to all the equipment - drums, tympani, music stands, bass fiddles etc - and overseeing the music library.

THOSE DANCING YEARS

Ashington went dance crazy in the years immediately before and after the second war. At least half-a-dozen dancehalls catered for all kinds of tastes.

If you were interested in old tyme then the Harmonic Hall was the place to go, but if it was the ultra modern jive or bebop that took your fancy, then the Princess Ballroom or Arcade Hall were just two of the dazzling palais de dance to try out favourite steps. The Walton Assembly Rooms, on Station Road opposite the Seventh Row, was always a popular venue. Welfare Halls at Hirst, North Seaton, Linton and Lynemouth were packed to the doors.

A supreme terpsichorean was dapper dancer, Vic Hindmarsh, self-styled 'professor of dancing', who participated in some bizarre contests upon the dance floor at the Harmonic Hall, where he held the lease for a number of years. In the space of six months in 1923, Vic, partnered by a Miss Russell, set some all-time records for 'Marathon Dancing'. On February 9th 1923, Vic and partner danced non-stop for 7 hours 1 minute; a month later that record went for a waltz when the pair extended that to an amazing 25 hours; but Vic and partner were to excel themselves in June, in response to a telegram challenge from Aberdeen-based Joe O'Connor. Vic Hindmarsh danced himself into the record books by staying on the floor of the Harmonic for a staggering one hundred hours. On hearing that the opposition - the Scot partnered by Miss Belle Dunn was dancing at the Princess Ballroom - were still on their feet, Vic managed to tango for another ten hours. Spectator receipts for that amazing feat of endurance amounted to one hundred and seventy-seven pounds and three shillings. A couple of years later, a rematch failed to engender much enthusiasm from the Ashington public, and Vic's expenses amounted to seven pounds more than the meagre takings of forty-one pounds.

By 1933, dancing was taking place three times a week at the Harmonic Hall. On the first night of this new venture 120 people passed through the doors. But the numbers fell dramatically with only 60 patrons attending the next time. A disastrous Monday evening on April 3rd, only one week after opening, saw only seven couples on the floor, and the management abandoned mid-week dances altogether.

ASHINGTON ART GROUP

The Pitmen Painters' exhibition is now housed at Woodhorn Colliery Museum which was officially opened by Mr Neil Kinnock in 1990. There to greet him was founder member **OLIVER KILBOURN.** Oliver recalled that there were 38 names on the first list of members. Two girls attended at the outset, but lasted only a couple of weeks: it was still very much a male-dominated Ashington on October 29th, 1934 when the first meeting was held. An earlier meeting that Oliver had attended was run by the philosophical society. He recalled:

It was called Experimental Evolution, and we used to go into the country looking in ponds and one thing and another for biology subjects; we used to seek such things as flints. There was a desire in all pitmen, I think, to learn a little bit more than what we were taught in school.

Mass Observation investigator, Tom Harrisson, described the set-up in the Group's headquarters next to the YMCA:

To paint in, they have the occasional use of a hut in a backwaste behind the Buffalo Cinema. There may often be singing from the tiny fundamentalist gospel on the one hand, while boys play riotous games in the room on the other side. For half a crown a time they have two naked light bulbs, two rough tables and hard wood chairs. On these they sit, with wood or paper balanced on knees, smoking, talking, whistling, everyone painting straight out of mind, without preliminary sketches or looking at things, yet often with such an accuracy and intimacy that one can scarcely credit it. It is one of the oddest sights, a little dilapidated room full of men in working clothes, all sitting round turning out these pictures without any effort, even in apparent thought.

In fact, the men were *not* wearing 'working clothes'. Harrisson's perception was based on how he mistakenly believed a miner dressed. Had he been more used to pitmen's apparel he would have realised that the suits, collar and ties worn by the men represented an effort to be 'properly dressed' for their artistic activities.

One of Oliver's finest works is centred on *foreshift*: a Boy's Day series of pen and ink drawings of himself, aged fourteen, leaving home in the dark, while his mother sees him off. Explained Oliver to his tutor:

I thought that by making the boy set off at dawn it would give more point to my story. I don't want anyone to think I have tried to make it look as though this lad leaving home in the early morning is something tragic or terrific; neither do I ask anybody to be sorry for him or any of the other boys who start in the pit when they are fourteen. They are not a bit sorry for themselves.

WALLAW PICTURES

Silent movies were shown at a number of halls in the early 1900s. Craigs's Buildings, as the present Ashington Post Office was once called, was used for showing pictures as well as providing a floor big enough to dance on. Another hall was situated in the present TSB building, once the home of the Oriental Bazaar, it became known as the Old Wallaw.

WALTER LAWSON was born in 1890, attending Bothal School, and later working as an electrician at Ashington Colliery. He was a big man, almost six foot, with very poor eyesight. In 1910 he met and married a young actress, Vera Maude Dale, in Stanley, County Durham. His wife, stage name Dot Parez, only four feet eight inches tall, taking a size-one shoe, was one of 12 theatrical children. Dot bore him three sons and a daughter. Only one boy survived, Christopher Sydney, who went initially to Hirst North School, and lived until he was seventeen before succumbing to double pneumonia. At that time the family were living in Hillcrest, beside Ashington Hospital.

Mr Lawson took his first steps into the movie business by humping a hefty portable cinematograph projector around from venue to venue, riding on a motor bike and sidecar, showing the best silent films of the day. After securing the lease at the Linton and Woodhorn Miners' Hall (the 'Old Wallaw') this became his first permanent base. But the war came along in 1914, and Walter, like the movie heroes on his screens, was eager to play a leading role in it. He joined the Royal Flying Corps and went across to Canada to assist their airforce. But his sight deficiency meant that he never actually flew planes in warfare, but by wearing goggles with specially-made lens, he took on the important task of training young pilots. In his absence, the cinema was looked after by his wife and sister Rita.

Returning from Canada, he went into partnership with four other men: Messrs John Craigs Jnr, J Gibson, Marshall, and McKenzie, who became directors of the Ashington cinemas under Walter's supervision. Company secretary then was Mr A W Purves. It was then that Wallaw Pictures Ltd took over the theatres at the Buffalo and Pavilion. Separately, with Newbiggin man, William George Carter, he also took a controlling interest in the Empire Theatre at Newbiggin, destined to become another 'WALLAW', using the first three letters of his christian and surname. Each shareholder was given a small yellow ticket which allowed two people into the cinema, free of charge. A dividend was also paid at the end of the financial year. When W G Carter died in 1930 his shareholding passed to his son, Carlton, who later became manager of the cinema at Newbiggin.

A balance sheet dated April 1st 1917, loaned by Elsie Page who worked for many years at the Wallaw and Regal, shows that the nominal capital of the company then consisted of 7,000 one pound shares, with a further 4,100 shares of issued capital. A dividend of seven and a half per cent was paid that year. Freehold land and buildings were valued at just over five thousand pounds. Gross receipts for twelve months were £7.609-5-11, with additional income from sweets amounting to £127-0-7. Salaries for the orchestra accounted for just over six hundred pounds, while other staff were paid £433-4-10. Film hire for the year came to £2,203-6-7, and the Inland Revenue took over one thousand pounds in entertainment tax.

The following article describing the Ashington Wallaw in the days of silent movies appeared in a 1927 Ashington Council booklet:

This is an up-to-date Picture Theatre, with seating accommodation for over a thousand persons. A first-class programme is always provided, and a special feature is made of music, classical and popular. Attention has been given by the proprietors to the heating and ventilation. A special system of ventilation is used that enables a change of air every fifteen minutes. The Wallaw is most comfortably furnished and modern in every way. One is always assured of an evening's enjoyment. Popular prices are charged for all parts. It is interesting to note that Walter Lawson, the enterprising and popular Managing Director of 'Wallaw Pictures Ltd', who has been catering for the public for nearly twenty years, opened the first Picture Hall in Ashington on the site now occupied by The Oriental Bazaar.

In 1921, Walter Lawson's wife, Dot, presented him with a girl, Dorothy. She told me:

In the beginning he brought in four directors who provided the capital, because he had no money and my grandparents had no money. His father was Christopher 'Kit' Lawson, a lay preacher, who died of consumption at the age of forty-eight. Kit's wife, my grandmother, Margaret Ann, had a hat shop. They lived in a house on the far side of Peoples Park, called Woodlands. My mother played instruments, danced, sang...the lot. She was in a troupe with her sisters. Grandma Dale, her mother, was married to a sea captain. Father could paint, and was very good with his hands, but everybody ridiculed him, so he got rid of all his paintings; the one I remember best was of some cherries done on marble. He used to help me with my drawing as a child. He often told of his time spent in Canada during the first war. He said he flew under the bridge at the Niagara Falls, and had numerous crashes; the airmen then lived in bell-tents in the snow, near Winnipeg. I started off my education with a tutor, Mrs Storey. Thelma Spence, the doctor's daughter, and I went together. The Storeys lived in Cresswell Terrace next to the railway line, behind the Fire Station. I used to go up into the signal box to play.
Our first car that I can remember was a Lanchester, then he went on to Daimlers. We lived at Lintonville first, then he had the house built at Hillcrest. Sidney was boarded out at a Quaker school at Great Ayton, Yorkshire; that's where he caught his pneumonia.
My father helped to build the cinema at Bedlington, because I can remember him being up on the scaffolding; it was the same at the Blyth Wallaw. He bought the Playhouse at Morpeth and the Colliseum where Captain Bradley was installed as manager; my uncle, Willie Anderson, ran the Playhouse, and had originally been in the Buffalo; he had one of those wide moustaches, and as a child I thought that the cinema was named Buffalo after him because of this enormous moustache. My father was in several Freemason lodges. He also gave a lot of money away to charity, but didn't broadcast it. Each year he gave managers a turkey at Christmas, and all the staff received extra money, too. Anyone who was off sick got full pay for several months. One member of staff was caught fiddling, but he was never prosecuted because he had been a faithful employee for many years. Father was a good business man, but quite ruthless, and couldn't stand fools.
Television had just started to become popular when father died in 1956. I went down to the Cresswell house to see the Coronation in 1953, and he had erected this massive TV aerial in the garden. But the reception was still dreadful, and it was difficult keeping my four-year-old son Chris occupied during the ceremony.
Father suffered a lot from bronchitis. Of course he smoked like a chimney, sometimes getting through 60 a day. He had some trouble with his heart and the doctors told him to give up smoking cigarettes, so he went on to a pipe. He had been poorly, but still insisted that he got out of bed one night to go to a masonic meeting, and that finished him. He was ill for about four days, and it was Johnny Allen, manager at the Regal, who told me he was in hospital and dying. I was living in Gosforth then. Father's funeral was like a cinema queue: there were hundreds of people there. He was cremated at Newcastle.
Noble bought us out in the end. The Wallaw company had been paying out twenty-five per cent dividend some years, yet all we got was a little over two pounds for shares which had been worth £4.50.

From the late 1920s, with the boom brought on by talking pictures, Ashington's cinemas had always done good business. Walter Lawson leased the halls for concerts, and some of the big names in variety and musical comedy trod the stage at his theatres. The Ashington Operatic Society and the 'Thespians' performed many of their shows at the Pavilion and Miners' Theatre, which Lawson took over and completely rebuilt, changing its name to the Regal, in 1939. As his staff multiplied, so Walter started up a football team in the Coquetdale League and a reserve squad in the Ashington Welfare League, both playing as *Wallaw United;*

Staff Dances and Socials were held each Christmas; outings were arranged regularly. Lawson was in the right industry at the right time, and he became highly respected throughout the area.

BETTY CARTER, daughter of Carlton, recalls how she was asked as a young girl attending a school at Gosforth to take as much as three hundred pounds in cash to the Inland Revenue office on Newcastle quayside. That amount was for one month's entertainment tax, which by 1947 had risen to a penny ha'penny for the stalls and eightpence ha'penny for the circle. Cinemas were compelled to show a quota of British films; another of Betty's tasks was to spend long hours wading through trade books, examining each new release for length of footage so as to comply with the unpopular regulations.

An avid film buff, Betty used her free pass practically every night of the week. She remembers that in the early days of cinema in the Ashington area, children could gain admission by handing in two jam jars. At some matinees, each paying child was given a counter which gave them free admission for their next visit. Film breaks and projectionist's errors simply added to the fun of a visit to the magical moving pictures. One night, Betty says that the villain in *Lorna Doone* was slain in one reel, only to turn up riding a horse, quite unharmed, in the next.

Cinema-going peaked in the immediate post-second-war years, and Betty remembers helping her father to pack over 700 people into the Newbiggin Wallaw: "To get them in out of the cold." By then, Walter Lawson owned, not only five Ashington cinemas, but those at Newbiggin, Bedlington, Morpeth, Blyth and Alnwick; he also booked films for Berwick and Galashiels.

Betty points an accusing finger at TV and Bingo as being responsible for the demise of the luxuriant picture palaces. By 1961, only five years after Lawson's death, people had begun shunning the movies, and showman Jack Richardson acquired three cinemas: Newbiggin's Wallaw, North Seaton's Hippodrome, and Ashington's Pavilion, running them simultaneously as Bingo Halls. Finally, as Dorothy said, it was the Noble Organisation, specialising in gaming machines and prize bingo halls, which bought out Wallaw Pictures Ltd in the late '70s, blacking out Ashington's screens completely in 1982.

When folks stop Betty Carter in the street now, complaining: "Eeh, it's a crime that the pictures are shut," she replies "I didn't see you going. You can't keep on losing money indefinitely."

Cinema buff **KEITH PROCTOR** has done an enormous amount of research on *Cinemas in Ashington*. Here are a few of his findings:

The Miners Theatre was built in 1896 to provide a centre for trade union business and to give the people of the town a large-scale hall for entertainments of various kinds. In 1907, the Ashington and District Sunday Leisure Society was formed, with music provided by the Harmonic Society Orchestra.

Cinematography, in its infancy, was called *The Living Pictures or The Bioscope*. The equipment merely rested on a trestle table at the back of the hall, roped off from the audience. Animal acts were not uncommon at the Miners, accompanied by lusty music. Bob Evans and Arthur Moody jointly managed the theatre in the early days.

The elaborate grand organ, installed in 1921, took up 300 sq ft of floor space and stood 20 ft high; a celebrated organist from Newcastle's Pavilion Theatre, Mr Harry Davison, came to open the programme. Feature films on the first night starred W S Hart in *John Petticoats* and Fatty Arbuckle in *Love* Harry Laws was manager then and Bobby Blaine was his operator. Several young lads were engaged as 'Chocolate Boys' (today's equivalent to usherettes) including Billy Page, Edwin Hicks and Andy Middlemass; local lass Winnie Haggerty was also employed in the 1930s.

In 1938 the Miners was demolished, destined to rise again as the Regal Cinema, with a large perpendicular sign and a new longer canopy; inside, the side circles disappeared together with unsightly pillars. First film to be premiered at what was then acclaimed as Ashington's No.1 cinema, capable of seating 1,422 patrons, was *Dodge City*, starring Errol Flynn. Managers in the fifties included Jim Stewart and J W Allan; Norman Dickinson was an operator, while John Easton and Bill Hindmarsh were assistants. The last house at the Regal came on a Saturday night in November, 1979, with *Elvis - the Movie*.

In 1914, plans were passed to build a new cinema near the Grand Corner, and the Wallaw was built on the site of old open cowsheds. Initially, the first four rows in the stalls were crude wooden forms, referred to as the 'plank-end', the cheapest seats in the house at thrupence. The Wallaw was the first of four cinemas of that name, the others being at Blyth, Bedlington, and Newbiggin. The cinema at Ashington found itself in a prime position when the United Bus Company took over Dungait's Farm next door and built a depot in 1936.

Jack Allen, destined to become Walter Lawson's right-hand man, began work at 11 years of age to help out the family after his father had been killed at the pit. Jack's first job was at the Portland Printing Works on Station Bridge, and he later worked in the telephone exchange at Ashington Colliery, and at the Time Office. He went from there to work at the Wallaw part-time, and after 14 years became manager of the Miners. In 1950 he was appointed general manager of Wallaw Cinemas Ltd., and became a director. Other names connected with the Wallaw were Harry Laws and Arthur Bishop (managers), Bob Hostler, Effie Godfrey, Doris Tindale, a secretary who fell through the roof during alterations, and Elsie Dunning, another secretary who also worked as cashier, in the pay box, and as sweet shop operator for thirty years. Jean Ledgerwood was an employee when she married Walter Lawson after his first wife died. When it closed in 1982 Jean Herron was manager with Denis Cleough as operator.

The Pavilion opened in 1910 as a 1,400-seater theatre. Like the Miners, it specialised in all kinds of musical hall acts, catering for touring companies, operas, and silent film shows. In 1920 the original building was replaced by a new and more up-to-date theatre. Plays were staged by the 'Pavilion Popular Players'. The 'Piv' became known as one of the best built and comfortable theatres in the country. In 1924 no less than 17 young actresses from the one company bedded down one night at lodgings near the theatre, the floor of the house being covered with mattresses and suitcases full of costumes.

Bob Johnson was manager in the 1920s, followed by Louis Stoddart who had been musical director at the age of eighteen. Some of the top show business names to have played at the Piv included: Flannagan and Allen; Gracie Fields who sang 'Sally' and was booed off stage (before she became a star); George Formby performed with his father; and Albert Burdon. The 'Royal Denville Company' gave the last 'live' performance at the Piv. When it became a cinema, pitmen in working clothes went into special matinee showings. The Piv closed on December 30th, 1961, showing three films a week, including *The Wages of Fear*. Some people who worked there when it was a cinema included Edith Lockyer and Myra Sanders, alternating between paybox and hall work. Tommy Garry, who had started as a 'runner' when there were eight lads employed to carry films from hall to hall, spent 25 years at various cinemas; Olive Thompson retired in 1990 after 25 years service; others were Vera Weddell, Elsie and Alan Davison, and Wendy Wonders.

The Buffalo was originally owned by the 'Buffs', a Freemason lodge. Joe Lamb and his wife Ethel, managed the place before it became a Walter Lawson hall. Ashington poet, Fred Reed claimed the Buff had the best accoustics in Ashington; his wife, Janet, worked as a cashier in 1927, and remembered the plush red carpet up the staircases. A nickname for the Buffs was *'Lovers' Cove'* on account of the double seats in the back row. It became known for the many cowboy films shown there which were extremely popular. Mr W Oliver was manager in 1935, followed by Lawrence S Allen. Mr Anderson, Walter Lawson's brother-in-law, was a previous manager, as were Bobby Blain, Jim Stewart, and finally Louis Stoddart, who had played at the theatre as resident pianist when only 15 years of age. Operators included Norman Dickinson, Billy Mather and Denis Cleough. The Buff closed in 1967 showing *The Family Way*, starring Hayley Mills and her father, John.

The Hippodrome, served North Seaton as well as Ashington. Sidney Prince was the manager in 1915 when a Bijou Orchestra played for the entertainment of the audience watching silent movies. Thursday nights became souvenir nights when postcards, tie pins, and brooches were given away. In September of that year there began *The Black Box*, billed as the greatest thing in pictures, a thrilling serial in 15 parts of 2,000 ft each, showing one part per week. An illustrated synopsis of the serial could be obtained on request. First-night patrons received a replica black box. Next door to the hall, Granny Weddell's sweet shop provided all the temptations imaginable to lure the youngsters.

Keith Proctor's father, Bill, remembered that when he was a boy the films shown at the Hipp were ideal for him and his mates. The goodies and baddies could be relied upon to slug it out the following week after a nailbiting finale. His favourite stars were W S Hart, Eddie Polo, Eileen Sedgewick, and Pearl White. If the lads happened to miss a particular episode it "nearly broke their hearts." Tommy Hindmarsh, operator then among his many other trades, painted cinema posters, as did Bill Proctor: spectacular reds, blues, greens, and blacks, all with sweeping curves, brightening the days and nights of all who saw them. Bob Wilkinson was manager in the 1930s; Winnie Haggerty worked there; Stevie Knight took tickets, and Bob Hostler was there for 13 years as a projectionist. Bob, a keen photographer, often took photos of some of the children doing 'turns' on the Hipp stage after they had been invited out of the audience to stop the noise they made while waiting impatiently for the matinees to start; one of the first young starlets was Sheila Armstrong. Keith recalls that Jock McGarry, one of the original bouncers, threw out whole rows of kids who misbehaved, and that he would be pelted with orange peel and peanuts when the lights went up at the end.

The Hipp closed in December 1960, last picture shown *Sink the Bismark*. Harvey Inchmore was the last manager. It was later opened by Jack Richardson as a Bingo Hall, only to close again in 1965. After being used by Freedman's as a warehouse for six years it was finally burned down in February, 1971, supposedly the work of children, perhaps disillusioned at not having the benefit of a cinema to keep them otherwise occupied.

MYSTERY BLAZE OF PRINCESS BALLROOM

ALEC CUMMINGS, one time musician at the Princess Ballroom, and now a chiropodist, took over the Harmonic Hall in the early 1950s. He recalls:

It was a billiard saloon when I got it, but it had been a dance and concert hall when it was first built. We took all the billiard tables out except one which was in a side room. When the Harmonic Orchestral Society had owned the place they put a clause in the sales contract to the effect that one table was to made available for their members at all times. Dr Gunn and business people like Gardiner the baker came in and used it regularly. Bill Henderson was teaching music then at the Hall. He taught all kinds of musical instruments, and always had stacks of sheet music of popular songs. He charged half a crown an hour, but sometimes people stayed all day! I set up the Al Cummings Band as residents there, but before that I'd played for Alf Shepherd at the Princess Ballroom.

Another musician, 77-year-old **LAURENCE SHEARER**, takes up the story:

I played guitar and saxaphone in that band at the Rink. My brother, Eddie, played, Billy Mason doubled on trombone and fiddle, his brother George was on clarinet, Jackie Hunter on trumpet, Bob Rochester, Bill Ord, Les and Bob Easton, Harry Hogarth on piano, Ron Teasdale on drums. The big band sound was all the rage then, with Glen Miller, Artie Shaw, and Joe Loss providing the right kind of music for dancing. We had a contract to play for six nights a week plus a rehearsal on Sunday mornings, and were paid £2.17s.6d - a lot of money just before the war - we all had day jobs as well. I didn't play for the duration because I joined the Durham Light Infantry.

The Princess Ballroom burned down on all the fours: 4th day of the 4th month, 1944. The story of the blaze which destroyed the Ballroom is one that is still recounted and argued about by the many musicians who played there, as well as members of the public for whom it became a Mecca several times a week. Built in 1909, it was a magnificent dancehall which doubled as a skating rink. It stood directly behind the Wallaw cinema, ugly to look at from the outside, but quite luxurious when viewed from within. Dancing was on a magnificent oak parquetry floor, hung from spiral springs, which gave it that light touch so necessary for ballroom dancing purists.

The *Rink*, as it was called, held novelty nights, carnivals, fancy dress balls, whist drives, supper dances, wedding receptions and boxing matches. Display dancing classes took place on Saturday afternoons during the season, and a dancing teacher attended most sessions. The Princess Cafe, adjoining the Hall, could accommodate 250 people at one sitting, and an American Soda Machine was installed in the Buffet in 1926.

When the second world war started, individual business premises in Ashington were responsible for arranging their own nightly firewatch team. A roster existed for the Rink staff which was never rigorously enforced, and on the night of the fire the two musicians next on the list were given the night off. On Thursday, April 6th, a headline in the Ashington Post read:

ASHINGTON BALLROOM GUTTED

An outbreak of fire, unobserved until it was firmly established, completely destroyed the Princess Ballroom on Tuesday April 4th, 1944. Five fire service units fought the flames for more than two hours, but the building was completely gutted; 6,000 sq ft of dance floor was irreparably damaged.

The first warning that anything was wrong came from P C Hastle who saw flames licking the roof of the building at 5.15 am. Ten minutes prior to that, three workmen had passed the hall and seen nothing to suggest that a fire was raging. All the circumstances indicated that the flames had been establishing a firm hold on the interior for some time before they burst into the open air. Fire-fighting was directed by Divisional Officer W S Symons and Superintendent J Worswick who had the Durham and Northumberland Rescue and Fire Brigade engines of Ashington, Morpeth, Bedlington, and Newbiggin on the spot within minutes.

At the height of the outbreak the roof collapsed sending flames and sparks shooting over 100 feet into the sky. Some danger to residential property in Lintonville was feared and occupants were warned to be prepared to evacuate immediately. However, the fire was confined to the ballroom itself. Some horses and cattle were removed to safety from a nearby stable by the police. John Morton, then living with his parents in Lintonville, remembers that the windows of their house, standing only yards from the fire, cracked with the heat. By 7 am the once magnificent Princess Ballroom had been reduced to a charred pile of twisted metal.

Some of the band had been away doing an ENSA concert that night for the troops, and there wasn't a dance at the Rink. When the musicians turned up the next day for practise the only thing left of the beautiful dance floor was a sea of springs, lapping in the breeze over the charred wood. Band instruments were totally destroyed, and Billy Mason recalls going to the Rink and picking up his long xylophone which had completely buckled in the middle. Thousands of musical arrangements had also gone up in smoke. It was a tragedy for the musicians and the town.

Rumours began to fly around. Some said it was the work of a jealous husband, others blamed a rival danceband leader. It transpired that there had already been a fire in September, 1939, the week *before* war broke out. On that occasion one complete side of the hall had been destroyed. It was said that owner, Alf Shepherd, had great difficulty in obtaining compensation from his insurance company on that occasion.

Less than two months after the 1944 fire, Ashington Council were debating why new plans to build upon the same site which had been put forward by owner Alf Shepherd, himself an Ashington councillor, had been turned down by the Ministry of Works. Cllr A Rogers fumed: *"The youth of the town are travelling all over the North East seeking dancing facilities, and are getting into difficulties with finding transport to get home."* Cllr Bobby Gray added his weight to the argument: *"We are expecting a goodly number of Bevin Boys in the town very soon and they should be housed in buildings near recreational facilities. This dancehall is needed."*

While sympathising with the proprietor Cllr Shepherd, Cllr Hugh Reilly wondered: *"Will it be wise in acting at this stage unless the case was exceptionally strong? Perhaps the proprietor himself should make the next move and ascertain why the M o W had refused his application."* Hugh Reilly held a senior position with the Ashington Co-operative Society, which housed the Arcade Dancehall, prime competitor to the Princess Ballroom.

Said Alf Shepherd in his defence: "*Why my application was not entertained was not made very clear. I know the estimates we gave were exceptionally economic in the proposed use of materials.*" Cllr Mick Bell was convinced that the anticipated 350 Bevin Boys would: "*Be at a loose end for long periods in the evening.*"

The Ministry of Works, never fast movers, allowed the squabble to last too long, and an exasperated Alf Shepherd finally used the insurance money from the burnt-out Princess Ballroom to acquire the more prestigious, and even more successful, Oxford Galleries in Newcastle. A new dancehall was never built, and Ashington Co-op built a new Works Department on the site.

ASHINGTON OPERATIC SOCIETY AND THESPIANS

The idea to form Ashington's first Operatic Society came in 1919 when a group of locals, which included musician Benny Creigh and butcher Weldon Laing, were coming back from having a very enjoyable evening at Amble. They had been entertained by the Amble Operatic Society, producer David D Kennedy.

A committee was formed which met at the Excelsior Club, and later the inaugural meeting was held in the Presbyterian Church Hall. Local businessmen showed an interest, and patrons queued up to join the new venture. Professional men such as George Arrowsmith, and Pentland the photographer put their names down; the first president was the ubiquitous Alderman John Craigs; Russell Cook became treasurer; and the first accompanist was Mrs M Neil.

It was decided not to be too adventurous with the company's first production, and the tried and tested Gilbert and Sullivan's *HMS Pinafore* was performed at the Miners Theatre from Monday May 10th to 15th, 1920; Dress Circle cost two shillings and sixpence; Circle one shilling and ninepence; Pits one shilling. The part of Josephine was taken by Miss Corinna Stimpson, while Mrs Russell Cook played Buttercup. The fifteen members of the orchestra included Bill Henderson on viola, J Floyd on cornet, and Harry Gordon on drums. After matinee performances, the cast met at the restaurant in the Arcade Hall for a meal, and the end-of-the-week's run was celebrated with a party and dance.

The production earned good reviews, and *Pirates of Penzance* quickly followed. But already there was dissention in the camp. Whenever such a large number of temperamental artistes are involved (there were 49 in the first cast) disagreements are bound to occur. A breakaway group under Russell Cook formed the *Thespians* in 1923, performing *Iolanthe* in January of that year. Productions were staged at the Miners and Pavilion Theatres which were fully equipped with orchestra pits, dressing rooms and ample-sized stages.

Both companies continued to put on at least one big production each year until 1939. The *Thespians*, however, had branched out into straight drama, not very successfully it seems from the reviews; performances of George Bernard Shaw's plays were poorly attended by the Ashington public. At the outset of war, the *Thespians* disbanded, never to be reformed.

Ashington's music lovers reeled in November 1952 when Normanton Barron announced that he was resigning from his position as musical director and organist at the Methodist Central Hall, a position he had held for over 20 years. Although the reason given at the time was that the retirement was brought on due to 'ill health', the decision came only a year after the Rev Harry Williams had banned the very popular Sunday evening celebrity concerts, saying that he wasn't against such concerts, but was against their performance immediately following Sunday evening worship. The Ashington Central Hall Concerts had been founded in 1944 by Normanton and the Rev Norman Glanville; the first artiste to appear was Miss Isobel Baillie.

Thankfully for the town, the man who had brought Joan Hammond, Kathleen Ferrier and Elizabeth Schwarzkoft to perform for the miners and their families, was back wielding his baton again within a few years. The concerts were also resumed, and as well as the famous, Normanton Barron was to give first chances to local lasses: Maureen Williams, Sheila Armstrong and Janice Cairns, three superb singers who went on to create spectacular careers for themselves.

In 1956, after a period of conducting augmented Methodist choirs of Ashington and Newbiggin, Normanton formed the Central Hall Choral Union.

GLADYS DAVIES' singing career began at the age of seven when she was asked by Miss Ella Jacques if she would like to sing solo at the Central Hall. She admits now, looking back, that it must have taken a great deal of nerve for a shy little girl to stand in such a large hall where some of the best singers in the world have performed. But, of course, Gladys came from a very outgoing family: the Boutlands.

Her grandfather, Harry, was a founder member of the Harmonic Orchestra when it was inaugurated in 1889, and was later conductor of the military section of the band. Harry, who played outside-left for Ashington when their home ground was at the Rec, had two sons: John, tragically killed in the first war, and Robert Boutland, Gladys' father. Bob played leading roles in many of the Ashington Operatic Society's early productions including Sergeant Major Miligan in *'The Dandy Fifth'* at the Miners' Theatre, in January 1930, and, keeping his military rank, as Sergeant Malone in *'Rose Marie'*, four years later. Bob was promoted to General for his part in *'Rio Rita'* in 1935, but then came the pinnacle of playing a Prince in *'Goodnight Vienna'* in 1937.

But way back in the days of silent films, Bob was once asked by Louis Stoddart, then playing piano at the Wallaw, if he would sing some lyrics to accompany a film. It must have been a real weepy because the song was entitled *'Angels - we call them mothers down here'*. Singing for six nights earned Bob an impressive seven guineas, with bucketfuls of tears being shed twice nightly. Gladys still treasures the original musical score of that song, and often performed the same number.

It was indeed 'Angels' which the seven-year-old sang at the Central Hall, ending to a spontaneous burst of applause from an appreciative audience which was very quickly quashed by the Reverend Meadowcroft, who thought it 'unseemly'. But it was as a dancer with the Ashington Operatic Society that Gladys next performed at fifteen years of age. With her father playing one of the leading parts, the show was a musical comedy entitled *'My Lady Mollie'*. However, in 1938, like all good fairy stories, Gladys was plucked from the chorus line to take the title role in *'No, No, Nanette'*, earning good reviews which staked her claim to be considered for the lead in the next show:

Ashington has a 'Jessie Mathews' of its own! With charming and refreshing youthfulness, Gladys Boutland sings and dances her way in scintillating fashion at the Miners' Theatre where the Ashington Operatic Society is making that racy show 'No, No, Nanette' its 19th production.

Unfortunately, the Operatic Society found itself caught up in the second war, losing many of its principal males into the services. Gladys and a few others combined with the Co-operative Players to put on shows for the troops at the various military bases around Northumberland. It was during a troop performance in 1940 that Ella Jacques, (married name Wade) was accidently burned to death while stepping over an electric fire. After the war, and by then married, Gladys took her leave of the Society, while father Bob, pleading old age, did the same.

A nucleus of four men: Jack Balsdon, Will Armstrong, Benny Creigh, and Jed Brown were responsible for re-establishing the Operatic Society in 1950. It was decided to perform HMS Pinafore again with Olive Weddell as the new accompanist, and scenery made by painters Oliver Kilbourn and Edwin Harrison. Productions once more became annual events with performances, initially, in the Arcade Hall. Since 1962, the County Technical College (now called Northumberland College) in Hawthorn Road, has been the Society's permanent base.

The Abercrombie family came from Wooler, and the Williams' clan originated in Wales. Between them, Curly Williams and Nellie Abercrombie produced one of Ashington's finest singers, and the first local after the second war to attend the Royal Academy for Music in London, **MAUREEN WILLIAMS**.

Nellie's uncle, Major Jonty Abercrombie, was in the Royal Hussars; her father, Joseph, was a miner. Her husband's father was a Welsh miner, and when I asked Curly (real name Isiaah but he hates it) which part of Wales he came from, he held his hands about six inches apart, saying: "I don't know what it was called, but it had a name that was this long!"

100

Curly was very interested in music and played the piano by ear. Nellie went to the East School, as did her husband, and daughter, Maureen, who was born in 1937. Said Nellie:

Maureen picked her music up at school from Miss Coils and the headmistress Miss Simpson. They noticed that Maureen had a good voice; they sent for me saying that Maureen should have her voice trained. She left school at fifteen and began work at Arrowsmith's with Normanton Barron.

I went to hear her sing at school one night, even though I had just given birth to my son - there was thirteen and a half years between them. Maureen sang an Irriskee Love Lilt. She began training under Miss Jennie Mordue at Ryton, then under Dr Hutchinson at Newcastle. Her piano teacher was Olive Weddell, and it was she who told Maureen that she should go for an audition with the Ashington Operatic Society. Maureen was snapped up straight away and was in the chorus for two productions before singing the part of Elsie Maynard in Yeomen of the Guard, in 1955, the year that Audrey Stimpson became the first accompanist.

Maureen herself said:

I always remember Ashington as being a town where there was so much to do. I went Scottish Dancing on a Monday - the band was all rigged out in tartan; on Wednesdays and Saturdays I went dancing at the Arcade. When I started at Arrowsmith's after I left school I worked in the men's department. We were all scared stiff of Normanton Barron; he was very strict.

But there was never any danger that I would end up as a permanent shopgirl. I always wanted to be a singer from being a little girl. While at the Royal Academy, I came back to sing the Messiah at my first Celebrity Concert for Mr Barron at the Central Hall. I received five guineas, and remember buying five Premium Bonds with the money, though they've never won me anything. Towards the end of my Royal Academy days I shared a house with Sheila Armstrong who had just come down to London. I was at the Academy for four years and was accepted for Covent Garden, singing with the chorus for four years, and absolutely loved it.

I married a Scotsman, John Bruce, a London policeman, and we later moved to Orpington. I had a baby, and it wasn't the done thing then to leave your child and go out to work, so I gave up singing. Eventually, I did go back to it with a group of six people who got together to raise money for cancer research. Through that I joined the Kentish Operatic Group. While singing the High Priestess in Aida for them, I was spotted by some of my old friends from Covent Garden, and the manager asked me to go back. Which I did, and for the last two years I have been singing in the chorus up until September, 1991.

But I have branched out now, and get the occasional walk-on part on television. I was in Melvyn Bragg's 'Time to Dance', playing the part of the solicitor's wife, and I have been seen, albeit briefly, in a couple of episodes of 'Spender.' I still do some singing for charity, but I don't think the 'top' is as good as it was. I am quite happy getting the odd one-liner on telly, and it keeps you in showbusiness. Would I come back and sing in Ashington? Well, nobody ever asked me.

Maureen has two sons, and now lives in North Yorkshire.

There must be something in the grimy Ashington air that lends itself to producing beautiful singing voices, because the town has launched a number of successful musical careers. **SHEILA ARMSTRONG** was only a young child when she was being hailed by London impressarios Bernard Delfonte and Val Parnell as a second Judy Garland. That had all stemmed from her stunning performance in the 1956 BBC television contest *Top Town*. She recollects:

They took me for an audition to the London Palladium, and I used a dressing room which had belonged to Alma Cogan. But I disliked the whole episode of going down to London. I stayed with my aunt, but was very unhappy and extremely homesick. It's probably because I am a very insular person - I don't enjoy being away from home for lengthy periods.

My father drove a bulldozer at Lynemouth Colliery. The earliest recollection I have of Ashington is walking from my home in East Villas, past the Hirst colliery rows, and seeing these big blankets hung up across the streets. It must have been VE Day, I was only about two years old, and the whole street seemed to be having a party. I went to the North School first, then to the East, but we moved to Norham Road, and it was then I went to the Park School. I was playing bass recorder in a quintet which won at the Morpeth Festival. As part of our prize for winning the Sample Cup, we all went along to Bothal Castle, and I remember being very thrilled by that. Mrs Ingram at the Park School was very keen on dancing and ballet, and I enjoyed that as well.

My intention on leaving school was to go into interior design, and I also studied singing under Dr Hutchinson at Newcastle, but mother couldn't afford to let me do both. There was no way that I would do shop-work, so I ended up going to Ashington Tech College - it had just opened - doing very badly at shorthand and typing on a commercial course. It was, as everyone told me, 'something to fall back on'. I later obtained employment as a clerk at the Ministry of Pensions buildings behind the Central Hall. But I was useless at it, and when they put me on the switchboard, I used to cross the lines and listen to the music on Rediffusion.

I won the Kathleen Ferrier and Mozart prizes, then, at eighteen, began studying music at the Royal Academy in London. Elizabeth Swartzkopf was a favourite of mine, but I adored Bill Haley and rock 'n' roll, like any other teenager, too. Opera singing does not figure all that highly in my career now. Singing opera means being away from home, doing perhaps twelve performances in two months, and I become horribly bored, needing the stimulus of doing something different. And I need to be in my own home. What I prefer now is singing oratorio - which I have done all over the world - doing recitals with just me and piano for a few months, and then singing solo soprano plus orchestra. I enjoy the change.

My advice to any aspiring singer would be: don't do it! The whole complexion of singing has changed, with singers fighting for sponsorship. It has become terribly expensive, and people can't afford to go to concerts any more. Young singers haven't got the benefit of recital work in which to gain experience. They need to win a big prize, and then they have no time to develop. Singers don't reach maturity until they are approaching forty. But nowadays there is nowhere to do the groundwork. It is very hard.

About twenty years ago Ashington Council gave me the equivalent to 'freedom of the town', and I was presented with a silver tray and glasses. I was made a Master of Arts at Newcastle University, but probably the biggest thrill occurred in September, 1991, when I was given an Honorary Doctorate at Durham University, which, apart from a CBE, is one of the highest honours which can be bestowed.

JANICE CAIRNS took her place at Ashington Grammar School in the mid-sixties, having previously attended Wansbeck School. She was then living in Station Road where her father, Ron, managed the John Collier tailor's shop, but became better known as the Handyman, with the woodwork shop at the top of North Seaton Road. As a young girl Janice was quite unaware that singing might be a career to pursue. Said Ron:

Janice was going for music lessons to Norman Spowart, and came in one day saying that she had been asked to sing at someone's wedding in Felton. I contacted Norman, and queried whether this could be correct. Up until then, I hadn't known that Janice could sing a note. It transpired that she had been running up and down the scales at Norman's when she was overheard by this gentleman who was getting married - he was a doctor working in Harley Street, London. This stranger had been so impressed by her voice that he had asked Norman to persuade Janice to sing at the wedding. I still hadn't heard her sing so I went to the church in Felton for the rehearsal. Norman asked me if I would sit in the pews to gauge if her voice was carrying. Janice sang Gounod's Ave Maria, and I cried my eyes out - it was wonderful!

Janice Cairns' first venture on to the stage as a soloist was in the school's production of *HMS Pinafore* as Little Buttercup. Her potential was spotted by music teacher Derek Hobbs, and for the school's next musical project it was decided, because of Janice's outstanding voice, that they would tackle a "real opera," Smetana's *Bartered Bride*, with Janice singing as Marenka. Janice explained:

I had no idea that opera singing was what I wanted to do. Of course the teachers encouraged me; Edna Robson came to our house once, saying "Oh, you must go to music college, you really must." I had sung in a couple of school productions and with the Madrigal Group. And I did a solo spot for a Carol Concert, but opera!

In the end, after passing my 'A' levels, I did get a three-year scholarship at the Royal Scottish Academy and, following on from there, another scholarship at Caird's in Dundee for a further four years; so I studied music for seven years in all. I suppose Maria Callas was one of my favourites, and I learnt a great deal from Tito Gobbi, while in Italy.

I have been away from Ashington for 20 years now, but I love coming back, and the children still call it their 'Ashington Home'. I remember the town as being warm, cosy, and secure, with friendly people. Normanton Barron was very helpful, giving me soloist spots at some of his concerts at the Central Hall. I trembled when I had to go into Arrowsmith's to see him as he sat behind his enormous desk.

Mid Northumberland Arts Group who have been running a very successful Festival of Arts since 1966 under the intuitive supervision of George Stephenson, were looking for a new President in 1988. Janice was asked if she would like to follow celebrities like Sid Chaplin and Owen Brannigan, and she readily agreed, saying:

I am absolutely delighted and honoured to have been asked to be President. It is a great honour; I only hope I can be as successful and make the same kind of contribution as my predecessors.

Janice had a serious accident in 1990, injuring her back when falling from the battlements in a scene from *Tosca*, at London's Colliseum theatre. She was laid low for 15 months, but is now (January 1992) rehearsing a part in Kurt Weill's *Streetscene*, which is to run at the Colliseum with a possible screening by BBC Television also lined up. Said Janice, finally: *"I have never done anything like this before, but I'm enjoying it."*

JIM HUNT was born in 1907 and joined the original Harmonic Hall band in 1923. Members then included Tommy Akenhead, Norman Lazenby, Peter Hollings on drums, George Hunt (Jim's father), and Tom Boutland Snr and Jnr. Other bands which functioned at the time from the Harmonic Hall were the Military Band and the String Band which had connections with the Ashington Operatic Society. Band practice was carried out in the police station yard just over the road. Says Jim:

My father came to the north east from Norfolk. He had seen an advertisement in the paper for a milkman with Vaux of Sunderland so he came up when he was sixteen. He met my mother at Ryhope, they married and had eleven children. Father came to Ashington in 1903 and worked at the Home Farm. His trade was that of dairyman, and that was what I became when I left the Bothal School at thirteen and a half.

I was always keen on music and had lessons from Bill Henderson. I was one of the original Arcadians in a band which included the four Gray brothers: Rowley, Harry, and Joe, an electrician with the Store Works Department; another brother, Billy, was killed in the second war. We played at the Arcade Hall in direct opposition to the Princess Ballroom. I played saxaphone, Hector Imrie was on trumpet, and Charlie Woolans played trombone.

One memorable moment was when I played on the Tyne Bridge at Newcastle the day it was officially opened. One band I played for was the 72nd Field Brigade - an army outfit - but I got out of that in 1938 when there was a chance that I might get called up.

We later got our own milk round and called regularly on Walter Berkely who had a smallholding at Hawthorn Cottage near the Ellington Road ends, plus a farm at Togston. We bought milk from Walter and sold it on our regular round.

My wife's father was a Proudlock. George Proudlock and his brother John lived at The Kennels, and had a haulage business in Lynemouth when the town was being built in the mid 1920s. John had a horse and cart, and cleaned out all the middens. Later, they bought motors and began a coal business from a depot at the end of Windmill Field.

JIM LOCKER was born in 1923 when the family lived at Myrtle Street. His father, Thomas, had arrived in Ashington at the turn of the century after having lived at Fenton near Stoke where he was a miner. Like many others, he had heard of how well the Ashington pits were doing, and decided to try his luck. He came out of the mines during the first war and joined the Marines. Having suffered dreadful deprivation at sea, he was invalided out in 1918 barely able to use the right side of his body. A fine musician, he had to resort to playing a 'left-handed' cornet.

He went back to the pit and worked as an underground engine driver on the haulage system. But his love of music was passed on to his three sons, Jimmy, Archie and Jack, as well as a nephew, Dick Hoskin. In later years, all became accomplished musicians. Youngest of the Lockers, daughter Helen, was taught the piano by her mother, and later worked in the music shop, Hall and Cardwells. Jimmy recalls:

The first memory of my father playing an instrument was when I was so tiny that I had to hold on to his shirt tails as he marched around the kitchen table playing his cornet. He taught the three of us to play - four with cousin Dick - and would come home from the pit, still black, and give us an hour's practise separately.

He used to play standing alongside the piano in the Central Hall before they had the Miners Theatre organ installed. That was when the Methodists had their own band. Every Sunday they would play at the Grand Corner, until one day they asked the minister - Rev. Meadowcroft - if they could have one Sunday in four off. The minister told them they could have the Sunday off...if it rained. They were not at all pleased, and the Central Hall Band disbanded.

I would be about ten when a new band was formed: the Ashington Public Band, who still played at the Central Hall as a Methodist group. I joined them in 1934, and played baritone in those early days, including one special occasion at Crystal Palace. But we had some excellent baritone players, so I was persuaded to go on trombone. I was too small for it really, but someone tied some bell-wire to the end of my trombone so that I could reach the 7th position.

The band attempted to get money from the Ashington Coal Company but they refused to levy one penny a quarter from the miners which was all it would have taken to fund us. We tried to bring in honorary members to boost the funds. I had about fifteen names, and would go knocking on doors asking for a penny for the band. But the folks were hard up themselves and I was often told, "Come back next week, son, and Aa'll give ye tuppence." Finding a rehearsal room proved difficult, too. We practised at Scouts' Huts in Lintonville and Green Lane, and for a time we were based at the Hirst Industrial Club.

In 1935, we were invited by the committee of the North Seaton Colliery Band to go and help them out. Officials then included Jim Wealans, Butch McLean, and Charlie Mavin. We were all in favour because our band had got into debt; we played with second-hand instruments and wore second-hand uniforms. North Seaton was just a small colliery, but at least they had made us the offer, so we went down en bloc, and with our own uniforms of black with a red and gold braid, didn't differ all that much from their original outfit.

Sammy Bond was our conductor then - he was a pitman - and he knew just how to get the best out of any musician. Even when we went for walks as kids down to Sheepwash, we would be whistling our band parts as we walked - that was our entertainment.

The very next year, 1936, the Miners Picnic was held at Newbiggin. North Seaton finished 4th in the competition, and got drenched into the bargain; it poured all day. But there were some great bands around then: Cambois, Netherton, Dudley, Newbiggin and Bedlington. Nearly every pit village had their own band, except the biggest of the lot, Ashington. That was when bands played a full selection of their own choice. We won the Picnic for the next three years running, although I was only eligible to play in the first win of 1937, because just after that I started work at the Store. The rules then stated that only miners, their sons or daughters could play in the competition at the annual Gala. But after the war they changed the rules and that enabled me to take part again in 1946.

Ashington Colliery, by now rather shamefaced at not having a band, asked us to go back and form one. They promised us a new bandstand, practise room, instruments, uniforms, the lot, but we told them to get lost - we were staying loyal to North Seaton.

At the beginning of the war I was in an exempt occupation, working for the Store Butchers. The Co-op then was acting as slaughterhouse for the Ministry of Food, and was looked upon as a reserved occupation. But I had always wanted to join the RAF so that's what I went in for.

I'd had a good education; from the South School I'd passed the scholarship, and gone to Bedlington Grammar School. In fact I passed the scholarship twice, but I was five days too young to take my place the first year, and had to spend the next twelve months running errands at the South School, getting in the milk, and even playing chess with the headmaster. But I was only at Bedlington till I was thirteen. I had captained the football and cricket teams, but when it came to playing away matches, say at Alnwick, my mother just couldn't afford the bus fares, and it was embarrassing for a young lad to say that he was poor. There were 15 lads and 15 lasses in my class at Bedlington, and I am positive that the miners' kids were treated as second-class citizens - as though we shouldn't have been there.

So I was set on at the Co-op butchers in 1941 when Jim Pyle was head butcher. I became a member of the Air Training Corps, meeting at the Mining School, under Flight Lieutenant McLeod, and took to Morse Code straight away. I used to play Beethoven's 5th, "da, da, da, daa", on a bicycle pump.

The Miners Galas had been discontinued during the war, but they started up in 1946, and I helped North Seaton to win the trophy again. As champions of the Northern Area, we qualified to play in what was then the Daily Herald Band Competition. From there we went down to London to compete against the likes of Black Dyke, Foden and Brighouse. We were the only band to wear the old-fashioned choker tunic, whereas the others wore dress suits. Malcolm Sergeant conducted that year.

I guested for several brass bands. I played in the Arcadians, straight after the war. Members of that band included the Gray brothers, Roly, Harry and Joe, Bob Henderson, Tommy Nichol, Joe Tomlinson, Dave Thompson, Charlie and Roy Lawson; Connie Allsop was a beautiful singer, and Eric Nichol did a good job fronting the band. The Arcade was very popular, with hundreds of dancers filling the hall two or three times a week. It wasn't until I'd had a few engagements with professional dance-bands that I realised how poor an outfit the Arcadians were. But Joe Gray did Ashington a real favour, because after the Princess Ballroom burned down, the Arcade provided the only means of young people getting together, socially.

North Seaton Colliery, being a small pit, was always hard up, so that when it closed in 1962 we were asked by Ashington Colliery to move up and represent them. They were full of promises of what they were going to do: new headquarters etc. but we were kicked from one place to another. We practised at the West End Club, the Bothal School, the Mining School, and even the old grandstand at Portland Park, but we were never really welcome at any of them. We did get a set of new uniforms - red ones made by Ashington Co-op, costing £2,000 - and CISWO assisted with the purchase of instruments.

I should think that the first girls we ever had in the band were Maisie Holland and Ann McIntosh, the police inspector's daughter. Now we have only one working miner in the entire group: Peter Scott, who works at Ellington Colliery.

It was a piece of good fortune when the German Vlometel Band from Schalkmuhle came across to play in Bedlington in 1971. They invited Netherton Band to go over there the following year but, when Netherton declined, we took their place on what turned out to be the first of several reciprocal visits. We have also played at Ashington's twin town of Remscheid.

In 1988, when Ashington pit closed, the band's name was changed to Wansbeck's Ashington Colliery Band. John Pearson from Newcastle is our conductor. I've been playing now for 58 years, and can cover up to ten positions when needed. But Paul Cutler is a very good trombone player, and I only fill-in when required.

It's still a very hard struggle trying to raise funds, but we have a marvellous lady's committee who run coffee mornings, social evenings, jumbles etc, and they are an indispensible source of revenue.

ASHINGTON TOP TOWN

The town went telly daft in the mid-1950s, especially when ITV started up in 1955. Prior to that, they had been privy to the Coronation of Queen Elizabeth II as thousands took advantage of easy HP payments to buy sets from local shops such as Little's, Grierson's, Dance's or Jimmy Bullen's. But the pinnacle of the small screen popularity came in 1956 when Ashington was invited to enter a squad in the BBC Top Town series. The show featured various kinds of entertainments, and was open to all ages between 13 and 103.

Auditions were held at the Arcade Hall and the West End Social club. Concert Chairman then, Jack Wallace, remembers that one young girl got stage fright at the last minute and refused to sing. He eventually cajoled her into letting her voice do the talking, and her rendition of 'It's Delovely', went a long way in persuading the BBC producer Barney (give'em the money) Colehan, to let the youngster, 13-year-old Sheila Armstrong, and the rest of the team take their chance in the first round against Bournemouth.

Some of the local talent on show included: the North Seaton Colliery Band; the Molly Metcalfe Dancers; Lilian Turner; the YMCA Gleemen (oldest member 72-year-old Ned Shearer); Milburn & Bacon; and Eric Nichol, Ben Cherrington, Bill Jordan, Doris Pearson, Alan Richardson, and Dick Slaughter, who together made up the 'Five Beaux and a Belle'.

Council Chairman, George Rogerson, got the job of driving one of the two coaches which carried the team to Manchester. Producer of the show was Ashington journalist, Alan Robson, and Arthur Leonard acted as secretary.

Organist Buck Milburn's dad went with the squad to Manchester where the show was to be televised live, and during rehearsals recognised international celebrity Frances Day as one of the judges. Forgetting the etiquette of a TV studio, he marched up to where Ms Day was seated, stared hard at her then returned to his seat, saying in a loud stage whisper, "Hey, man, she's two days older than a Store pie!"

Just before the show was about to begin, there was consternation in the Bournemouth camp when someone discovered that their mascot, a lucky black cat, was missing. Ashington performers strongly denied that they were responsible, and it was Ned Shearer who found the poor animal, cowering behind a studio partition.

Ensuring the team's success with her tremendous singing of 'June is bustin' out all over', the diminuitive Sheila Armstrong attracted a number of offers of contracts, including one from the BBC. Her mother had already rejected an offer of a summer show at Butlin's in Filey, because she considered Sheila to be too young.

Lilian Turner, of whom judge Dorothy Ward said: "This young lady will go far," went to school at the same time as big Jack Charlton. Working at Shepherd's Department Store when singing with the victorious Ashington team, she recalls:

Up till then I had worn dresses that I had made myself, but I decided to lash out for the TV show on a Norman Hartnell creation of black velvet. I found it lying on the floor during a sale at Moses in Newcastle. I am sure it brought me luck.
I owed my soprano voice to the training I received from Miss Welch at Newbiggin. My voice was more suited to light opera or musical comedy, but Barney Colehan insisted that I sang 'Sailor Boy', one of the trendy songs of the day.

The country's imagination was captured by this head-to-head meeting of coal town versus seaside resort, including the *Illustrated* magazine writer, Elizabeth Frances, who went a tiny bit OTT with this extract:

Lilian Turner is a girl with stars in her eyes. A girl whose pale golden beauty was reared in a mining town and shone for one and a half minutes on television screens when Ashington, Northumberland, was Top Town. Nobody knows yet if the end of the story will be written in lights, but whatever happens, these were minutes that Lilian Turner will remember for always.

However, for Lilian and the rest of Ashington's would-be stars, the lights went out three months later when they were beaten by Blackburn in the next round of the competition. But Lilian remained philosophical, and I am positive she spoke for the entire team when she said: *"It was great fun...while it lasted"*.

Following on from their success in the Top Town series, singers Sheila Armstrong and Lilian Turner appeared with many talented locals in Variety Fanfare at the Arcade Hall in October, 1957. The programme featured the following:

> Joe Gray and the Arcadians;
> YMCA Gleemen conducted by Eddie Hall;
> John Ellison with harmonica selections;
> Molly Metcalfe Dancers with Mrs Race at the piano;
> Lilian Turner singing 'Vilia', 'Out of my Dreams', and
> 'Waltz of my Heart';
> The Dent Brothers - Four Boys in Harmony;
> Jack and George Shepherd - Songs and piano;
> Tom Camsell, selections at the piano;
> Sheila Armstrong singing 'Show Business', 'I'll walk with God',
> and 'Allegro' (Mozart);
> Central Hall Choral Union, conductor Normanton Barron, singing
> 'All in an April Evening'.

The show played to packed appreciative audiences for two nights, and all proceeds went to the Ashington Hospital League of Friends.

This was only the second public appearance for the 53-voice Choral Union. They made their debut on the same bill at the Central Hall as that wonderful soprano, Jacqueline Delman, who described the new choir as *"Absolutely wonderful! The tenors were particularly good, and good tenors are usually hard to find."*

The tenor voices that Miss Delman singled out for praise belonged to:

> J Robert Coombs, Robert Coombs Jnr,
> Alan Dobson, William Gibson,
> Ronald Gibson, Robert Hetherington,
> George Matthews, John W Moffatt.
> Albert Morton, Roland Whinnom.

The choir was accompanied on piano, as on so many occasions, by Miss Audrey Stimpson.

In May, 1964, the Harmonic Hall was taken over by a former Ashington FC centre forward.
RONNIE HARRISON was born in Hebburn in 1923. His father worked for North East Marine at Wallsend. Ronnie took a job as a fitter at Reyrolles on leaving school and played for the Jarrow and Hebburn boys' team which won the All England Cup. It was Raymond Poxon, then Ashington's club secretary, who signed him as a part-time pro for Ashington. Ronnie recalls:

I was still working and living at Hebburn, and Ashington paid me £4 a game plus a win bonus of £1 with ten bob for a draw. And, of course, you got your expenses as well. There must have been more than half the team who didn't actually live in Ashington. We only came together on match days, but in my first season, 1948/49 we went eleven games without losing a match. You couldn't hope to compete with the likes of Sunderland or Middlesbrough Reserves who invariably won the League title every year, but we more than held our own with the rest of them.

When playing against West Stanley in a Cup game, I broke my leg for the first time. I went for a fifty-fifty ball with their goalie and his boot went over the ball and crashed into my shin. It was Gordon Dent who ran over as I lay on the ground. "What is it?" he asked. And I think his face went even more grey than mine when I told him the leg was broken. Jackie Dryden was trainer then, and he helped to carry me off.

I had just been married a few months earlier and Betty, my wife, was having complications with our first child, so it looked for a time as if we would both be in the same hospital. They said I would be out of football for a year but I was back in five months. But before that, they had a benefit match for me and I got all the proceeds from the sale of programmes which came to over £30 - when you realise that programmes were only threepence then you can see how big a gate it was.

I then had spells playing for Darlington and Gateshead, before coming back to Ashington to live in Green Lane, just over the road from the Grammar School where both of our sons, Graham and Paul, attended. I had always been interested in running dances since working at Reyrolles - I had a big dance at Bishop Auckland for about eight years and another at the Morpeth Parochial Hall which later became the YMCA. It was in April 1958 that I took the plunge and left Reyrolles to start up full-time on my own.

The lease for the Harmonic Hall came up when the owner, Curtis Absolam, died. Alec Cummings had been there for a year or two. The idea to rename the place came from my wife. Betty spotted that the address was 111 Station Road, so that became its new name, 'The Three Ones', although we never had a sign put up.

It was Ashington's first real nightclub with dancing, cabaret and casino. We had a grand opening night, and after that we had lots of the big names in showbusiness then like Englebert Humperdink, Little and Large, and Emile Ford. We had a resident band with Eric Nichol as compere and the girl dancers from the Blue Parrot. In 1967, Jackie Milburn's testimonial spilled over into the club, and we had lots of big names there that night including Brian Clough.

As well as having that place, I also ran the Old Ship Hotel at Newbiggin. It was while Alcan were setting up their works at Lynemouth, and we had one hundred per cent occupancy at the hotel every week with 14 bedrooms.

One of Ashington FC'S directors, Albert Anderson, had asked if I would like to join the board at Portland Park which I did, buying 500 shares. That was in 1963 when the football club had been approached by a London-based firm who wanted to develop the ground. It was then that the greyhound people were given notice to quit.

Other directors at the time included Bill Kell, from the Portland, Hylton Laing, the butcher, and Eric Nichol who had a haulage business. Not long after I joined, the team got the chance to join the Northern Premier League which was the brainchild of Peter Swales who is now chairman of Manchester City, but who was in charge of Altrincham then. With Hylton Laing and Eric Nichol, I went to a meeting at Hillsborough to finalise Ashington's acceptance into the league, and a young fella who was helping out as the Sheffield Wednesday coach took us on a tour of ground facilities. His name was Laurie McMenemy!

With Ronnie Harrison and the other local entrepreneurs running it, the club took on a prosperous look for a while. A new brick grandstand was built. Officials ran a 200-Club which guaranteed £200 coming in every week irrespective of gates. But then things began to slide. The new grandstand was burned down. Gates slumped. Players' wages and heavy expenses to away matches in the Premier League began to eat into the club's reserves. A league trip to Bangor meant that everyone had to lose two days work.

After only a few seasons, Ashington FC had to pull out of the league. There was talk of either going 'amateur' or going under. The football club made a gift of Portland Park to Ashington U. D. Council, and Ashington FC's shareholders, including Ronnie Harrison, lost their money.

In 1973, with his ten-year lease almost at end, Ronnie pulled out of the nightclub business in Ashington, and the Harmonic Hall, the town's 19th century chameleon, changed its colours once again, becoming a car showroom.

ASHINGTON PHOTOGRAPHERS

One of the first 'pages' in Ashington's history was Sally Page whose father arrived in town from Evenwood in 1876. Sally became friendly with Nurse Burt of Ashington Hospital, and it was she who eventually introduced Sally to her future husband, **ALF JENSON**.

Alf, Swedish son of a ship's engineer, was born at sea *en route* from Gothenberg to South Shields. His mother, a Shield's girl, always travelled with her husband on board. Other children by the marriage were Christine, Willhelmina, Arthur, and Jimmy. After his father was drowned at sea, Alf lied about his age and began working at Ashington Colliery as a cable repairer. But it was as a pit photographer that the young lad came to prominence. Sally remembers:

The first photos Alf took underground were on 'touch-paper' - a very primitive method - but later he was using two very sophisticated Leicas. I became quite proficient myself after he taught me how to use one of them; I wish now I had never given his enlarger away. He was often asked to take photos of pit life, and Cllr Jack Mather was hardly ever away from our house with requests for photos. Weddings were a speciality of his, and I could buy a bungalow with the money people still owed him for their wedding. Northumberland County Council commissioned Alf to keep a photographic record of Ashington Technical College being built in the 1950s. After he retired in the late 1960s, Alf and Bill Harrison, then an Ashington librarian, teamed up and took lots of photos of the changing face of Ashington.

Many other men were responsible for ensuring that the town's history was recorded on film. Early photographers included Pentland, Barnard, Curry and NCB photographer Johnny Briggs. As the years wore on so new names came to the fore: Cud Stephenson, Bob Johnson, Jackie Laws, Jack Wallace, and Bill Harrison who has built up a vast array of old photographs and postcards. Interest in camera work saw organisations such as the Ashington Co-op Camera Club come into being, with Bob Hostler playing a leading role, together with Ron Staines; Ken Morton runs a similar club from Ashington High School; Brian Wade is a freelance professional who provides a steady stream of photos for the council and local press; Mick Critchlow and Keith Hobbs have had many photographs exhibited around the area.

And you can still see many amateurs like Reuben Daglish, camera at the ready, roaming Ashington and its surrounding areas, ever on the look-out for the unusual; unwittingly, perhaps, ensuring that the Ashington of today will find its way into the historical photo albums of tomorrow.

MILLICAN & NESBITT

If you were to have asked any of Ashington's 22 workingmens club's concert chairmen which act was certain to fill the club, there would have been a unanimous vote for Alan Millican and Tommy Nesbitt.

Alan Millican was born in 1930 at the Winning in West Sleekburn. He had a love of music, and was soon singing his first solo *'In the bleak mid-winter'*, with the school choir. He had a very high-pitched voice then, in fact it was soprano, but when his voice broke at fifteen it came down to light tenor. At his home in Bedlington in April 1991, he recalled:

My first job was at Newcastle. My father had always wanted me to have a trade, and he spotted this job advertised, so we went through and I was set on at a garage. I was supposed to be an appentice, but I spent most of my time riding around on this bicycle as an errand boy. There were lots of trams in Newcastle then, and I used to grab hold of the rail at the back and get pulled along on my bike. That job only lasted a twelve month, and then I started at the Winning pit as an apprentice blacksmith.
I joined the Youth Club along with two of my brothers, Bob and Derek. It was there we teamed up with Tom Nesbitt and his cousin Ray. We all liked having a singsong, and someone suggested that we form a group. So

with Ken Smith and Jimmy Munroe we called ourselves the 'Millican Sextet'. Kit Brown was another member, and he played piano.

In 1948 we got our first big break when we won the Carrol Levis Discoveries Show at Blyth. We were over the moon with winning, and celebrated at the North Seaton dance that night. We began to get bookings at workingmen's clubs, all over the area. Cambois Club was always our favourite, cos it was like being on home ground. We had a permanent booking every Christmas and New Year. It was great!

My brother Derek got married and moved up to Whittingham to work on a farm, and that was the start of the Sextet splitting up. It was a fella called Joe Wright who suggested that me and Tom Nesbitt combine as a duo. We did quite well, Kit Brown still played piano for us, and we continued playing the clubs.

The way we finally broke into the 'big-time' in 1973 was unusual. It all stemmed from Alf Robens who was chairman of the Coal Board at the time. He was having this big do on at the Isle of Man for NCB officials and union men and such. John Freeman, a friend of ours who was 'high-up' in the NCB, had put in a good word for us, so Robens invited Tom and me to form the cabaret. We were caught unawares by this, and we had to go to Dormies in Newcastle to hire dress suits for the occasion. We did our spot, and Lord Robens, as he is now, came over, and said how much he'd enjoyed it. He asked us if we'd ever considered trying to get on Opportunity Knocks which was the TV show for new acts. Of course, we said no, and he said he would have a word with a friend of his, Hughie Green, who was presenter on the show.

We came back home - I was working as an underground blacksmith then at Bates Colliery - and thought no more about it. Then I received this letter saying that we had to report to Thames Television in London for an audition. We waited ages in this long queue of hopefuls, sang 'Moonlight and Roses', and caught the next train home. There wasn't a sign of the great Hughie Green.

Months went by and we gave up hope of being called. It was while we were playing at Morpeth Club that we had another piece of good fortune. Tom ......, a company director from Morpeth, was at the club, and he asked if we had considered Oppnox. We told him that we'd already been down, and he said he would speak to a man who produced the show. That started the ball rolling again. We got a letter from Leeds this time asking us to go down again to audition. Hughie Green was in the theatre - it was just a big church hall really - but he read his newspaper during every act, and never looked up once.

We went on and sang 'Moonlight' again, and I noticed that Hughie put his paper down. After we had finished, he complimented us: "Very nice, boys," then he turned to his producer and said: "Why haven't I heard this act before?" The upshot was that he asked us to do another number, which we did, and sang 'Anna Marie'. He must have been very impressed because it wasn't long after that when we did our first Oppnox. We were asked to go down on the Thursday night, rehearse on Friday and Saturday morning and record the show on Saturday afternoon. Again we sang 'Moonlight', thought we had done ourselves justice, and caught the train back to Newcastle Central.

The show went out on ITV on a Monday night, and the result wasn't known until the Thursday. The voting then was all done by postcard. Whey, there wasn't a card to get by the time everyone had gone into the shops and emptied them to vote for us. People were fantastic! A garage at Stakeford used to give out cards with the petrol and tell all of their customers to vote for us. When the cards ran out altogether, the Welwyn factory at Bedlington began to make their own cards - brilliant!

But it wasn't just local votes - we were getting votes from Scotland, Wales, all over the shop. It was because we were two working class lads, you see, the people must've identified with us.

I was down the pit when the call came through that we had won. Someone called us up on the blower, and said: "You've done it lads, you've won!" And that happened eleven times. We won the show eleven weeks on the trot, and that was a record.

Things began to happen at an incredible pace after we won the first time. I would get a call on a Thursday night from Bob Sharples - a great musical director - and he would say: "What song are you going to give us this week for the show?" And me and Tom would sing it over the phone to him from Guide Post club. Dickie Slaughter, resident organist, would play alongside us. We recorded that on a tape, and then phoned the recording down the line. Sharples would record it at the other end, and say: "Lovely fellas I'll get to work on *the arrangements and see you tomorrow." And when we got to the studios the next day, there would be this magnificent 30-piece orchestra playing a wonderful arrangement of the number we had sent from Guide Post. Amazing!*

Thames TV produced a manager out of a hat for the two north-east lads. They'd never been managed before, never saw the need, and now here was a man talking about getting them a recording contract and bookings at night clubs - what could they do? They were just two pit lads, and here was someone offering them the moon. Alan and Tom accepted. From that moment, for Millican and Nesbitt, the crooning colliers, everything was truly *'Moonlight and Roses'*. They recorded a single for Pye, and it went on sale within a matter of weeks. Everything happened at breakneck speed. Their schedule each week was a nail-biting Monday to Thursday at the pit, waiting for a call from the TV studio.

That one phone call meant everything to Alan and Tom, beckoning either the dazzling lights of stardom at the top or the prospect of a life spent in the obscurity of the pit. Luckily, the calls were ones of victory - triumph for the lads and their faithful followers. Then it was the mad rush on the train to London, the rehearsals, the show, then, for Alan, back to the reality of living in a council house at Guide Post and working an eight-hour shift down the pit. It seemed to everyone else that it was the high life for Millican and Nesbitt, but the reality was that the pair were not all that well rewarded by Thames. Alan continued:

We were well catered for with good digs and suchlike, though it would only be about forty pounds that we got for each performance. But, of course, the record had begun to sell, and we expected the 'big money' to be in the pipeline. It was our manager who suggested after we had won Oppnox for the eleventh time that it was time to ditch the show. He said we'd gone far enough with it and, besides that, he had got us a two-week contract at the London Palladium with Vic Damone and Arthur Askey.

Again we took his advice. Starring at the London Palladium - wouldn't anyone? The thoughts of following some of the great names who had tread those boards frightened Tom and me, but we jumped at the chance. Vic Damone took us to one side and said: "Hey, how come I've been working for 25 years and this is my first invitation to appear here, and you guys have made it after only three months?" He had a point - we were overwhelmed by how quickly things were progressing.

It was then that we packed in our jobs, in 1974. I left our litle council house behind and bought a house on Leech's Estate at Stakeford. Our manager provided us with two big Granadas, and we were so new-fangled that me and Tom would travel to our gigs in convoy, taking both cars. Not long after that, we recorded 'Via Condios' which got into the charts, in fact, it won us a gold disc. Later we were awarded two silvers for other albums. We appeared on Top of the Pops, with Leo Sayer and Slade; there was Stars on Sunday; the Golden Shot; all the big shows on telly. We got radio work as well, the Charlie Chester Show among others. That same year, we got our first pantomime work as the villains in 'Babes in the Wood', at Stockport.

Our manager said it would be a good idea to do a promotional tour of Canada to get ourselves known across there. That was the first time I'd been on a Jumbo Jet - I was scared. When we were in Toronto, we appeared on a TV show called the Pig and Whistle, which was fine. But the thing we enjoyed most was when a pal of ours, Bill Tait, who had emigrated to Canada, called in to see us, and invited us to his home. We were fed on roast beef, yorkshire puddings, veg, the lot - just like being home.

When we were due to come back, our manager said that there was a strong possiblity that we could play a summer season at Las Vegas. Me and Tom were thinking: "Hey,...this is it...the money will be rolling in...we'll be millionaires". But he came back later with another option: we could either do Vegas or Blackpool, so we chose Blackpool!

They were the best 26 weeks of my life. Me and Tom were booked into adjoining flats. I brought my wife, Nell, and the three kids, and Tom brought Thelma and their family, and we had a great time. Of course other members of the Millican and Nesbitt clan came for weekends and such, and either stayed with us or we booked them into a hotel. Fantastic! We played the theatre on the North Pier with Mike Reid - he's on Eastenders now - and Paul Melba, the impressionist. Melba was a bit put out when we got top billing, but he soon came round. We sang six nights a week at Blackpool with two matinees, and then did a Sunday show mebbes in Wales or the Midlands. We thought we were rolling in money. We got a thousand pounds a week, which in the 1970s was a lot, but never actually saw the cash - they used to send a cheque home each week to the wife. It was when they began to bounce that we suspected we were being taken for a ride. But that didn't come till 1980. From winning Oppnox in 1974, we had seven years on the road. Did we enjoy it? Every minute of it! We played at all the big night clubs in Britain - you name it, we played it. And audiences! I can honestly say that we never had a bad audience or an empty seat. They were wonderful years!

When the scandal of the missing money eventually broke in 1981, the pair hired themselves an accountant who told them exactly how much they had been conned. They were advised to take their manager to court which they did, but it was a waste of time. In spite of everything, Alan was not bitter:

Tom and me just came home and began looking for work. Everyone we asked said that we were too old to employ at fifty. Tom eventually got fixed up as a porter at St George's Hospital in Morpeth, but after a very short time, him and Thelma emigrated to Australia - they have a son who lives there. In time, I got this job as a caretaker at Meadowdale School in Bedlington. I love it. I still sing, mainly for charity now.

They say that opportunity knocks only once, but before he died in August, 1991, Alan Millican discovered a brand-new challenge in his charity work, helping others. His gold and silver discs were the only tangible evidence of past glories. But he had a headful of wonderful memories and songs, and a silver voice, which, he said: "is reward enough for anyone."

ASHINGTON YMCA

Ashington YMCA dates back over one hundred years. This was verified through an inscription: *'Presented to the Ashington YMCA by the Author, June 1888'*, found on the flyleaf of a book, *The Voice of the Year*, written by Andrew Simon Lamb. In 1954, the then secretary, R J Vince, attempted to follow up this lead, and from his research discovered that the YMCA had begun in 1886, two years before the book's publication.

The title of the first Association contained the words *Hirst Station,* and consisted of one room given free of charge. Archive records dated 1886 obtained from the YMCA headquarters in London, showed that: *"Three brethren, Mr W Hind-Smith, Mr Henry Thorne and Mr J C Moor, have been occupied in the work of visiting the Associations throughout England."* A summarised report of the labour of these members is presented as follows:

Ashington: Mr J C Moor paid two visits, met friends, and addressed them with a view to formation of a branch. On his second visit he formed an Association.'

There were 76 members in the early days. One compulsory Religious Meeting was held each week which attracted an average of 11, whereas the weekly Literary Meeting drew over 50 members. The initial base was open all day and evenings. It contained a Reference Room and Circulating Library. Income for the first year was five pounds, and expenditure accounted for two pounds. An honorary secretary was responsible for the day-to-day running of the Association.

It was never established what connection Andrew Simon Lamb, Scottish Advocate of the Inner Temple, had with Ashington YMCA, but his inscription certainly established the opening date of the group. The first tangible evidence of a permanent H/Q for the YMCA next to Portland Park, again comes from London's archives which states that:

The hut which was erected in 1919 at Ashington had served throughout the first world war in another part of the N E Division. It was transferred to the site at Ashington belonging to the Duke of Portland, who granted a 99-year lease at a peppercorn rental. The Duke later granted a further lease of land which ran concurrently, because on it was another hut which was formerly used as Ashington Post Office and which was purchased locally for sixty pounds with the original intention of using it as living accommodation for the Secretary. When the cost of alterations was gone into, however, it proved too much and was therefore used for small meetings.

Mr Francis Priestman, son of Jonathan, was the prime mover in the upkeep of the establishment which was a direct responsibility of the National Council of the YMCA.

For many years there appeared a debt in the Ashington Balance Sheet which represented cash loans of over three hundred pounds to the National Council. But a further fifteen hundred pounds had been ploughed into the Ashington YMCA during the first ten years of its life. The local Women's Auxiliary did staunch work in those early days in raising money to pay off the debt.

The next year of note in the YMCA's history was 1921. It was then that Princess Marie Louise "whose devotion to the YMCA movement was unstinted," visited Ashington to officially open the new H/Q. The following extract appeared in the December, 1921, issue of *The Red Triangle:*

On Thursday, the Princess took up the role of coal-hewer among her many engagements. Crossing the Tyne into Northumberland, she descended a coal mine at Ashington. A young driver presented her with a hazel yard-wand, used by officials when walking along the galleries underground. As a light to her feet she had a Davy lamp, which was made of silver.
Quaint and picturesque were the party. The ladies and the burly Dean of Durham being robed in white overalls. At the coal face the Princess took a pick and hewed some 'black diamonds' which were quickly picked as souvenirs. She then fired an electric shot, and later visited ponies in their stables. Soon she was aloft again, and after hearing the children sing a greeting at Guide Post, she went on to Bedlington to re-open the YMCA and grounds.
Returning to Ashington, after another civic welcome, Her Highness opened the new Ashington Red Triangle Club which has cost £2,000, towards which the local colliery have donated £500. Over 400 members joined the Club on opening day, since when another thousand have joined.

One of the founder members from the 1921 opening was Bill McDonald who was fully employed by the Red Triangle Club, a name popularised by the late Sir Arthur Yapp after the 1914-18 war. Three years later, in 1924, McDonald emigrated to Australia, but visited the area in 1954, finding the Ashington YMCA hut "little changed."

R J Vince, had with him a very dedicated team who kept the good work of the YMCA very much to the fore in the immediate post-war years. Regular reports appeared in the Ashington Advertiser informing the public about sporting events, carnivals, concerts, drama evenings and dozens of other social happenings. On the sporting side, the YMCA produced some of the best athletes for miles around. YMCA news on Saturday February 8th 1949, observed:

Social Hour attenders last week enjoyed the programme provided by Joe Dalkin and his Rhythm Boys, with Alan Richardson as soloist. Next Sunday evening we welcome R Millican's Sextet.

Ivor Bird, of the dentist family based in North Seaton Road, proved himself an excellent snooker player, helping the YMCA to lift many trophies. Ivor also excelled as an all round athlete, a fine runner, and member of Ashington's rugby club. He later became a grower of champion gladioli, winning many cups for his fine blooms. Playing snooker alongside Ivor in 1946 was Bill Shiel, still a dab hand with the cue, and turning out regularly in the Veterans League.

In 1959, the YMCA's ramshackle wooden hut was demolished. A sectional building was erected on the same site and, once more, a member of the Royal family, Rose, the Princess Royal, was invited to launch the new headquarters. A massive Carnival was organised in her honour with floats of every description on parade. Pitman artist, Oliver Kilbourn, was commissioned to paint a mural depicting a typical Northumbrian scene, which can still be viewed in the cafeteria.

LEEK SHOWS

The first Leek Show in Ashington was held in 1893, organised by the Portland Leek Club, six years before the the Portland Hotel was built. As each of the 22 workingmen's clubs were built they in turn began their own leek competitions.

The White House (Unique) Social Club promoted its first Show in September, 1909. Isaac Russell was the judge, and club officials that day were Matt Taylor, president, Bob Thompson, treasurer, and M Hennessey, secretary. The twenty-five pounds in prize money was shared among the 33 stands. The winner proved to be John Moncaster, while other highly-placed entrants included: Joe Wardle, Sam Coe, Andrew Johnson, and Fred and George Smith.

The West End Club had run a Show in its very first year, 1902, but the year 1909 was, according to the *Ashington and Hirst Press*: "*So far as the quality of the leeks was concerned the show was considered to be the best yet held at the club.*" Alexander Crow, proving almost unbeatable in the town, won for the second year in a row with a stand measuring 106.26 cubic inches; Sam Coe took second prize. The Excelsior Show of 1909 had prize money of thirty pounds at stake for the 42 entries. Thomas Thompson and Thomas Robinson took first and second prizes. Tommy Boutland, who later became club secretary, was down in 17th place.

The 1909 Show at the Portland Hotel saw the greatest number of entries in Ashington that year. The 56 men also shared the largest prize money, sixty pounds. A silver cup donated by the landlord, Sylvester Strong, was won outright by Mr R Brown of Widdrington who had carried off the trophy in three years out of four. His leeks measured 116 cubic inches. Alex Crow was the highest placed Ashingtonian in sixth position. Showing how keen the competition was at the Portland, Tommy Thompson, who had won the Show at the Ex, could finish no higher than 26th.

Another club which had its first Leek Show in 1909 was the Hirst East End. First prize went to J Gibson, with Henry Woodmas, and shopkeeper, Moses Sixsmith, taking a substantial share of the twenty-five pounds in prizes.

DICK FREEMAN was born in 1923 and is featured on that now famous photograph of the Hirst East Boys football team of 1936, playing alongside Jackie Milburn. Dick went on to gain many medals for his footballing skills, but it is for his ability to grow prizewinning leeks and vegetables that he has become better known. He took over his father's allotment just after the second world war, winning his first leek show in 1946. He recalls:

My garden then was one of two owned by the Premier Club. There were five social clubs on the Low Market, and each had a couple of allotments at the back. I lived in the second block of Chestnut then, three doors from the Milburns, and, like Jackie, I was football daft. But my father said: "never mind football, lad, it'll not keep you." And he took me down to help him as a young laddie.
My first win was at the Comrades, and I received seven pounds and ten shillings. When the council wanted to build a car park behind the clubs I got a garden down Green Lane, but never liked it so I moved up to the Woodhorn Allotments when I took over a really good garden that had belonged to Jack Douglas. They used to call me 'young Dick' in those days, but now it's become 'old Dick'. I've managed to set up house with the prizes I've won over the years.

Hilda Freeman's house is evidence of her husband's winning ways. Clocks and bureaux; china cabinets chockablock with cups and trophies; bedroom suites; three piece suites, the lot. It was once said that Dickie had won enough to start up TWO houses. Hilda tells of the trouble with having a man about the house who is a garden fanatic: "You've no idea what it's like. I've seen the hallway full of leek seed heads, hanging from the ceiling for the next year."

Tyne Tees TV covered Dick's fantastic run of success in a documentary. He tells of winning the NCB Best Vegetable Collection ten years on the trot in the sixties:

It got so embarrassing that I had to stop taking my best stuff down to the Hirst Welfare so that someone else could win. I have won the vegetable collection at the Universal Club for 19 years out of 22. In 1961, I won the Leek Show at four separate clubs: the Comrades, Linton and Woodhorn, Excelsior and the old Northern. I'm not doing all that well at the minute only 6th at the Comrades - and the last show I won was at the Catholic Club in 1987. It's hard to get to the top, but it's even harder to stay there.

There was never any secret of my success, no magic formula, it was all down to getting a good strain of leek, then after that a general feeding was all that was needed. It does tend to take over your life. Normally I pull the leeks on a Friday night, but one year I decided to wait till the Saturday morning, and you know, I never slept a wink that night. I got up while it was still dark at 4.30 am and pedalled down to the allotment. I had to use the light from my bike to scrape away the soil so that I could see how big the leek was.

But I was never in it just for the prizes. There was always a certain satisfaction and a big thrill to be gained from beating a fellow gardener, someone who was keen, like yourself. That was the best part of it. Today any novice can win a Leek Show; all he needs to do is go down to Durham where the best strains are, and buy himself a dozen leeks. But he couldn't do that with vegetables. It takes skill and years of experience to be able to grow good carrots or celery. That's where a real gardener comes into his own.

There have been funny moments. My brother Harry used to show from my trench, and we entered the Industrial Club one year. I went up at six o'clock on the Saturday night after the judging to see how we had fared. When I got back home, Harry came around and asked: "How did you get on?" "Oh," I says, "I got second." "Who won then?" he asked. "Who do you think," I says, "it was you!" Harry offered to give the prize to me, but I told him that he had won fair and square.

Another time, the CIU were holding their show at the West End. I was preparing my mixed vegetables for putting on the table at the club when a top show man, a fella called Ridley from Bardon Mill, says: "You'll not win with that lot." "How's that?" I asked. "Because you've dressed your onion and the conditions state that onions have to be fresh dug."

I said to my son, Les, who would only be fourteen: "Les, jump on your bike, go down to the garden and pull one of the biggest onions from the middle row." He did as he was told and was back in about ten minutes. I switched the onions just before Jimmy Eke, a grand gardener, came in and said: "I hear you're gonna be disqualified for having a dressed onion." "Not me, Jimmy," I said, "take yourself a look." He had to laugh, and said that that was the first good turn that particular man had done for anybody.

I've had a good time with the various shows, but it hasn't been easy. If you have to go three times a day to stoke up your solid fuel boiler, it's no joke on a winter's night when it's pouring with rain. But things change, I've got a gas cylinder in the greenhouse now.

ASHINGTON FOOTBALL CLUB

Ashington FC was affiliated to the Northumberland Football Association for the first time in 1888, and became a Limited Company in 1914. They took over their present ground, Portland Park, in 1909. The Colliers, playing in the same black 'n' white stripes as Newcastle United, have a footballing record second to none in the area. Steeped in tradition, they have provided many brilliant players who have graced the biggest stadiums in the world.

Initially, the team competed in the Northern Football Alliance, which at that time (1902-1914) was the premier league in Northumberland. After finishing runners-up in three consecutive seasons, they eventually won the league title in 1914. At the beginning of the first world war they were promoted into the North Eastern League, which they contested until 1921 when they gained admission to the Third Division North of the Football League.

On January 12th, 1924, they reached the First Round Proper of the F A Cup (this was equivalent to reaching Round Three today). They were drawn against the first division team, Aston Villa, at home, and a capacity crowd of 11,837 cramming the terraces of the little ground saw them go out of the competition, but still managing to score a goal against their illustrious opponents - the only goal that Villa conceded on their way to Wembley. It was a magnificent effort which drew record gate receipts of £806-10s-0d. Three years later, on January 8th, 1927, the Colliers were again on the Wembley trail in the Third Round Proper when they lost at home to Nottingham Forest before a massive crowd of 9,242.

It was around this time that fortunes began to wane for the Ashington team who drew many of their players straight from the pits. They gradually dropped lower and lower down the league until they finished rock bottom in 1930 and were relegated back into the North Eastern League. It was a disaster for the Colliers to drop out of the Football League. Soccer success seemed to correlate directly with the town's self esteem, and heads visibly dropped.

Ashington FC appointed its first full-time manager in 1934. Billy Hampson, a former Newcastle United full-back, helped to lift the team during his two seasons, but he left to take up a more lucrative position as manager of Leeds United. At Leeds he formed a formidable team using John, George and Jim Milburn in his defence, as well as bringing in their brother-in-law, Jimmy Potts, to keep goal for them. Custodian before Potts arrived was another Ashington FC player, Billy Down, father of the 1946 Powderhall winner, Dusty.

Many former Ashington FC players jumped at the chance to 'get away'. The long list of old timers includes:

GOALKEEPERS:
Tommy Rigg	Middlesbrough, Watford, Gillingham
Gordon Mason	Sunderland

DEFENDERS:
Stan Milburn	Leicester and Rochdale
Eddie Ramsey	Lincoln City
R Ferguson	Chelsea
A Todd	Newcastle Utd
R Day	Aberdeen
K Finlay	Aberdeen
J Rutherford	Tottenham
J Trainer	Leeds Utd, Southend
Billy Hogg	Sheffield Utd
Jack Hindmarsh	Sheffield Utd, Burnley, Notts Cty
Copper Reed	Burnley

FORWARDS:
Bobby Cummings	Aberdeen, Newcastle Utd, Darlington
Ray Henderson	Middlesbrough, Hull City
Jimmy Randall	Derby County, Bradford City, Bristol City
W Banks	Liverpool
Ron Harbertson	Darlington, Lincoln, Wrexham
A Smith	Leeds Utd
M Metcalfe	Aberdeen

Jack Dryden	Newcastle, Sheff Utd, Burnley, Bristol City
J Moore	Barnsley
Jim Bumphrey	Birmingham City
W Beadling	Grimsby Town
Bobby Gibson	Aberdeen, Hull City
J Duff	Newcastle, Rochdale
P Spooner	Bradford City, York, Sheff Utd
E Joice	Everton
R Jefferson	Leeds Utd
W Turnbull	Manchester City, Chesterfield
Joe Bell	Middlesbrough, West Ham, Millwall
W Haley	West Ham
C J Hayes	Ipswich, Bradford PA, Burnley
W R Wallbanks	Aberdeen, Grimsby, Luton
Bobby Farrington	Bradford City
Arthur Bolton	Sunderland
Cyril Brown	Brentford, Sunderland, Notts City, Rochdale

As well as the above list of former Ashington FC players, the town provided many more who were very successful at club and international level:

GOALKEEPERS:

Jim Potts	Leeds Utd, Port Vale
Ron Routledge	Burnley, Sunderland, Bradford PA
Bobby Moore	England schoolboy
Kevin Carr	Newcastle Utd,

DEFENDERS:

Cecil Irwin	Sunderland
John Milburn	Leeds Utd, Norwich
George Milburn	Leeds Utd, Chesterfield
Dougie Graham	Newcastle, Preston, Lincoln
W Pierce	QPR, Carlisle
Tom McLain	Sunderland, Northampton
George Prior	Sheffield Wed, Watford
Jimmy Jackson	Newcastle, Aldershot, England schoolboys
Jack Charlton	Leeds Utd, England
Jimmy Adamson	Burnley
G Johnson	Sheffield Wed, Reading, Watford
J Stevens	Stockport County, Brighton
H Waller	Arsenal
John Patterson	Derby County
Sid Hutton	Newcastle Utd
Bob Whitehead	Newcastle Utd

FORWARDS:

Bobby Charlton	Manchester Utd, England
Jackie Milburn	Newcastle, Linfield, Yiewsley
Billy Gray	Orient, Chelsea, Burnley, Notts Forest, Eng. B

J R Richardson	Newcastle, England, Huddersfield, Millwall
Jack Prior	Sunderland, Grimsby
Andy Smailes	Newcastle, Bristol City, Sheff Wed, Rotherham
J Martin	Aston Villa
W Scott	Newcastle Utd
R Thompson	Sunderland
John Elliott	Notts County
Neville Black	Newcastle Utd
W Watson	Carlisle, Rochdale, Accrington Stanley
J M Turnbull	Barnsley, Gateshead
A Taylor	Gateshead, Chelsea, Bristol Rovers
Ken Prior	Newcastle, Millwall, Berwick Rangers.
G (Dusty) Down	Hearts, Third Lanark, Guildford

Many of the above also went on to successful managerial posts in the Football League and local football.

In 1942, when Ashington FC found itself in the middle of yet another crazy war, the directors decided that it was unpatriotic for games to be played when so many men were fighting and dying. The team was withdrawn from the NE League with the promise that it would return as soon as hostilities ceased.

And so it was that the 1945/46 season saw the Colliers back in action again, and that is when I began to take a personal interest in the town's football team. My first entrance into the ground was through selling programmes at thrupence each. The man responsible for their distribution was 'peg-leg' Ossie Mathews who, as his name suggests, stomped around outside the ground in Lintonville Terrace for about an hour before each game was due to take place, selling the flimsy pieces of paper. There were half-a-dozen young programme sellers, and we received a penny for every 20 programmes that we managed to sell. It wasn't a fortune, but alongside the commission was the extra bonus of being allowed into the ground free of charge.

Often I went behind the goals as a ball-boy - a much sought-after position. Jack and Bobby Charlton often took turns at recovering the ball for first-team keeper Tommy Rutherford, too. Stan Milburn, Jack Charlton's uncle, was playing at left-back then, and he encouraged young Jack and Bobby to carry the pail containing the magic sponge on to the field.

Another good player then was Raymond Poxon who had accompanied Jackie Milburn when the pair went for a trial with Newcastle United in 1943. Wor Jackie, who scored six that day, went on to become a folk hero, and Raymond, forced to play with the Stiffs in that game, later went to Sheffield Wednesday for a short time before returning to play for the Colliers and later their long-term rivals, Blyth Spartans.

In June, 1947, the tall rangy Scotsman, Jimmy Denmark, former Newcastle United and Queen of the South centre-half, took on the position of Ashington's player/coach. In the opening game of the season he took the extraordinary step of moving the regular pivot, Jack Clough, into the forward line while he himself took Clough's place in the centre of the defence. But Cloughie had a dismal time up front, and in the second half he dropped back into his usual role, Denmark moved into the attack, and suddenly the team clicked into gear. The Scotsman, the first man I ever saw at Portland Park wearing gloves during a game, stayed for a couple of seasons before moving on and leaving local favourite, Bobby Gibson, to take up the job as player/manager.

Bobby had been a Newbiggin schoolboy whose rumbustious bustling style of centre-forward had made him a crowd pleaser when he later signed on for Ashington in 1945. His goalscoring ability was noticed north of the Border in Aberdeen and Bobby spent a couple of seasons there before heading down to Hull City. He returned to take up the Ashington job at the beginning of the 1949/50 season.

That season was a turning point for football in the town. The team began the season badly, hardly winning a game. But as the year wore on, so they brought in new players. Gordon Dent came into the side after a spell at Derby County; Ronnie Harrison, who also had Football League experience, bolstered up the attack; long-time favourite, Sammy Scott, began to buzz. Ashington's football future looked bright again. In the First Round of the FA Cup the Colliers were drawn away to third division Halifax Town. Ashington supporters booked a special excursion train and almost two thousand hopeful fans travelled to the Yorkshire mill town.

A local poet of the day, Robert Straughan, sets up the opening minutes of the game in verse:

"Howway Ashington!" the cry rings oot
as fifteen hundred Geordies shoot.
Just then wor little ootside reet
beat two opponents, varry neat,
then crossed the baall, did winger DENT,
GIPPER nodded an' in sh' went.
Just after half-time in a raid,
young DENT anuther oppenin' made.
He weaved his way wiv clivvor tricks
an' swung her ower 'cross the sticks,
where SIMPSON met it sure an' true,
an' banged it in - that med us two.

After going two up, Ashington came under pressure from Halifax who pulled back the Colliers lead with goals from Glaister and Core. Charlton in the Ashington goal performed well, making numerous fine saves. With the seconds ticking away, our humorous versifier takes up the story again:

Wi fifteen hundred Geordie yells,
alaang wi' corneycrakes an' bells,
The Colliers, egged on wi the din.
wor still aall oot ti try an' win.
Then waat an uproar - waat a shoot,
when SCOTTIE scored wi size-six boot.
It chuck sum reel hard play indeed
ti keep thaat one goal in the lead;
the home side tried, withoot a doot,
but wor defenders kept thum oot.
There was nee way that they'd relax
that one-goal lead at Halifax.

postscript
If wor lads win the FA Cup
I'll mek a few mair vorses up.

On December 9th, 1950, an all-time record crowd of 13,199 packed into Portland Park to watch the lads take on another third division team, Rochdale, in the Second Round of the FA Cup. All the local league games had been moved to the morning to allow players to support Ashington. I jostled for room under the ramshackle corrugated iron roof on the 'popular' side of the ground - amazingly, two fans perched upon the stand itself. It was a jovial, good-humoured crowd with staunch supporter and critic, Pat Haley, blasting his trumpet of a voice across the muddy swamp that ran through the middle of the pitch. Opposite, the wooden grandstand groaned under its seating capacity of 250. All was set for the tussle which Ashington folks were convinced would see their team climbing another rung of the Cup ladder.

What a roar greeted the black 'n' whites as they trotted out on to the field. Track-suited trainers, Jack Dryden and Joe Bell - familiar bald head gleaming in the winter sunshine - took up their positions in the dug out. It was the perfect setting with an imperfect result. With Ashington two-one down and seconds to go, Norman West sent the ball whistling goalwards, Gipper lunged at the ball which flew into the back of the net. The roar was heard at the White Elephant, but so was the groan when the referee decided that it was a 'Hand-of-God' effort from Ashington's player/ manager, and disallowed the strike. Ashington's glorious run had come to an end, and our poet put down his pen for another season.

On the February 14th, 1964, it became apparent that a blazing row was looming between Ashington Football Club and the Portland Park Greyhound Racing Company. The football club alleged that the owners of the dog track - managing director J W Lavender - had broken a number of their conditions of lease. When the lease came up for annual renewal, the football club opposed it. The rent being charged at the time was £250 per year.

Jack Johnson, FC secretary, said that Lavender had "failed to keep the stadium in good order; was constantly late in paying his rent; had allowed the premises to become dilapidated; and that the water had been cut off through non-payment of water rates." An offer to spend £8,000 on improvements by Mr Lavender was rejected. He also stressed that the gambling game of 'Legalite' was not now being played.

The last dog programme to be run under the Ashington Greyhound Stadium management was on Easter Monday, March 30th, 1964. With the withdrawal of the scratch dog, *Big Blizzard*, the final race turned into a four-dog event won by the 7-2 chance, *Jackpot*, from *Twinkletoes*, in the mediocre time of 30.26 seconds.

Lavender's pleas for a reprieve went unheard and on April Fools' Day, the entire assets of the Greyhound Racing Company went under the hammer at Portland Park. In two hours of glorious mayhem, one housewife bought a set of five enamel pails for thirteen shillings, while another picked up a piano for ten bob. Modern track lighting valued at £5,000 was sold for £150, and dog traps worth £600 fetched only £40. Forty-eight feet of bar counter went for £18.

But that wasn't the end of the giveaways. All the dogs ran in trials and Ron Goldsworthy, a miner, bought a brindle bitch called *Blithe Heroine* for ten and a tanner. One of the best dogs at the track, *Town Topic*, fetched the top price of a meagre £31.

If it hadn't been so pathetic it would have been laughable. Greyhound racing had been a way of life for hundreds of Ashington folk; it provided a chance to have a flutter - to take a chance. Thirty years of the 'sport of pitmen' was squandered in the space of one morning.

In an open letter to the people of the town, published in the Ashington Advertiser, Mr Lavender, who had run the stadium for five years, castigated the football club for its folly. He said: "*Without greyhound racing to prop it up, the football club, with its dwindling crowds, will lose at least £50 a week.*"

He went on: "*Almost everyone is now familiar with Mr J Stafford's visions of a super stadium for Portland Park. Their only major asset is the ground which is owned freehold by 6,000 shareholders. Don't they realise that with greyhound racing discontinued, a certain amount of status will be lost to the town.*"

Jack Stafford, FC chairman, countered by saying that it had not been all that long ago when the Greyhound Racing Company had tried to obtain a controlling interest in Portland Park. He said: "*I am delighted that our supporters have got their football field restored to them. And as for status symbols, I think that a brand-new sports stadium will give us that.*"

On the first of May, 1964, at a Council Meeting, it was revealed that, following the closure of the dog track, a 200-space car park was to be built at Lintonville Terrace at a peppercorn rent of £1 a year. Permission was also granted for Ashington FC to go ahead with their plans to incorporate into their present buildings a cafeteria, casino, dancehall, covered market, and public auction rooms. Mr Boundy, council surveyor, also agreed to the building of a new grandstand with an overhanging canopy.

Pavilion Theatre, Hirst. 1913.

Arcadians. 1948.

Ashington Colliery Band. c. 1970.

Sheila Armstrong.

Maureen Williams.

J. Normanton Barron and Janice Cairns. c. 1972.

Millican and Nesbitt. 1973.

Ashington F.C. 1948.

Harry Harle wins at Powderhall in 1950.

F. Loss wins Morpeth Half Mile. 1949.

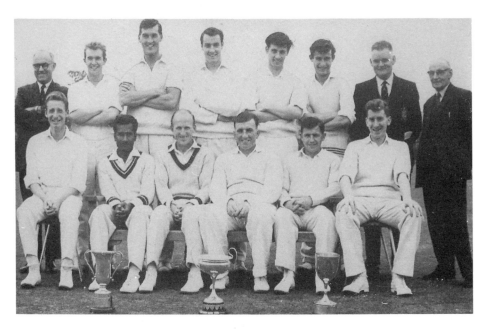

Ashington Cricket Club. 1965.

Celebrity Charity Cricket match at Pegswood. 1952.

Ray King	Tommy Rigg	Neville Black	Jackie Milburn
(Port Vale & England B)	*(Middlesbrough)*	*(Newcastle Utd.)*	*(Newcastle Utd. & England)*
Jack Watson	Ken Prior	Cyril Brown	Bobby Charlton
(North'd C.C. Club)	*(Newcastle Utd.)*	*(Sunderland F.C.)*	*(England Schoolboys)*
Jimmy Scarth	Bobby Gibson		'Dusty Downs'
{Tottenham Hotspur}	*(Aberdeen & Peterborough)*		*{Hearts F.C. & Powderhall Winner)*

A young Jackie Milburn. 1943.

Milburn won 13 caps up to 1956.

Jack Thompson, M.P., Jackie Milburn family group. c. 1937.

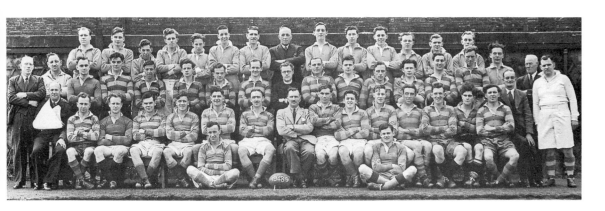

Ashington Rugby Football Club. 1948-9.

Linton Dynamos Ladies F.C. c. 1958.

Charlton Brothers return to a hero's welcome. 1966.

Oliver Kilbourn's YMCA mural unveiled 1960.
(From right to left: Cherie Mills, secretary; Alan Steele, Chairman; Oliver Kilbourn; Julie Finlay; Michael Lavelle.)

WOR JACKIE MILBURN

JOHN EDWARD THOMPSON MILBURN epitomised the honest working class man. Son of a miner, he was working as an underground fitter himself when he began knocking in some of the greatest goals ever seen at St James's Park, Newcastle. I was the last person to interview him and he recalled:

I was born in no. 14 the 6th Row, Ashington. It was my grannie's house, but Presto has a supermarket there now. The house overlooked the tankey shed, and the engines used to puff, puff, puff, all day, and all night 'n' all, but you got used to it. Ashington has always thrown up some great footballers. I counted up one day and I got as far as forty-seven Ashington lads who had made the grade in League football. And I mean First Division - none of your lower league stuff. It was football, football, all the time with me. I knew nowt else. I got away to play, but I was lucky. In fact I've been lucky all through my life.

I remember the day I started school. My mother took me to the North School. And she had knitted a special outfit. You know what it was like before the war - I'm talking about 1930. Anyway, she had knitted a thing with a knitted top, and I cried my bloody eyes out because I hadn't a pair of pants like the other lads. I felt as if I was a jessy with this knitted stuff on.

It was always football, cos I was brought up kicking a ball. My whole family, my father...there were six brothers and six sisters on my father's side, and everyone one of 'em played football. Ladies and men played organised football. So we knew nowt else right from the start. At that time I had three cousins: Jack, George and Jimmy playing for Leeds United, and later young Stan went to Chesterfield. Their sister is Cissie Charlton, mother of Jack and Bobby.

My first job was as a kitchen boy in a big house at Dorking in Surrey. I ran away the first morning! They caught me, put me to bed, and I got up and ran away again. My father had always wanted me to get a trade so when the second world war broke out and they began to shout for miners, he was instrumental in me getting an apprenticeship at Ashington Colliery. My first job was in the saddler's shop, making knee-pads and all the horses' bridles. I was fifteen-and-a-half. Then I started my apprenticeship as a fitter. It was magic, because you got six months at least in every part of the profession: six months on cutters, six months on general, six months in the loco shed, six months in the garage. You covered every sphere of engineering. I didn't mind going down the pit, but that's part of the reason I left. The first time I went down the pit I left my top-coat on. This was my first time with the fitter, and we walked about four miles inbye; me with my top-coat and scarf on! The sweat was pouring off me. I didn't know, what it was all about, you see. I didn't have a clue. But he didn't have the sense to tell me to take my coat off - daft bugger!

I was still working full-time down the pit and playing professional football for Newcastle United. I used to start at twelve o'clock on the Friday night to finish at seven the next morning, and then turn out at St James's in the afternoon. One time I was working at Woodhorn Colliery and the whole pit was going to come out on strike because the manager wouldn't let me off on a Saturday. Mick Bell who was in charge of the Mechanics Union then, told the gaffer that every engineer, every fitter and electrician were coming out on strike unless he gave me permission to get off.

The last time I was down the pit, I was servicing this coal cutter. I had to go on the face, take the jib off, which was in the cut, and then I had to sylvester the cutter right out to the barrier, cos I couldn't get the lid off on account of it not being high enough: it was an eighteen inch seam. And I was playing the next day! This was on the Friday night and we were playing West Bromwich on the Saturday afternoon.

Whey, you know what it's like when you're down the pit by yourself. The props are popping and creaking; the stone's falling and the roof's laying on. I says to myself: "Hey, Jack, this is your bloody last! To hell with this! That's my finish!"

Jack Milburn went on to win thirteen caps for England, three FA Cup-winners medals, and the hearts of millions of football fans all over the world. He was Ashington's first and finest sporting ambassador.

THE CHARLTON BROTHERS

The town of Ashington made world news on July 30th, 1966. England had won the Jules Rimet World Cup, and two of Ashington's favourite sons, Bobby and Jack Charlton, had helped them to do it.

Cissie Milburn came from a soccer-mad family; her father was Tanner Milburn; her four brothers Jimmy, George, Jack, and Stan, all played as professional footballers; her cousin was Jackie Milburn, the Ashington Flyer. There was never any doubt in her mind when she gave birth to her first son, Jack, on May 8th, 1935, that he would continue to uphold the family name.

But it was No 2 son, Bobby, two years younger, who first attracted the scouts of a multitude of First Division managers. Bobby, then going to Bedlington Grammar School, was a regular player for East Northumberland Juniors, a squad that had thrown up dozens of extremely talented footballers. Being a ball-player, he had a hankering to join that most amazing of football conjurers, Len Shackleton, at Roker Park. Indeed, a Sunderland scout did check up on young Bobby, but instead of snapping him up, went instead for the goalkeeper, Ronnie Routledge.

Said Bobby in his autobiography:

My first memories of playing football are when my four uncles used to come to my home in Ashington. They'd say to me: "Come on, Bobby, we'll show you how we beat Arsenal yesterday." I went to the North School, and when I was ten I was picked to play for the junior team. We didn't have strips, and played in anything we, or our mothers, wanted to. Then, just after the war, the school bought a supply of red shirts and one of the mistresses made a set of black shorts from the blackout curtains. When I was eleven, having passed the scholarship, I was supposed to go to Morpeth Grammar School where they didn't play football, only rugby. Mr Hamilton, head at the North, managed to get me into Bedlington Grammar instead. I didn't get the same kind of help there, and I found that football isn't a career they have in mind for you at Grammar School.

In fact, it was through his brother Jack's headmaster at the Park School that Bobby eventually signed for Manchester United. The Mancunian-born headmaster arranged for Joe Armstrong, a Man. Utd. scout, to have a look at young Bobby. Joe was so impressed that he was able to persuade Cisse Charlton that her son could do no better than sign for them. Said Bobby:

I was fifteen then, and I think eighteen clubs were keen to sign me. Newcastle United took it for granted that, because I was local, I would sign for them. When Newcastle did make a move they sent my cousin Jackie Milburn over to persuade me using the family lever. He said that I was assured of a job working for a Newcastle-based newspaper. But then he was completely honest and said that Newcastle United was not such a good club at that time (1953) and that what organisation they did have was inefficient. In the end, it was my mother who helped me make my final decision to join Manchester United.

It is well-documented history of how Bobby became one of the Busby Babes, survived the Munich Air Disaster which wiped out his Manchester United team-mates in 1958, and went on to gain over 100 caps for England, setting up a goalscoring record for his country.

Success did not come so easily to his big brother, Jack. Not an intellectual by any means, this gangling Charlton lad had to be content with a very good, but basic, education at the Hirst Park School. Like his father, Bob who worked at Linton pit, he signed on for work at the colliery. He told me:

In the days when Jackie Milburn grew up, and then, a while later, me and our kid, the only way you could get away from Ashington was to play football. Or, like some of my pals, you could go away to London to find a job and sort something out for yourself. Out of the lads I knocked around with, maybe half of them left home - the rest are still in Ashington, and have been all of their lives.

As kids, me and Bobby played for Ashington YMCA. The pitch was at Reyrolles factory down North Seaton

Road, and it was like kicking up one hill and down another. We got murdered every week! In one season all we managed was a draw.

We had a football, which was through having uncles who played the game. And we took it over to the Hirst Park on a Sunday morning and got kicked to bits. If you wanted to go home for your dinner they would talk you into leaving your ball, and they promised you would get it back, which you never did.

I didn't mind going into the pit or doing something within the mining industry. It was just that you were glad to leave school and go and get a job. Obviously, in Ashington at that time there was only the pits - there was very little else. I worked on bank for a while, first on the screens, then in the weigh-cabin at Linton Colliery with Jackie Summers. I enjoyed that.

One of the things about going away to play football was that you were worried that you might not make it, and get sent home again. Then you went back as a failure. This was probably why I worked so hard when I went away from Ashington. In the first two years I was at Leeds I only played about once in the Central League before I went to do my national service in the Coldstream Guards.

Amazingly, it was big Jack who 'got away' first. Cissie remembered that she was watching her rangy long-necked son playing for Ashington YMCA Juniors when she was approached by the only other person in attendance. He introduced himself as a scout from Leeds United, and asked Cissie if he could take Jack down there for a trial. Said Mrs Charlton in her book, *Cissie*:

I was amazed! Going for a trial at Leeds! Wor Jack! Although Jack enjoyed his game of football, he just wasn't the same calibre of Bobby. Jack was a good enough to play for East Northumberland, but he hadn't made it to the County side. He was due to go down the pit on the Monday to begin an apprenticeship, but instead he went to Leeds.

And, of course, the world and his wife now knows the name of Ireland's new patron saint. Saint Jack has done for the Irish what he could do for the people of Ashington: make them believe in themselves again.

ASHINGTON WELFARE FOOTBALL LEAGUE

Mining and football were inseparable - you couldn't do one without at least trying the other. And so it was, as Raymond Poxon said: *"Out of a population of 15,000 males, if they weren't playing football then 15,000 males were thinking about it."* Right from its inception in 1920, the Welfare League attracted some of the best players in the area. At the Hirst Welfare, no less than seven pitches accommodated the many outlying villages, workingmen's clubs, pit squads, organisations such as the YMCA, churches, and in the late twenties there was even a team representing Wallaw United. It was a well-organised league, with appointed officials keeping a firm control on each match. Competition was fierce, and the Final of the Booth Cup drew almost as many spectators as did the professionals at Portland Park.

I began playing in the Welfare League in 1952 for the Central Club. I was eighteen, and had served my footballing apprenticeship in the Junior League playing for the newly-formed Hirst Villa Juniors, run by Louis Rogers. One junior game was played at Bomarsund, and our goalie, Josie Jones, was kicked in the head and suffered concussion. I went between sticks and let in eight sloppy goals. After the game, Josie regained consciousness and enquired about the score. Realising he couldn't remember a thing, I said: "We got beat eight and nowt, Josie, and how *you* could have let in so many goals I'll never know!"

My first game as centre-forward for the Central was in mid-season when they hadn't won a game. In my first match, a cup game against Seaton Burn, I scored both of our goals in a 2-0 win. After that we went eleven league games without defeat and I scored in every game, but in the twelfth, against Coneygarth Rangers, a team we were expected to hammer, we were held to a goalless draw. It seemed that I carried the can and I was dropped for the next game. In a fit of pique, I stopped playing altogether.

One of the mainstays of the league was **GEORDIE CAVE**. Geordie had cut his teeth on junior football in West Sleekburn. He served on the Northumberland Football Association for many years. Jack Charlton told me:

I walked into the Football Association's Headquarters one day at Lancaster Gate, and was shown into their committee room. And there was this chair, a beautiful thing with plush leather. And do you know what...engraved on the back was this name...George Cave!

JOE GRIEVE was a well-known character around the playing fields of Ashington. Born in Duke Street in 1923, Joe attended the old Bothal School and later moved to Wansbeck School on the first day it opened. Always keen on the land, he began his working life on Douglas's Farm, which, as the Ashington Farm, is the oldest building in the town. Above the door is still an insignia of the Crow family which dates back to the 17th century. Because of the poor wages, Joe only stayed for a couple of years, and he tells this story:

I fancied farmwork, but moved away because the money was so bad. My mates were all working at the pit, getting good money and it's awful when you cannot even pay your turn. So I started with the Colliery Farm when Sloan was manager. It must have been about 1950 when I took on the job of groundsman at the Rec. Dickie Howe was Welfare Organiser at the time, and I was under Geordie Mordie. There was no new-fangled grass cutters then - I had a horse that pulled a shearing machine, and it took ages to get around all that grass. It was while I was at the Rec that I started up my first football team: High Market Juniors.
After ten years there I moved to the Hirst Welfare when Tom Crosskey was in charge. He had been a professional footballer and a cricketer. There were three groundsmen for seven football pitches, four tennis courts, a cricket ground and an athletic track. Then they held the dances in the old Welfare Hut, the 'Shack', when Joe Dalkin played. When Crosskey finished, the Welfare Committee decided that I should take over as Organiser, but only on a temporary basis. After a year in charge, they advertised the post again and Tommy Taylor from Newcastle got the job, But after only two years he died from a heart attack and I was appointed Welfare Organiser on a permanent basis - that would be in 1968. Tommy Douglas and Ted Hall were two of the groundsmen; Tommy was responsible for the Athletics Club.
It was during my stay there that I began the Ashington Joint Welfare Committee Flower and Vegetable Show. Ernie Wallace was its first secretary, then it was taken over by Bob Coombs. I retired in 1988.

Ashington always provided many young footballers for the East Northumberland team. One spectacular game in 1948 at Portland Park saw over five thousand spectators witness a great final of the Sunderland Children's Hospital Cup, between East North and Hetton Boys. The burly County Durham lads notched up two quick goals to go in at half-time leading 2-0. But a spirited comeback by the local laddies, cheered on by their staunch supporters, saw their international schoolboy, Percy Armstrong, pull one goal back, and his Hirst Park colleague, little Jackie Robinson, brought the house down with a late equaliser. Controversy spoiled extra time for the home side when an Armstrong goal was disallowed by a dubious offside decision. As a very partisan Ashington Advertiser reporter saw it:

East fully deserved to have been victors. Their recovery after early reverses was amazing. Both teams, however, fully deserved the loud and merited applause of the large crowd, which could never wish to witness a finer display of football ability, grit and determination.

East Northumberland's team was: Miller (Morpeth), Billy Robson (Hirst Park), Sid Hutton, (Hirst East), Jim Hill (Hirst East), Cyril Beddard (Hirst Park), Jimmy Jackson (Hirst East), Graham (Newbiggin), Pud Barnfather (Guide Post), Charlton (West Sleekburn), Pussy Armstrong (Hirst Park) and 'Sammy' Robinson (Hirst Park).

ASHINGTON RUGBY CLUB as it stands today was founded in 1922. Fred Booth's son, Robert, who went on to be Linton Colliery's manager, was one of the founder members and played in the club's first season. But the history of Rugby Union in Ashington goes back at least to the turn of the century when the town had two separate teams: Ashington and Ashington Hirst United. Both sides won different versions of the Senior Shield in 1908. Ralph Howard was a committee man with the Hirst team at the time they won the trophy. Ralph was one of these invaluable people who did a thousand and one jobs such as line marking etc. Unfortunately, he was one of thirteen miners who lost their lives in the Woodhorn Pit disaster of 1916.

The rugby ground, initially, was a few hundred yards down what was then known as the Lonnen, now Lintonville. When Commander Kemp was given the job of starting up the various Miners Welfares in 1920 the club moved to its present ground at Ashington Rec. The Recreation ground had always been in existence as common land. When the coal boom got under way, it was used for exactly what the name suggests: a place where miners could get away from the close confines of a shabby colliery house, and relax with friends among the fields and trees. The Ashington Coal Company decided to fence it off in November, 1886, and a hall was built three years later. Ashington poet, Fred Reed, a former drawer down the pit, who had just joined the Welfare Department, painted this eloquent word picture of the Rec in 1929:

I stood at the Recreation Hall and looked over the playing fields towards the power plants, workshops, engine rooms, shaft wheels and chimneys of the busy colliery, and I searched for a word to describe the impression the scene made upon me.

The high chimneys, mighty monuments to years of toil, towered up into the clear sky, while the boisterous wind, snatching at grey smoke issuing from their craters and hurling it impetuously away into the distance beyond vision, seemed to visualise a vigorous optimism sweeping away the grey clouds of doubt and worry. And the noise of clanging hammers, of falling shaft 'keps', of the chug, puff and shriek of shunting engines, and the sissing and whistling of vented steam impressed upon me the meaning of dynamic and creative desires. Here was each link in the chain that pulls the mineral from the bowels of the earth and into the markets of the world. Then I knew that the word I searched for was Romance. For once upon a time a dream had arisen and the finger of desire had pointed to a spot in the midst of the green fields of England, and that this scene before me was the panorama of materialised dreams.

One dream which had yet to materialise in those early days for the Ashington rugby club was a permanent base. The clubhouse used today by the rugby team was once the house of Ashington Colliery's policeman. Later, it was taken over by Ashington Farms, and, indeed, a past chairman of the club was R S Sloane, Ashington Colliery Farm's manager. Present secretary (1992), Stan Leithead, who joined the club in 1937, recalls that the Rec once played host to a feast of sporting activities:

As well as football and rugby pitches, it had some of the best tennis courts in Northumberland, a hockey pitch, and around the perimeter was a cinder track for bicycle racing. Geordie Mordie was the groundsman we knew best - he took over from Anty Watson. If Geordie saw you on the pitch when you shouldn't have been there, he let you know in no uncertain terms. The miners were very protective towards the place - the members had tuppence a week kept off their checks. Woe betide any strangers who tried to use the facilities without paying their dues. The place was all locked up at nine o'clock, and people respected the Rec then.

Asked to nominate a couple of men who had given great service to the Rugby Club, Stan had no hesitation in putting forward the names of Percy Bates and Tommy Noble. Tommy arrived from Consett looking for a job at the colliery in 1934. He found work with the Mines Rescue Brigade, and later became Safety Officer with Bates Pit then Pegswood. He played for Ashington as a second row forward when the team got going again in 1945 after the war ended. Lots of grounds had been taken over during the war for military purposes. Tommy later became a referee and was secretary for a number of years before he died in 1983.

Percy Bates' association with Ashington rugby dates back to 1922. A founder member, Percy was the team's county representative for many years. When he finished playing he refereed, became club chairman, and was a past president of the Northumberland Rugby Union. In 1929, Percy, together with team mates A Smith, C Chester and W Knight, won the half mile Rugby Relay Race which took place that year in Durham. Carrying the oval ball under his arm on the last leg, Percy caused an *Evening World* cartoonist to report: "Bates runs so fast he makes the dust fly on a wet night."

The sport of rugby continued to thrive in Ashington during the twenties. The following is a report taken from the Colliery Magazine:

Anyone who saw the match between Ashington Welfare's first team against Gosforth at the Rec on Saturday 23rd February, 1929, will not in a hurry forget the muddied mass of sportsmen who heaved and strove in one of the toughest tussles of the season. We are indebted to the keenness of our lads who provided such a grand exhibition of clean wholesome play and ended up winning by 11 points to 6.

The town of Ashington was justifiably proud when John Ellerington, son of Mr W Ellerington the assistant farm's manager, became one of their first rugby internationals. John, who attended Morpeth Grammar School, was a county player before gaining his cap for England boys playing Wales on March 23rd, 1929.

The team continued to do well in the post-war period. The following is a summary in the Ashington Advertiser of a Northumberland Challenge Shield Second Round game against North Shields, on February 21st, 1948:

From the kick off the home team went into the attack and K Rogerson, Ashington full-back, opened the scoring with a penalty goal. With a heavier pack, North Shields were getting more of the ball in the scrums, but the keen tackling prevented their backs from completing any movement. The visitors drew level with a penalty by Burns.

After twenty minutes play in the second half, Ashington had the misfortune to lose S Shilitto, a forward, who had to retire with an injured shoulder. With determination, Ashington took up the attack again and increased their lead with a try by Eric Bird. A penalty by Ken Rogerson enabled the home team to run out winners of a hard fought game by 18 points to 9.

Team for next week's Second XV v Seghill in Junior Cup: E Scougall, G Elliott, Ivor Bird, D Hedley, W Williams, A Molesworth, F Spare, J Smith, S Wingate, J Jackson, G Henderson, J Lynn, L Hayton, T Noble, J Telfer. Reserves Tom Glasper and F Millar.

The Ashington rugby club was once housed in the old gymnasium situated not far from the steps of the wooden bridge which provided a crossing over the railway line between the colliery rows and the ground. Committee meetings and after-match socialising took place at the *Middle Market Club* right up till 1962 when the rugby club moved into a wooden hut which was their first permanent home.

Originally, it had been a sectionalised house standing on the outskirts of Morpeth. Members dismantled it, brought it back, assembled it, and were drinking beer there within a very short time. Stan Leithead pointed out that the original coal owner, Jonathan Priestman, had placed a covenant on most of Ashington forbidding the sale of alcohol on any premises. Because of a loophole in the fine print, this did not apply to the thirsty rugby players in their new clubhouse. In 1976 the club acquired the building they now use, together with a small triangle of land, from the National Coal Board for the sum of £1,500.

The local team did provide an international in 1985 in the formidable shape of Kevin Clough who represented England Colts on their tour of Canada that year. Kevin attended Hirst High School where the first-hand knowledge of his sports teacher, Alan Mole, himself a stalwart member of the club, proved invaluable in Kevin's approach to the game.

More recently, the royal blue and amber hoops have been seen as far afield as Hull and Pontefract as they fulfil their fixtures in Division Two, North East. Further promotion would see the team have to travel way beyond even Yorkshire, and it is evident that the added expense incurred would cause problems.

What does cause immediate problems at the minute is the lack of pitches. With five teams now operating, some fixtures have to be played at Hirst Welfare which is very inconvenient as players still strip at the Rec. But bulldozers in an ajoining piece of ground - once the site of the colliery fitting shops - are busy levelling out another two pitches for the club as players and supporters look forward, at least for the game of rugby, to a very rosy future.

ASHINGTON CRICKET CLUB began in 1892, although it is recorded that matches were being played in the village 20 years earlier. Their present ground at Langwell Crescent was presented to them by the owner of the field, the Duke of Portland. He decreed that no development of any kind could take place, so preserving a very valuable piece of real estate for the town's cricket lovers. The team has had a number of pavilions built over the years, with the present building going up in 1960. It was then that the 1914-18 War Memorial panels were brought from Ashington Hospital to form part of the pavilion.

The name of Ashington Cricket Club and Stan Levison are practically synonymous, in fact not many people can remember when he *wasn't* attached to the Langwell Park organisation, but he can, vividly:

I first went to Ashington in 1941 when the team was playing in what they called the Northumberland Wartime League. But my first interest in the game had come when I was at St Aidan's RC school from a teacher called Pat Grimes. He was a good all-rounder and played football in the local Welfare League. The school didn't have all that much gear and we played our games on the Peoples Park which wasn't an ideal ground. My first taste of organised cricket came with Lynemouth who had two XIs in the Alnwick and District league. I was a wicket keeper and opening bat when I played my first game for them at 14 years of age.

Two Ashington Cricket Club committee men, Jimmy Davison and John McCoy came to ask me if I would play for Ashington which I did. I was then living at Lynemouth and working at Ellington colliery. During the war years we weren't allowed to travel, so we would play a team like Percy Main at home, but we couldn't have an away fixture there. There was never very much money at Langwell, but we had a wonderful backroom crew who worked for nothing. Sightscreens were made by colliery blacksmiths, players bought their own gear, there was always a great camaraderie in the squad.

After the war, the transport problem didn't get all that much easier. To get to a place like Tynedale, we had to catch a bus to Newcastle then a train to Hexham. Many a time I left Lynemouth at eleven o'clock on a Saturday morning for a 2.30 pm start away from home, then didn't get back till the last bus at 10 pm from Ashington.

A lot of our finance came from a Lottery which we ran. We were well advised by Dick McLaughlin, the Trustees Savings Bank manager, and Charlie Chisholm, a local bookmaker.

The following is a resumé of the 1949 cricket season at Langwell, as noted by the Ashington Advertiser correspondent in September of that year:

Winding up this weekend is one of the best seasons in the history of Ashington Cricket Club. No honours have been acquired, but there have been golden days at Langwell Crescent Ground this year, and a consistently healthy atmosphere of bustling activity. The highlight was the refusal of Ashington to bow the knee to the mighty County Club, with its galaxy of star players. It was a rude shock for the invincible County when, on their own ground, the lads from the pit place walloped them with six wickets to spare. Batsmen who took toll of the County bowlers were Arthur Teasdale (80 not out) and D Tanner (53).

In the return match, Ashington, with a weakened attack, were in a most stubborn mood, and the County were obliged to be content with a draw. Arthur Teasdale bowled magnificently, and the batsmen, with John Robinson in his glory as an obstructionist, just wore 'em out.

The Seconds also beat County when 15-year-old Jim Turnbull, son of the club chairman, scored 100 not out, and G Gray took 8 wickets for 61.

Throughout the season various players have jumped into the limelight. W Johnson in the first match had the astonishing figures of 8 wickets for 3 runs, and the club presented him with the ball. Several batsmen made scores just short of the half century: J Robinson (47), J Davison (42), S Levison (41), W Roberts (46), D Gibson (48), B Coleman (48).

Among those who passed the 50 mark were A Teasdale (79), J Barnes (70), H Carr (58), J Hill (56), D Tanner (54), J Robinson (52), T E Crowe (50). R Wright (50).

Most exhilarating knocks were those of the popular professional Jack Watson, whose 76 at Benwell and 69 at home against Tynedale, sparkled with lusty six hits and boundaries. During the season he became a regular choice for representative county matches, and Arthur Teasdale was also accorded the honour of a county outing. During the season, Jim Turnbull and Grant Stobbart, two of the club's up-and-coming youngsters played for Northumberland Public Schools against Durham.

Gala day was the benefit match for Jack Watson when guest teams included some footballers of whom Ashington's Jack Milburn was the natural 'star turn'. To the delight of scores of small boys, the great Jack scored 41 and took two wickets.

The introduction of Sunday cricket has provided hundreds with a pleasant afternoon, and it was in one of these matches that we saw the 'lesser-lights' tried out. The club president, Mr W Proudlock, and secretary Dick McLaughlin, both appeared, the latter getting two wickets with his unorthodox googlie bowling.

ROHAN KANHAI was already a world class batsman when the then president of Ashington Cricket Club, Charlie Chisholm Snr, announced that the West Indian was the man to put the colliery town on to the cricketing map.

The popular West Indian made his debut in May 1964, against Percy Main in the Northumberland League. Ashington's team that day was: S Levison (capt), C Cairns, A Crooks, P Cummings, R Kanhai, A McGrady, R A Saunders, K D Smith, F Suffield, G Walton, K Walton.

A cavalier batsman with a wealth of stunning shots, Kanhai began the season in great style scoring 50 in his first innings. He followed this up with knocks of 55, 80, and 106 against Alnwick to put Ashington into second place in the League by the end of June.

Kanhai brought the entire West Indian test team to Langwell Park on the 5th July for his first benefit match. Tom Boutland in his diary noted that: *"200 cars turned up and a collection raised over £105."* By the end of the season, Kanhai had broken the league record by scoring 1217 runs with an average of 93.62, enabling Ashington to win the League as well as the coveted Wilson Cup.

At their annual meeting, the Cricket Club with its membership of 308, was said to be thriving by J Morris, Chairman. *"The signing of Rohan Kanhai is a good thing for the club and the town,"* he said. *"We now need to put in a lot of hard work to raise the extra expenditure."* Officials elected for the following season were: Chas Chisholm Snr, president; J Morris, chairman; S Levison, vice chairman; R Southcott, secretary; A K Chambers, treasurer; and team selectors H Conn, R E Davison and R Southcott.

Stan Levison observed:

Kanhai was a brilliant batsman who definitely developed Colin Cairns from being a good player into an outstanding cricketer. But he was good for the town as well; spectators flocked to the ground to see this little West Indian who was a world-class player. We played at a little ground at Belford one day and the place was packed. Afterwards we holed in at the local pub and couldn't get moved. Rohan sat behind the bar out of the way, signing autographs.

But a memory I will never forget was the day I declared with Rohan Kanhai on 196 and heading towards his first double century for the club. On paper it looked as though I was the villain of the piece, but the way it happened was that we were playing Backworth at home and had built up a massive score. Rohan was then on

174, and I said I would declare at the end of the next over. So, with it being teatime, all the players in the pavilion took off their pads and boots.

But Kanhai's score was up to 196 by the end of the over. I thought that a few minutes more would make no difference, and decided to let them have another over so that he could get his double ton. But Kanhai's batting partner, George Walton, got himself stumped, and I had no-one else ready to go in to bat, so I just declared the innings closed. You would have thought I had just declared War! Spectators were screaming for my blood, Kanhai was blowing a fuse as he stormed off the pitch, my wife was almost in tears. Still, we won the match.

Ashington Cricket Club has always tried to provide the best that was going in the cricket world. We brought Fred Trueman to Langwell for a Benefit Match in 1961. He fielded an excellent side which included Phil Sharpe and Peter Parfitt.

In my opinion, men who have had a definite influence on the game at Ashington are players like Tommy Simpson, a great favourite with the fans, George Walton, a Minor Counties batsman together with Colin Cairns, and Arthur Teasdale, Stuart Miles, (a great left-arm bowler), Don Hall, Jimmy Davison, and one of the very early ones Bart Conn. Richard Dreyer was a good player; Steve Williams is playing well; and I rate our captain, Stuart Tiffen, an excellent leader. Our professional, Collie Solomon, is performing great things with bat and ball.

Highlights of my career? Well, as a player it has to be the 96 I scored against Tynedale, and the 48 catches and stumpings I achieved in 1958. But even after I stopped playing about 25 years ago I have had some memorable moments: umpiring in the Minor Counties, and for the last ten years standing at the Cricket Festival in Jesmond started off by the Callers Brothers. You name the players and I have umpired for them. The great players never questioned a decision; they might raise an eyebrow as if to say 'Stan Levison! what does he know about cricket?'

Modest as always, I think the people of Ashington know the answer to that one.

ASHINGTON's MOTOR CLUBS

Motor cycling was always a very popular pastime in the town. The first club to be formed in the 1920s was Wansbeck Motor Club. These daredevils performed a number of stunts during the annual Hospital Carnival, all in the name of charity. In 1928, one of the most interesting events was a Motor Cycle Football Match. The match, according to a report in the Colliery Magazine, "attracted a large and appreciative crowd of spectators, who were treated to an exciting and skilful display of machine and ball control." Noted as goalscorers were: G Watson, J C Bell, and G Oliver. The squad that day consisted of: E S Brown, L Deans, A J Hunt, G Downie, J C Bell, G Watson, G Oliver, R Scott, F Smart, W Mather, J Gray, and W Ogston. J J Hall, the Colliery Agent, was then president of the club.

But Wansbeck Motor Club, like so many organisations, closed shop when the second world war broke out. Its revival was 'mainly' due to motor biking fanatic, Jimmy Main, who became Club secretary. A report in the Ashington Advertiser of March 5th, 1949 shows that the Club was still going strong:

With the approach of the light nights and good motor cycling weather, the Wansbeck MC is well ahead with its plans for the forthcoming season. Social runs are to be held frequently but the meagre petrol ration will necessitate them being relatively short. A treasure hunt is to be held in the Rothbury district, and several camping weekends which proved popular last year. Organisation is already under way for the Wansbeck MC Gymkhana. This is to take place in July, and should be great entertainment for both motor cyclists and public alike. A Consistency Hill Climb is scheduled for May. The Club meets at 8 pm every Tuesday night at the Mortimer Club, and the meetings are always lively and well attended. All motor cyclists are invited to come along - they would be made more than welcome by the Wansbeck Members.

Yet another motor club, this time calling themselves, the Ashington Motor Club, became very popular after the second war, being formed in 1946. It catered mostly for motor cycles although a few cars did turn up for the many rallies which the club organised. They found themselves in direct competition for members with the Wansbeck squad. The AMC's first trial in Sheepwash Dene was held in October, 1948, won by club member C Stansbury of Rosalind Street. He was presented with the 'Torch Bearer' Trophy. Fixtures for 1949 included an Open to Centre Sprint Race on Druridge Sands. A two-week tour of the Continent was planned for later in the year. Secretary then was R Johnson of Sycamore Street.

AMC's meeting place for a long time was in the *Comrades Club*, which was very handy for one of the energetic members, Harry Crowe, who lived next door. He joined the club in 1951 as an enthusiast when scrambles and hill-climbs were being held at farms in Ulgham and Whittle as well as the popular Wellhead Dene at Sheepwash. The Ashington Motor Club members and their families enjoyed many social outings and holidays together before it eventually folded in 1970.

ASHINGTON WELFARE TENNIS

The tennis courts at Ashington Recreation and Hirst grounds were among the finest in the county. Equipment could be hired at the Welfare Office for a small fee, and many people took advantage of what, till then, was very much an upper middle class sport. An editorial in the August 1928 edition of the Colliery Magazine noted:

We would like to congratulate our first county tennis team on winning their group and to express our admiration of the work of the Committee in organising such a successful tournament. The point which stands out in tennis is the way in which the game has been taken up at Hirst. Great credit is due to the young and energetic members for the Saturday American Tournaments which they have been organising. What matter if the courts are not resplendent with flannels and blazers, or if during the week there are stockinged feet in place of shoes. It is the game which matters - all these other things will be added in good time and when times become good.

The 'American Tournament' referred to was won by Miss Jean Ridley and Mr J Lennard, with Messrs R Lowdon and R Tait as runners-up. A tournament held the following week was won by Miss Jean Robson and Mr George Hewitt.

It was around about then that 17-year-old Winifred Garvie came on to the Welfare tennis scene. She had been given a mis-shapen raquet as a child - a present from her father on coming back from the first war. After teaching herself to play by banging a ball up against the coalhouse wall, Winifred, found herself playing for her school, Morpeth High. On getting a new raquet, one of her four brothers quipped: *"Let's see if you can play without your old bucket!"*

She *could* play, and proved it by winning tournaments at Ashington Welfare in 1929, then continued playing and winning for a number of years. She often went down to Commander Kemp's house in Wansbeck Road to play on his tennis court, partnering Frank Gairdner's wife who lived opposite. In 1938, the year she married conductor and organist Normanton Barron, Winifred won the women's tennis singles as well as the doubles, partnering Mr E M Clark. The following year she won all three sections of the same tournament as well as taking the singles of the annual Northumberland LTA at the Osborne Road courts in Jesmond, Newcastle.

ASHINGTON HOCKEY TEAM

JOE CURRY came with his family as an eleven-year-old in 1924. His father had worked at the Starr Gate pit in Blaydon, but as news spread of the good seams being worked in the Ashington area, he became a stoneman at Linton colliery. Joe recalls:

It was through my father that I got set on at Linton. In those days it helped if you had someone to speak for you. At first I worked on transit, and later I went to Linton where I eventually ended up as surface electrical engineer.

I played quite a lot of sport, like most of the young people at the time. I was sports daft. They used to say I either had my pit clays on or my sandshoes. Trouble was, if you were a good tennis player and a good cricketer you had to choose one or the other; same in the winter, some were good at football and others at hockey. A lot of talent was lost because you needed to specialise.

I began playing hockey in 1934 and didn't finish till about the 1960s. The team in the early days consisted of Arthur Robertson, captain, Ben Tinkler and Ed Gladson, all Northumberland County players, and others like myself, Joe Ward, Jackson, Davison, Williams, Thain, and Tapson. Doug Wallace played after the war.

But hockey never really counted in Ashington, not like rugby. We had to whitewash our own hockey balls. Geordie Clemerson, who ran the Welfare then, thought we had a good chance to bring the Northumberland County Headquarters to the Hirst, but the day before the meeting our old hut burned down, so they went to Morpeth instead.

I played with the badminton team up at the Rec because the Hirst hall wasn't big enough. Our mixed doubles team in 1937 was Bob Patterson and Peggy Jameson (now Howe); Hindmarsh and Mrs Robson; and me and Ethel Blandford (now Mrs Dodds).

The Ashington Welfare Hockey team which met Tynedale at Hirst Welfare on Saturday February 1st 1947, was chosen from the following men: R Beddard, W J Fowler, H Shaw, A Robertson, R Cutter, J Gladson, R Wardhaugh, H Boutland, E Curry, J Curry, J Harrison, and R Davison.

On Saturday January 22nd 1949, the Ashington Ladies Hockey team defeated Lloyds LHC by ten goals to nil; scorers were: I Davidson 1, C Hall 2, V Donkin 2, D Hindhaugh 2, J Hay 3.

The Ladies team to play LNER Accountants the following week was unchanged: I Charlton, E Togo, Mrs J Chrisp, J Fox, L Ryder, R Riddell, I Davidson, C Hall, J Hay, D Hindhaugh, and V Donkin.

The men's hockey team had their ups and downs, and it was mainly through the work of long-time stalwart Ed Gladson that it kept on as long as it did. It finally folded in the middle sixties, and Ed began coaching the Ashington Ladies Hockey squad.

ASHINGTON NETBALL CLUB

A Ladies Netball Club was formed in the town in 1947, and shortly afterwards several players went for County Trials including: P Neary, who became a regular, M Sharp, E Hallowell, and I Brown. Practises were held throughout the summer at the North School on a Tuesday and Wednesday evening. The team won a Rally organised by the Northumberland County Netball Asociation on July 9th, 1949. Players taking part were: P Neary, M Sharp, M Elliott, J Pratt, E Fuge, I Brown, and M Ternent. The club captain, Miss E Hallowell, was unable to attend, and her place was taken by M Ternent. Chairperson of the Ashington Netball Club in 1949 was Mrs M Gregory, who, as Marion Tapson, held the same position at the club's inauguration, as did the treasurer, Mrs G Sharp.

ASHINGTON's CYCLING CLUBS

Cycling as a sport in Ashington dates back to the 1890s when an ash track was laid around the Ashington Recreation Ground. It is recorded that 100-mile races were commonplace, taking most of the day to pedal round and round the short circuit. Two of the best-known Clubs formed to cater for these two-wheelers were the Merryfellows and the Clarion, but other organisations such as the Royal Order of Ancient Buffalos also entered teams into the various competitions which were arranged.

The programme for Saturday August 16th, 1926, included the following events: a Grand Parade, meeting at the Hirst Welfare, with prizes awarded for 'Best Decorated Cycle'; 'Best Comic Costume'; and

'Oldest Cyclist in Parade'. The next day all clubs and unattached cyclists met at the Ashington Colliery Farm for a Church Parade, held at the Harmonic Hall, where the president, F L Booth, placed a wreath on the War Memorial. The Parade then proceeded to the Recreation Ground, accompanied by the Harmonic Band, for a Service conducted by the Rev P T Hutchinson of Newbiggin.

Clubs which took part in the procession were: RAOB, Merryfellows, Ashington Juniors, Central Hall, St George's Rovers, South Benwell Wheelers, Newbiggin PM, White Star Ramblers, and St James of Newcastle. Prizewinners on the Saturday included: J Kent (RAOB), W Weddell (Merryfellows), and L Dobinson, aged three, judged the best 'Youngest Cyclist on Parade'. Because the Parade occurred in the middle of the 1926 Strike, the relatively small sum of £12 was collected in aid of Ashington Hospital.

ASHINGTON ATHLETIC CLUB

Like the rest of the sporting activities, organised athletics took place from the early 1920s. Runners then called themselves the Welfare Harriers. An entry in the Colliery Magazine of May 1926 observed:

The Annual Championship Race was run on Easter Monday over the Longhirst Course of 4 miles. Twelve juniors started, and the run resulted in a win for G Brown with W Anderson in second place. The senior race went to J Coombs with G Chilton second. At the AGM the following officials were chosen: G Murdie, J Occleston, R Rump, G Chilton, G Brown and R Guy.

Ashington Joint Welfare Athletic Club staged its first big meeting on August 20th, 1949, at Hirst Welfare. Events such as running and discus throwing were joined by the more unusual quoits and tug-of-war, with entries confined to miners. Cycling's *'Devil take the Hindmost'* and a display by the local gymnastic team concluded the day's sport.

One of the finest of Ashington's long distance amateur runners began his career shortly afterwards. Ernie Slaughter, wearing a Morpeth Harrier vest, ran himself into many record books, winning for himself a sideboard full of trophies.

ASHINGTON BOXING

Boxing in the Ashington area was very popular amongst the mining community. Pitmen's Champions at each weight emerged in the 1930s, such as Andy McLauchlin; the O'Keefe family from Lynemouth produced some great fighters; Hirst Premier Club had its own pugilists, trained by Jack Bacon, these included: Tom Bacon, Larry Lavelle, Bob Parkinson, Joe Swinhoe, Tommy O'Keefe, Andy McLauchlin, Joe Denwood, Kid Barnes, Bill McLauchlin, Nick Carr, and John Rogers. One man from that era is **BILL GIBSON**, born in 1921. He recalls:

I trained with the likes of Andy McLauchlin in the upstairs room at the Premier. As kids we used the old hut in Hirst Welfare. The trainer then, Geordie Clemerson, arranged four wooden benches in a square to form a boxing ring. Then he threw two pairs of gloves at us young lads, and whoever picked them up had to fight each other. I later went down to London and boxed as a pro for £3 a fight.

Ashington Joint Welfare revived boxing after the war. It was their intention to build a top-class team. To facilitate this in 1949 they enlisted the services of Tommy Todd, NCB flyweight champion of 1947, and Sammy Morgan ex-RAF champion.

BILLIARDS AND SNOOKER

The game of snooker was just in its infancy when I joined Priestman's Institute in 1947 with Charlie Wendt, a delightful left-handed potter of the ball. The building then - erected as a Memorial to Francis Priestman - was split into three: a large rectangular room housing six billiard tables, a games room for darts and dominoes, and a reading room full of books, daily newspapers and periodicals.

There was to be a Christmas Handicap, and although we weren't old enough - rules stipulated a minimum age of fourteen - Charlie and I both placed four entries at a cost of threepence each. Being unknown quantities we were both allotted the maximum mark of 28 points start. The handicappers then were Bill Shell, caretaker, and committee members Bill Staines and Tom Mason.

Still very much a novice, I went out in the first round, but Charlie, potting like a demon, cued his way to three of the first four prizes, beating old-hand Wally Waldock in the final. Jealousy was rife among the older members, and there was talk of a disqualification owing to Charlie's tender years, but, after a 'stewards' enquiry', the result was allowed to stand.

We kids were still very much in awe of the older men who could make massive breaks at billiards on No 1 table which was reserved exclusively for the first team. Men like Norman Harrison and Bill Staines seemed to have the red ball on a piece of string, always bringing it up the table to the exact spot they wanted.

Ashington turned out some excellent cuemen - John Sinclair was British Youths Billiard Champion in 1952, and Bruce Butters held the title at a senior level. Players had the choice of a variety of billiard saloons, as they were called.

My initiation came at Marchi's which was housed at the Harmonic Hall, opposite the police station, which had eight tables, many with torn cloths resulting from patrons standing on the table to play a difficult shot.

A much more regimentally run establishment was Docherty's above the tobacconist's shop in the middle of Station Road. The atmosphere here was lighter, although clouds of cigarette smoke still hung over the green baize like stour after a shot had been fired. The top facade of the building is still intact, with the inscription: 'CENTRAL BILLIARD SALOON 18 TABLES'.

The 'Top Tute' billiard room - still unchanged to the present day - was another which produced many fine players. Workingmen's clubs such as the *Mortimer* and the *Excelsior* also had billiard rooms. One smokey saloon with a dozen tables was Kellets, above Shepherds, at the Grand Corner. A great deal of money changed hands here in the course of a day as players would 'crack out' their marras: "I'll give you two blacks for a dollar." The game of skittles was a money spinner, too. A dozen pieces of wood were placed around the table, each carrying a certain value. Sixteen players could take part at sixpence a go, and the first to reach 31 points took the kitty. Much cheating went on, and the games often ended in controversy.

I became friendly with Ivor Bird - always known as 'Ivor Bird, the dentist's son', whose practice was just over the road from Priestman's. By sleight of hand with the 16 alleys (marbles), the blonde six-footer would ensure that I was always first player with 16 start when we teamed up to play skittles.

Another gambling game on the table was 'Peter', a cut-throat affair played rather like the game of 'Killer' at darts. The 'Peter' ball was the pink, and each time someone shopped it you lost a tanner. 'Crash' was yet one more sure way of losing your pocket money.

A familiar game at Priestmans was two-ball partner golf. Four players split into pairs with the object of getting round the 'course' of six pockets before their opponents. Side bets of one or two shillings made for some intense games, and rivalry was fierce among the men who played against each other on a regular basis. Some games were hilarious, especially when little Hennor Eastlake and Tom McGee paired up. The spectators could be guaranteed a performance to rival that of Laurel and Hardy as first Hennor and then Tom would complain of his partner's poor shots.

Priestman's was a very popular place immediately after the second war with prices for a game - sixpence for half an hour - subsidised by the Ashington Joint Miners Welfare Committee. The six tables were fully booked with long waiting lists from opening time of 10 am right through for another twelve hours until it closed. A glass awning built on to the front of the building, proved an ideal sunspot for men to sit and discuss the events of the day while waiting for the bookie's runner to turn up and take their bets.

Shortly after I joined Priestman's I was 'put on the books'. This meant that I was reported to the Committee for unruly behaviour. I had been playing on No. 6 table which was right next to the cubicle used by the manager. I tried a difficult, forcing shot, which sent a red ball flying off the table, bouncing on to the counter where a number of bottles of Vimto were standing. The ivory ball cannoned into the pop bottles sending them crashing down like nine-pins. Thick-set boxer, Sammy Morgan, who was caretaker then, was in no mood for explanations, and he immediately suspended me pending my appearance before my betters. I was let off with a caution.

In the late 1950s, I eventually scraped into Priestman's B snooker team, led by Jimmy Henderson; there were two leagues operating then in the area. We played at venues like Pegswood and Moscardini's, catching the United bus at the 'stand'; the four of us: me, Jimmy, Andy Patterson, and the late little Jackie Lawson, our cues held upright in long metal cases, like Roman soldiers carrying spears in search of realms to conquer.

PROFESSIONAL RUNNING

The area's history is knee-deep in the sport of pedestrianism. First records of a Geordie participant concern George Wilson of Newcastle. In 1813 he walked a record 50 miles in 12 hours around the recreation yard in Durham Gaol - he was interned there at the time for bad debt. The early days of the sport were enacted upon a colourful canvas populated with outrageous characters. A Red Indian of the Seneca tribe, named Deerfoot, competed in the 1860s wearing nothing but a loincloth and a feather in his hair.

Handicaps were run from May to September when footballers had thrown away their boots, and begun looking around for other types of competition. Summer games such as golf and tennis were alien to the putters of Pegswood, the brickies of Bedlington, and the arc-wall cuttermen of Ashington. Many looked around for alternatives and discovered horse racing and whippets. But the majority of men in those days were participants: doers, not cut out to be spectators. They worked in an all-action environment before mechanisation made brains obsolete along with picks and shovels; where body and mind co-ordinated perfectly, and were constantly in use. Miners were required to be fast thinking, but above all they needed to gamble.

Gambling with his life every working minute meant that, for a miner, any other game of chance came naturally to him. To go from one day to the next without a wager of some kind was to leave many a man gasping as though craving a cigarette.

The Powderhall Gold Medal Handicap, held annually in Edinburgh on New Year's Day, was the 'big one' as far as professional runners were concerned. It was - and still is - the pro-runners Olympiad. For at least a month prior to Powderhall, likely lads were taken on a prep or 'keep'. For week after week, somewhere on a remote farm on the borders of Scotland, sprinters were fattened and fussed over like prize bulls. Pitmen, painters, plumbers, and clerks, anyone, in fact, who was thought to be in with a chance was seized by faceless backers who paid a proven trainer to take the runner away from his working environment, his wife and bairns, to produce him on the day fit to run the race of this life.

I was introduced to running in 1944 while living in the first block of Pont Street. It was a typical colliery row, separated from the houses in Milburn Road by a back alley flanked by a long row of outside toilets and bin corners. These were our goalposts during the soccer season, when the rap of a tennis ball on the netty door, brought out a stream of abuse from within. But in the summer months every lad - and some lasses - became budding sprinters.

Bob Miller, 'Roy of Ashington', lived a couple of doors away from us. It was he and a chap called Geordie Poole who would get the streetlads together for a series of races. It was commonplace to see fathers and mothers betting on their offspring to win the handicap. To me, this was the norm. When you are young you think that everyone lives the same lives. There is security in like minds.

At St Aidan's RC school, we Catholic kids might have been rich in spiritual grace, but when it came to sport we were definitely the poor relations. We went into the concrete schoolyard for half an hour a week doing PT - pigs' torture - jumping up and down on the spot and waving our arms around as if participating in some ritualistic war dance.

The school had access to only *one* battered football, and games lessons consisted of the entire school trooping the hundred yards past the cemetery to Peoples Park where the two best footballers were told to pick teams. Those not chosen had to sit on the grass and pick their noses while the twenty-two lucky ones belted the ball around the Park for half an hour.

The school team invariably got thrashed even playing against the other schools' second teams. In my last year - the leaving age had risen to fifteen - I was appointed by Mr Rutherford, teacher of Standard VI, as captain of both the football and cricket elevens. I think I became wicket keeper because I was the only one with a pair of old motor-bike gloves which took the sting out of the hard corker.

The year 1948 saw the first Ashington inter-school sports day held at the Hirst Welfare. Four schools were entered for the event: Bothal, St Aidans, Hirst East, and Hirst Park, but the Park dropped out at the last minute because of some dispute. I remember being pleased that they didn't turn up because I knew that Percy Armstrong, their English Schoolboy International, could run far better than me, so that was one less to worry about.

But there were others. The East school at that time had some of the best footballers and fastest runners than at any other time in their history. The only Bothal runner of note proved to be John Sinclair who later went on to distinguish himself at the more sedate sport of billiards. He made a quick exit, which left me against five lads from the East. One was Jimmy 'Chinky' Jackson, another England schoolboy; Sid Hutton, later to play for Newcastle United; Jimmy Hill, an East Northumberland regular; a lad called MacPherson who could run like the wind; and Jimmy Brown whose massive frame seemed to float over the ground.

As I lined up with them I noticed that they were all wearing spikes and colourful running strips, while I sported my school colours of faded yellow and pit socks. I wondered if the colour of my shirt would disguise the streak which began to run down my back when I first saw the opposition.

As they all crouched down to their marks I vowed to do what any other young Pont Street lad would do in my position: cheat! I stood poised in what I imagined to be the classic start position and kept my eye on the neutral Bothal schoolteacher with the gun. As soon as I saw him clench his firing finger I was off like a gazelle. When the bang went I was already five yards down the track! Whether the starter didn't have any other means of stopping the race, or whether, being impartial, he took pity on me as I was the only runner who wasn't from the East school, but he let the race go on. Cries of 'Shame' or its equivalent rang out from the large crowd, but I raced on. It was only an eighty yards dash, and I was still clear with only ten yards to go. Alas, cheaters never prosper, and one by one the pack devoured me as I lunged in vain at the tape.

I had run a close, if not honourable, race. Eyes lowered, I walked up to take my prize for reaching the final: a book entitled 'A Voyage to Vineland'. I shamefacedly accepted the praise heaped on me by the Hirst East headmaster: "Well done, lad. I've never seen anyone start as quickly as that. You gave our lot a real fright."

The following results of that Sports Meeting appeared in the Ashington Advertiser, July, 1948:

SUNSHINE FOR SENIOR SCHOOLS SPORTS

There was a good crowd at Hirst Welfare grounds, Ashington, on Tuesday evening to witness the Senior Inter-school Sports, which had been postponed last week owing to the bad weather.
Sunshine on this occasion brought out many supporters and friends to enjoy an excellent programme of events. The chief results were:-
Senior Boys, 80 yds: 1 J Jackson, East, 2 S. Hutton, East, 3 J. Hill, East.
Long Jump: 1 J. Jackson, East, 2 J, Hill, East, 3 R Little, East.
220 yds: 1 McPherson, East, 2 R. Johnson, East, 3 (tie) T. Stoddart and S. Hutton, both East.

Senior Girls, 80 yds: 1 M. Stevenson, Bothal, 2 J. Reilly, St Aidans, 3 Thompson.
Girls Potato Race: 1 V. Robinson, East, 2 S Appleby, Bothal, 3 B. Cook, Bothal.
Boys Potato Race: 1 T. Johnson, Bothal, 2 Joe Conroy, St Aidans, 3 J. Dickinson, East.
Junior Boys 80 yds: 1 M. Robinson, East, 2 J. Dickinson, East, 3 Brian Hall, East
Junior Girls Sack: 1 M. Ternant, Bothal, 2 J. Thompson, St Aidans, 3 P Turnbull, Park.
Summary of Results:
Boys: 1 East 72 points, 2 Bothal, 23 points, 3 St Aidans, 18 points.
Girls: 1 Bothal, 39 points, 2 East, 29 points, 3 St Aidans, 17 points, 4 Park, 15 points.

From that day on there was never any doubt in my mind that I would take up professional sprinting when I left school. That happened in 1949 when fate decreed that this was the year that runners were unable to use a *nom de plume*. And so it was that the name M Kirkup first appeared on a handicap programme at Longhirst alongside that of F Loss, running in a boys' heat. Right from the first bang of the starting pistol it should have been obvious to me that I was destined *never* to win a race. My handicap mark was very poor in comparison to F Loss - real name Eddie Poxon - I think I had to give him start which was ludicrous. That rainy day on the ploughed field at Longhirst, F Loss went on to take the £100 prize while I skulked away having been thoroughly thrashed.

OSSIE SWORD is a name that figures prominently when talk turns to foot-running in this area. He remembers:

I was chargeman on the Screens at Ashington colliery when I got into my first final in 1936. It was at Portland Park and I was positive that I'd won the race, but Tommy Lyons, the judge and handicapper, gave the verdict to a lad called Frank Gardiner. Whey, all hell let loose then and one of my marras, Butcher Robson, was going to thump Lyons, but he was dragged away by a policeman.
I suppose running was popular because it was something anybody could have a go at. We certainly weren't in it for the prizes. I only got twenty-five pounds for winning at Choppington in 1939, but we cleaned up with the betting. What a heat there was - all nine runners were trying - and we got 3-1 for wor money. I won my cross-tie in a slower time than the rest because I was 'puttin' the short ones in', you know. Come the final, the bookies were laying 40-1 against me winning. I won pulling up!
Later, I got into four finals at Powderhall between 1941-45; the closest I got to winning was a second place in the Consolation Final of '42. I was the trial-horse for Bob Miller, (R Roy) in 1946. He should've won that year; he was two yards faster than Dusty Downs, and Norman Pentland. But he slipped over on his marks and couldn't recover. Bob could've won everything, but he didn't take it seriously enough - he liked his pop and his fisticuffs - and you have to be committed to succeed at anything.
I drifted into handicapping. My first chance came at Seaton Burn Flower Show in the late forties. Charlie Lyons, Tom's brother, was the official starter. He used a double-barrelled pistol - one shot to start the race and the other to call the runners back if there was a false start. He was stemming one barrel between heats when the other side went off taking away two of poor Charlie's fingers with it. I took over and stayed with the job until Tom got his other brother, Bill Lyons, to take the gun.
I had to pack in running shortly after the war because of an ulcer. It was then I concentrated on the training side - I did a bit of bookmaking as well! I had some great times along with Jackie Dryden, we brought some good youngsters through to win big handicaps. The first big winner was Eddie Poxon, running as F Loss. He won the big sprint at Longhirst in 1949.

Probably the unluckiest loser at the big New Year's Day Powderhall meeting was *Berwick of Ashington*, real name **JACKIE THOMPSON**. As an apprentice butcher, young Thompson had won the big'un at the grandly-named Morpeth Olympic Games in 1947. But he had the misfortune to run up against Australian champion Eric Cummings in the 1951 Edinburgh final. In a head-to-head tussle through a January blizzard, the well-built *Wizard of Oz* got home by the width of a snowflake. Soon afterwards, a great future in the sport was curtailed when the be-spectacled Ashington runner was involved in a motor cycle accident at the end of Woodhorn Road, and died from his injuries.

Christened **ROBERT MILLER,** *Roy of Ashington,* was born in 1922. Now living in Chestnut Street, Bob still has vivid memories of past glories:

I started sprinting when I was about twenty-two. We used to train in a field behind Seaton Hirst churchyard. Afterwards it was only a short trip to the White Elephant for a pint. We never took training all that seriously, not like nowadays. How could we? I worked as a filler down Linton colliery. You canna do a job like that and hope to be as fit as the fellas today. We had no running strips; I just wore a pair of football shorts and vest. One of my marras, Kenny Gray, who trained with me had two short arms; his middle name was Roy, so that was the nom-de-plume I took. I used to do a bit of boxing as well; there was this back garden in Garden City Villas, and the whole neighbourhood turned out to see the bouts we used to put on - just for a bit of fun, like.

I only once went to Powderhall, in 1946. A fella called Tom Potter took me, Norman (Pentland) Main and Ossie (Oswald) Sword as a workhorse on a month's prep. I got beat in my heat; tripped over when I started, but Dusty Downs (Mitchell) went on to win the final, and Pentland won the 220. We stayed in this big house near Carlisle, but I didn't much like being away from home, and when they asked us the following year, I just refused.

I was always the backmarker, and must've won about five handicaps: two at Portland Park, one at Peoples Park, and Bates Welfare - I broke the clock there! Then there was an Invitation Race at Morpeth during the war which I won from Jackie Milburn and a coloured chap who ran under the name of Coffee. I had a bit of gamble each time, and my brother, Ralph, put the bets on; sometimes a fiver or tenner, a lot of money in those days. I only once put leads in me shoes - never again, I said. I was just in it for the sport, you see."

TOM McLAIN was the youngest of seven children, born in Linton, 1922, son of a colliery overman. He told this story:

I went to Linton school, and played football for them and East Northumberland. We had a great team. I always liked Linton - the miners built it themselves, you know, during the 1926 strike - and although I've travelled all over the world, I still have a soft spot for the place. From school I went to work for the Ashington Coal Company's Welfare Department. Commander Kemp was still running it then. He had heard that I was a bit of an all-rounder at sport. As well as being an athlete, I boxed and even did a bit of weightlifting. I was like a trainee manager for the scheme.

My father's middle name was Penrith, and I had always wanted to win something for him. There were seven of us in the family, all athletes, while he hadn't done anything in that line. He had trained runners at the Old Vic grounds in Newcastle, but his one claim to fame was that he had a fast whippet called 'Paste Egg of Pegswood'. So I decided to run as 'Penrith of Linton' when I took up the sport professionally.

I enlisted in 1941. The recruiting office then was in a school in Newcastle. It was quite an adventure going into town on my own. I went into the RAF, and worked on erecting radar aerials. It was while I was stationed near Liverpool that I ran in a major sports event held under AA rules. It was sponsored by a big commercial company. I entered every event: 100, 220, 440, half mile, and came away that day with a stack of prizes: electric iron, barometer, all sorts. But winning that 100 yards final had a great effect on my life. I was running against this coloured lad who everyone said was good. I beat him, and I knew from then on that I could run a bit.

And it was while I was abroad in South Africa, that I realised that I could play football as good as the best, too. I played for the RAF, and I was chosen for a Combined Services eleven. Sunderland's manager then, Bill Murray, had this sergeant acting as a scout for him. And this fella must have wired back about me and a little winger called Tommy Reynolds because I was told that I would be approached by Sunderland just before I was demobbed. In fact, five or six clubs were after me following the publicity given to the games we played, but I knew that Sunderland were offering the best terms, and that I was guaranteed a first team place.

But it had always been my ambition to win at the Morpeth Olympic Games, and I knew if I signed for a First Division team then I would never get a good mark again - I was due to run off 14 yards. So I told Sunderland's manager that I wouldn't sign until after Morpeth.

I ran a trial at Newbiggin a few days before the race. We waited until 10.30 pm, and it was almost dark as I raced alone on the Moor. A local man who was very good with the watch did the timing. Afterwards we went into the Cresswell Arms for a drink, and it was there my brothers, Jimmy and Alec, said that I was not going to win at Morpeth. I asked them why and they said that, with my mark, I couldn't fail to win Powderhall. But I was adamant - it was the Morpeth Olympics I wanted. Besides, I reasoned with them, my mark will go down as soon as news leaks out that I am to sign for Sunderland.

We argued long and hard, and it almost split the family apart. But I wouldn't budge, so they reluctantly fell in with me. We got a Pegswood bookie called Tom Robinson to place some big bets with Wanless and Pallister at long odds of 28-1. We must have come away with more than three thousand pounds in winnings.

My brother Jimmy was a likeable lad, but a bit of a rake. At that time he had just got himself engaged, and he was thirty-three. He had over three hundred pounds saved up, and he drew all but £25 of it out from the bank. Then he said to Vera, his fiancee: "Pet, I'm putting the lot on our Tommy to win at Morpeth, and if he gets beat the wedding's off!"

But I won easily enough, by about three yards. Afterwards, Tommy Lyons told me that if he'd been handicapping I would only have got 6 yards. I was still so far up the handicap that I reckoned I was a certainty to win at Ashington the following week, but the damned thing got rained off. I only ran for a season or two after that.

I played for Sunderland until joining Northampton. It was there I teamed up with another Morpeth winner, Roberts of Amble, who had won the big'un in 1938. Roberts, in fact, was Bob Dennison who had played for Newcastle and Sunderland, and he was then the Northampton manager. I still meet up with my ex-Sunderland mate, Len Shackleton, at Tenerife when we go there for our holidays.

Tom McLain, a very fit-looking 70-year-old, is now retired and living at Hauxley with his wife Phyllis. The name of Tom's house? What else, but *'Penrith Lodge'*.

Still a very lithe and fit-looking man, **GEORGE DOWN** was born in Ashington in 1922. In a varied and chequered career he has been an colliery electrician, a professional footballer, a soldier, a bookie's board clerk, a builder, and a club steward. But it is as *'the first Ashington man to win the Powderhall Sprint'* that 'Dusty' Down will always be remembered. George came from a footballing family. He said:

My father played in goal for Burnley before the 1939-45 war, and the whole family - I had three brothers - moved down there. I had been educated as an infant at the Wansbeck School. Michael Craig, the solicitor's son, was in my class. I can remember going to Turf Moor and seeing all these old-time players. Jimmy Potts, from Pegswood, followed my father into the team. We came back to live at Kenilworth Road, and I went to Bedlington Grammar School. Then my father - Willie Down - played for Ashington, in the North Eastern League.

My first job was at the colliery as an apprentice electrician - you had to serve about six years then. I played inside forward for the Electricians, Lynemouth and Linton, in the Welfare League. Coincidently, I played in the same Trial Match at St James' Park when Jackie Milburn scored his six goals. He was signed professional and played against Bradford City the next week. I only signed as an amateur, and played for Newcastle United reserves against Gateshead; Albert Stubbins was in the team that day.

It was while I was a kid in the colliery electric shops that a boxer called Dusty Montana was fighting. Nicky Hancocks was chargeman then, and he shouted at me one day: "Hey, Dusty, hand us that screwdriver," and that nickname followed me to this day. I remember a couple of years after winning Powderhall, this journalist had travelled all the way from Manchester, and he walked on to the track shouting: "Where's Dusty? I want a picture of Dusty." I didn't know where to look.

I think my first run as a pro would be when I was seventeen. It was soon after that when big Jock Marshall and Davey Moore who were looking after me took me down to the Birtley Handicap. It was to be run in the afternoon, and Jock and Davey wanted to go to Sunderland dogs that night. Jock approached the handicapper about entering me - it was only a fifteen pound prize. "Can he run?" asked the man in charge. Jock and Davey just shrugged and said: "Not that much - better put him off ten and a half yards." And he did! Whey, when I got a look around, I was getting start from fellas that I could give three yards to. The lads saw the chance to make a bob or two to take to the dogs, so they told me to go through and win. I was in a heat made up from lads who had entered on the track, and it was to be run after the official last heat.

I had to get ready in the dykeside because there was no tent. I won the heat easily, but as I pulled up, big Jock shouted: "Quick, young'un, get your clays on and let's get oot of here!" I didn't find out till later that they hadn't managed to get a penny on 'cos the bookies were already laying on the cross-tie. To cap it all, I had just about smashed the clock in trying to win. We didn't go back there again.

When I did eventually win my first sprint it was at Newbiggin - only fifteen pounds. Norman Anderson of Ashington was in that final, with a couple of Scottish soldiers who were on leave.

Powderhall was always going to be the goal. For a couple of years I ran with a harness which went over my shoulders and around my waist, and it was stuffed with lead in pouches. I had to run in a football strip to avoid being found out. I'm not kidding you, I could hardly trail my legs, let alone run carrying that lot!

The year I won Powderhall (1946) I was trained by Jimmy Muir who was a past winner himself. I took eight weeks off work and went on a prep financed by Newbiggin bookie, Davie Gibbons. Ray Bowart, another Ashington lad, came along as a trial-horse. We stayed in digs just outside Edinburgh. Davie fixed it up with a backhander to the groundsman for me to be able to train on an ash and cinder track at Hawkhill Stadium which was normally used for bike racing.

Unfortunately, Ray injured himself and never pulled on a pair of spikes for the whole eight weeks. Jimmy Muir had to arrange for a policeman who was the Edinburgh police force champion, to come and act as a hare. He thought he was better than he was. I used to give him three yards start in training, but when we sat down on our marks Jimmy used to give me the wire, and I would move back another couple of yards before the gun went off.

Davie Gibbons got 7-2 for me in the final. It was reported later that he had won ten thousand pounds. I had made sure that I won my cross-tie in a slow time so that we could get a price. My timing was all in the head. The final wasn't due to take place for three hours so Davie arranged for a taxi to take me back to the digs, and I went to bed for a rest. The final was a good race, but I knew I had it won after we'd gone halfway down the track. You did notice after winning the gold medal that people would nudge each other if they saw you coming, and even now I am stopped by strangers who say: "I know you - you won Powderhall".

The only trouble with winning was that I ended up in the army! It was a time when the pits were a reserved occupation and a miner couldn't be conscripted. But, having taken eight weeks off work, I had gone back on my contract, and was eligible for national service. I wasn't the only one from Ashington that year. Norman Pentland ended up in the Navy; Ray Bowart had to join the RAF; and Ossie Sword got his call-up papers, but managed to wriggle out of it by saying that he had flat feet!

The name **RAYMOND POXON** figures prominently when talk in Ashington comes around to sport. He was born in 1925, son of a Woodhorn Colliery miner. Raymond went to the Park School, and later served his apprenticeship as a mining surveyor with Ernie Little, among others. He was keen on athletics, but it was as a footballer that he got his first break when he played for Ashington at Portland Park because the lad who had been first choice was injured down the pit. One highlight of Raymond's career in Ashington's black 'n' white strips was in 1945 when he scored five times in the Colliers' defeat of Carlisle Reserves. As a professional runner he ran as *Raymond of Ashington,* winning the Morpeth Rescue Sports 100 yds handicap in 1945, gaining for himself a fifty pound prize which he used to propose to his future wife on her 21st birthday. He recalls that day:

I turned out for the heat wearing a pair of old running pumps and some tatty football shorts. I did the same in the semi-final, and by the time the final came around I was an outsider at 14-1. But come the final, I threw away the old togs and got dressed in some flashy gear that I had packed away. I won the final which included Pentland and Neal of Ashington; around that time I was with John Nixon, whose father Sid, and Arthur Middlemiss, were the trainers.

One day at Seaton Burn I was running against Edwin Dodds, the horsekeeper at Ashington. He was a veteran at that stage, and we thought we could win easily. Edwin spread the word around that the only one he was frightened of was me. Sid Nixon was the man putting our money on, but at the last minute Arthur decided that I wasn't to try so they switched the money on to Edwin. But the poor old fella froze on his blocks, and we all lost out - there was an almighty row after the race.

The NCB surveyors had their headquarters at what is now the Minto Lodge Hotel in Newbiggin which then acted as the NCB Group Office. One of my apprentices was a young North Seaton lad called John Hall. At one 'do' I went to lately I made a speech saying that of all the people to pass through my hands as a surveyor, John Hall would have been my choice as the least likely to succeed. How wrong could I be!

HARRY 'PEACHY' HARLE, with stature belying his three score years and ten, was born in 1922 at 27 Sycamore Street, Ashington. His father was a coal teemer at the local pit. He recalled:

The first handicap I ran in was at Throckley in 1946. Jackie Dryden persuaded me to join his school of runners. It was Raymond Poxon who suggested that I should have a go with the running pumps. I just kept my vest on and Frankie Kenyon threw me a pair of football shorts. I nearly smashed me neck, wearing spikes for the first time. Tommy Lyons was handicapping when I first started. He just looked at me and said: "Do you play football?" Of course I said I did. "You should be fit then," he said. "I'll put you in off twelve and half yards." And that was my first mark.

I decided to call myself Harry Short, which was my mother's maiden name. My grannie had always called me her 'little peach', and the nickname 'Peachy' stuck for life, too.

I was still with Dryden two years later when I had a go at the Morpeth Olympic Games in 1949. But I ran up against a great runner, Ray Surtees of Morpeth, who has just retired from being headmaster at a West Sleekburn school. It was a close race, but I only managed second place. And it was the same later that season at Jedburgh, when I again finished second.

A Blyth man called Jackie Stephenson called at the house to see me - he was a tic-tac man for Billy Mitchell of Saltcoats. This Mitchell had sent Jackie to see someone else about going away on a prep before Powderhall, but this fella had been refused time off work, so he came seeking me. He asked if I would be willing to go up to Mitchell's dogtrack in Saltcoats and run a trial. I had just been married and wasn't all that keen to be away. He said it would be for three months if they thought that I had a chance of winning.

And so it came about that Peachy Harle and his young bride, Peggy, were separated for 12 weeks. She was sworn to secrecy; no-one on any account was to be told that her husband Harry was locked away in a Scottish hideout being fed on prime beef, chicken and fish. *"It was awful,"* she admitted. Harry, still a chunky six-footer, continued:

You wouldn't believe some of the meals we had. On the first morning for breakfast I ate two fish, two eggs, two steaks and two slices of toast. They gradually built up on the toast so that by the time of the race I was eating fourteen slices with my breakfast. I ate everything they put in front of me, but I had to say no when tripe appeared on the menu. "Not for me," I says, but I said "yes" to a whole rabbit!

All I did was eat and train. My weight went up from 12 stone 7lbs to nearly 14 stone. Training consisted of exercises and short bursts up to 40 yards, which later built up to 100 then 130 yards. Youngsters today don't know what training is. I would walk for an hour in the evening and smell the fresh air, maybe see some rabbits in a field. It was worth it, those twelve weeks away.

My father and brother Jim came up to Edinburgh, but even then I had to have a 'minder' present when I talked to them in case I let it slip that I had a good chance to win. They had booked me into a lodge very near the track, and I was able to come back and rest after the cross-ties. I was full of myself and told the trainer that I would raise my arms as soon as I knew I had the final won. He was biting his nails about this. "You do that," he said, "and I'll be right behind you with a boot up your backside." But I won the final by over a yard, and from the winnings me and Peggy were able to buy our house in Council Road, beside the Town Hall. I could stand in my garden and follow the greyhound results from Portland Park. Great!

Said Peggy:

I was pleased to have him back, and being able to buy our own house made it all worthwhile. But I still wasn't able to afford the nice little telly that I kept looking at in the window of Hall and Cardwell's...that had to wait.

W. WEAVER was another fine Ashington sprinter. Born Billy Lyons in 1926, he attended the North and Hirst East schools before starting his working career on a milk round for the Ashington Coal Company based at their farm. It was while he was there that Billy palled up with yet one more Ashington flyer. Jackie Milburn, then an engineering apprentice at Ashington colliery, would leap over the perimeter fence at the Rec after his shift had ended, and the speedy pair would treat amazed spectators to the sight of miner versus milkman over one hundred yards.

After working for the Coal Company for a number of years, Billy and the rest of the milk roundsmen were in dispute with the gaffers and walked out *en bloc* to join the Co-operative dairy at the bottom of the railway station bank. Son of Bill Lyons, official caller, and nephew of handicapper, Tommy Lyons, Billy burst into prominence after the second war, winning numerous handicaps including Seaton Burn. He was greatly fancied for Powderhall in 1949 when he prepared for the race with Albert Grant, clocking 12.14 off 8 yards. He returned the next year, but ran up against a fierce competitor, *Harrington of Brownhills,* in the cross-tie.

It was while preparing for the big Edinburgh race in 1951 that Billy became great friends with Eric Cumming, one of the many visitors who came across from Australia to take on Britain's best runners. Billy and Eric made a strange looking pair training up at Peebles. The massively-framed, tee-total, non-smoking sheep farmer from Acheron, Alexandria, stood six foot and weighed a hefty 13st 10lb, while Billy was of a much slighter build. The following year, 1952, although not even acknowledged as the champion in his own country, Cumming succeeded where others from abroad had failed and won the coveted gold medal. *Berwick of Ashington* was narrowly beaten into second place with Billy Lyon unplaced, causing Walter Meeds of the *Sporting Chronicle* to write: *"Finalist, Billy Lyons, from Berwick's home town of Ashington, and as bonnie a sprinter as one could ever hope to see, suffered from his lack of inches. But I have never gazed upon his superior from the holes."*

Not long after that Billy suffered an appalling injury to his hand, falling on a broken glass bottle which left his right hand virtually useless. He had to have two fingers of his right hand stitched to his palm, and never regained the strength to hold himself in the *'set'* position. Billy was unable to keep his job on the milk, but Jimmy Little, who was then the foreman painter at the Co-op Works Department, arranged for Billy to drive one of the vans. Billy's widow, Stella, remembers that he came in one afternoon after work and asked: *"Hey, do you think I have a dark suit somewhere?"* She asked him why, and was told that he had been asked to assist at a funeral by the Store's funeral director. Stella says that Billy was completely taken by this new job. She laughed as she recalled how a trainee undertaker on his first solo funeral went with Billy to a house in Wansbeck Road. *"Where is the deceased, madam?"* asked the young lad, solemnly, on entering the house. Billy nudged him and muttered under his breath: *"He's in the hearse, you daft bugger!"*

Billy stayed with the Co-op until ill health caused him to leave in 1989. Sadly, Billy Lyons died in his home town of Newbiggin by the Sea, one year later.

One of only two men ever to win gold medals at both the sprint and half mile at Powderhall is **EDWIN (NOBBIE) POXON**. Born in Beatrice Street in 1931, he went to the North School, passed his eleven plus and went on to Bedlington Grammar. Nobbie remembers:

I competed in a lot of sports at Bedlington Grammar school, and ended up Victor Ludorum one year. I played football and it was through that that I met up with Jackie Dryden in 1947 when he was Ashington FC's trainer. He and Ossie Sword realised that I could run a bit, and I didn't need any prompting when asked to join their school of runners who trained at the Hirst Welfare. Pro-running then was frowned on by the Welfare management, and we were banished to train on a piece of ash track at the side of what was then football pitch Number One. Of course it was at a time when runners used an alias so Jackie asked me what I wanted to call myself. I had a border terrier called Floss, so I just says to him: "I'll run under F Loss," and that's how the name came about. People have been calling me Fred Loss ever since.

Right from the outset Jackie said: "Nobbie, we are going to set our sights on only one thing: winning a gold at Powderhall." And after that everything was incidental. He was only interested in me winning the big' un, but that's not to say that I didn't try every time I ran at a small meeting. Oh, I tried all right, but I wore 'heavies' each time. My favourite running pumps were bought for thirty shillings at Ashington Co-op. Jackie used to have the lead weights all set out for his runners - there were about ten lads when I first started - and he knew how much weight could slow a runner down, right to the last inch. With me being a big lad, it took quite a weight in each shoe to make any impression, but to one of the smaller lads, say Copper Reed, a lighter piece of lead was sufficient to do the trick. Jackie used to get the weights custom-made at the colliery blacksmiths.

I think we got about 10-1 at long odds that year I won Powderhall, and because I was holding back in the heats, I was still a 7-2 chance in the cross-tie, but the odds had dropped to 6-4 favourite by the time the final was run. Luckily, there were no incidents and I won quite easily. Part of the money was spent on buying a wedding ring, and great play was made of it in the Press with headlines like: 'Cupid strikes Gold' and suchlike. After that I began to get noticed, but never received what could be called 'appearance money' for turning out. Spence, as British Champion, was the only one who could command a fee.

Having achieved one lifetime's ambition, I set about to try for another by winning the gold for the half mile, which had only ever been done once before. The secret in winning the distance race - which I did in 1962 - was to have as easy a race as possible in the heat, because running a gruelling heat went against you in the final. I was nearly conned in my heat. A stablemate of a fancied runner tried to run the legs off me for 660 yards. He set off at a tremendous pace, and if I hadn't had this in-built clock in my head, I might have been tempted to follow him. But I kept it steady, and reached the final which I won by about six yards.

I did very little competition running after that and went back to playing football for Ashington, mainly in the reserves. I had played for them intermittently since I was a lad. But I never turned out at the beginning of a season - I always waited until after New Year's Day and Powderhall. That was where the priority lay.

And now...Powderhall is still top of my list, but as a trainer. Have I got a future gold medalist? I'm hoping...just hoping.

JIM CHARLTON, born 1934 in Charlton Street, Ashington, is one of those rare breed of local professional runners who wasn't a sprinter. Jim was a middle-distance specialist who won many handicaps over 880 yards and one mile. However, he was quick to point out:

I still managed to win a couple of 80-yard sprint heats at Seghill and Seaton Burn. I was training then with Jackie Dryden and his running school of Johnny Minoughan, Neville Black, Eddie Poxon and Copper Reed. It was through Jack Agan, brother of another runner, Les, that I first went with Dryden in 1957. I'd met up with Jack Agan when we were both conscripted into the Northumberland Fusiliers in 1952. I worked for British Rail then, and I was eligible to be called up.

While I was in the Army I ran against the Kenyan national squad. When I was demobbed, Jack Agan told his brother Les about me running for the Army, and Jackie Dryden heard about it. When I went over to the

Welfare to meet him he said: "I hear you can run a bit - want to join us?" Of course I agreed. But training with the sprinters on that strip of ash over at the Hirst Welfare wasn't really suitable for a middle-distance man, and it was mostly for the companionship that I stuck with them for a couple of years.

Then I got hold of a book by Franz Stampfl who was training Gordon Pirie at the time. His training methods revolutionised the sport, and as Pirie was one of my idols I decided to follow his routine according to the book, and from then on I just trained myself. It must have paid off because in 1959 I won Grasmere off a mark of 50 yards. I only got £30 for winning, but wasn't really in it for the money.

I went up to Annan in Scotland and won the half mile the same day as Alan Benson of Bedlington won the sprint. In 1960, I won the mile at Jedburgh off 100 yards, from a field of 45 runners - my father got money on at 3-1 for the race. And I think it was the same year that I won both the half and one mile in one afternoon at the Whittingham Games.

We had a good touch in 1961 when I travelled up to Annan in the same car as Charlie Harrison and Norman Brough - Ossie Sword and Joe Dryden came that day too. We all won that day, and Norman won the 220 yards final.

After I packed in competing I began to train young lads, and must have had about 32 winners of various handicaps over all kinds of distances. In 1974 a West Sleekburn lad, Stuart Freeman, aged 22, won the final of the 110 metres at the Selkirk Games; Bob Ferguson, a fireman from Ashington, ran second in the fastest ever run 800 metres at the Powderhall meeting when it was held at Meadowbank in 1976. In 1979 he went on to win the richest-ever 800 metres at the Grangemouth Christmas meeting. In 1988 Kevin Appleby, then working for the Welwyn, and son of Innes, won the £400 first prize for the 110 metres at Morebattle.

But it's only in the Borders and further north in Scotland that the sport of pro-running still exists. It was sad when the north-east connection dropped out of the sport in the late 1950s. It was probably due to more affluence, more cars, more choice on how to spend your time and money.

Jim Charlton still cares passionately about pedestrianism, witness his carefully-documented scrap book. He can still be seen jogging around the town's outskirts, and though the step might not be as sprightly, his memory is still as razor-sharp as ever as he recalls that he was in the last final to be held at the prestigious Morpeth Olympic Games in 1959, and that he won the last-ever Houghton Feast Sports the same year. Happy days.

And, of course, they *were* happy days. Not only for the talented pro-runners, footballers and entertainers, but for the whole community. Those years spanning the forties and fifties proved to be a turning-the-corner period. Backs were turned on the bad old days of the hungry twenties and angry thirties, and eyes were fixed firmly on the prosperity that people were convinced lay ahead. It was a time when people had a sense of purpose in achieving their own personal goals. But it was also a time of collective civic pride in a town which had come to terms with itself, recognised its shortcomings, and decided, for better or worse, that Ashington, as Will Cain had said in 1927, *"wasn't see baad."*

Woodhorn Colliery. 1920.

Linton Colliery and village. 1924.

Ashington Colliery. 1954.

Co-op Women's Guild at Ashington Colliery. 1958.
[From left to right: Connie Wilkes (Croydon); C.M.D. Pringle (Training Officer); Mrs. Gregory (Croydon);
Will Owen, M.P.; Nellie Middlemiss & Millie Davies (Ashington Co-op Women's Guild); George Nelson (N.U.M.)]

Ashington coal leaders at safety award presentation. 1949.

Ashington Colliery tradesmen. c.1959.

Coal wagons at 1937 Coronation Parade.

Durham & Northumberland Mines Rescue Brigade. 1935.

BLOOD ON THE COAL

JONATHAN PRIESTMAN AND THE ASHINGTON COAL COMPANY

Whether he planned it or not, the town of Ashington, 'warts 'n' all', was the creation of Jonathan Priestman and his like-minded Quaker followers. And, whatever his intentions, the lives of all Ashingtonians, past and present, were shaped and coloured by *his* early decisions and philosophy.

The Priestmans owned the Newcastle District Bank which failed to meet its creditors in 1857. Following agitated negotiations between shareholders and officials, the family took over Consett Iron Works which was also on the verge of collapse. This was with the proviso that the family business took on the Iron Works' debts in return for release from the Bank's liabilities. Luck changed for the Priestmans and Jonathan went on to manage the Consett undertaking for a decade, also becoming involved with the running of a pit at Rowlands Gill. The two industries were perfectly matched and prospered side by side. The Quaker religion manifested itself in the interest he showed in his workers both socially and spiritually. Jonathan Priestman was drawn to the Ashington area in the early 1860s after acquiring a substantial amount of shares in the Ashington project when his father died. He immediately bought other shares until he held a commanding position on the board of directors.

The valuable seam of coal, revealed when the Bothal Downcast shaft was sunk in 1867, also brought in William Milburn who became a principal shareholder in the first coal company, known as 'Milburn, Priestman, and Partners'. The Milburns were a highly successful wealthy family with control of most of the north-east shipping lines. Large tracts of land to the east of what is now known as Milburn Road all became part of the Milburn Estate.

From the outset, Priestman sought to bring in fellow Quakers as part of his management team. Mr H Richardson, Robert Booth and Edmond Southern, captained the team which laid down the solid, no-nonsense foundations from which the colliery grew into such a huge and immensely profitable undertaking. There was reward for the resolute disciples, but swift punishment for anyone who trod a path other than that furrowed by the 'masters'.

And yet, with all their professed convictions of fair dealing, the Ashington Coal Company - re-named in 1898 - were blatantly concerned in fostering their own image as humane, charitable masters, dedicated to the well-being of their workers. Discreetly hidden from public view was the unacceptable face of capitalism: the pursuit of profit at the expense of long-term security for its workforce. Right from the first day it was palpably obvious that the company were after 'easy pickings'. The owners pinpointed the most commercially profitable seams and proceeded to run them dry. Coal of inferior quality: the seams of Middle Main, Bottom Main, Top Yard and Maudlin, were ignored until it was far too late. Some might argue that entrepreneurs are in business to make money quickly and that the company's only guilt lay in its hypocrisy; others, including miners leaders Will Lawther and Joe Gormley, were less inclined to be so lenient with the early private coal-owning regimes of Britain.

Five shafts were sunk at Ashington in the space of less than twenty years: Carl Upcast and Downcast in 1873; Bothal relief shaft in 1877; Duke Downcast in 1885; and the Bothal Downcast in 1890. As well as these, there were further sinkings for new collieries at Woodhorn in 1894 and Linton in 1896.

Capital investment was heaped upon the development of the new pits with easy shaft access to the prestigious High Main, Yard and Low Main Seams. George Hetherington, the colliery manager almost 100 years later, observed:

Ashington pit came to be seen as the main administrative site with facilities such as the central stores, new workshops, and brickyard, used for servicing the expanding group of collieries...it is obvious that they (ACC) had no intention to work the inferior seams of the upper measures nor those below the Brass Thill.

In the first mad rush, nothing was spared in bringing innovatory machinery into Ashington Colliery. One of the first coal cutters ever used underground, manufactured by the Yorkshire Engine Co., was installed in the Carl Yard Seam in 1895; conveyors were used for the first time in the Bothal Yard Seam in 1905; a mechanical trough for washing small coal for use on the boilers was built on the surface in 1896; wagons capable of carrying 40-tons travelled the company's private railways in 1902.

It was a hectic period, and in the scramble for jobs the workforce multiplied ten-fold in as many years. The quiet hamlet took on the look of a 'Boom Town', with only the black of the coal dust lying in the unmade streets distinguishing it from gold. A great deal of profit was made in those early years, with Priestman and Milburn making use of their commercial contacts to provide an infrastructure which carried the coal to where it could be sold at a premium. At no time would the original owners have envisaged such a project surviving more than a few decades. Of course it was a large undertaking, but the belief had to be that it couldn't last. Why else would they exploit the easier rich seams? Profitability was the aim of these pragmatic socialists who quickly presented themselves to the world at large as the caring coal company.

They provided a major share of the capital needed to establish the town's first school which opened its doors in 1873. Yet it cannot have gone unnoticed that this occurred only a couple of years after Forster's Education Act had made elementary schooling compulsory for children. It was the ACC's first bitter taste of government intervention, yet the medicine had the desired effect. The Bothal National School, built in the High Market area, catered for children up to the age of fourteen, or thirteen if the child could prove that he/she had a job waiting.

The job that was waiting for these often underweight, sickly children, was a miserable lifetime of drudgery and darkness.

Children were being used in the pit, some less than ten years old. A Royal Commission was set up in 1842 to look at conditions in the mines, and the following evidence was given:

JOSEPH TURPIN *Aged 11. (very little) Broke his arm down the pit some time ago, and was kept off about five weeks. Here he broke his thigh by rolleys (tubs) squeezing him, and was off eight weeks.*
THOMAS STUBBS *Aged 14. Greases the rolleys. Gets one shilling and thrupence a-day for that. Has been down the pit four years; drove at first for two years. Never was bad (ill) at all. Knows easy words, cannot write. Was at school only two years before he was a pit boy. Was lamed last year, falling stones breaking his thigh in two places. The same year the rolleys ran over his leg, and he was off three months from both accidents.*
JOHN CLARKE *Aged 10. (very little) Cleans the 'way, getting a shilling a-day. Goes down the pit at 3 am, coming up again at 4 pm. Has been down nearly three years. About a year ago he got amongst some water in the pit where he was keeping a trap door, and he got cold, and was off some days. Reads easy words, cannot write his name. Father is a hewer.*
GEORGE SHORT *Aged nearly 16. Hoists a crane and is paid one shilling and sixpence a-day. Has been down the pit for six years. It is bad air where he is, and makes him bad; makes small spots come out upon him, which he thinks is from the air, and he takes physic to stop them. His head works very often, and he feels sickish sometimes, especially if he sits down. Twice he has worked three shifts following, of 12 hours each shift. Never came up at all during the 36 hours. Was sleepy, but had not time to sleep. Has many times done double shifts of 19 hours. Gives the money to his father who does not like to see him stay down so long. Can read (fairly). Goes to Sunday school chapel now and then. Father is a deputy. Has had one brother killed by rolleys running over him.*

The youngest boys were mainly employed as *trapper lads*, responsible for opening a wooden ventilation trap-door when they heard the coal driver and his pony approaching. It was a dismal, lonely existence, often spent in complete darkness when the two candles provided by their father were spent. This job had also been done by women and young girls in earlier days. A piece of verse written at the time, voices the despair of a young trapper lad:

157

Father must I go down with you
Into that dark and dismal hole
And leave the sky above so blue
Buried amidst the blackest coal?

Why must I sit behind the door
So many hours away from you
And hear the putters shout and roar
And nought but shut and open do'?

The very dark and that small low*
You gave me soon will burn away
And I'm afraid and tremble now
To think of biding there all day.
* low - candle or small light

As the boys got bigger they were given more strenuous jobs to do, often working with pit ponies. A driver transported pit props and other pieces of equipment to the coal face. It was looked upon as a step up the ladder for a young lad, as seen in this next piece of verse entitled 'The Driver'.

I sit on my seat with my whip in my hand
And I crack it so often and loud
That the King on his throne, and the Lord of the land,
Are neither more happy nor proud.
If I fall from my seat, I meet with a 'laming'
But I get up again in a trice
If I don't break my head, then it's not worth the naming
And I don't want the doctor's advice.

From driving, the lads went on to coal putting. It was a form of piece-work, providing the filler with empty tubs. The young putter pushed the tub along the narrow-gauge railway to the face and brought out a full tub of coal. For every tub, he received an extra penny or two in his wage packet.

By the time the Ashington pits started, ponies had been introduced into the low seams where it was impossible to instal machinery. At the end of each shift, the drivers and putters leapt astride their gallowas (bred on a farm in Galloway) and galloped outbye to the stables. It was an illegal act, but this did not deter the young would-be jockeys from racing their own Pitmen's Derby.

EARLY LIVING CONDITIONS

In 1891, a census was carried out at Ashington Colliery giving the breakdown of house occupancy. This showed that 846 houses had been built, and practically all of them were within a stone's throw of the colliery yard. This figure included all the rows from the First to Eleventh, Long, Cross, and Stable Rows, and the Six Houses. At the time only 775 were occupied.

Accommodation varied immensely; of the 100 houses built in the 10th Row, 63 were two-roomed dwellings, while the remainder had a third room added. This contrasted with the spacious 5-roomed houses in the 1st Row, five of which housed the manager, undermanager, and three overmen. It was to these dwellings that a reporter from the *Newcastle Weekly Chronicle* was directed on September 4th, 1873. But they were far from being the typical pitman's house which he had asked to see. Understandably, the writer described the officials' dwellings in glowing terms, after setting the scene with this description of Ashington:

Notable indeed has been the change within the last few years in the district north of the river Wansbeck. Where, formally, only a few landsale pits existed, we now see large collieries, with gigantic pit gearing and towering chimneys springing up like huge blue-topped mushrooms.

Such has been the fate of Fell 'em Doon, the old has given way to the new system, and money has not only given it a new name but has also infused new life and energy into it so that it now keeps pace with most of the pits in the county.

Ashington, together with Sheepwash, formed a township of only 76 in 1861. In the twelve years up to the reporter's investigation it had risen to little short of 1,400. The original Fell 'em Doon shaft had ceased to be used although its old gearing still stood as a reminder of the town's origin. In 1867 the activity had moved half a mile to the east, and new shafts had been sunk. A pit village had sprung up, which, observed the writer: *"has not as yet done growing."*

The primitive accommodation initially comprised of two old-fashioned back to back rows, standing at right angles to each other. In the muddy backstreet were half a dozen ash-tips and privies for the use of the entire community. Each house was built for two families; there was no through ventilation; the windows were small, and during the hot summer they were, *"like so many ovens erected for the baking or kippering of the numerous families who had been packed into them like so many herrings."*

But as houses became vacant, partitions were broken down making the meagre dwellings double their size. The end house of the 2nd Row was used as a school, but on the day of the reporter's visit it was closed and had been for some time. He continued:

Since Mr Forster's 1871 Education Act, a splendid set of Church schools (Bothal School) have been built in Ashington, and will shortly be open to the children of the village.

His Grace the Duke of Portland is the owner of the soil, and however the dissenters of the village may strive to get an unsectarian school in the place, they may depend upon it there will be no site for them to build on.

There are several pleasant foot roads through the fields from Ashington where we noted numerous tall posts bearing in large characters: NO ROAD THIS WAY. It is important that Ashingtonians stick to their right of way; for however important it may be that hares shall breed unmolested, to provide sport for the leisure hours of the aristocratic person, it is of much greater importance that the small rights of way which the plebian public still possess should be protected.

At Ashington New Colliery, as the village was first called, operations were being carried out at breakneck speed. Only the High Main seam of coal was worked, employing nearly 250 hewers. They sent to bank some 600 tons of coal per day, running it down the waggon-way to the North-Eastern Railway's main line at Hirst station. From there it was despatched to the Blyth or Tyne staithes, or to *"such other places as the requirement of the market may demand."*

A new shaft had just been sunk to the low seam. The writer noted: *"As we looked down the abyss of some 250 feet, we saw a host of adventurous bricklayers suspended on a platform doing their work by the light of candles, looking like brilliant fireflies."* He continued:

Ashington is a compactly-built village, each row standing in a regular succession, like a regiment of soldiers. There is plenty of space between each row for all sanitary arrangements required, and space also for the pure air of heaven to blow through the houses.

The row facing the road (Long Row), with gardens in front, may be taken as showing a fair sample of the sort of cottage which is required by our pitmen now-a-days. The majority contain a good sized kitchen, with cement floor, a pantry, large enough to hold provisions for even a large family with large appetites. Down at the backside runs an open drain, which seemed objectionable, but we were informed that all these drains are kept under strict supervision, and no filth is allowed to accumulate.

The upper storey is reached by a narrow stairway which seems to have been made for Chinese feet. It is divided into two comfortable rooms, one of which may be available as a sitting room, if not required as a bedroom. Five houses in this row contain each five rooms, and it has not been our lot to see five more comfortable colliery houses anywhere. Such houses as these could not be had in Newcastle for less than eighteen pounds a year.

From his description it is clear that Ashington was thought to be "*a model young village.*" But there were many drawbacks, principal among them being the availability and quality of the water supply, which was drawn underground from the Duke pit, and was dependant upon the working of the colliery engine. If the pit worked and the engine ran, that was fine, but when it stopped, so did the water supply. At weekends, a sufficient stock had to be drawn from a standpipe in the backstreet. Queues formed, and women waited patiently, passing the time of day, before carrying and storing the water in the house in buckets until the pit started again.

If the Newcastle reporter used superlatives in his praise for the mining operations, he wrote disparagingly of the inadequate facilities for shopping and, by implication, the ineffectiveness of the local landowner:

There is but one shop near the place, and it is away at the old place (Fell 'em Doon). Such restriction by the man who owns the land (Duke of Portland) is an insult to the free inhabitants of what we fondly deem a free country. The men of Ashington are co-operators, yet they cannot get a store on the estate. Therefore we are not surprised that a large number of miners here are members of the Choppington Store, three miles away, or that the carts of the omnipresent Cramlington Store, penetrate even into the sacred preserves of his Grace of Portland.
There is, however, a reading room in the village with a list of 102 members who entertain a confident hope that the owners may be persuaded to build them an institution and leisure room worthy of the colliery.

Having been, at times, highly critical of the Ashington of 1873, our anonymous reporter now turned his attention on nearby Pegswood. Mining had begun in Pegswood around 1810 when the Bank's Colliery shaft was sunk. Since then the Royalty had passed through various hands, and in 1873 was owned by S. H. Frazer of Newcastle.

Pegswood Colliery then employed 160 hewers, winning some 380 tons per day. Coal was shunted from under the screens on to the North Eastern Railway, which passed close to the pit. At that time there was no station for the villagers. Morpeth, the nearest station, was three miles away, and as there was no shop or store in Pegswood, the reporter claimed: "*A weary distance has to be trudged every weekend by those who desire to go a-marketing.*"

The old workings which passed out of use when the new pit commenced in 1867, stood about half a mile further to the north. They had become unworkable because of their susceptibility to flood. At one time the men employed in the new workings became alarmed in case, wrote our reporter: "*The near approaches to the old workings should let the water in upon them, and drown them, like so many rats, without a chance of escape.*"

In all there were seven rows of houses near the colliery, but many of the miners employed in the pit lived: "*In villages at a distance, some of them even walking from Morpeth.*"

As a village, Pegswood was said to: "*Lack the neatness and quaker-like precision of Ashington.*" The rows of cottages were more closely built, straggling at all sorts of angles from each other. Two rows contained houses of two rooms, one on the ground level with a cement floor, and an upstairs bedroom reached by a narrow ladder built in like a staircase.

Ashpits and privies were built on the space between the back sides of the rows. On the day of his visit, the reporter observed: "*It would seem that many of the inhabitants are too lazy in their habits to throw their refuse into the proper receptacles.*"

160

The miners leased their dwellings from the Duke of Portland, and a group of four, situated at the top of the Quarry Bank: *"May be safely taken as the worst specimens of the human habitation to be found within the whole length and breadth of Northumberland."* The writer continued:

Four wretched bothies are there, with low walls of brick and stone, open in places to every breeze that blows, whether it be the balmy air of summer or the biting breeze of winter. Miserable floors of brick, stone, and wet clay; covered with old thatched roofs, which admits the rain through a hundred gaps, and dimly lighted by little more than one square foot of glass.

In one of these houses we found a miserable-looking Scottish woman, whose shortened locks told of recent fever. In apologetic tones, as though she were afraid of being turned out even from the semi shelter of those miserable walls, she admitted that they were, "awfu' places," but still they were better than, "oot bye a'thegither".

The next apartment was vacant but someone from Morpeth was to come over and take possession of it ere night. Part of its walls had fallen or been blown down, and a good gap had been simply fitted with loose stones. Next door to this was a similar kennel, which a broken-down looking woman in vain attempted to make decent by a plentiful sprinkling of the damp uneven floor with sand, a process which only served to show the course of the rivulets which had flowed from the walls to the pool in front of the fireplace. In a quavering voice she informed me that she had lived eighteen years in the place, and now would not like to leave it.

These kennels stand upon ducal ground, and doubtless ducal hands receive rent for them. Such miserable dwellings are a disgrace to our civilisation, and reflect eternal shame upon the men who not only suffer them to deface the landscape, but leave them upon for human beings to dwell therein.

As at Ashington, the same desire to keep education in the hands of the Establishment prevents the erection of a school here in Pegswood. Neither is there any chapel, and children must trudge to Bothal or Longhirst to learn their catechism, and be taught due reverence to their betters. The only break in this dark social cloud is a Mechanics Institute in course of erection at the village. This much the miners have been allowed to do - a small mercy for which the men of Pegswood can never be sufficiently thankful to his Grace.

A few years after this barbed slice of investigative journalism was published, a diary kept at the Pegswood Colliery School emphasised the problems of that tiny village:

8-6-1877   *Some children have left school in consequence of their parents leaving the colliery.*
14-6-1878 *Colliery getting very uneasy - school closed for one year.*
23-1-1885 *The people of Pegswood have this week begun to remove to Ashington - many of the new houses there being ready for use.*

But the new houses referred to could barely keep pace with the population explosion. As the Ashington pits expanded and new collieries came into operation, so the need for adequate housing for the workforce grew. The Ashington Coal Company began a programme of house building on an unprecedented scale. But they needed to run just to stand still.

A pitman on the colliery house waiting list in 1898 could expect to wait an average of 5 years and 3 months to be housed. By 1913 that wait had lengthened to 7 years and 8 months.

Based on notes from a Memorandum of Ashington Coal Company 1889-1929, here are some details of early house building:

July 3, 1889   New cottages contracted for : twelve 3-roomed cottages at east end of 8th Row, price £65-10s. £1 10s 0d. extra for iron down spout.
Feb 6, 1890   37 double houses at east end of 9th Row, price £103. 1s. 0d. per house extra for 18" oven instead of 17".

Oct 1st 1897 J & G Douglas to build 76 flats on 38 sites in Sycamore Street. With enclosed yard, for £119-19s a pair.

W G Gordon to build 27 4-roomed cottages in Laburnum Terrace for £93-10s-0d, bricks supplied by Coal Company.

For cottages built in Medway Street use white bricks.

For cottages built in Severn Street use red bricks.

(Medway later became Maple, and Severn was re-named Sycamore).

July 12,1898 W G Gordon to build overman's house at Linton and one at Woodhorn, price £260-10s-0d (we will find bricks)

(the last named, known as the Red House, was put on the market in 1991, asking price £125,000)

Jan 18, 1899 J & G Douglas to build 25 3-roomed cottages in Pont St £75 ea.

J & G Douglas to build 25 4-roomed cottages in Mersey St £98.

(Mersey was later absorbed into Milburn Road).

July 12, 1899 W G Gordon to build 3 5-roomed cottages Woodhorn at £110 ea.

It is easy to see why there was such a housing shortage when comparing the growing labour force of the Ashington Group of Collieries over 30 years:

	1898	*1909*	*1919*	*1927*
Ashington	2867	4059	4957	4254
Woodhorn	499	1796	2284	1730
Linton	476	1156	1045	1348
Ellington		59	1215	1347
Lynemouth				17

WORKING CLASS PIONEERS

In 1920, by order of the government, one penny a ton on all coal sales was ploughed into the setting up of a Welfare Scheme for the miners. The money from the Ashington Coal Company's vast profits was used to set up Welfare Halls at Ashington, Hirst, Linton, and Lynemouth. Football, cricket, hockey, and rugby pitches were laid; tennis courts were built; gymnasiums sprang up. At the same time, ACC subsidised the printing of a monthly colliery magazine. But it became the voice of authority, cajoling the men to work harder, keep off the booze, demand less wages, and save on materials. It was pure propaganda. Yet, for all that, the magazine, printed between 1922-41, has provided important information on the infant town and its pioneers.

One of the first working class voices to speak of old Ashington is that belonging to **JOHN MARTIN**, born on Guy Fawkes Day, 1853, in West Allen, Allendale. He wrote:

I was brought to Ashington - Fell 'em Doon as it was then - in the first week of February, 1854. My parents were encouraged to come here by Messrs Lee and Henderson, owners of the pit.

Things started badly. On our arrival, we found that the furniture had not turned up. So we spent our first night in what was called the 'Swankey Shop' (Swankey was a type of beer). Next morning mother went to look at the house we were to live in, but as soon as she saw it she wanted to leave immediately. For better or worse, we stayed.

There were only seven houses where we lived in the Cross Row. A house at the end of one row was made into a school with a Mr Larmouth as its first master. As a child, I had to get up at seven o' clock every morning and go to Coney Garth Farm for the milk. I soon tired of school and was only nine years of age when I applied for work at the pit. I started on the screens where there was no shelter of any sort, and I stood picking stones from the belts in all weathers for eleven hours for which I was paid one shilling (5p) a-day.

In the following year I went down the pit to look after a trap-door, after which I became a driver. There were seven heavy horses down the pit and eight putting ponies. A nine-hands pony called Duke often wandered down to the shaft and if he got half a chance he made off with someone's bait. He liked the warmth and sometimes we found him lying asleep on the loose coals in front of the furnace at the bottom of the shaft.

I became a putter when I reached thirteen and was paid three shillings a day. The pump went night and day down the pit, but we couldn't get any drinking water until the end of the shift. Only two brakesmen were employed, and they had to stand twelve hours each shift. Nobody worked about the pit at nights except one brakesman who often had to put up with the company of tramps.

There were only two fatal accidents at the old Fell 'em Doon pit. Robert Brown was killed through falling from the pit heap; and William Temple, a driver lad, also lost his life. The former left a widow, a son, and a daughter. The owners bought the widow a mangle, and she sold powder at the Magazine which stands by the Railway. Her son later became an overman at the Bothal Pit.

The Bothal was sunk about the middle of what is now the Fourth Row, but they found nothing but clay and water and the shaft was filled up again. At the next boring (1867) when the coal was reached, I went down with the sinker to see it, and the same night there was some jollification - a barrel of beer and beef being provided.

The common land about Fell 'em Doon was cultivated by the local men free of charge, and a man could have as much land as he wanted. A lot of it was worked, for the produce was of great value, especially when the pits were working short time as they often did in the winter.

There was a public house at Bothal when first we came, named the Castle Inn. There was talk of Cooper's Ghost. A certain Mr Cooper visited this inn every Saturday night, and it is said that the grisly spectre met him at the bottom of Bothal Bank and followed him all the way to his home at Cooper's Shop.

At that time the people of Choppington district came to Bothal on Sunday nights. On the south side of the river were sale gardens kept by Mr Thomas Milburn. At these gardens one could get a cap full of apples for a penny. The keels came up the river to the quarry to be loaded with sand stones, which they carried down to North Seaton where they were loaded into ships. Coal from North Seaton colliery was loaded into ships on the Wansbeck, too.

My father and mother had a family of ten - seven sons and three daughters - and not one of them has left Ashington. My wife was born in the Long Row, so we are a real Ashington family. We have two daughters, the elder being a nurse in the Royal Victoria Infirmary, Newcastle, for thirteen years; the younger one is a dressmaker.

John Martin lived at 40 Fifth Row, and retired on February 28th, 1928, after working at Ashington Colliery for sixty-four years.

SAM SNOW was a regular contributor to the Ashington Colliery Magazine. He recounts of how he arrived by train bound for his new home in Newbiggin:

Accompanied by two school chums, I came to Ashington for the first time on Saturday, April 1st 1894. We arrived home via Cambois, Blyth and Newsham, late on the same night. Where the Grand Hotel now stands was a neat three-feet wall enclosing grassland, and a little further east we came upon workmen engaged to build the first eight houses at the North end of Hawthorn Road. Seated in a trap was a gentleman whom we learnt was Mr Charlton, Chief Engineer of the Ashington Coal Company. I approached the gentleman and asked for employment, obtained it, and commenced work helping to make the railway line to Linton on April 4th, 1984.

Soon I was employed in the Colliery Yard at Ashington. We were receiving and despatching all kinds of machinery to commence sinkings at Woodhorn and Linton. I was sent to Longhirst Colliery and found, as near as possible, an old time family pit. The fireman had to blow the buzzer and all the surface workers ran home for their dinner, even the onsetter. Later on, when Linton got to draw coal, Longhirst was closed down.

In May, 1894, I saw Mr Richardson, Agent, cut the sod for Woodhorn No. 1 Pit. As I passed over the Blyth and Tyne Railway by the fields path to Woodhorn Village I had seen a group of men laying down the points and making ready for the sidings on April 1st.

Soon we were all agog with the Boer War and the rising cost of living together with the clamour for higher wages. I was paid six shillings and eightpence halfpenny (33p) a day. A shilling per ton levy was imposed upon all export coal to raise war finances. Basic wage for firemen was three shillings and fourpence halfpenny for an eleven-hours-per-day shift and thirteen hours night shift."

GEORGE MASON, three of whose sons, George, Billy, and John, all played in the same danceband, remembered the early days at the turn of the century, while talking to BBC Radio Newcastle:

The hardest work that was ever done in the pit in my time was done by the putters - that was youths from 16-20 years of age. They were strong-built; they had to be! They had to go down the pit at seven o'clock in the morning and they didn't get to bank till half past five. It meant, in the wintertime, they didn't see sunlight from one weekend to the next. Their mothers had the dinner ready when they came home - no pithead baths in those days - and I've seen some of the boys who were so tired lie down on the mat in front of the fire before they got their dinner and fall asleep.

All coal at that time was produced by pick and shovel with as little explosive as they could afford to buy. Miners bought their own picks; they bought their own pick shafts; they had to buy their own drilling machines and drills, and their own worm and handle to turn the drills in. They were all bought at the Co-operative Stores.

The Miners Union bought the explosives wholesale, and it was stored in a specially-built building erected by the coal owners. Once a month, each miner used to send down to the Powder Magazine for sufficient powder to keep them going.

The powder used was ordinary, loose-grained gunpowder. This had to be made into cartridges. I watched my father many a time making these cartridges to go to work the next morning. He cut old newspapers into triangular shapes and rolled them on a stick. He left an inch at the end of the stick to be doubled up, beaten hard on the cement floor to make a bottom, then he filled it with the loose gunpowder up to the size of cartridges that he wanted for the next day.

He put these into his shot-box; then he had his candle-box - usually three candles - which used to serve the miner his shift. It was all naked flame working in those days. There was supposed to be no gas. At the age I was, I hadn't the sense to be scared about explosions.

Every colliery house had a pantry where the powder was stored on a shelf to keep it dry. What surprises me now was to think of how father used to stick a candle - no electricity then - into a lemonade bottle, or a beer bottle if he was lucky enough to have beer in the house, and he used this light to see while he made his cartridges. And the candle wouldn't be passing twenty inches away from all this gunpowder. There was enough gunpowder in the colliery houses of Ashington to blow the whole place to smithereens!

For leisure in the early 1900s there were many miners interested in music. There were three brass bands, and a brass and reed band. Lots of miners joined these bands and learnt how to play a musical instrument. They played good music and I enjoyed listening to them. And miners had their own gardens which they tended, and sometimes entered their flowers and vegetables into the local Show.

The miners had one day off in a fortnight. They had a pay weekend and a Baff week when they didn't get paid. Everybody got paid on a Friday night and the next day was when all the football matches, cricket, and all kinds of sport were played.

Trips took place on that Saturday. It used to be regular practice for about fourteen men to hire a horse-drawn brake and arrange for a trip on a Saturday morning in the summertime. Before they set off they put a box of beer into the brake, and they would drive from Ashington maybe as far as Felton - about 14 miles. They would loose the horses off, put them into a stable, then go into a pub and have their sandwiches and a drink or two of beer. After about an hour, they would cut away from there across country eastwards to Warkworth and Amble where they would do the same. They would land home at the Portland Hotel, probably about nine o'clock, and that gave them a couple of hours to have a drink or two - it was eleven o'clock closing then. It was a really good day out which they would talk about down the pit for the next fortnight - and they had only travelled 25 miles!

George Mason, a Woodhorn colliery Master Shifter, worked for over 50 years and served for many years as a Co-operative member on Ashington Council.

GEORGE MATHER was the first District Overman at Ashington Colliery. He arrived in the town in 1889 after working as a boy for a short time in Durham and later in Broomhill. He related this story in 1936:

When I arrived at the High Market there was a brassy heap on the site where the villas now stand at the junction of the Ellington and Morpeth roads. The railway line in those days ran right down the front of the Long Row. At this time there was a quarry opposite the Cooper's Shop. There were no houses in the Hirst - just the old castle, Black Close, and two dwellings near the site of the Grand Corner.
We got very severe weather in the early days. I mind of how folks in the Cross Row had to fight to keep out the water, blocking up nooks and crannies with clay while they stood in eighteen inches of water in the kitchens.
I remember a snowstorm in 1886 which brought a very heavy fall. The snow was still lying in May, and to give you some idea of its depth, a light engine near Acklington was lost in it for three weeks. The heat of the engine melted the snow around it, but it froze again and formed an impenetrable cover of ice.
On 'Windy Friday', a day of cyclonic fury in 1900, the scaffolding of Dr Beaton's house in Lintonville, which was in the process of erection, was all blown down, and havoc was wrought everywhere. That same day, at Newbiggin, a wreck was lifted by mountainous waves and hurled up on the hillside where Bay View houses now stand; the sea swept through the streets and the froth of the angry waves stretched right across the links.
I was on the original Hospital Committee which was formed before the erection of the Ashington Infirmary. We began to build it just before the 1914 war broke out. There was all sorts of trouble with the foundations which had to be laid below a bed of quicksand. Then building was halted because of the war.

Mr Mather, who also served as Secretary for the Children's Sports and President of the Northumberland Branch of the Club and Institute Union, retired in February 1936 after serving the Ashington Coal Co. for 48 years.

JOE BELL, or to give him his familiar name, Joe the Sinker, arrived in Ashington around 1910. A Durham man by birth, Joe sank pit shafts the way some men sink pints of beer. A real character, he spent many years in Russia, opening up new collieries, and boasted that he had lived in 55 different houses. He was encouraged to write down some of his experiences, now housed at the County Records office, in 1952. Here he recalls:

I was working on my knees down Newbiggin pit when a stone fell on my back and heels. It measured ten feet by four, and was a foot thick. Both of my boots were doubled up, and two big toes put out of joint. My chest was forced down between my thighs, almost thrusting the hip joints out of their sockets. I screamed to attract the attention of two cuttermen, but they couldn't hear me until they switched off their machine.
For those terrible injuries I was allowed eighteen shillings a week compensation. After being off work for eight weeks, one of my mates tried to mingle with a crowd of men outside the pit office so that he could take the usual gathering of sixpence or a shilling for anyone who had been out of work. But someone with a big mouth shouted: "What? For him! He doesn't drink or smoke or gamble. He's better off than we are." So I got nowt!
I went up to Ashington from my house at Newbiggin to be interviewed by the Company doctor. On the way there I had to get someone to help me on and off the kerb, because I was so bent - I had thrown my crutches away by then. The doctor said: "Mr Bell, you mustn't even think about work. When you do get a job you'll need a chair to sit in." Within a twelve month I was back doing my same work.

ROSS MILES was born on the fourth of December, 1902. He was the seventh in a family of nine - all girls apart from him and his brother Dickie - although two of his sisters died as babies. His father was the man who ploughed the field before it became Peoples Park. The Duke of Portland had made a present of the site to the people of Ashington, plus one nearby for the Holy Sepulchre Church, in 1885.

Ross recalls:

I was born at 13 the Cross Row, but most of the family were born at Sparrow House Farm. My grandfather had worked at Coney Garth Farm and he was the first Granary foreman for the Ashington Coal Company before he retired in 1900.

In those days you could leave school at thirteen if you could prove you had a job to go to, but my parents wanted me to get the best out of any education that was going so I stayed on till I was fourteen. In fact, I even attended night school during my last year, doing the same kind of subjects but at a more advanced level. In those days, Morpeth Grammar School was the place to go to, but selection was not based on any examination rather on who you were.

My first job was working for my father in the 'choppy house' at the Granary. It was called choppy because this machine used to chop up the corn into small pieces. During the whole of the 51 years I was employed at the colliery, I never worked harder than I did that first year. It was because my father was the gaffer - I needed to show the others that I wasn't getting preferential treatment. My first wage was one shilling a day but, as it was wartime, everyone got a little extra because the war had shoved the prices up.

When I was sixteen, I started a five-year apprenticeship as a fitter. I attended the Day Continuation School for three years to learn the technical side of mining. Ned Lewis, the Company's chief draughtsman, took us for technical drawing. The school then was held at the Priestman Memorial Hall in the 2nd Row. John Murray was the Principal, and a very fine job he made of it.

The first big strike I remember was in 1921 when the men had their wages reduced from £1 a shift to six shillings and ninepence halfpenny. That was done by the Mine Owners Association of Northumberland and Durham, it wasn't just the Ashington Coal Company. We were lucky because, although I was on strike, my father was ranked as an official and kept on working - the ponies still had to be fed, work or not.

Ross was a very active member of the Boy Scout movement. An article in the *Ashington and Hirst Press* of 1909 charted the progress of Ashington's first troop:

Six members of the 1st Ashington Troop of Boy Scouts are now bearers of the 2nd class scout badge. The examination was held in the Club Rooms, Ashington, before Acting Scout Master F Maughan, Acting Adjt C Bell, and Quartermaster R J Oliver. The successful members are: Patrol Leaders J Boutland, J Beattie, J Graham, M Bell, Corporals T Scott and J Robinson. Sadly, John Boutland later lost his life in the first world war.

Ross explained his involvement with the movement:

I became interested in scouting at a very early age. The first troop in Ashington (1st Ashington) often met in our house because my brother, Dickie, became their scoutmaster. But he went into the Army in the Royal Engineers during the 1914-war. He shouldn't really have been allowed in because, as well as being undersized at 5ft 1in, he had flat feet and was C3 on his medical. He was later transferred to the Flying Corps. By then I had taken over the troop and Jack Dorgan had begun the 1st Hirst.

In 1920 I was one of several local scouts chosen to represent Northumberland at the first International Scout Jamboree being held at Olympia in London. Ashington Coal Company decided to put on an exhibition showing how coal was won, so Will Cookson designed a massive structure, built by Harry Turnbull representing a full-blown colliery with a cage descending through rock strata, displays of haulage and mine rescue, the lot - they even took three ponies, Baby, Tulip and Topper, to demonstrate putting with gallowas. We

166

had a great time in London, and stayed at St Peter's School, near Victoria Station. One day, when we were chattering away on a bus going to the exhibition, our dialect sounded so strange that a lady asked which country we came from.

Quite by chance I took over the running of the 1st Pegswood Troop. Harry Grieves and I were on the bus going to Morpeth for the day. We decided to break our journey at Pegswood. Getting off the bus, we heard this dreadful commotion coming from the Mission Hall. When we entered the Hall it was bedlam; young lads were romping around all over the place, completely out of control. It seems that the curate at Bothal, Arthur Wasey, had ideas for starting a troop in Pegswood, but he hadn't turned up.

Me and Harry got the lads sorted out doing knots and other kinds of scouting activities. In walks Arthur who ordered us out because we were strangers. However, when he saw how well his young Pegswood boys were behaving, he asked me and Harry if we would like to run the troop, and we agreed, staying until 1931.

While I was there, the Duke of Portland gave permission for us to use the title: '1st Pegswood, the Dukes Own Troop'. Lads who were members included: Bob Frazer, Andy Thompson, Peter Devon, Tubby Nuttal, and Billy Bell who later became headmaster of Newbiggin Secondary School.

It was through the scout movement that Ross met up with Molly, his future wife, in 1929. She explained:

There was a North East Scout Exhibition on the Town Moor and my troop, 71st Newcastle, were picked to put on a series of Jungle Dances for the spectators.

A friend of mine introduced me to Ross and he asked if he could visit me at Newcastle. Of course, I said "yes" and he came through on the bus. At the end of the evening he asked if I wanted to visit him at Ashington the next day. I told that I would, but that I didn't have the bus fare. So Ross gave me his return ticket and bought another return for himself on the way home. At the end of the next day he gave me his other return ticket to get me back home again. In the end, to save ourselves about six shillings a week in bus fares, we got married! My father was a publican - he had The Byker Tavern - so I never ever went into full-time employment. I was the skivvy around the place; lots of lasses were like that in those days.

Ross and Molly were married in 1930, moved into their house in the Colliery Scheme, and are still living there after sixty years. A curious feature of that estate - the first built by the Coal Company for private sale - is that the names of the eight streets (taking the initial letters) spells PARK ROAD

Park Road	Ridsdale Square
Arundel Square	Oakland Terrace
Rutland Street	Ashbourne Crescent
Kenilworth Road	Darnley Road

JACK HARRISON, now aged eighty-seven, and living in Ariel Street, joined the Ashington Art Group, he says "*in its declining years.*" He recalls of how only he and founder member, Oliver Kilbourn, sat waiting in their old hut to welcome anyone who was interested in art, but no-one came. He has written down some of his discerning observations on life in Ashington's bygone days:

I remember the pit village of my youth, good friends, neighbours, workmates; the yellow brick houses, row after row; the unpaved streets, roads made out of stone from the pit and burnt ash from the stone heaps. There were no motor cars or buses, just horse-drawn carts, rolleys, and traps. I remember the bogies and the bogie lines along every row and back street. Huge horses pulled four full tubs of coal to the miners' coal houses. By day, and at night, horses pulled four midden bogies to the open middens; the bogies were filled by men shovelling in the ashes, rubbish and shit, and then hauled to the tips in the fields to be emptied.

I remember the blackened fly-papers hanging in every house, and the battle at meal times chasing the flies from the food. I remember when home from the pit, the tin bath in front of the fire. No back was ever washed "It weakened the back", the wise men said. There were no pithead baths.

Education was on a low level. Only the pits for the boys and domestic service for the girls. "Give 'em Scripture!" "Blessed are the poor". "Teach 'em Spelling". "DANGER, PRIVATE PROPERTY - KEEP OUT" "Give 'em, Tables". "Twelve pence, one shilling - twenty shillings, one pound". "That's all they need to know."

I remember the oil lamps and candles that lit the homes - no electricity or gas; no washers or spin driers; no electric irons for wash day, just the old-fashioned flat or box irons. There was no running water, only two outside taps to serve the long streets; no inside toilets - across the road was a wooden box toilet, and open middens. There was no radio, or video, or television, or telephone, or fancy carpets - the well-off had linoleum and home-made hooky and proggy mats.

There was no sliced bread, but fresh home-baked bread and stotties. We had one good meal a day of either beef, mutton, bacon, sausages, black and white pudding, or liver, served with onions, tatties, boiled suet puddings, broth and dumplings. On baking days, I remember my mother' kneading the dough; the dough in the tins, rising in front of the fire before going into the oven to bake; the granny loaf and scones; the lovely smells when she opened the oven door.

We menfolk thought women were lucky; they didn't go down the pit; they were never in the two o'clock foreshift! Now I know how wrong we were - they were on call twenty-four hours a day.

I remember washing days; the big iron pan was on the fire all day, heating the water for the washing. Then came the thump, thump of the poss-stick, bounced up and down in the poss-tub, beating out the dirt from the clothes into the boiling water; the big wooden-rollered mangle squeezing out the water; on rainy days the clothes line stretched back and forwards across the kitchen, hung with wet clothes drying in front of a roaring coal fire, thick steam clouding the air. I remember the evenings, mother patiently ironing the clothes, then folding them into drawers; darning thick pit stockings, mending and patching pit pants and coats - the menfolk must go to work clean and tidy. In between these jobs, roasting big potatoes or toasted cheese sandwiches; something tasty for supper, pan of boiled onions or leeks. If someone was in foreshift, putting up their bait in a newspaper parcel.

I remember how my mother and sister washed pit stockings; cleaned and greased pit boots; dadded coats, pants, and shirts against the backyard wall. On Fridays the oven door and fireplace had to be blackleaded and polished; the fender, fire-irons and brasses had to be gleaming for the weekend. I remember them cutting up cast-off clothing, making clippings for the mats. But I can't remember my mother ever taking it easy, even when she was ill; and I can't remember ever telling her how much I appreciated her many acts of goodness and kindness, or how much I loved her. I didn't need to tell her - she knew.

"A strike's aalreet but by gum Aa wad
rather be at work."

Deputy: "Lad, d'ye knaa them men in theor hev a
shipload o' coal?"
Putter: "Wey then, gan in an' tell them to set sail"

MINE DISASTER
THIRTEEN LIVES LOST AT WOODHORN
A GAS EXPLOSION

These were the headlines in the Newcastle Daily Journal & Courant on August 14th 1916. The Hirst area of Ashington was plunged into mourning by a serious mine explosion which had occurred the previous day, resulting in thirteen men losing their lives. The blast happened at Woodhorn Colliery, a mine in which over 2,000 men were employed but, as it was a Sunday, only about 30 were in the pit at the time.

First indications that something calamitous had happened came at 6.45 am when a dull booming sound cleeved through the quiet of a typical Ashington Sunday morning, sending tremors as far afield as Bedlington. At first, it was thought that one of Kaiser Bill's Zeppelins had strayed too far north and crashed. But then came the speculation that the only possible reason for the explosion was an accumulation of gas, though how this could have happened when the pit had been inspected only hours before remained a mystery until evidence was put forward at the resulting Inquest.

At that time Woodhorn Pit had three seams: Low Main, Yard, and High Main. The calamity occurred in No. 2 pit in the Low Main seam. Of the following thirteen men killed, eight were deputies:

Daniel Harrison,	152 Maple Street
George Hodgson,	33 Katherine Street
George R Hudson,	43 Katherine Street
Ralph Howard,	288 Sycamore Street
George Marshall,	12 Rosalind Street
Thomas Armstrong,	25 Rosalind Street
David Armstrong,	38 Rosalind Street
Robert Hindmarsh,	41 Rosalind Street
Edward Walton,	118 Rosalind Street
Joseph Harrogate,	Hirst
Walter Hughes,	146 Hawthorn Road
George Blair,	Allison's Yard, Newbiggin
George Patterson,	137 Sycamore Street

The hand of the spectre of premature death had knocked many times upon the doors in the colliery rows of the town, but never so greedily, never so violently, never so mercilessly.

Youngest of those killed was 21-year-old George Patterson, a single man, and the oldest was 66-year-old Robert Hindmarsh. Edward Walton, a stoneman aged 47, left a widow and nine children, ranging from William aged 24, serving in the Royal Navy, to 2-year-old Joseph Adrian.

Reacting immediately, the Rescue Brigades of Ashington and Elswick were quickly on the scene of the disaster, but were hampered by afterdamp and heavy falls of stone, some of which measured over eighty yards in length. Heavy steel arch girders and wooden props were completely stripped by the blast. Ventilation systems were also destroyed. It was apparent soon after the Brigades went down that no-one could have survived such a blast.

The dead were all part of a working party sent in to erect steel girders. They descended the shaft at six am. Some safety lamps recovered later were found to be tightly secured, and as no shots would have been fired, the cause of the explosion remained a mystery.

Ten bodies were found after a lengthy search. Two men, Walter Hughes and Daniel Harrison, were found alive, but died later after admittance to Ashington Infirmary which had just been built. The body of George Patterson was not recovered until the next day; the dead man, aged twenty-one, was found, together with his pit pony, crushed beneath a fall of rock.

Mr Charles Percy, coroner for Northumberland, opened the Inquest on August 14th at the Harmonic Hall in Ashington. In his opening address he expressed sympathy and condolence to the bereaved families.

Mr Waddilove, on behalf of the royalty owners, said: *"This is the first bad accident in the Ashington area for eight years."*

W Weir of the Northumberland Miners Association commented: *"There is scarcely a home in which hearts were not being wrung with sadness and sorrow; the calamity at Woodhorn had come as a rude shock to them as they awoke that fateful Sunday morning."*

The Home Secretary, Mr Samuels, sent a telegram saying: *"I regret the loss of life at Woodhorn colliery and send sincere sympathy."* There were also messages of condolence from the Miners Associations of Durham and North Staffordshire. The Northumberland Coal Owners expressed: *"Our deepest regret of the serious disaster at Woodhorn."*

As a mark of respect, No. 1 and No. 2 pits were closed for one day. Evidence of identification was given by relatives, and the Inquest was adjourned until August 21st.

Five of the men, all Church of England, were buried at midday on August 16th at Seaton Hirst Churchyard: David Armstrong, Thomas Armstrong, Daniel Harrison, Robert Hindmarsh and Joseph Harrogate. Long before noon, large crowds of people approached Ashington by road and rail. Milburn Road, which led to the cemetery, was packed with sympathetic spectators. The Reverend L D Griffiths and W E Renwick, curates at Seaton Hirst, officiated at the funeral.

Mourners included one Member of Parliament and representatives of many organisations. For Ashington Coal Company: Frank Priestman and Fred Milburn; for Priestman's Institute: Mr Hall, secretary, and T Jacques, treasurer. Many wreaths were laid including two from the Universal Social Club for members Daniel Harrison and Robert Hindmarsh; one from the Fell 'em Doon Club for David Armstrong; and one from Priestman's Institute for member Thomas Armstrong. George Blair was buried the same afternoon at Newbiggin. The remaining seven were interred the following day.

In his opening address at the resumed Inquest, Mr Charles Percy said:

I want to say at once, I propose to adopt my usual practice of giving a very wide latitude for the calling of witnesses - any person having an interest may call and produce before this Court what he considers will be any evidence which may assist us in coming to a conclusion. I want not one jot or tittle of evidence omitted which may throw a light on this terrible calamity.

From evidence given, it was possible to build a picture of the events which led up to the explosion. A ventilation fan had been switched off at the end of the Friday shift, and no written report had been made of this - contrary to existing safety regulations. This particular machine, together with a compressed air fan, ventilated the two main headings in the working which was being opened out.

The main fan was worked by a steam engine, fuelled by eight boilers. Four firemen normally kept the furnaces stoked during each shift. But 500 Woodhorn men were away fighting at the Somme, as was Major Milburn the colliery manager; the pit was left short-handed, and only *two* men turned up to fire the furnaces on the Saturday night before the explosion. The two who did get to work that night could not cope, and the steam pressure dropped accordingly. Insufficient air was being pumped into the Main Seam where the 13 men were due to work. Had this fan been working properly, the gas might never have been ignited, as probably only a small amount was being given off, which would have been carried away had good ventilation been maintained.

The written reports required under the Mines Act were never made out for these 'special shifts' when deputies and others went in to do work such as setting girders, as the dead men had been doing. It seems that Woodhorn Colliery was not alone in disregarding the writing of such reports, and that it was common practice throughout the Northumberland and Durham coalfields to disregard them.

A Mines Inspector was heard to say: *"So long as we have coal seams there will always be the danger of gas making an appearance. I am of the opinion that the time will come when no naked light will be allowed in any mine."*

Last witness called was Mr Granville Pool, H.M. Junior Inspector of Mines. According to W Straker of the Northumberland Miners Association, by the time Pool had finished:

"The opinions of all who had gone before him appeared almost fantastic. He brought out so clearly the evidence in support of his conclusion that all in the Court were convinced that the opinion which he had formed was probably the truth of the matter."

Poole's view was that, due to lack of air pressure, there had been a build-up of methane gas which had probably been ignited when the man furthest inbye had held up his candle to the roof to see where to position the first girder. A broken clay pipe was found where the first explosion occurred and spots of fresh blood on the coal. As there were eight deputies in the working party, it was not made clear who had the responsibility of going into the working first and examining for gas with his safety lamp.

The Inquest Jury were out for only 50 minutes before returning with the following verdict read by the Coroner:

That the 13 men were accidently killed on the 13th day of August 1916, while working at Woodhorn Colliery, by an explosion of gas in the main seam, and that such gas had accumulated through want of sufficient ventilation, and exploded through contact with a naked light and before any fall of stone took place. The Jury are of the opinion that the management should see, in the future, that written reports should be made for every shift, special or otherwise. The Jury are also of the opinion that there has been a certain amount of laxity on the part of the management in not seeing to sufficient ventilation being maintained."

Writing his memoirs many years later, the late Joe Bell, a shaft sinker, who was working on Ellington pit shaft at the time, made this uncorroborated statement:

These thirteen men went up a steep incline from the bottom seam. They stripped off their clothes and sat down for a few minutes to cool off and have a smoke, which was a regular occurrence, but this was not mentioned at the Inquest.

What did come out was that firemen were idle (absent) at the boiler-house on the surface, and the only fireman at work had so strenuous a time clearing the slag from his furnaces that he had forgotten to start the ventilating fan, therefore, the seam was standing foul with gas. The official in charge of these men had failed to test the atmosphere with his safety lamp. On previous occasions the fan had been started before the men arrived.

A Memorial Service was held for the dead at the Miners' Theatre, Ashington on Sunday September 12th, when about 500 people attended. The Service was conducted by Mr Charles Fenwick M.P. According to a local paper: *"The Ashington Choir Party rendered some remarkably fine pieces of music suitable for the occasion."* Mr G H Warne of the Woodhorn Branch of the N.M.A. in moving a vote of thanks, said: *"I am sure that all who are present are better men and women for having being at this Service today."*

At a meeting in October, the amount of compensation asked by the N.M.A. on behalf of the dependants was disputed by the Owners, who eventually agreed to the following rates: £300 for each married man killed in the explosion, and £40 for the two single men, Joseph Harrogate and George Patterson.

Soon after the disaster, a group was formed to suggest ways in which a suitable Memorial could be erected. Heading the first committee was Mr E Edwards, who soon moved on to Burt Hall; into the Chair stepped G H Warne, but he was replaced when he was elected to Parliament; the man who finally saw the project through to the end was John Harrison. D Marshall was appointed as Treasurer, and H Poll filled the post of Secretary. Surveyor to Ashington UDC, George Beattie, offered practical help in planning the Memorial.

The task of designing the plinth went to W H Knowles FRIBA. It was square in form rising from a two-step foundation of granite. Built of grey granite, the 20-feet high shaft was placed on a heavy granite base and finished with moulded cornice. Aloft on the plinth, cast in bronze, was placed the figure of a 'typical Northumbrian miner'.

Except that this was not strictly true. Up until then, whenever the statue of a miner had been erected it invariably showed him carrying a safety lamp in his hand which hung by his side and a pick, held in the other hand, balanced on his shoulder. However, as the majority of men killed at Woodhorn were deputies, it was decided that the figure would represent 'a Deputy', holding up his lamp so that 'His practised eye can, by the action of the flame, recognise the presence of gas and so warn the workers of possible danger'. The purpose of that particular pose was 'to convey to all the imperative reminder that *Safety First* should be the watchword'.

Bronze panels were cast on two sides of the shaft, one depicting the Pit Head, the other with an inscription and names of the thirteen men who lost their lives.

The inscription read:

ERECTED BY THE MINERS AND DEPUTIES TRADE UNION BRANCHES IN THE ASHINGTON GROUP OF COLLIERIES (ASSISTED BY DONATIONS FROM THE ASHINGTON COAL COMPANY, THE NORTHUMBERLAND MINERS ASSOCIATION, THE DEPUTIES ASSOCIATION AND FRIENDS). IN MEMORY OF THEIR FELLOW WORKMEN WHO LOST THEIR LIVES IN THE WOODHORN COLLIERY EXPLOSION ON SUNDAY AUGUST 13th 1916.

Placed either side on the Monument were two drinking fountains with artistic drinking cups. The statue itself was modelled and designed by John Reid ARCA of the Armstrong College of Art in Newcastle. Contractors who erected the Memorial were Henry Walker and Son of Westgate Road and Gallowgate.

The total cost of the structure was £1,070, and donations were as follows:

	£	s	d
Ashington Coal Company	100	0	0
Northumberland Miners Association	100	0	0
Northumberland Deputies Association	50	0	0
Ashington Federated Collieries	441	2	3
Ashington Federated Deputies	18	13	6
Duke of Portland	10	10	0
Mr.G H Waddilove	10	10	0
Alderman John Craigs	1	1	0
Mr Wm Straker	0	10	0
Major Milburn	0	10	0
Mrs. Morgan	0	5	0
A Friend	0	5	0
Ashington United Social Clubs	56	4	0
Anniversary Collections	43	9	8
Sale of Memorial Cards	8	18	9
Bank Interest	105	9	5
Ashington Industrial Co-op Society	10	10	0
Ashington Equitable Co-op Society	5	0	0
Newbiggin Co-op Society	5	0	0
Hirst Priestman Institute	5	0	0
TOTAL	£972	18	7

Ashington Federated Collieries decided to donate the shortfall of £120.

The Memorial was officially unveiled at a ceremony in Hirst Flower Park on August 18th 1923, by Robert Smillie MP. Among those present were G H Warne, Member of Parliament for the Wansbeck Division; Ridley Warham, Managing Director, and Capt. C E Pumphrey of the Ashington Coal Company; W Straker, E Edwards, W Hogg and W Weir of the Northumberland Miners Association; Samuel Coulthard of the Deputies Association; John Harrison Chairman of the Memorial Committee; Ashington councillors John Colvin, and J R Tomlin; and Mrs R Smillie.

Bob Howard, now aged eighty two, is the only survivor of the five children left on the death of his father, Ralph in 1916. He recalls that the accident occurred the day before his seventh birthday: "*I didn't have much of a birthday that year.*" In his spare time Mr. Howard was an official with the Ashington Rugby Club. "*He used to have this long stick with a brush on the end, and he would go around painting the lines on the pitch,*" said Bob.

The fact that their father was killed at Woodhorn did not deter Bob or his three brothers from going there straight from school at thirteen years of age. He says: "*We were brought up to it, so never thought a thing about going down the pit. What else was there to do?*" He counts himself lucky not to have been killed underground. "*I was working on with the cutter with a marra of mine, Bill Carey, who didn't know the cutting blade had been left in gear. When Bill started it up, the picks flew around and sliced the poor lad's leg off, and I ended up in a heap under the cutter.*"

Bob's wife, Annie, says that accidents were the norm in those days: "*My father brought some detonators home from the pit, and he was messing around with one of them in his hand; it went off and blew two of his fingers away. We found his thumb the next day under the sideboard!*"

Young Bob Howard's wage underground in 1923 was nine shillings, and he recalls feeling like the richest lad in the world when he got his first two bob pocket money. He said: "*I was waiting to get into the Wallaw cinema, second house, when this lass came around rattling a tin and selling flags for charity. I put my hand in my pocket and pulled out this two shilling piece thinking she would give me some change. But when she grabbed the coin and hoyed it into the tin I went straight home and cried my eyes out.*"

It was in 1989, when the disused Woodhorn Colliery was in the process of becoming a museum, that Bob wrote a letter to the local press suggesting that it would be the natural place for the Memorial to be placed. When the transfer was finalised, Bob expressed himself as being "well pleased".

When word got around that the widows of the eleven married men were to get three hundred pounds in compensation (about £30,000 by today's standards) it set some men thinking that here was a nest-egg too good to miss. A stranger from Wallsend turned up on one widow's doorstep and began courting the distraught lady whom he married very quickly, later attempting to strangle the poor woman in order to get at her Co-op passbook. It transpired that he had served a 16-year prison sentence for murdering his first wife.

The late Ann (Nancy) Walton was ten and living at 118 Rosalind Street when her father died. She remembered:

We were all getting ready for nine o'clock Mass when our neighbour, Mrs Hamilton, came in. "Is your Ned at work this morning?" she asked mother. "Aye!" my mother said, "how's that, like?" The woman lowered her eyes: "Oh, I just wondered," and left.
There was a colliery policeman lived near the top of Chestnut Street who eventually brought word about the accident. By then my mother was on the way to the pit - we'd all heard the explosion, you see. We never did get to church that Sunday.

Nancy said that the broken bodies were taken to Ashington Infirmary, and she heard later that some of the nurses were sent home suffering from the effects of gas being expelled from the lungs of the dead men as their remains were being stitched into white sheets.

Her brother, Ned, was allowed to leave St Aidan's school at the age of twelve and a half so that he could begin work. Nancy said:

173

With the eldest lads being away at the war, our Ned had to become the breadwinner. He went down Woodhorn Pit same as my father, but didn't settle - he came out of the mine a few years later and joined the army.

My mother had to take in lodgers in order to keep the colliery house or we would have been evicted. She went through to Morpeth once a quarter for her widow's pension from Judge Greenwood. He was a gentleman, and told my mother: "Mrs Walton, I think it is degrading that you have to present yourself here every three months for this pittance of a pension." All she got was three pounds and eight shillings.

I know that for many years after the Memorial was erected in 1923, mother took us children to the Hirst Flower Park on the Sunday set aside to commemorate the tradgedy. The brass bands played, somebody said a few words, and we enjoyed that. I'm really pleased that the Monument was moved to Woodhorn Colliery Museum - it's like coming home."

The work on bringing the monument *home* to Woodhorn Colliery Museum began on 28th February, 1991. It took three days to dismantle the 20-feet plynth and remove the statue, now sadly without pick or lamp because of vandals. Said one of the workmen employed by Lowry's the contractors of Gallowgate: *"They certainly built this one to last - just take a look at that cornerstone."*

THE LASKI LETTERS

Long before the phrase 'public relations' was coined, the Ashington Coal Company missed few opportunities to present themselves as benevolent employers, and the grimy pit town became headline news nationwide. The pit owners who looked after all aspects of their employees' work, leisure, and spiritual activities, attracted the cream of the country's intelligentsia. The 1920 ACC Welfare Scheme was on a scale far above what Robert Owen had attempted in his brave new world at New Lanark, almost a century before.

Harold J Laski, one of an increasing band of socialist intellectuals based in London, paid many visits to Ashington, mixing and talking to miners at outdoor rallies and in the tiny institute. Here are extracts from two of his letters to Justice Holmes.

September 26th, 1924

I have had a dazzling time in the North, full of more genuine pleasure than I can remember in a long time. In Ashington, I stayed with a miner (Sam Snow) who began by discussing Kent with me, with a knowledge and an insight which must be rare outside a group of dons.

I gave four lectures to about 200 miners, and their questions and arguments were as searching as I ever met. Each evening I was there my host had in a dozen men for talk, and I frankly can rarely remember such talk. What was the value of Lester Ward's work? Where did Hardy stand in the pageant of English Literature? And was security, as Bentham said, more important than freedom?

Imagine a dozen men furiously smoking around a fire, and the questions beginning almost before I could think of the answers. And it was all done with the courtesy and modesty of really great gentlemen. Many of them had not had a day's schooling after fourteen years of age. They all belonged to a little society (Literary & Debating Society) where week by week they met to discuss intellectual problems.

September 15th, 1925

I have just come back from my annual weekend with miners at Ashington - a really thrilling time. I gave them four lectures but I learned more than I could ever teach. I stayed again with Sam Snow and his three thousand books, and talked each night with them until the dawn came.

It was sometimes grim talk, for there are hard times ahead for the mining community in England. But in general it was of books and men. Floyd tells the others that Nausicca makes other women futile - he being a bachelor; Snow says that Hazlitt on the English comic poets is the best dramatic criticism ever written; while

174

McIntyre is prepared to prove the certainty of sin before the world. They are wonderful people.

The dozen fellows I know best are all around sixty years of age, and like all men who live isolated and in the face of perpetual danger, they have really thought about the universe. These twelve, every Friday for thirty-six years have met to read and discuss a book. They argue grimly and you have to know your piece to get by them. They were saddened while I was there by the death of a miner who was found killed by a fall of stone; in his coat was found a translation of Thucydides.

From Ashington, I came back to London to an amusing dinner with Ramsey McDonald.

The Ashington Literary and Debating Society produced some remarkable men of letters, not least the anonymous poet, writing under the *nom-de-plume* OAP, responsible for this very powerful verse:

AN ODE

Oh, Ashington! The name synonymous
With all that's gritty, dirty and unclean,
Did the old sponsors at thy christening
Cremate thee there and then, imagining
Thou wert not worthy of a name at all
And spread thine ashes o'er the plebian place
How then? Thou didst by rise all purified
From out the scathing fire. For came wise men
Who tested, probed thee, to thine utmost parts,
And found the very heart of thee. Thy heart
The which hath lain for aeons undisturbed
Within the bosom of its mother earth,
The Great Creator of the Universe
We know did place it there. The Great 'I Am'
Created Nature's self, and doth provide
Things seen and unseen, for His people's good.
The wise men found it good. From its rich veins
Thou sendest light, and warmth, and mighty power
Throughout the world, on land and on sea.
Now hath arisen miles on miles of streets
Wherein do dwell brave toilers at thy depths,
And who repose on thy pulsating breast,
Thy splendid shops, and thy palatial stores
Speak of vitality, and do uplift
The hearts of all thy brave inhabitants.
Thou once wert insignificant, but now -
Thou art no plebian, Thou, Oh, Ashington!

PITCH 'n' TOSS

Until the introduction of Welfare organisation facilities, there was very little that the pitman and his family could do together. The man, as master of the household, was *never* called upon to do any of the mundane chores associated with housework. Male leisure time was taken up by visiting his club for a gill or two, having a bit crack with his marras, then back home for a fish supper before rolling into bed.

But some men followed the Methodist ethic of temperance, and kept away from the many drinking establishments which were springing up along the Low Market. The more energetic had allotments, and spent most of their spare time tending vegetables, a creeful of pigeons, or perhaps a few hens and pigs.

Saturday afternoons were set aside for following the Colliers, their local team. Few miners had motor transport, so visits to see Newcastle United perform were rare, and Ashington FC was always very well supported when members of the Third Division North.

Many miners gambled away their pocket money playing pitch n' toss. Although it was a game of pure chance, the rituals behind the simple tossing of two pennies in the air were very complex.

Half the men - often a game could atttract over 100 miners - bet on the two pennies which were tossed into the air coming down *heads,* while the others backed *tails.* The man throwing the coins was often chosen for his skillful technique by a wealthy backer. To save the thrower's back, a *'bebber'* was employed to pick the pennies out of the dirt, dust them off, and hand them back to the thrower. The bebber was usually paid a percentage of the winnings at the end of each session.

Hundreds of pounds were wagered in the space of a Sunday morning at one of the usual haunts, the Three Fields, now part of North Seaton Estate. A lookout was always posted to watch for the local bobbies, but they usually turned a blind eye on the entire proceedings.

In 1975, I wrote lyrics for a musical called *'Song of the Coal '* which included a pitch 'n' toss song:

'Heads ye win, tails ye lose,
then ye gan to bed wiv a bellyful of booze'

And that was what happened. After the game had broken up around noon, the gamblers would pour into the nearest club, or perhaps the White Elephant pub, to either celebrate their good fortune or drown their sorrows. Then it was home for the roast beef and yorkshire puddings, and heaven help the poor wife who had let the dinner overcook in the oven.

THE 1926 GENERAL STRIKE

The 1920s loomed dark over Ashington, shrouding the mining community in clouds of depression. As the decade wore on, a world-wide trade recession began to bite into the Coal Company's profits. The mini boom, which had occurred at the end of the 1914-18 war, fizzled out, leaving countries with huge bills to pick up. Very few ships were being built, and manufacturing companies laid off thousands of workers. The demand for steel went down, and with it, inevitably, the need for coal.

Ashington miners, like their brethren nationwide, were forced to take a pay cut. Moderate in viewpoint, most of the pitmen of Northumberland tightened their belts, muttered amongst themselves, and got on with the job. Miners elsewhere were more militant and they had a leader, A J Cook, who was thirsting for a fight. Some, however, looked up at the sky of bleak prospects and saw a silver lining beckoning on the other side of the world.

Many local pitmen emigrated to Australia, Canada, New Zealand and South Africa. They tended not to go as families, but as individual pioneers, taking with them the traditional mining community qualities of thrift and endeavour.

Back home, the pitmen's representatives, The Miners' Federation, urged other trade unions to back the miners by coming out on a General Strike. For nine days Britain was at a virtual standstill. No trains or buses ran; ships were left unloaded, their cargoes rotting at the docks; mail went undelivered. For a while it looked as though the strike might succeed. But the Tory government brought in the Army to get things moving again; high-born ladies and college students began to drive buses and taxis. The miners held firm, but one by one the other workers drifted back into employment, leaving the miners to their own devices.

The General Strike of 1926, called for May 1st, set the pattern for industrial action in the 20th century with the miners at the sharp end of the fray. It was their leader Arthur J Cook who led the rest of the country into the stoppage when the Federation of Mineworkers was in its infancy. Just as it was another Arthur - Scargill - who led the National Union of Mineworkers to a disastrous humiliation in 1984/85.

Managing director of the Ashington Coal Company, Ridley Warham, pleaded with his workers *not* to back the rest of the country's miners, through the medium of the monthly Ashington Colliery Magazine:

APRIL, 1926
The Coal Trade is disorganised owing to the present uncertain position, and we have lost some good orders recently to our foreign competitors. It is clear that a very serious crisis is facing us on May 1st. Our special difficulty on the North East coast is that our usual markets are just those which are most exposed to the competition of foreign coal produced at a very much lower level of wages than in this country. We are in a very desperate position. The alternatives seem to be the acceptance of a minimum rate of wages such as would enable us to carry on, or almost universal unemployment in our coalfield.

Clearly, the threatened stoppage hadn't dampened the spirit of some contributors to the magazine. This joke was printed in the same issue:

It was dole day and Geordie was at the Dole Office for his money. He discovered that he had been paid a day's money short, and asked the clerk to explain.
"Well, Geordie," said the clerk, "did I not see you hawking a load of firewood last Thursday?"
"Firewood be hanged," screamed Geordie, "that waas me fornicha - aa waas shiftin'."

When the strike began, a system of self-help was organised. Allotment holders arrived at workingmen's clubs with barrowloads of cabbages, leeks, onions and peas. Women got to work making soup, and for a couple of hours around mid-day the clubs became makeshift soup kitchens. Corner-end shops, ever reliant on local custom, extended their credit to the pitmen's wives. With so much time on their hands, sporting events such as the Booth Cup Final were attended by thousands. Ladies' football matches, always popular, were used to collect funds. Warham continued to warn the men:

MAY, 1926
Whether we have a stoppage or not this threat of trouble has been enough to drive away our trade. There will be little enough for the Northumberland collieries to do in May and June whatever happens now. In our opinion, we should never have got into this desperate situation if we could have settled our affairs in the friendly atmosphere of Newcastle instead of London.
JUNE, 1926
The first month of the stoppage is nearly over. The damage to the trade by which we live has been enormous. We see our business, so carefully got together by many years of work, scattered to the winds. Our oldest customers are getting used to German and Silesian coal and we shall find it very difficult to get our markets back. The pity is that our workmen must know they are fighting and suffering for an impossibility. It is entirely futile for the Miners' Federation to ignore economic facts. We have offered terms which will not only give us no profit, but will show a definite loss.

Hard times call for drastic action. Men and boys gathered in numbers on the pit heaps of Ashington and Woodhorn. They scrambled up the festering piles of hot ash, scratching away with their bare hands, searching for pieces of coal to light their fires, to keep the family warm.

One wag in the magazine told this story:

Geordie went to the doctors one night to have his eyes examined. The doctor gave him the once over and asked if he had been reading a lot lately.
"Noa, Aa canna say Aa hev," says Geordie.
"Do you know anything that might have strained your eyes?" asked the doctor.
"When ye cum ti speak of it, doctor, Aa've been leukin for coals lately on th' heap," admitted Geordie.

Another joker chipped in with the following verse:

I've heard of 'Busman's Holidays', and seen some funny sights;
a college student swotting during long vacation nights;
a postman on a walking tour; a doctor suffering pain;
an engine driver's holiday spent riding on a train;
but tis the strangest sight of all to see men in the role
of Miners who are out on strike fetching and carrying Coal.

Warham was not amused. As the strike maintained its momentum, he began sniping at the Federation, making out that it was *they* who were to blame for the Ashington miners' problems:

JULY, 1926

We are beginning the third month of this disastrous stoppage of our industry. The wiser heads among the workmen of Northumberland must realise that the bulk of their trade - four fifths of our coal has to find customers abroad - is going or has gone. It will only be possible to recover it by still greater sacrifices. And they now know that the goal for which their Federation is fighting means living on the dole or emigration for half a million miners, among whom 80 per cent of our people in Northumberland. This is what they are fighting for.

Warham was right about mass emigration from the area. My father's family were hit very hard by the stoppage. He worked at Woodhorn Pit with his father and two brothers, Larry and Sid. His mother, four sisters, and a baby brother, made up a family of eight, living frugally without money coming in.

With no signs of a let up to the strike action, the whole family contemplated going to Canada. The men were no strangers to working on the land, and thoughts of getting away from the claustrophobic pit kindled visions of the wide open spaces of Canada. But my grandmother Agnes baulked at the idea of travelling with the youngest son, Denis, a baby of only ten months; she argued that she would be unable to work and look after the baby as well.

It was decided that my father should go alone, see what the prospects were like, then report back. After working in a remote part of Saskatchewan on a sheep farm for almost three years, he wrote to say that Canada, with its bleak winters and spartan conditions, was no easy solution and that he was coming home.

Meanwhile, Warham continued to wring his hands:

AUGUST, 1926

The position, unfortunately, is quite unchanged. Our trade is slipping away from us more and more as the weeks go by and the only result of the stoppage has been to bring prosperity to the Coal trade of other countries. As a County, we have asked the workmen's representatives to meet us to discuss the situation, but they are tied to the Miners' Federation and cannot do so. We shall have to meet sometime. Would it not be better to have a consultation than an inquest?

On September 1st, Winston Churchill, then Chancellor of the Exchequer, joined the debate in the House of Commons: "*We must have an offer from the miners showing a sincere desire to face the realities of the situation by men who are responsible and can deliver the goods.*" For the Liberals, Lloyd George countered with: "*London is a bad place to judge the condition of the mining industry. It is no use putting the thermometer near the radiator.*"

There were now signs that the strike was not one hundred per cent solid; in Durham, 150 miners at Heworth Coal Company signed on for work. The Minister of Mines, Colonel Lane-Fox, reported that 7,600,000 tons of coal had been imported into Great Britain between May and August. A J Cook, the Miners' Federation secretary, was still adamant that his men could win. He coined the phrase: '*Not a penny off the pay, not a minute on the day*', and urged the miners to fight on.

Nearer home, lack of food and adequate sanitation began to take its toll on the innocent victims of any strike: the children. At a Council Meeting held in Ashington on September 2nd, Dr Bruce, Medical Officer, reported:

Smallpox is on the increase. Six of the 22 cases reported come from one family. Five contacts in a family of six have refused vaccination. Because of this, other families are being infected, due to visiting neighbours. I propose that, as precautionary measures, we open a male/female discharge room, bathing accommodation and a hot-water system at the Isolation Hospital at North Seaton, at a cost of £800.

G Bowen, Chairman of the Hospital Committee, argued: *"This hospital is little better than some of the shacks used abroad in times of war."*

Alderman John Craigs, reported that rates were already twenty-one shillings in the pound, and that: *"The Council is not at the end of it yet. With the strike still going on, no rates are being paid by the colliery. I urge that expenditure be postponed."*

Bowen interjected: *"It has always been my object to transfer this hospital from a lethal chamber into a decent institution. At the moment, one out of every seven persons admitted dies."*

"Ah, but," argued Ald Craigs, *"that was during the typhoid fever epidemic."*

While this penny pinching squabble was in progress, Ridley Warham asked his workforce to disregard what was happening nationally in his next address to the Ashington colliers:

SEPTEMBER, 1926

It was made quite clear at the meeting in London on August 19th that no National Settlement of our difficulties was possible. We wonder how long our men in Northumberland will take to see that the dispute can only end by negotiations in the County, and that the longer the stoppage lasts the more difficult will become the conditions with which we have to deal. There can be only one end, because the workmen are not fighting the owners, but are refusing to recognise the hard facts of the situation. The fact that you cannot get more than a pint out of a pint pot will be as true six months hence as it is today.

OCTOBER, 1926

We are still idle. No one can doubt that the way to peace lies, and has always lain, through District Settlements. During the last five years we have had experience enough of National Settlements. They have meant nothing but continual uncertainty and strife, conditions which must ruin our industry and bring inevitable distress to all the people depending upon it. We should put aside old prejudices and consider first and last the efficiency of the concern. And the sooner we get on with it the better for everybody.

William Straker, Northumberland Miners' Secretary, addressed a meeting of local miners on 15th October. A 'Notice of Eviction' had gone out to several families. One man, a father of six, who raised the issue, was told by Straker: *"Ignore this Notice! We will order that victimisation pay be given to any man who is put out of his home."*

But some Ashington families *had* been evicted from their colliery homes in previous strikes. Agnes Mason, then a little girl of eight, remembers with revulsion the sight that met her eyes one afternoon on coming out of school:

I was walking past the Hirst Park - it wasn't a park then, more like a great rubbish tip - and I was amazed when I saw all these tents which had been erected. It was like a tented village. Whole families were living there; clothes were hanging from washing lines; open fires were burning and women cooking meals; children were crying - it was awful.

In the Newcastle Journal on October 16th, a banner headline noted:

230,603 MINERS GO BACK TO WORK

In spite of the stoppage, the Journal reported the same day that for the town's sport it was a case of 'business as usual'. The Ashington FC team to meet Rochdale in Division Three of the Football League was: Elliott, Ferguson, Hamilton, Price, Grieves, Chipperfield, Dalkin, J Turnbull, Johnson, Randall, and Watson.

To keep idle young hands busy, a Boys' Unemployment School was set up in the Hirst Welfare Hut. Its purpose: 'To combat the serious depreciation of character that takes place in boys compelled to spend periods in idleness'. The curriculum included: 'classwork and organised games in the gymnasium'. Some boys made step ladders, stools, and pokers, which they could purchase for the cost of material only. Youths were asked to attend during the hours of 9-12 and 1-4. Free buses were laid on from Bedlington, Blyth, Morpeth, and Newbiggin. Girls were not catered for.

Ridley Warham now sounded exasperated:

NOVEMBER, 1926
After nearly six months of idleness, finding that the leaders of the men refuse to enter into any negotiations with us, either as a county or at our own collieries, we have thought it right to re-open Ashington Colliery, where a large number of workmen signified their willingness to resume work. Unfortunately, the Union does not approve of this action and a large number of those who wished to work have dared not do so. During these six months our competitors have been set on their feet again, while our workers have lost over half a million pounds in wages. We are in a far worse position to pay good wages in the future than we were six months ago, and the longer we go on like this the worse it will be.

DECEMBER, 1926
We write as the arrangements for a ballot on the terms accepted by the County Executive are being made and we have every hope that the result of the voting will be a general acceptance. In that case we shall have re-started before this is printed and this long and disastrous stoppage will be over. The losses to both owners and workmen are appalling and will be felt for a long time to come. If we both do our job properly, we shall get back to prosperity once more. If we don't, we shall not only bring ourselves down to ruin, but drag down our country with us.

Reluctantly, the miners returned to work. The long and bitter layoff had won them nothing. Settlement Terms released on November 29th showed how much they had lost:
1 an increase in shift from 7 to 8 hours;
2 surface men increased 2 hours;
3 substinence wage reduced from 7s. 7d. to 6s. 9d.
4 a 20% reduction in the percentage addition to basic rate of pay;
5 abolition of the National Wages Board (Miners' negotiating body)

The town reeled with the after effects of the strike. On February, 26th, 1927, J J Hall, Chairman of Governor's at Ashington Hospital, reported:

The Hospital has suffered a very severe set-back this year owing to the industrial crisis through which we have passed. The building programme, which it was hoped would have been by this time commenced, has unfortunately had to be postponed indefinitely. It was hoped that at least some of the extensions would have been carried out. These hopes have been shattered and the work must be held up pending some change for the better in the matter of finance.

The hospital then was funded mostly by a levy of one penny from each miner's pay packet, and if the pits were idle that source of income disappeared. The annual subscriptions from workmen's levies for 1926 came to £2,145 - a drop of almost £2,000 on the previous year.

Private subscriptions for 1926 amounted to a little over one hundred pounds. These included:

G Arrowsmith, 1 Woodhorn Road	£1. 1s. 0d.
F L Booth, The Hawthorns	£1. 1s. 0d.
J Chrisp, 80 Station Road	£0. 10s.6d.
B Creigh, Station Road	£1. 1s. 0d.
J Craigs, Station Villas	£1. 1s. 0d
Donkin, 4 West View	£1. 1s. 0d.
Dr Spence, 126 Woodhorn Road	£1. 1s. 0d.
M Wilkinson, High Market	£0.10s. 0d.

Staff at the Hospital in 1926 consisted of Frank Gairdner, Superintendent Surgeon; house surgeons David Campbell and James Durie; matron, Miss Jean Richardson; sisters M Dixon, L Vint, M Wilson, P Richards; in the orthopaedic department Miss C Maudsley and Miss B Swanson; and nine probation nurses. Gairdner, in his annual report, observed:

The work of the Hospital is hampered for want of room. The Out-patient Department is specially crowded. A new X-ray unit is an urgent want. Our inability to house nursing staff is also a constant difficulty. Extensions are necessary in order to attain the standard which I know the public wants.

The average daily number of in-patients in 1926 was 30.9, which gave a yearly cost per bed of £156. 15s. 11d. One thousand and sixty three in-patients passed through the hospital that year with an average stay of ten days, at a cost of £4.11s 2d each. Operations for tonsils and adenoids (103) topped the 1926 league table with 'Diseases Peculiar to Women' coming a close second. Least successful of the operations was for 'Abdominal Conditions' when, out of 21 operations, five people died. Eighty miners were admitted 'for conditions caused by accidents at work'.

Repercussions of the 26-week stoppage were still being felt two years later. In line with County policy, Ashington Coal Company fixed a minimum price for their coal and adopted the policy of *stopping* the pits rather than accept anything less. The Duke Pit was closed for a time. This had the short-term effect of preventing a further fall in revenue, but it caused vast unemployment in the town. Families began to emigrate in droves.

"*It is a disastrous state of affairs for all of us,*" said Ridley Warham, on July 28th, 1928.

My mother's brother, Jack Talbot, married with four sons, emigrated to Australia; her sister, Nellie, single and only nineteen, went unaccompanied to New Zealand. Neither returned. Next it was the turn of my mother's brother, Dick, to try his luck in Canada. With many others, he was recruited to assist in harvesting the country's vast wheatfields. He recalls:

I had every intention of staying for good. Things were cramped at home - there were still eight of us, including two of my brother Jack's sons who didn't emigrate straight away. I looked on it as a kind of adventure. But I changed my mind when we were put on a train after the ship docked. It was one of these trains with open-sided carriages, and we sat on long wooden benches looking outwards at all this grass for as far as the eye could see. It was when we passed through little stations and these Canadian fellas started pelting us with rocks and yelling 'Scabs' that I realised that we had been taken on as strike-breakers, cos they were involved in a dispute as well.

I came back and got started at Woodhorn pit. During one holiday I went with four others to pick tatties on a farm in Kent. There were a lot of students there as well, and they were amazed that we wanted to work during our holidays. I told one of them that to get out into the fresh air was a holiday in itself.

Old bell pit. c.1800.

Pony and driver. c.1930.

Ashington screens. 1924.

Fillers in 3ft seam. c.1930.

Duke of York at Ashington Colliery with Coal Company officials. 1928.

Voice: "Is thor anybody in there?"'
Geordie (in flooded place) : "Aye,
Robinson Crusoe. Send in ma parrot."

Duke Pit Plessey seam, 1970.

Ashington pit trainees. 1940.

Trainees in underground stable. c. 1940.

Jack Charlton (centre back) with 1951 pit trainees.

Power loader, Woodhorn. 1980.

March back after strike. 1985.

Bedlington Miner's Picnic, 1982.

Ashington Colliery's last shift after 130 years, 25th March 1988.

Cast of 'Song of Coal'.
From left to right: Dave Loveday (hidden); John Wilson; Jared Johnson; Ted Liddy; Jim Askell.

A PUBLIC SCHOOLBOY'S VIEW

Ashington Colliery continued to attract great attention. In 1936 it was the turn of a group of public schoolboys from 'down south' to visit the pit and see first-hand just how the coal was won. One of the young lads, Peter Mennell, obviously impressed by what he saw, penned the following article for the Colliery Magazine:

You must be quite used to parties of strangers intruding into your mine, but you may remember not so long ago a party of seven boys, in the usual caps and white overalls, who were not the normal intelligents. You noticed the expressions on their faces: "Where shall we go? What shall we do next?" They noticed the look on yours: "Poor fools, why on earth should they want to come down here? They'll know better when they come up again."

Perhaps it is difficult for you who live in and know those strange surroundings to understand the answer to that "why?" But here it is. To the outsider there is something strangely fascinating in those two huge wheels which turn and stop, then jerk and turn again; in these cages which go down with empty trucks and come up with them laden with coal; in these cages which drop and rise with you on either side. Where do they come from? Where do they go to? These are questions which must be answered, and somehow a book on mining, or the manager's description, will not do. Even photographs will not satisfy, but only increase curiosity to know. "Does it really look like that?" although the camera is reputed never to lie.

To anyone who has ever sat by a fire in the evening, to anyone who has watched the lines of coal trucks trundling down a railway, to anyone who has watched tramp steamers passing up and down the seas with their cargoes of coal, to anyone who has any imagination, who has seen these things and then finds himself in a world of slagheap mountains, there is only one way of answering his questions and realising his images, and that is to go down into the mine. That is why "they'll know better when they come up."

And so they did. Far better. But not with any regret. They knew of the endless conveyor lines; they knew of the cool air entering and the hot air coming out; they knew of the conveyor bands and of the strange machine for cutting coal. They had heard the distant roar of an approaching convoy of trucks; they had heard it grow louder till it burst on them and the trucks came rattling and swaying past them. They had seen the lights of other men shining beyond a dark unlighted passage, and heard the voices, solitary, distant and clear. They had waited in suspense for the loud explosion of charge, then had been surprised by the dull thud which came. They had watched the clouds of dust and smelt the strong odour of cordite. They had stumbled through miles of passages not half as tall as they were, tramped in pools, bumped their backs and their heads, and tripped over rails. They had smelt the warm smell of the stables, and seen the ponies of which they had heard so much. They knew how coal became what they knew as coal, and knew what you were when they heard of miners.

And now when they watch their fires, or the dirty colliers, or the railway trucks, they know how, where and why it all is. As you have always been able to imagine how the coal is worked after you use it, so now they, when they use it, are able to imagine how you work it.

THE MINES FIRE & RESCUE BRIGADE

BOB MOORE, now a very active septegenarian, remembers his days spent in the service with the Durham and Northumberland Collieries Fire & Rescue Brigade, based at Ashington:

I had been a coal putter first of all with a pit pony when the chance came up to join the Brigade. In those days the headquarters were under Ashington Council Chambers, and it was split into four flats. There was a kitchen on the premises, and three of us who were single men used to live there. We were the only Fire Brigade for miles around, and other councils had to pay the coal-owners a yearly fee for us to cover their area.

The equipment we used was right up to date. We used a 600 gallon per minute fire engine, a rescue tender with liquid air bottles, and 20 hp Bedford van. Fourteen men made up the Ashington force under Supt. J Worswick.

I left to go to war on Motor Torpedo Boats. Not long after I had come back to the Brigade when the war finished, we were involved in a major disaster in the William Pit at Whitehaven in August 1947. Me and three others, Joe Otterwell, Albert Robbins and Frank Ramsey, were on duty when word came through that a gas explosion had rocked the Cumbrian pit. Although they weren't part of our district, the calamity was such that they wanted every available rescue team to go there.

Roads were bad in those days and the journey took four hours in the Bedford van. When we arrived we found that about fifty rescue men were involved in two-hour shifts trying to get some kind of ventilation into a pit that was registering 9.6 of methane - way above the safety limit. Two hours was the limit of our oxygen masks. It was a little pit village and practically everyone had someone who was down below. Thirty-six hours after the accident there was still a crowd of people at the colliery gates waiting for news.

When we got down down the pit it was obvious that the explosion, which had occurred some two miles inbye, had propogated: that means a gas explosion at the coal face had picked up the coal dust all the way out to the shaft causing massive falls of stone. A young lad's body lay at the shaft bottom; he had been picked up by the blast and his head had been dadded against the rock. Only three men out of 108 survived. One of them was an old hand who had been involved in an explosion before. He told the other two to sit tight in an old working and not come out again for 24 hours. I hadn't time to be frightened myself, that came afterwards when I sat down to think about it.

THE COAL LEADERS

FORSTER PROUDLOCK was born in Coronation Street, Newbiggin in 1905. The only boy with four sisters, he later moved to Chestnut Street, then called Clyde Street, and attended the South School until he was thirteen. He said:

My first job was as an errand boy for Worthington Milburn, a grocery shop in the Hirst. I earned about half a dollar (12p) in wages. I was always keen on motors and driving, and my first licence was to drive a motor bike. Then my mother bought a van with a soft top which could be converted into a car, and we started to hawk fish. She would be waiting when the cobles came on to the sand at Newbiggin and she would buy the fish and then go hawking it around all over the place, but mostly in the Rothbury area, Powburn, Glanton and suchlike. You see, there were already people with fish rounds in the Ashington area, so mother had this idea about going further afield.

I taught myself how to drive the van, but I wasn't all that clever at going down through the gears - I could go up champion! One day I got onto this bank, couldn't get the gears right and fettled the rear axle. I had to leave it to get help, but when we came back someone had pinched the engine.

Ernie Smith at Stakeford ran a bus sevice, and he asked me if I would like to drive one of his coaches - Ashington to Lynemouth - in direct competition to the United Bus Company. That would be in the 1920s, I used to work seven days a week, morning till night, but one day I finished at four o'clock, and that was my day off! There were a few buses on the road then: Jack Scott of Ellington and a fella called Armstrong, Bob Britain and Jimmy Gordon of Stakeford had the County Motor Services, and of course there was the United. I was getting about two pounds five shillings in wages by then.

It was then I moved to the Ashington Coal Company when George Proctor was Transport Manager. I told my wife, Dora, that we would be better off, not financially cos I only got six shillings and ninepence halfpenny a shift, but we would get our coals free which was quite a big help. And I had an allowance of four shillings and sevenpence for rent. I already had a licence to drive any kind of bus, single or double deckers, but I got my HGV when I started the Coal Company, that would be just before the second war. My first wagon was a Ford V8 with five compartments carrying 13 hundred weights of coal. You used to have a second man who would jump out of the wagon and pull the chain to release the coal outside the folks' coalhouses. The hoyers-in then were Jack Harris, often referred to as Jack the Coalman, Jimmy Hume who had this massive carbuncle on his head, and later there was Johnny and Joe Green.

When the war broke out a few of the drivers who had been in the Territorials were called up. Wilfy Kirkup was captured straight away and spent the duration in a German POW camp. Charlie Spare went into the army. Other drivers then were Joe Foster, Joe Hays and Arthur Taylor, Tommy Tinkler was a second man and so was Larry Bell who formed the Boys Club behind the Regal cinema. Larry later became chargeman at the Duke Street Depot, where they led the coals from. After he left in the sixites, Ronnie Henderson then Geordie Charlton got the job. Coal hadn't always been led from Duke Street. Way back when the coals were delivered by horse they had a depot in the Sixth Row and one behind the Central Hall. Coal was loaded into four bogeys and transported on a two-foot railway gauge into the back streets. Jimmy Little was on the wagons and he became the first manager at Duke Street, he had a house right outside the depot in the Tenth Row. He was followed by Billy Mason who had the dance band with his brothers. During the second war I was given authorisation from the manager at Ashington Colliery to dump all of the pit's explosive powder in the river at Sheepwash; this was to be done at the first sign of invasion by the Germans.

Private hauliers began delivering coal in bags in the 1950s to the houses where you couldn't drop coals outside. First bagged delivery contractor was Jimmy Dungait who had a farm where the United Bus terminus is now. He had six wagons and a great set of hard-working lads like Andy Casson, Ronnie Scott, and the Turnbull brothers. When Dave Moody of Choppington took over the round the drivers just transferred to him. Dave got started through having a mechanical shovel which he hired out at Lynemouth. He later had a fleet of lorries. Other local coalmen then were Geordie and Jack Nichol, followed by Eric; and then Ken Parker.

ARTHUR TAYLOR was born in 1909 in Greenside, County Durham. His father, Jack, was head horsekeeper at Wardley Colliery until moving to this district in 1925. Jack had come to work at Ellington Pit, but, because there was no accommodation ready, the family was housed for a time in the crudely-named Cement Row, Widdrington. Young Arthur had worked on the screens at Wardley, but went straight down the pit at Ellington as a coal putter. He recalls:

I had only been putting for a short time when the foreman drainer, Joe Mitchell, asked my father if I would like to be a 'second man' on one of the coal wagons. Of course I was very keen to get out of the pit, and was delighted to begin with the wagons. A man called Jack Carr taught me how to drive a truck. Later, I had Tommy Tinkler as a second man. Tommy had come from the timber yard. He stayed with the wagons for some time before working in the depot at Woodhorn, and in 1960 he moved to the Duke Street Coal Depot, in charge of the loose coal deliveries to the workers and veterans in colliery and council houses.

There were fourteen Fodens on the road in the 1930s and '40s: dark blue, sit-up-and-beg motors, each individually numbered. At that time, 'Tink' was inexperienced, and tells of how he was the only driver ever to drive a coal wagon using 'L' plates, which was within the regulations so long as the total weight was less than three tons.

It was Jim Maxwell's task to take all the joiners, builders and plumbers out in the morning and drop them at their various jobs, sometimes to Bog Hall farm, Blakemoor or Broomhill. They were transported in an ordinary Foden with the inside boards extracted and a tarpaulin draped over the top as sparse protection against the prevailing north-east winds. For the rest of the shift, Jim hauled material, often from the limeyard or colliery stores. Some of the wagons were unsteady when the back was raised for tipping coal, hence the 'sit-up-and-beg' nickname. Each driver learnt the little eccentricities of individual drops, and Jim remembers always leaving a house with a particularly vicious dog until the very last drop so that he could release the pin at the previous coal house and make a quick getaway.

Arthur Taylor progressed to driving dumpers. He later went back down the pit at Woodhorn as a haulage worker until Stanley Hall, the undermanager, asked him if he fancied a job as assistant horsekeeper under Mr Sixsmith. Arthur had always enjoyed working with ponies, like his father, so he readily agreed. There were two stables down Woodhorn Colliery then, each housing about fifty ponies. Arthur surfaced again with his old job as dumper driver. But Jack Thompson, Traffic Manager, asked him to go on the Dragline, which was an entirely new piece of machinery - a huge gaping-mouthed excavator, used for winning new drifts. Arthur explained:

I became quite proficient with this machine and became an Area Driver, digging out at all the new drifts which were being opened out in the 1950s. I started Stobswood Drift, Coneygarth, and the new Bothal Drift which was actually in the Ashington Colliery yard. The gaffers used to come around, and I had to give exhibitions of how the machine worked.

In 1966 Arthur was working with a humble caterpillar bulldozer when he was asked to take over the prestigious position of personal chauffeur to J J Hall, the Agent, who lived at Longhirst. He agreed, put on his best suit, and drove the silky smooth limousine until retiring in 1972.

ARTHUR LANCELOT BELL, youngest of a family of ten, was born in 1899 and died in 1986. His father was known as Durham Jack, coming from the village of Evenwood. He was called that because of a profusion of Bells living in the town. The main reason Jack had come to Ashington was to organise one of the bands - he arranged his own music, and played eight instruments, but refused to play drums, saying: "Any stupid beggar can beat a drum." Arthur left the Bothal School when he was thirteen and began work on Ashington Screens. The family then lived at number 10 Chestnut Street. In those days he called himself Lance, but his workmates began to call him 'Larry', and it was as 'Larry Bell' that he became known throughout Ashington.

One day Larry saw a steam traction engine being brought into the colliery yard, immediately fell in love with it, and asked for a job on the 'Engines'. He was told to go to Woodhorn and help 'feed' a portable engine which was being used to drive a sawmill. When he was sixteen he progressed to 'Steersman' on a road traction engine and a year later was driving a Foden engine and a 'Showman's' engine. This latter was such a brute in size that the vibration from it caused gas mantles to fall from the premises in Station Road whenever it rumbled down the main street. Always mad keen to drive a 'proper' motor, Larry begged Hughie Naismith to let him have a go in Mr J J Hall's converted car which was known as a 'Ford Flat'. He was taken down to Woodhorn where he jumped into the cab and drove back to Ashington - he was now considered competent to drive.

Larry drove the first colliery model T Ford, and was one of the earliest of the motorised coal-leaders in the area. On one Hospital Carnival Day in the 1920s, his wagon was used as a float by the Women's Temperance League. But the wagon's message condemning alchohol failed to amuse the judge, Sylvester Strong, the landlord of the Portland Hotel, who awarded the prize to someone else. According to Larry's daughter, Jean, it was just after the second war started that Larry began Ashington's first Boys Club:

At first it was called the 'Ashington Athletic Boys Club', and in the beginning it was run from our back yard. A couple of lads, Alan Robson and Jimmy Graham, came to our house at 17 Park View, and said they were interested in boxing. Dad got hold of an old kit bag, filled it full of sand, and suspended it from his garage roof: that was our first punch bag.
Soon we were run off our feet with about 300 youngsters turning up every night of the week. We were cramped for space so the Middle Market Club gave us free use of a hut which stood at the back, and became our canteen. There was a billiard table in there and dart board, as well as the canteen. A retired Co-op tailor called John Clark came to stay with us, and when it was decided to re-name the Club, 'Larry Bell's Boys Club', he went out and bought a huge red Russian flag, cut off the hammer and sickle, and printed LBBC in large gold letters on the flag. We used to run it up on a flagpole for special occasions.
As well as boxing, the Club had Jimmy Randle - a well-known soccer player - running three football teams at one time in various leagues: the Swifts, Rovers, Rangers, and the youngest lads were known as the Midgets.

Dad could never play football at all, but he was grand at blowing up the old-type leather balls. Jackie Milburn came in one day and asked Dad if he would blow up a couple of balls for him, which he did. Some time later, Jackie came back carrying a brown paper bag. He stood it behind the door, and left without saying a word. And do you know what was in the bag? A beautiful leather football which Jackie had had autographed by all the celebrities he had come into contact with; there was Wilfred Pickles, Violet Carson, Arthur Askey, as well as the well-known footballers. The ball was raffled later for Club funds and was won by Tommy Dawson. I heard later that Peter Grenfell, now an undertaker, used it for kicking around the backstreets as a laddie.

When the Coal Depot moved to Duke Street in 1934, father was the first chargeman there; Jimmy Little was in the office then. Dad always liked Shilbottle best coal, and used to say to my mother: "Bella, I would love to have a load of them coals," but, of course, the best coal was just for the gaffers, so the nearest he got to a load was when he filled his haversack up and brought it home; our fireback was burnt brown from the heat.

ASHINGTON'S BEVIN BOYS

In December 1943, because of an acute shortage of coal, the coalition government, led by Winston Churchill, decided to hold a secret ballot among young men who had enlisted in the armed forces. The men whose names were drawn out were to be conscripted into the mines. The term 'Bevin Boys' was born, and the 30,000 draftees included among them such household names as Brian Rix and Jimmy Savile.

Locally, such men were looked upon as suspiciously as one would view a pair of new pit boots - not quite sure if they would fit straight away, but to be given the chance, anyway. They were named after the man whose brainchild it was, Ernest Bevin, a Labour politician, who as Minister of Labour, formed part of the coalition government under whom mining was a 'reserved occupation' which meant that although miners didn't need to go to war, unsuspecting young men working in non-reserved jobs were liable to be sent down the pits.

One such lad was Ron Keene, born in 1925 and brought up in the Hendon area of London. His parents were working class and lived in a council house. After passing his scholarship, Ron went on to grammar school which he left in 1942 to take up a position with the Inland Revenue at Wembley, as a clerical officer. Like any other patriotic chap at the time, he registered for military service on the day of his 18th birthday. Having passed his medical A1 he was interviewed and accepted into the Royal Navy for training as a wireless telegraphist. But to his horror he was subsequently notified that, under the special conditions applying to the Conscription for Work in the Mines Act, he had been selected from the first ballot of names. After being prepared for the worst in the Navy, Ron was shocked into disbelief when he thought of what might await him down a dark hole somewhere north of Watford.

There was an Appeals procedure which the frantic Ron immediately applied for. He had a second medical, appeared before a tribunal, and told them of his application for the Navy. His plea counted for nothing. The Mines Conscription Act and Ernie Bevin carried far more weight than any Navy contract.

Ron explained his frustration:

Most prospective conscripts were appealing and clogging up the system. I attended a local labour exchange one Saturday afternoon, and found long queues of reluctant miners. Yet we had to sign on the spot for travel warrants, and were given instructions to meet at Kings Cross railway station the following week.

On May 8th, 1944, Ron and about a dozen other young Cockneys were met by a Ministry of Labour official and put on the train bound for Newcastle. He bunked down with a lad from Walthamstow in lodgings on the Blakelaw Estate at Cowgate. He was made very welcome, and to his surprise found conditions similar to those back home. Each day a bus called for the two lads and took them to the old Lamb Pit at Cramlington. The month's training was very basic, consisting of shovelling duff into rail trucks destined for one of the power stations. Underground experience consisted of two trips to the shaft bottom. These were followed by afternoon lectures which failed to introduce the raw recruits to anything like the deprivations and dangers of a realistic pit life. The main theme, according to Ron, was one of fitness:

Getting us fit was in the hands of two drill sergeants, one army, one RAF. PT took place in the Drill Hall at Seaton Delaval and on the local soccer ground. Games consisted of 50-a-side football matches which were always popular. Like all military men, our instructors were fond of route marches, and neighbours must have wondered about the funny-talking young fellas, wearing pit helmets painted with names of girl friends. We were fit, even if our pit knowledge was minimal. The losses during and just after our training were very high. Men simply disappeared, sometimes returning for another bout of training. It was all down to lack of discipline and the absence of sanctions. It served to reinforce the general lack of interest and purpose, surely the pre-requisite to any training programme.

After a month's training we were allocated to working collieries. Three of us were billeted in Melton Terrace, New Hartley, and went to work in Hartley Main Colliery. We had two weeks on bank, unloading pit props and sorting stone from coal on the screens. My first experience of underground working came in foreshift in June, 1944, on haulage work. I worked at the shaft bottom with Jackie Hunter who, with incredible skill, could slow fast-moving sets of tubs with the well-aimed throw of an iron dreg. I was also impressed by the high level of skills required to maintain the haulage system which was constantly breaking down due to the effects of excess water. And all the time in the background I was aware of the terrible history associated with the Hartley Pit disaster.

I never saw the coal face as it was so far inbye; face workers were taken down a separate drift entrance. The environment was wet and roadways low roofed, but worst of all were the frequent changes of shift.

My landlady, Mrs Barnes, a women in her sixties, served up excellent food, but the conditions and facilities differed greatly from those we found at Cowgate. Here, we only had one external water tap shared by six houses. All water was brought in by pail to be heated in the boiler at the side of the coal-burning stove. There was no electricity - all lighting was by gas. Outside toilets were next to the wash-house across the back street. Washing in a tin bath placed in front of the fire was an embarrassing affair. I once sat for an hour while the landlady chatted with neighbours before starting my bath. Our southern susceptibilities were pandered to on special occasions when we were able to take the bath into the front room which gave a little privacy. I think the washing arrangements were the most difficult aspect of my time in Hartley.

My landord was a great character who kept the nightshift, never washed his back, and constantly puffed at an old clay pipe. He made sure we enjoyed ourselves, organising visits to the British Legion and the Newsham club. Before my call-up I had played for Hendon FC, and he it was who put me in touch with a local football team at Shankhouse. I signed for them in the 1944/45 season, and this widened my contacts, giving me a chance to travel around the district. One of the team was Jackie Clough who later played centre half for Ashington and Blyth Spartans, and Newcastle United winger, Tommy Walker, guested for us on occasion.

But the landlady could barely cope with two lodgers, and we were told to transfer to the Miners Hostel in Ashington.

The Miners Hostel was situated at the rear of the Central Hall, catering specifically for Bevin Boys, miners with no accommodation, and open-cast workers. There were a number of facilities laid on for the men, which made the Hostel very attractive. Many others used lodging houses in the town.

Facilities at the Hostel included: a canteen and buffet; laundry; showers and bathrooms; reading and writing room; a dozen Nissen huts with sleeping accommodation (up to 12 men in each), personal lockers and drying facilities for pit clothes. There was even a small area of open space which often accommodated a friendly game of cricket. The mixture of occupations among the men was tremendous. In Ron's time there were opticians, accountants, civil servants, shipyard workers, barrow boys and stall-holders from Petticoat Lane, labourers, musicians, and ex-Royal Navy personnel. Accents varied enormously, with some of the men coming from Glasgow, Greenock, Hawick, Cumberland, Gateshead, Durham, Ireland, and even India.

Ron Keene was allocated to work at Linton Colliery. He recalls:

Linton was ultra-modern compared to Hartley; and the Hostel facilities in terms of baths, electricity and open space, superior to Melton Terrace. I also had other contacts and I was still travelling to Shankhouse as a member of their football team. The town of Ashington pleasantly surprised me with its facilities for shopping, entertainment and sport. The transport was good with road and rail connections to anywhere in the county. The surrounding countryside was pleasant, and Newbiggin was an easy walk away in the summer. For recreation we went dancing, swimming, dog racing, or perhaps to the Central Hall for an organ recital or band concert, and there was always the five cinemas to choose from. After a Saturday evening at the pictures, the Nissen-hut group would relax, discuss and recount in detail the afternoon's soccer games - one of the locals would invariably have visited Roker Park.

The Hostel members even organised their own soccer team for the 1945/46 season, playing as 'Bevin United' in the Ashington Welfare League. A group of us helped out with a lot of the secretarial work, organising grounds etc. Members tended to congregate in small groups, but generally, the whole community got on well together. In our hut we always had at least three local men and the atmosphere was always friendly. One of our men, an optician from North London, was a budding financier. He soon spotted the opportunities offered by the Co-op dividend of 2s 6d in the pound. He was the only one I knew with a Co-op Account, and he encouraged everyone to use his number for any purchases we made. No errand was too small for him, but the Co-op drew the line when he attempted to draw our entire cigarette rations and put them on his account.

At Linton Colliery we were in contact with both transport and face workers. I felt that the systems of pay, designed to reward the fillers at the face and coal-drawers at the shaft, rather unfairly squeezed the haulage workers in between. Pressure was always on the shifter to keep the tubs flowing and the conveyors working. However, the spirit was good and a healthy competition existed between shifts. I often wished in my subsequent work experience that one could have developed such good team spirit stemming from interest in the work situation.

I played football for a very successful Linton side in the 1946/47 season. It took me out of the Hostel from Saturday lunchtime onwards. That Linton team included: Tommy Rigg, Sugar Mordue, Bob English, Stevenson, Mac McHale (another Bevin Boy), Tom English, Bobby McGee, George Donnison, Josh Gray, and Tom McLain who later played for Sunderland. If the match was at home, I was invited by John and Pat Hume into their home to change and get ready. After the game there was always a hot bath and a huge meal laid on. The kindness was almost embarrassing. Many of us BBs visited local homes where there was a shared interest. One in particular, with a great interest in music often visited a friend for gramophone sessions.

After the war finished, many who were covered by the same demobilisation rules as the army, left as soon as they were able. A few returned, and at least one married locally. I left, like most of them, I suppose, because I had never conceived of any other action. I am sure that this applied to our employers, too. My family ties were in London, together with career opportunities. Perhaps I didn't appreciate what the growing coal industry had to offer. I had been studying by correspondence course for the Civil Service examination while at the Hostel, and had sat one of the exams at Newcastle. In the event, I never took the position on offer.

I was destined to end up back in the coal industry until 1956; first in the Headquarters Planning Office, then as an Assistant at Coal Industry Social Welfare Organisation H/Q, and finally as Social Welfare Officer in the Kent coalfield. But I married an Ashington girl, Joyce Jobling, and never lost contact with the town and its developments.

PITS NATIONALISED

When the coal industry was taken over by the National Coal Board on January 1st, 1947, the Ashington Advertiser editorial sounded a cautionary note:

There is need at this moment of change to take stock, need for a sober estimate of future prospects, and the first essential is to avoid expectations of miracles. The machinery of public ownership will have to face the same sort of human and mechanical problems as their predecessors had to face, and neither consumers nor workers should be tempted into making early judgements.
Nationalisation in the first week, the first month, the first year, may not fill up our empty coalhouses, or give industry all the coal it needs. Nor will it provide mineworkers with an era of ease, of bacon and eggs for breakfast in bed.

But all was optimism at Ashington Colliery on New Year's Day when a 30-second triumphal blast on the pit buzzer signalled the unfurling in the colliery yard of the brand-new blue and white flag of the NCB. It replaced the previous banner which had served for 40 years with its bold text and vivid tableaux making a demand for nationalisation. Miners marched into the pit yard behind the Lynemouth Colliery Band to a ceremony to mark the transfer of the mines to public ownership. Mr J Elliott, president of the Ashington Miners Federation, was in the chair, and local arrangements were in the hands of Cllr Frank Millican.

Fourteen-year-old William (Buck) Ferguson and 70-year-old Thomas Nicholson were chosen to represent youth and maturity. Thomas had served for 58 years and worked in every pit in the group, while Buck, who began as a driver of a horse and cart when he left the East School, had just completed a seven week stint on the screens before going underground.

Nationalisation, said many wise tongues, was long overdue, and that placing the coal mines in the hands of the miners themselves, was a victory as tremendous and as worthy of celebration as VE Day. In 1942, Will Lawther, then President of the Miners Federation, had no doubts as to which way the industry should be heading when he wrote:

Nationalisation would win the complete confidence of the miners and their families. Generations of suspicion and hatred would be wiped out, and an entirely new attitude developed towards the coal industry. How can you run an industry efficiently, and get the best out of it, if every miner loathes his industry because of its owners; if every miner's wife swears "her boy will not go down the pit"; if in every miner's home the pit is looked upon as an accursed thing?

Yet, when it came, what did the Nationalisation Act really achieve? According to Sir John Hall, brought up in Railway Row, North Seaton, it gained the men nothing:

The men didn't have the managers to put in charge, so they couldn't take over. They sacked the Ashington Coal Company one day, and gave them their jobs back the next. And what had it won the men? Absolutely nothing!

Former Ashington Colliery manager, George Hetherington, takes a different stance:

Nationalisation was looked upon by most Northumbrian miners as being a victory over tyrannical owners. The Miners Union's influence in the corridors of power grew rapidly, unpopular owner figures disappeared from the scene and were replaced by men such as James Bowman, an ex-Ashington face worker, who had moved through the ranks to become General Secretary of the Northumberland Miners' Federation in 1938, and later Chairman of the National Coal Board itself.

Government intervention began to be noticed all around Ashington. The Furnished Rent Tribunal was set up to adjudicate on complaints regarding room rent charges; a Reinstatement Committee acted as arbitor on disputes between employers and employees arising from the restoration of jobs to ex-Servicemen and women; and the Local Fuel Overseer set fixed prices on the sale of sea coal. Petty bureaucracy immediately set in at the collieries. The Ashington Advertiser of February 1947, reported:

A girl clerk at a local colliery, needing urgently a supply of official forms, was recently involved in nine telephone calls to departments in Newcastle, only to be finally referred back to the department she had first contacted.
For Press purposes, the Coal Board have carefully classified subjects and allocated them to various Divisional Officers in Newcastle. Instructions have gone out to local collieries that this arrangement is now functioning, with the result that everyone is gleefully denying responsibility for answering even the most simple question of fact.

One boon which did arrive in Ashington, courtesy of the newly-formed National Union of Mineworkers, was the inauguration of the five-day week and the granting of a full week's annual holiday. Prior to this, the pits had worked on Saturdays, initially for a full day, then, later, till noon.

The five-day week had a profound effect on the miner and his family. Pre-war, mining communities had accepted a degree of isolation. Working on a Saturday, even till mid-day, meant that getting away for the weekend was almost impossible. Activities tended to be confined to their own localities. Miners stayed at home most of the time, earning for themselves a reputation for solidarity, while still being an easy prey for the vices of narrow parochialism.

But radical changes were on the way. The family suddenly had far more mobility. A Saturday afternoon excursion to Newbiggin or Whitley Bay was no longer the limit of their scope for entertainment. They determined to make full use of their new freedom. The Whitsuntide break of 1947 heralded a mass exodus from the town. This was seen as being so big a threat to a horse and pony racing event due to be held at Peoples Park in May, that the fixture, which was to benefit the Northumberland Miners' Homes, was duly cancelled. Immediate effects were felt by the home town's football team, as gates slumped to around 2,000. One reporter said:

Ashington, while high wages prevail, may become a town of week-enders. The bonds of community life may be loosened, and group activity broken up by counter attractions.

By the time the pit holidays of 1949 had come round, a pattern of movement by residents during the miners' one-week holiday was taking shape. Special trains, carrying thousands of people, were leaving Ashington from early Friday morning until Saturday evenings to spend their holidays in places of their choice. By far the greater number headed for Billy Butlin's fun-type holiday camps, with Filey on the Yorkshire coast being the favourite. Two special trains en route to Filey left Ashington Station before eight o'clock on Friday morning.

The more adventurous headed for Scotland, Ireland, Wales and even the Continent. One group, members of Ashington Motor Cycle Club, some with wives and girl friends perched precariously behind them, left the Grand Corner on a round trip of 3,000 miles which would see them motor as far as Switzerland. Club leader, Mr S Mordue, was given a *grand* send off by their President, Dr Andrew Irvine. A party of Sea Cadets travelled to a Fleet Air Arm base at Warrington to indulge in sea and air training. Seventy locals, many of them Catholics, left Ashington Station for Stranraer, next stop Ireland.

Banks in the town were said to have paid out a collossal £30,000 to fund the miners' families on their seven-day jaunt. But many people stayed behind, and United Buses reported a brisk trade on the popular routes to Newbiggin, Whitley Bay, and Newcastle's Town Moor for the *shows*. Many Ashingtonians were spotted returning home from the Hoppings laden down with tea sets, cigarettes, and even watches, which had been won on what was then called the 'Housey Housey' stalls. As the last bus (10.50 pm) headed back from Newcastle, many people thought that they would be stranded and made a mad dash for Newcastle's Manor Station where the last train for Ashington left around midnight. On the Monday it was back to work in the dreaded foreshift (1 am till 9 am) contemplating another 364 days of mindless drudgery, with the one bright sparkling thought of *next* year's holiday to light the way inbye.

My schooldays ended the day before Good Friday in April, 1949 and I started work at Ashington Colliery on the Tuesday after Easter Monday. It was my mother who had informed me that I was to go down the pit. I didn't argue; there were no histrionics; I believed that *all* Ashington lads went down below.

Nothing can prepare a 15-year-old boy for the first dreaded step inside the pit cage; or the sudden drop into the shaft as the *keps* are pulled away; or the long silent flight, down, down, ever deeper. And all the while, invisible dust clings to eyelashes, and clogs the nostrils with the foul smell of an underground tomb. After the initial headlong plunge, the descent eases until the cage settles with a gentle bump at the shaft bottom. Then the first tentative stride into the pit itself. A small step forward for a boy - a giant step *backwards* for mankind.

The Bothal shaft bottom was unexpected. It was high, over 20 feet, breezy from the rush of air, and electrically lit. Tubs of coal were standing everywhere, waiting to be loaded into the cage. Empty chummins, greased and ready, waited for the short trip inbye to the loader-end of the Middle Main conveyor. I worked at the shaft for six months, coupling tubs together, *hanging on and knocking off* - new words to learn, new skills to acquire. No chance to play truant here. But men didn't do that anyway, and I was no longer a boy. Soon it was time to move on to timber leading, working with a pony. Again, a new expertise and vocabulary were needed. More words to remember: *'Beah'* for stop, and *'Bastard'* for when the pony refused to stop, and the timber tram jumped off the way (railway track). Then on to coal-putting, strenuous, back-breaking work, ever reliant upon your four-legged friend. This was piecework, when every full tub brought out to the flat meant another few pennies in the wage packet.

Soon I was eighteen, and it was time to go on the training face. Back to school again, but this time it was the back that did the work, not the brain. All aspects of pit work were taught: Drawing, Cutting, and Filling. Cutting was the worst; crawling on my belly in a three-foot seam, over a heap of duff spewed out by the sharp-toothed dragon of a machine; sticking in wooden chocks to prevent the coal face from settling; and all the while breathing in the dust that had killed Ashington miners for over a hundred years.

Fillers were the elite down the pit - the coal-eaters. Sets of about a dozen brawny young men attacked over one hundred yards of coal with their picks and shovels; hoyed the coal on to a moving rubber conveyor belt; got their timber in, then spent the rest of the eight-hour shift sharing a bit *crack* with their marras.

When I had finished my six-week's training, I was absorbed into a spare-man's set, which was a collection of odds and sods who were not attached to any of the regular sets. The first shifts spent filling were gruelling sessions. I had to conquer, not only the physical obstacles presented each day, but the mental torture that gnawed away in my head, frightening myself into thinking that every creak of a pitprop was the signal that the roof would collapse on top of me. It is bad enough working in tunnels deep under the earth away from fresh air and sunlight, but miners work with a mountain of rock half a mile high hanging over their heads. The strata above and around the workings are never still, but always exerting pressure on the roadways, twisting steel planks into the most grotesque shapes imaginable and breaking wooden timber into jagged splinters. The roadways were built to a stipulated height of five feet, but the constant pressure of the strata often heaved the floor up to within a couple of feet of the warped arch girders.

During one week I found myself on the same face as my father. By then he was a Deputy, in charge of the firing of shots and general safety of the men. There were cries of derision when he came along and helped me to fill off the last few yards of my *stretch*. "Oh, aye," my marra shouted, "got to get yor owld man to help ye oot, eh!" My face blushed crimson red under the coal dust. Coalfilling put thirty-two scars on my hands in two weeks; I sat for an hour one day when the belt was broken (as it often did) and counted the small

199

cuts and bruises which I had incurred getting the coals on to the conveyor. One day I was attempting to pick up a huge lump of coal when it broke into pieces just when I had it at shoulder height, and the force of the effort plunged a large jagged piece of coal into my face. My lip split into an ugly red slab, trapping a particle of coal which I carry to this day in my top lip - a blue scar medal which proves that I was once a miner.

While working on the coal face in the 1950s I had to get timber under the roof as soon as I filled away a yard of coal, but then, in the days before power loaders, there was always a stretch of roof - the cutter track - left unguarded. The majority of serious accidents were due to 'falls' of stone, where an undetected *cat* (a fossilised tree trunk) would fall and crush an unsuspecting miner. The coal faces of the post-war years got thinner and thinner as the better seams ran dry through over-production by the coal-owners, greedy for quick profits. This meant that I, and the other Ashington fillers, had to adopt a crouching position for much of the working day. I lay for hours at a stretch on my side or belly, using a pick and shovel in a space barely two-feet high from roof to floor. Cramp and stiffness of the joints soon became a regular feature of the day's work. (The arthritis that I have today can be traced back to that period) The long walk from the shaft to the coal face - average nearly a mile in 1925, but far longer in my days - had to be done doubled up so much that my hand could trail on the ground as I walked. Some men, including myself, hitched a ride on the back of tubs connected to the haulage system. As well as being illegal, it was highly dangerous, with moving wire ropes and run-away sets of coal providing only two of the hazards.

As the seams got deeper so the air deteriorated. Men worked stripped to the waist, losing pints of sweat in the space of a shift. Other mines were wet and cold, with water continuously oozing through crevices in the roof. Inflammable *firedamp*, or methane gas, caused terrible explosions year by year. In 1942 alone there were three serious explosions which claimed a total of eighty-two lives. A similar disaster in 1947 at the William pit in Whitehaven interred 105 men and boys in a cold, early grave. But barely a single day went past in the north-east coalfield when a miner *wasn't* maimed or killed. Again in 1942, there were 166,639 injuries to miners in the UK which caused them to lose three days or more of work. Earlier records for 1937 showed that 280 youths under sixteen were killed over a ten-year period, and 59,853 were seriously injured. It was bloody carnage on an unacceptable scale that somehow failed to make the headlines.

Indeed, the deaths went practically unreported. It did not make good news, especially to the fifty-one members of parliament in 1938 who held 109 directorships between them in iron, steel, coal and engineering companies. In the Conservative Party, mine-owners holding important places have *always* been amongst the most influential, the most vocal, and on many matters the most reactionary men of their day. Successive Prime Ministers Stanley Baldwin and Neville Chamberlain both came from families with long associations in steel and coal.

The mine-owners with their strong aristocratic connections have always understood the need of a powerful political organisation to back up their economic power. Their own organisation, the Mining Association, campaigned hard on every issue touching their profits or sovereignty. The Coal Mines Bill of 1938 gave the government power to compel reorganisation of the industry. But the coal baron insiders took advertising space in all the national newspapers, and circularised colliery shareholders and managements to agitate against the Bill. In the event, the Bill was considerably watered down. Part of it relating to coal royalties was also amended in favour of the coal-owners after a debate in the House of Lords, in which coal-owning peers like Lords Gainford and Dudley played leading roles.

The immediate post-war crisis of 1945/46 in the coal industry occupied huge chunks of newpaper column-inch, carrying claims issued by the Mining Association which alleged that absenteeism and laziness by the pitmen were at the root of the troubles in the industry. The Daily Telegraph closed one of its leading articles concerning the coal crisis by saying: *"An end must be made of all this trifling in the hour of the nation's need."* But the unwarranted space given to the coal-owners' views can be directly attributed to the traditional associations of some newspaper owners with mine ownership. Lord Kemsley, one of the Berry brothers who ran a powerful coal combine in South Wales, owned a fleet of newspapers nationwide, as well as the much-read local papers: the Newcastle Journal and Chronicle. Together with his brother, the family held directorships with the Daily Telegraph, Daily Sketch, Sunday Graphic, Western Mail, and Financial Times.

Editorials of these papers continuously put forward their ideas on all questions of politics as they affected the small and privileged groups to which they belonged. Forget the idea that the 'dirty-tricks brigade' has just been invented - the coal-owning Fleet Street barons had them all...and used them, ruthlessly.

Each quarter the men had to *cavil* for seams. In the Bothal Pit, the Yard Seam was considered to be a far better location than the Middle Main which was lower with an unpredictable roof. Cavilling was like taking a lucky dip. The name of each set leader was put in the overman's hat and he drew lots to see who went where. Good cavils were very precious to the fillers as they could make a big difference in take-home pay which in the early 1950s hovered around the £25 a week mark.

Keepybacks made up a high proportion of some miners' pocket money. On pay-day Fridays, men queued outside the Ashington Colliery Wages Department for their well-earned cash. Each man handed over his pay slip through a small window, and a cashier produced the individual wages wrapped up inside a small brass cup. Men who wanted to keep back a pound or two rummaged around on the floor for a pay check that showed two or three pounds less than their own. And this was presented to the wife on getting home. But pitmen's wives were not as green as they were cabbage looking, and many an argument followed if the husband was suspected of cheating on the family income. If the man was successful in duping his gullible spouse, he then had the problem of hiding his extra money. Toilet cisterns were only some of the ingenious hidey holes used by the men.

Allotments were being bulldozed beside North Seaton Road to make way for a new council estate. For a time, the area became a favourite haunt for small boys scavenging among the ruins of pigeon lofts and hen crees. My brother John, then a typical 12-year-old, and his friend, John Bell, rushed into our house in Chestnut Street one day shouting "Treasure! Treasure!" The two lads had stumbled upon a large biscuit box stuffed with crumbling ten-shilling notes and mouldy half dollars - over two hundred pounds in all. The horde was obviously the accumulation of many years keepybacks. The find was reported in the Newcastle Journal, and an embarrassed owner came forward to claim his money, saying he had *"forgotten it was there."* I often wondered if his wife believed him.

In 1954, after being five years a pitman, I decided that I wasn't meant to spend the best part of my life spitting out coal dust, so I handed in my notice. By then I was working with the Weddell twins at Coney Garth Drift whose long wedged snout stuck out into the green fields like a monster coming up for air. Not being qualified for anything, I looked at the prospect of joining one of Her Majesty's Services. I ended up in the RAF, signing on as a five-year regular.

When it came to choosing a trade, I was asked to take an IQ test, similar to that shown on the hilarious *'Frank Spencer'* TV series. Depending on how well you perform, you are offered a list of trades from which to choose. I must have done all right because I was shown a long list of titles ranging from Armaments to Telegraphist. The term *Radar Operator* struck me as being something which could be interesting, having seen all those black and white movies with young WAAFs plotting little arrows on a giant map. What I hadn't realised was that, although the radar aerials revolve on pretty, grassy hillocks, the radar cabins are hidden away from prying eyes, some fifty feet below the ground. Oh, no! After having spent most of my youth buried away in the pit, I was now sentenced to the same punishment for *another* five years.

I was demobbed from the RAF in August, 1959, having seen service in Germany, Cyprus during the Suez Crisis, and British West Hartlepool. I began looking for work immediately. In the Ashington Post I spotted a job going as a Wages Clerk at Ashington Colliery. That was perfect for me, I reckoned; no more going down below. My letter of application was posted at the Humber Terrace Post Office. Humber had been the original name of Hawthorn Road, but when it had changed, because of a technicality, the name of the Post Office had to remain unaltered. By then my mother had called a halt to our many moves and we lived at 187 Chestnut Street.

I sat back and waited for them to give me the job, filling in most of my spare time at Priestman's Institute where my potting improved immensely even if my immediate job prospects did not.

Two months later, when I was seriously considering re-enlisting for another five years, a letter dropped on to our doormat inviting me to go to the colliery office for an interview. The interviewer was Jack

Spowart, a kind man who put me at ease straight away. He said that a vacancy had come up, not as a Wages Clerk as advertised, but one which demanded a certain degree of accuracy with figures. No problem, I thought.

"What are you like at percentages, Michael?" he asked. "All right, I suppose," was my diffident reply. "Can you tell me what fifty per cent of a pound is?" I breathed a sigh of relief. If all the questions are as easy as this, I thought, then I'm quids in.

"Ten shillings," I proferred, confidently. "Very good," said Jack. "And twenty-five per cent of a pound?" Still easy! "Five shillings," I replied. "What about fifteen per cent?" he asked, gently. My face went red, and then redder. "Well...er...it's a long time since I did percentages, you know."

Jack smiled, but was not taken in. "Of course," he replied, "but I'm sure you'll soon get the hang of it when you start."

Start! I had the job. But I didn't even know what kind of job it was. Thoughts of my underground radar operating days flooded back. "Er, where exactly *is* the job?" I stammered. "It's at Duke Street Coal Depot, looking after the bagged coal deliveries. Seven o'clock Monday morning all right with you?"

It was still dark when I arrived at the miniscule cabin that was Duke Street Depot. Already a long line of lorries clogged up the narrow street, filling the air with suffocating fumes. The original manager, Jimmy Little, still occupied the gaffer's swivel chair. An enormous clock-faced weighing machine dominated the room next to Jimmy's desk. On the opposite wall was a welcoming coal fire. I settled into my seat and waited for instructions.

ASHINGTON COLLIERY'S TANKEYS

JOHN ELLIOTT served in the Coldstream Guards during the second war, and on being demobbed took a job as a fireman on locomotives with the London North Eastern Railway. He moved to the NCB in a similar capacity, and eventually ended up as Rail Traffic Controller at Ashington Colliery between 1960-80. It was an important position which had been successfully filled by Tommy Tapson and Tommy Temple before him. He stressed that tankeys not only satisfied an industrial need but also a social one, saying:

A blind eye was turned to those who had missed the last bus to Linton or Ellington as they mingled with the foreshift men on the Hirst platform. Wives, mothers and daughters also used this transport on Fridays to draw the menfolk's wages. During heavy falls of snow, the tankey - one was fitted with a snow plough - made many emergency journeys with stranded shoppers, as well as carrying much-needed domestic goods.

The main users of the tankeys, however, were the miners travelling to and from New Moor, Linton, and Ellington. The carriages then were ex-LNER stock. Some are still in use on private railways. They were worked 24 hours a day to a precise timetable. Another function was to supply all loading and tipping points with empty and full NCB and British Rail wagons. All movement was in the hands of Rail Traffic Control at Ashington Colliery.

BR often used 20-tonners, called Blues because of their colour. These were filled with household, industrial, and shipment coals. 24 tonners carried small coal for Power Plants; while POW's (Privately Owned Wagons) contained landsale coals for domestic use. The engines also brought in a steady supply of material needed to run the pit efficiently such as steel girders and pit props, not forgetting the choppy vans, used for transporting food for the many pit ponies. During Ashington Colliery's peak period of coal production in the 1960s, about thirty trainloads of coal were transported each day to all parts of the British Isles. Before the first war, coal was led via Coney Garth and Pegswood station, mainly directed to Doncaster.

If there was a shortage of NCB wagons then BR's stock had to be used, but this proved very expensive especially when a wagon had to be left loaded; this was known as demurrage. Many ploys were used to cover up this useage, trying to keep BR in the dark. Sometimes they found out, and sometimes they didn't. The supply of empty wagons was jeopardised in wintry conditions; points froze, as did the coal in the wagons. So solid was the frozen pack of coals that, at Duke Street Depot, a man had to literally jump into a wagon and hack away with a steel rod until a few pieces of coal crumbled then dropped into the lorries below. At other times a fire was lit under the trucks in an attempt to free the coals before they were lowered into the hoppers. Another hazard was the wind. Strong off-shore winds prevented ships from leaving or entering Blyth Port, and shipment was often halted. This meant that a backlog of wagons full of coal was held up. The only alternative was to tip the coals on one of the many sites allocated. Coal was loaded into lorries and stockpiled at New Moor fields; a costly operation, both to the Coal Board and the environment.

Stones and shale provided another major headache. They were driven in lorries to the Transporter at Lynemouth. A private contractor employed men to pick coal from the belt which fed stones from the tippling point. From there the shale was dumped on what was once part of the beautiful coastline of Lynemouth, known as Strawberry Hill. Another eyesore was the Ashington heap which was created by transporting buckets of shale on an overhead ropeway. These buckets could not keep pace with the shale coming from the Washer, so railway wagons were used to keep the shale bunkers clear. When the Washer ground to a halt so did the pit, and that is when the telephone lines became red-hot with the management wanting to know the reason why. No engine was allowed to pass the ropeway without filling this small standage with wagons; it was like feeding a donkey with strawberries!

Raw coal was led from Linton, Longhirst, Coneygarth, and Woodhorn to the Duke Hoppers at Ashington where it was tipped then fed by belt to the Washer or Coal Preparation Plant. It was cleared of stones then graded, making it one of the busiest points for tankeys in Ashington Colliery.

I had a good view of the coal hoppers while working at the extremely busy Duke Street Depot. Coal merchants were supplied, and NCB as well as private hauliers despatched coals to the boilers of hospitals, schools, and factories. By 1960, the Depot had a new manager when Billy Mason was promoted on the death of Jimmy Little. The late Tommy Tinkler moved in from Woodhorn Depot about the same time. Once there were no less than six of us beavering away in a room less than two square metres. But the worst blow came when our comforting coal fire was removed, only to be replaced by an electric night storage heater. It was a crazy situation. There we were, responsible for sending 2,000 tons of coal out of the depot yard every day, yet we had to rely on electricity to warm the place. At peak times a queue of lorries stretched up to the Harmonic Hall, making life miserable for the residents of that congested street, as the noisy, dirty vehicles trundled past their back doors every day.

John continued:

Most of the rail wagons inherited by the NCB were defective, especially when braking by hand. Once on the move such a wagon could only be stopped by letting it collide with another wagon or when derailed at the jack points. These points were always left open to prevent runaway wagons careering into adjacent running roads. Derailments were commonplace, needing the assistance of platelayers and often the crane. Empty wagons were quickly re-railed, but tankeys and full wagons needed the help of BR's crane and breakdown crew which was based at Greensfield Loco Shed in Gateshead. When called out, the Durham team brought three carriages with them which were used as a rest-room and for cooking meals. They were expensive, but the NCB was insured for breakdowns of this kind. Reasons for derailments were many, but some were never explained.

A set of carriages went a'main (loose) and crashed through New Moor and Portland level crossing gates before ploughing into a loco at Linton Colliery, killing the driver and fireman. One tankey fireman refused to go to the new sidings at Coneygarth during the hours of darkness because he was convinced it was haunted. I can just imagine me explaining to the colliery manager that the job hadn't been completed 'because of ghosts'.

LYNEMOUTH PIT ON FIRE

During the summer of '64 it became apparent that something was drastically wrong at Lynemouth Colliery. Temperatures in the lower level workings soared, making the miners' task an absolute hell. It happened when things had being going so well at the Ashington group's newest colliery which sent a milllion tons of coal to bank regularly each year.

A highly combustible situation was diagnosed a mile out to sea. It was decided to seal off a complete section of the pit, starving the burning workings of oxygen. It was hoped that this would avert a major fire occurring which could threaten the entire undersea coalfield; safety officers from other local pits supervised round-the-clock operations for six weeks. The ploy failed to keep the burning under control: the pit was on fire. In November of 1966 all of Lynemouth's 1,800 men were laid idle as a disaster was feared imminent. But there were still almost one hundred pit ponies to get out, and time was running out.

Management ordered that the fans be reversed to pump air to keep the ponies alive until they could be brought to the surface. But even before then, to get food to the animals, men had to trail bags of choppy underground from Woodhorn Colliery. Dougie Lewins was one of the men who helped with the operation, eventually getting the ponies to safety in the middle of the night. With the district sealed off it was hoped that that was the end of it, but worse was to come. On November 15th fumes from Lynemouth seeped into Woodhorn Pit and the men were laid idle for a week; on November 16th, Ellington Colliery withdrew men and ponies because of a build-up of fumes - this lasted nine days; on November 19th, fumes filtered into the Bothal Pit through the old Yard Seam workings which had been mined in the early 1920s - four men were overcome and had to be stretchered out from the Bentick Seam. It seemed for a time as though the Lynemouth fire would close all of the local pits.

Water pipes were laid from the shafts to the river at Lyneburn: the pit was to be flooded in a last desperate attempt to put out the fire. Four fire engines pumped non-stop until more than 200 million gallons of river and seawater filled the lower level workings. It was an imaginative engineering accomplishment which left the lower seams completely under water. Lynemouth Pit was officially closed on November 16th, and the last two men out were H Turnbull and Cush Todd, who had tended the pumps underground. Because of the threat to nearby Ellington Colliery, two new shafts were sunk, one of which was to be used as an escape route. No more coals were drawn from Lynemouth shaft.

A vast operation to open up a drift into the higher level of Lynemouth Colliery was set in motion. In the meantime, many of the Lynemouth men were found jobs in other pits, a few being retained in key positions until the pit re-opened. The first coals trickled to the surface up the massive Bewick Drift, built specially to avoid going into the lower levels. Lynemouth Colliery survived for a time, but coal production never reached anything like its projected targets and, inevitably, the pit closed in 1983.

If my visit as a teacher back down the pit taught me anything it was that I was glad to be out of it. The blackness and the smell hadn't changed, but the sense of camaraderie seemed to have gone, vanished into the stale air with the picks and shovels. The pits of the seventies seemed to be mechanised almost to the point of robotics. The men appeared to have lost the *feel* for the job along with the physical contact of the coal itself. It was the era of push-button mining. Another man who shared my view was yet one more 'pitman poet', Bill Coombs.

He voiced his feelings with the following, calling it *'The Pitman's Lament'*

They've tyen hard work from oot the pit,
Wor fathors wad have laughed,
Nee calloused hands on which t' spit
T' howld the greasy shaft.
Machines noo rive coal stretch b' stretch
And flacker not an inch,
But once bruised and tortured flesh

Weell knew the way t' flinch.
They've tyen the pownies oot as weell,
Replaced for gud nee doot,
B' noisy heartless things o' steel
T' bring the full-uns oot.
But Aa miss the steamin', heavin' flank
That Aa was wont t' pat,
When safely up the steepest bank
Me lab'rin' powny gat.
There's somethin' else forbye the graft
They'e tyen from oot the pit,
A thing caalled pride of work, a craft
That needs nee special wit,
Just applicashun, work, and will,
Wor fathors had that pride,
So its best ere sloth their spirits kill,
They, unbeknawin', died.

A report commissioned at a cost of £5,000 by Northumberland County Council, and published by Newcastle University in January 1973, told the miners of the town what they had known for years: *"The pits in the area are not employing as many men."* The figures showed that, between 1961 and 1970, the number of pit jobs registered at the local labour exchange dropped by 51 per cent. A warning was also given that there would be further colliery closures, and that by 1975, a record 15 per cent of the male population would be out of work.

One of the big problems was migration by young people. A big recruiting drive by the NCB resulted in scores of young men and their families moving to the more prosperous mines in the Midlands. In 1961 there had been 15,640 miners in the Ashington area but by 1970 the number had fallen to 8,276. Another major dilemma was that the proportion of the population aged 60 or over had risen from 15 to 21 per cent. The old town was beginning to feel its age. The report concluded: *"It will be better to spend money on new projects than help declining industry."*

In June, 1973, it was finally admitted that the pit heaps which had plagued the town for decades had to go. At a cost of £1 million, plans were approved which would give the go ahead for the removal of more than seven million cubic yards of shale, ash, and other toxic materials. The 740 acres involved included the aerial ropeway pit heap and the Woodhorn heap. When the huge operation was completed it was hoped that a vast 40-acre lake would be created surrounded by 60 acres of woodland which would attract tourists. Said Roy Nuttal, Town Clerk:

We are excited about the project. Our first priority is to make the area attractive to live in and then to attract business. The plan will disprove the image that some people have of Ashington.

Ashington Colliery's ropeway heap, half a mile long, quarter of a mile wide and 100 feet high, was the largest in Northumberland. It was intended to spread the waste material over an area of 570 acres. The project, which it was thought would take three years to complete, would create 138 acres of parkland, 376 acres of arable farmland, 38 acres of woods and 120 acres of grassland. The Department of the Environment were asked to approve the tender which qualified for an 85 per cent grant. The project was named the 'Queen Elizabeth II, Silver Jubilee Park', and was officially opened by the Queen Mother on October 18th, 1979.

Due to mounting public pressure, Ashington, long recognised as *'the biggest mining village in the world'*, held its first-ever Miners' Gala on June 14th, 1975. The Northumberland Miners' Picnics had been held since 1867, but mostly in Morpeth and Bedlington, although Newbiggin did play host once, on a rainy day in June, 1936. All police leave was cancelled to marshall the 1975 parade from Peoples Park led by the Brentford Nylons Band which had won the band contest the year before. Altogether, 12 bands took part in the competition. Not to be outdone, 15 jazz bands entertained the public at Hirst Park. Roy Jenkins was the main speaker, together with Shirley Williams, and miners' president, Joe Gormley.

Plans to pull down the Linton and Woodhorn Miners Hall were laid before the council on November 23rd, 1981. A big factor in the decision to demolish the building was that the pits after which the hall had been named had both closed: Linton in 1968, and Woodhorn in February, 1981.

MINERS STRIKE 1984/85

The years of 1984/85 were among the blackest in coal-mining history. An all-out strike by the country's miners was called by the NUM's leader, Arthur Scargill. The incredibly bad timing of the strike - high summer with immense stock-piles of coal lying all around the country - doomed it from the outset. As in the 1926 stoppage, public attitude soon became hostile. The 'winter of discontent' in the seventies had done nothing to raise the esteem of the pitmen's union as innocent families caught up in the strike saw their electricity switched off, and businessmen watched impotently as their factories were plunged into a 3-day week.

Apart from the hardship that the twelve-month stoppage brought to the town there were far more insidious repercussions, with father set against son, family against family, friend against friend. But the miners' wives stood solidly behind their men. Gwen Newton, who edited some of the women's stories of the stoppage, had this to say when the strike first flared alight:

We were just ordinary housewives when our men came out on strike. We came from different backgrounds, but with one thing in common: our men were miners and we were proud of them. Nearly everyone in our community has someone who has worked at the pit. There comes a time when you have to say something. Ashington will soon be a ghost town if we do not do something about it. I think a lot of women realised this and we were all behind our men, all the way.

Months passed and the bickering continued. Mrs Thatcher's man, Ian McGregor, proved to be stronger than his frail physique suggested, holding out against the doubtful tactics of Scargill and the so-called flying pickets. Nationwide condemnation followed when the NCB chairman was seen on TV to be bundled over a fence at Ellington Colliery by a sudden surge of pickets. It was a pathetic attempt at mob rule which lost them many friends. In mitigation, many of the men who caused much of the trouble did not come from any of the north-east's pits and some, indeed, were not miners at all.

In the end, all confidence in their leader gone, the Ashington and Ellington miners trudged back to work, as did their forebears of 1926, no better off. But the main difference between the two strikes was reflected when hundreds of Ashington's disillusioned miners took the golden handshake of redundancy and left the industry. In 1926 there had been no such luxury. The strike of 1984/85, with its resultant exodus of men from the pit, damaged the future of an already ageing town which now found a predominant portion of its male population over fifty years of age out of work and without any further hope of future employment.

On March 25th, 1988, the unthinkable, yet inevitable, happened when Ashington Colliery, around which the very town itself had been built, ceased to bring any coal to bank. It was a move which had been forecast back in the 1950s, but was no more palatable for all that. For many years it had been running at a loss. Manager, Tom Burns, who had also been in at the demise of Bates Colliery in 1986, commented philosophically:

The pit was not viable - it had to close. What we have to ensure is that something else is developed on the site. The saddest thing about the closure is the lack of opportunies for employment in Ashington now.

In line with British Coal policy, no compulsory redundancies were involved, and of the 346 men on the books when the closure was announced, only 78 opted to leave the industry. In the last full year 1986/87, 554 men produced 306,652 tonnes. At its peak in the 1960s Ashington Colliery was producing one million tonnes a year. When asked about the future of the site, a British Coal spokesman said:

Talks have been held with Wansbeck Council, which is keen to see the site developed for light industry. It is possible that funding could be available for such a project from British Coal Enterprise.

Folk hero Jackie Milburn was present to shake the hands of the last shift of Ashington Colliery workers as they came to bank. I interviewed the modest man in his home at Bothal Terrace in June, 1988 - the last person to do so. It was to get material together to write a musical on his life. Sadly, he died on October 11th, unaware that the script of *'Wor Jackie'* had won a major award from London Weekend Television. At his funeral, three days later, the route the cortege took from Ashigton to Newcastle was lined with mourners; grown men were seen openly weeping. Thousands of fans blocked the Newcastle streets around St Nicholas Cathedral. With the end of Ashington Colliery coinciding with the death of its favourite son, a remarkable era had come to an end. The legend lives on.

"Wor Jackie"

Jackie Milburn! He's.....
Venerable Bede
in a black 'n' white strip.
Saint Cuthbert
in an England cap, and
Saint Aidan
in a pair of size six football boots, all rolled into one.

He's.....
Bonnier than Bobby Shaftoe,
Bigger than the Lambton Worm.

Whey...the man's a legend.

Extract from 'Jackie Milburn in Black and White' by Mike Kirkup

EPILOGUE

Many illustrious historians have pilloried the early operation of the mines. They have highlighted the abysmal existence of small boys crouching in the blackness of narrow roads, opening doors to let the drivers past, terrified by dark, loneliness and rats; pitmen hewing and shovelling among foul water and stone dust, denied the most elementary safety precautions, their families housed in hovels where coal owners would not stable their horses; punished by eviction when they dared to complain against their inhuman conditions. This was the early history of the mines as noted by Marx, Engels and the Webbs.

And it has become obvious from my own experience and recent research that Ashington's coalminers and their families *never* had the rewards that should have been theirs by right. Pre-nationalisation, there were so many wasted years of neglect, when time almost stood still, when no progress of any kind was made in remedying the social injustices which pervaded the town. The coal owners had every opportunity to provide better conditions for the miners and to ensure efficiency in the mines. Yet wages remained low, technical development lagged far behind other countries, expenditure on research by the industry was negligible, and only profits and dividends were advancing. So long as the coal kept flowing, the coal industry took so much, but gave so little in return. And when they eventually tore out the pits, they tore out the heart of whole communities.

Apportioning blame is too easy. Ignorance and lack of education condemned our forefathers to work in the pit. No-one should depend for a living in an occupation which threatens their very lives. Ineptitude and exploitation by the 'masters', left the workforce suffering the squalor and deprivation of soil middens and open drains, and they endured the huge tips without a voice to air their grievances.

In a fascinating interview with entrepreneur Sir John Hall, he expressed his thoughts:

I used to say to my father: "Why don't you vote Communist, and change the bloody system? It's wrong!" "Lad," he said, "the communists will never do anything for you and me; for the Party, 'Yes', but not the individual." I used to think that he wasn't wise, but full of wisdom, and it wasn't until many years later that I knew what he meant. Our parents never had anything; they were a section of society who missed out; they never had the good times; they always had the bad times. They had a few good years with the Labour government after the War, and then when the pits got into trouble they were the first to suffer. The wages they did have were poor. Miners got a week's holiday, then a fortnight's holiday - so what! They didn't have any money - perhaps a few quid in the Store Bank. But they had no chance to save; they couldn't save, not like today when people have surplus income.
Whole generations of my family were in mining; my grandfather helped to build the shaft at North Seaton Colliery; my father worked as a filler, after having gone through all the tasks of datal hand and putter. In the end - and this is what made me disillusioned with the pits - he was moved from North Seaton when it closed, to Newbiggin, then to Woodhorn, then Ellington. Like the other miners, he was told by Robens, then NCB chief, to keep moving on, to go where the jobs were. Father died on £12 a week and a pound a week pension; my mother had his Certificate for 50-years service, and I have it now. And I wonder: what was it all for? Their generation definitely missed out.

Inevitably, one feels angry, like Sir John, when covering past ground. But now it is time to look forward. Ashington children are growing up with far more freedom to do what they want. They face new challenges, and need to find new ways of doing things for themselves. But always looking ahead, never back; always vigilant, on the look-out for opportunities for *their* children.

Ashington, as we have seen, has changed; as time goes by it will change again...but it must never be forgotten that it was once *the biggest mining village in the world.*

Michael Kirkup. 1993.

BIBLIOGRAPHY

Bibby, Roland, Bothal Observed.

Charlton, C., Cissie.

Feaver, W., Pitmen Painters.

Gormley, Joe, Battered Cherub.

Heinemann, Margot, Britain's Coal.

Hetherington, G., Ashington Colliery Past and Present.

Hough & Richards , Battle of Britain.

Kelly's Directory of Ashington, 1927.

Leifchild, J.R., Coal and Coal Towns.

Newton, Gwen, We are Women.

Purnell's History of Twentieth Century.

Reed, Fred, An Undine Overture.

Wallis, J., History of Northumberland. 1769.

Northumberland County Records Office.

Royal Commission Children in Mines, 1842.

Ashington & District Advertiser, 1940-70.

Ashington & Hirst Press, October 1909.

Ashington Post, 1944.

Building News, 1913.

Newcastle Daily Journal, August 1916.

Newcastle Journal & Chronicle, 1972-92.

Newcastle North Mail, Sept, 1926.

Newcastle Weekly Chronicle, 1873.

Newspost Leader, 1990-92.

St.George's Gazette, 1916.

Sporting Chronicle, 1952.

BIBLIOGRAPHY

Ashington Coal Co. Log, 1889-1939.

Ashington Colliery Magazines ,1920-40.

Ashington Grammar School Log, 1959-

Ashington Hospital Report, 1926-27.

Ashington Mining School Log, 1931.

Ashington Operatic Society, 1982.

Ashington YMCA Scrapbook.

Bothal School Centenary Booklet, 1973.

Central Hall Souvenir Booklet.

Northumberland Miners Association Circular, 1916.

Northumberland Miners Union Centenary.

Pegswood Colliery School Log, 1877.

Proctor, Keith, Cinemas of Ashington.

Salvation Army History.

St. Aidan's School Log, 1931-51.

St. John's Seaton Hirst Booklet, 1949.

Thompson, Bob, History of Ashington F.C.

Wanless, Colin, South to Welbeck.

Warn, C.S., Buses in Northumbria.

Wise, D.J., Presbyterianism in Ashington.

The diaries of Tom Boutland and George Caisley, together with the scrapbooks of many individuals mentioned in the text.

IMPORTANT DATES

1842 Wm Dickenson sinks bore hole at Black Close.

1844 Northumberland coal owners introduce Monthly Bond which sparks off 20 week strike.

1846 Duke of Portland awards lease for Pity Me.

1847 A parliamentary bill for better ventilation of mines is ridiculed by 'coal kings'.

1849 Shaft sunk at Fell 'em Doon and named 'Portland West Hartley Colliery'.

1859 North Seaton colliery opens. Wooden railway bridge built over Wansbeck.

1861 Mines Inspection Bill now in force. Hewers' wages four shillings per shift.

1862 Hartley Disaster - 204 men and boys killed. Second outlet from pit became compulsory.

1863 Northumberland Miners' Union founded.

1866 First picnic at Polly's Folly, Shankhouse.

1867 Bothal downcast shaft sunk. Jonathan Priestman becomes major shareholder of Ashington Coal Co. with William Milburn.

1873 Carl Pit shafts sunk. Bothal school opened.

1874 Thomas Burt elected MP for Morpeth.

1876 Wesleyan chapel built. Ashington New Pit Co-op formed.

1877 Miners locked out for refusal to arbitrate on question of free house and coal. Further lockout due to refusal to accept 12 per cent reduction in wages.

1885 Duke Downcast shaft sunk. Charles Fenwick elected MP for Wansbeck, becoming first miner to go straight from coalface to Westminster.

1886 Ashington Rugby Club formed. Duke of Portland gives £150 towards building of Recreation Hall. Ashington coal shipped to Blyth 144,983 tons.

1887 Holy Sepulchre church consecrated.

1888 Ashington becomes its own parish.

1889 Jonathan Priestman dies. Ashington Football Club formed.

1890 Bothal Upcast shaft sunk. John Marshall becomes first Ashington policeman; salary £80 plus boots.

1891 Robert Booth dies, succeeded by Edmond Southern as manager of Ashington Colliery. Fred Booth starts as assistant surveyor.

1892 Portland Hotel built. ACC agree with Portland manager, Thomas Forbes, for use of his large hall every Wednesday for miners' meetings. Ashington Cricket Club formed.

1893 T B Dixon builds sewer from New Hirst to river Wansbeck. Coal tonnage now going to Blyth 729,247.

1894 Grand Hotel built. Miners theatre built. St. Aidan's R.C. school built. Floods bring down Sheepwash Bridge. Telephone link made with Woodhorn Colliery.

1895 Fifth Row houses destroyed in fire.

1896 Ashington Urban D Council formed. Work begins on Linton Colliery.

1897 Harmonic Hall building commences. St. John's church, Seaton Hirst, consecrated. Constables in newly-built Police Station to receive one cartload of coal a month in consideration of giving protection to Company's property.

1898 Hirst Mixed School (the North) opened. H Boutland first leader of Harmonic Band. Woodhorn Colliery shaft sunk. Colliery house waiting list now 5yrs. 3 mths.

1899 Coal output at Ashington Colliery 960,271 tons. Russell Cook opens shop at Grand Corner.

1900 North Seaton added to Hirst. Ashington Aged Miners' Homes built. Dr. Seaton of Ashington paid extra £20 per annum on account of large number of accidents at New Hirst.

1901 Census shows that population of Ashington has risen in 100 years from 88 to 13,972.

1902 First workingmen's clubs open : Grand Street, West End and New Hirst (Mortimer).

1905 St. Aidan's RC church built.

IMPORTANT DATES

1908   South School opened.

1909   Princess Ballroom opened December 22nd. Royal Club erected on site of Dr. Goldie's house, later changed its name to Universal. Ellington Betty pit sunk, June 4th. Stakeford Bridge built.

1910   Eight Hours Agreement came into operation.

1911   Miners strike against three-shift working. Hippodrome Theatre opened July 18th.

1912   Minimum Wage strike.

1913   Hirst East school opened. Ellington Colliery draws coal for the first time. First agreement for men operating cutting machines.

1914   Great War begins and 12,000 Northumberland pitmen enlist. John Craigs lays foundation stone for new Ashington Infirmary. Wallaw Pictures Ltd formed by Walter Lawson, directors: Frank Marshall, John Craigs Jnr, J Gibson and McKenzie, painter and decorator.

1915   Eight-hour shift suspended owing to urgent demand for coal. Ashington Aerodrome opens on Longhirst Road.

1916   Ashington Hospital opened with 39 beds. Thirteen men killed in Woodhorn explosion. Ashington Male Voice Choir formed. Teachers in Ashington "Starving on less than one pound a week." Miners' Picnic not held, but rally at Peoples Park makes plea for nationalisation of mines.

1919   Death of Charles Fenwick, Wansbeck MP for 32 years. Ebby Edwards stands for vacant seat but loses by 547 votes. Sankey Report recommends mining industry be nationalised and a six-hour day for miners. The Seven Hour Act passed into law.

1920   Tynemouth Water Co in control of water supply. Hirst Welfare field bought from Milburn Estates - 13 sq acres at 32 shillings an acre. Ashington Operatic Society's first production 'HMS Pinafore'. Levy of one penny per ton on all coal sales to go towards new Welfare Fund.

1921   Miners out on strike for 13 weeks. Wages reduced by two shillings per shift. Ashington population reaches high of 29,000.

1922   Ashington Coal Company begins work on welfares in Ashington, Hirst, Linton and Ellington. Death of Thomas Burt. G H Warne elected MP for Wansbeck.

1923   Bob Smillie elected MP for Morpeth on death of John Cairns. Constitutional Club is the last of 22 workingmen's clubs built in Ashington.

1924   Plans laid for 200 houses to be built at a new village to be called 'Lynemouth'. Wembley Field laid to coincide with opening of Exhibition at Wembley stadium in London.

1925   Thirty-eight men and boys killed at Montagu. Average wage for underground datal hands : four shillings and sevenpence a shift.

1926   Owners seek to enforce a reduction in miners' wages. Strike lasts from May to December. New houses built at Linton and Lynemouth. Chairman of Ashington UDC: John Wallace, Medical Officer of Health: Dr Matthew Bruce, Inspector of Police: Thomas Scott, Railway Station Manager: John Aitcheson.

1927   Coals drawn from new Lynemouth Colliery. Twenty seven Ashington fish shops now trading. Top of the league for accidents to boys down Ashington pit is "Being run over with tubs."

1928   Death of G H Warne MP for Morpeth succeeded by George W Shield.

1930   Ellington Pit baths - first in Northumberland. Ashington Colliery's 'buzzer-time' ends. Ashington Institute opened by Manny Shinwell.

1931   Seven and a half hour Coal Mines Act passed. Death of A G Crook, secretary of Miners Federation. Death of George Arrowsmith whose shop dominated the Grand Corner for over 50 years.

1932   First Ashington & District Advertiser printed. Electric wiring installed in 118 Ashington colliery houses at a cost of £2. 18s. 0d. each. Former Hirst East schoolboy J R Richardson plays leading part in Newcastle United's controversial FA Cup win. Pit Pony races at Peoples Park.

IMPORTANT DATES

1934 Water connected to officials' houses in 7th Row. Ist Row houses already connected. Duke St. Depot opens. Jimmy Little - manager. April - Florrie Ford stars at Miners Theatre. Report on Nutrition reveals that miners should have an intake of 4,600 calories a day.

1935 Bob Taylor elected MP for Morpeth and held seat until he died in 1954. First safety helmet worn at Ashington pit. Nichol, Trobe and Fitzpatrick buy Harmonic Hall for £1,400 with lease on Billiard Room of £1 per week.

1936 Dog racing begins at Portland Park. Northumberland worst county in England for overcrowding of 60,000 working class families.

1938 Agreement on miners' holidays with pay. 2,125 pits now operating in UK, a drop of over one third in twenty-five years. Coal industry only attracts £18 million investment compared with four times that amount for retailing. Survey shows that fifty-one MPs held 109 directorships in coal and allied industries.

1939 Second War starts - pupils taught privately. First air raid alert in Ashington, lasts for one-and-a-half hours, in December. Miners' Theatre becomes the Regal Cinema, North Seaton Colliery band make it a hat-trick of victories at Miners Picnic.

1940 Wallaw Pictures shows 'Pinocchio' film for first time, price fourpence for children, sevenpence for adults. Plane crashes on 5th Row. German plane brought down at Cresswell. Cosa Maite champion greyhound at Portland Park. BSA motorbikes cost £49. 10s. 0d. at J Main's. Hirst Progressive Club donates £100 to War Effort. Frank Millican, union secretary, gives talk on 'Working after the siren blows'. WAAF recruitment at Ashington Employment Exchange.

1941 Ashington miners receive no pay on February 21st owing to severe snow storm. Two land mines explode at Sheepwash. 'Advertiser' closes for duration. Compulsory pit inspections introduced. Coal mining now 'Essential Work'. Bombs drop on Woodhorn Colliery fan and at Coney Garth Farm.

1942 Greene Award adds 2s. 6d. per shift to all underground workers above 21 years. Bombs drop at Sparrow House farm. White paper says that increased coal output could be achieved by concentrating more men in the more productive pits and seams.

1943 Secret ballot made in December to decide which men are to be conscripted into pits. Incendiary bombs drop on Long Row.

1944 Miners' Hostel at Ashington caters for influx of 'Bevin Boys'. Porter Award announced. Hartford Hall opens as rehabilitation centre for miners. Last of 237 air alerts in Ashington. Priestman Group now includes Ashington Coal Company, and owns seven pits in Durham as well as the five in Ashington.

1945 Formation of National Union of Mineworkers. Alf Robens elected MP for Wansbeck (later Blyth). Ashington Business and Professional Women's Club formed with Eva Stimpson as first president.

1946 First post-war Picnic held at Morpeth. George 'Dusty' Down becomes first Ashington sprinter to win gold medal at Powderhall. Tom McLain (Penrith of Linton) wins big sprint at Morpeth and John Nixon (Marks of Ashington) wins 80yards dash.

1947 January 1st, Vesting Date under Coal Nationalisation Act. UK coal-owners to get £66 million in compensation. May - Introduction 5-day week. French children stay with members of Larry Bell's Boys' Club. Liz Taylor stars in 'Lassie' at Wallaw, and prices now increased to ninepence for adults. Ashington Male Voice Choir gets new conductor : Mr. Jack Dawes. Berwick of Ashington (Jack Thompson) wins big 'un at Morpeth Olympic Games and Jim Williamson gets 80yard title. Ashington Council now in full charge of ground at Portland Park. Best selling record at Grierson's Station Road record shop : 'Oh, My Beloved Father' sung by Joan Hammond. December - National Wages Increase.

IMPORTANT DATES

1948 "Butlins at Filey is favourite resort for Ashington miners" says spokesman at J Chrisp, booking agent. Price of 8-day holiday : Ashington to Ireland £14. 17s. 6d. at Weatherstone's Travel Agents, 2 Park Road. Aluminium bungalow allocation for Ashington cut from 200 to 80. Homeless women complain of conditions at North Seaton Hall.

1949 Jackie Milburn and Jimmy Jackson, both from Hirst East school, capped for England soccer teams, senior and boys. Rediffusion broadcasting system connected to many Ashington homes at weekly rental of two shillings. Ashington now has 20,000 voters. Unveiling ceremony at Ashington Hospital of 1939-45 War Memorial. Council deplores indiscriminate dumping of refuse in Hirst back alleys. Ashington Co-op pays dividend of two shillings and threepence in the pound. Coney Garth Drift opened.

1950 James Bowman becomes Chairman of Northern Division of National Coal Board. Frankie Millican appointed Labour Director. Bob Main, secretary of Ashington Mineworkers' Federation, becomes General Secretary of Northumberland NUM. Ashington FC go out of FA Cup in front of almost 14,000 fans.

1951 Second increase in Wages Agreement - miners head table of industrial workers' earnings.

1952 Inception of Mineworkers' Pension Scheme. Transfer of Welfare Schemes to Coal Industry Social Welfare Organisation (CISWO). Ashington population now 28,470. NCB apprentice, John Sinclair, wins British Youth Billiard Championship.

1953 Television set installed in Excelsior Club. Longhirst Drift opened.

1954 Will Owen elected MP for Morpeth. John Minoughan wins Ashington Flower Show sprint.

1955 Jackie Milburn scores Wembley goal in record time and picks up his third FA cup-winners' medal in four seasons. Prime Minister Anthony Eden visits Lynemouth. River Wansbeck blocked by ice, January 23rd.

1956 James Bowman appointed Chairman of National Coal Board - knighted in following year. Ashington goes on TV Top Town trail. Bothal Drift opened in Colliery yard.

1957 Ashington Old People's Festival and Exhibition begins. Area Workshops begin to clear site, June 25th. Fire guts Grand Street Club, March 31st.

1958 Conchi billiard table removed.

1959 Compensation scheme for miners compulsorily retired at 65 or over. Billy Gray wins FA Cup medal with Nottingham Forest.

1960 New cricket pavilion built at Langwell.

1961 Divisional Engineering and Mechanisation Centre (Area W/Shops) opens at Ashington. Alf Robens takes chair of NCB on retirement of Sir James Bowman. Dickie Freeman wins four individual club Leek Shows.

1962 Inception of Inter-divisional Transfer Scheme for miners. Mechanics unofficial strike. Hippodrome and Pavilion cinemas close as Jack Richardson introduces daytime Bingo. New legislation sees dozens of 'little men' opening betting shops on corner-ends. New road from Cooper's Shop to Sheepwash Bridge opens at a cost of £25,000. 27 houses demolished in west end as part of new town development. Fred Trueman brings international cricket to Ashington. New Midland Bank opens on Station Bridge, manager Alan Proud. Work begins on colliery house modernisation in Hirst. New post office built - has been on present site since 1923. Proposals made for new Wansbeck area to merge Ashington with Newbiggin and Bedlington.

1963 Universal Club renovation costs £30,000.

1964 Over 3,000 fans see Rohan Kanhai testimonial. Ashington shopgirls - apart from the Co-op - win five-day week. The Three Ones becomes Ashington's first nightclub on May 8th.

1965 Rohan Kanhai and Colin Cairns set record opening stand at Langwell Crescent of 242.

IMPORTANT DATES

1966 Charlton Brothers, Bob and Jack, get heroes' welcome on return from winning the World Cup. MP Will Owen returned with increased majority. Lynemouth Colliery fire - everyone evacuated. NCB to dump 400,000 tons of waste from coastal collieries , such as Lynemouth and Newbiggin, into the North Sea. Cost of haircuts in Ashington rises to three shillings and sixpence. After closure of the pit, it is announced that the entire village at North Seaton Colliery is unfit for human habitation.

1967 Buffalo Cinema closed. NCB spend £780,000 on new coal preparation plant at Ashington, but pit is still classed as having a 'doubtful future'. July : Ashington Hospital opens maternity unit.

1969 Station Bridge strengthened. Last shift worked at Longhirst, March 14th.

1970 Cosmopolitan Social Club becomes first of Ashington's 22 clubs to close. George Grant, miner, takes over from MP Will Owen who is involved in leaked secrets scandal.

1971 Ashington Colliery Band win their first ever prize under that name at Miners' Picnic. Ashington FC grandstand burned down, October 31st. Derek Ezra takes over as NCB chairman.

1972 Alcan aluminium smelter commenced. NUM call their first national strike.

1973 United Bus Company premises enlarged. Grand Hotel demolished, April 2nd. New Leisure Centre opens in Ashington, and so does Riverside Park. Clearance begins of unsightly pit heaps.

1974 Ted Heath puts British industry on 3-day week because of miners' overtime ban. Death of Andy McLaughlin - Pitmen's Boxing Champion. Ashington finally merges with Newbiggin and Bedlington to form new Wansbeck Council. Miners Strike from February 10th, with 81 per cent in favour, 19 percent against. Heath loses 'Who governs Britain?' election. A £45 minimum pay for faceworkers puts the miners at the top of the pay league once more.

1975 Northumberland Miners Gala held at Ashington for the first time. New Grand Street club re-opened May 16th.

1977 J Normanton Barron dies in February.

1978 Death of William Nixon Craigs, MC, aged 86.

1979 Miners basic wage now £84.95.

1981 Woodhorn Colliery closes in February. Arthur Scargill succeeds Joe Gormley as President of NUM.

1982 Wallaw Cinema show its last movie, August 2nd.

1983 New War Memorial unveiled in Library Park. Jack Thompson, mining engineer for 39 years, becomes MP for Wansbeck. Lynemouth pit closes.

1984 Death of George Grant, former Wansbeck MP. National strike by miners but Nottinghamshire men stay at work.

1985 Miners go back to work after almost a year's stoppage.

1988 Ashington Colliery closes in March. Death of Jackie Milburn in October.

1989 Central Hall demolished.

1990 Experimental ban of Station Road traffic. Neil Kinnock opens Woodhorn Colliery Museum.

1992 April 9th, Labour's Jack Thompson voted back into Parliament, but Neil Kinnock quits. Wansbeck councillors "concerned over plans to have more opencast mining in the area". Central Hall site used for car-boot sale. June : Miners Gala comes to Woodhorn Colliery for the first time. October 13th: Thirty one pits to close, but Ellington gets reprieve.

Costumes - Blouses - Frocks
Baby Wear - Etc. Etc.

SEE THE NEW SPRING STYLES
AT
WALKER'S

15, STATION ROAD - ASHINGTON

HOLIDAY TRAVEL, 1938.

CRUISES

To Mediterranean, Madeira and Canary Islands, Norway and Northern Capitals
From £1 per Day.

MOTOR - COACH - TOURS

In Scotland, Ireland and Wales.   Also South Coast of England
From £4 - 7 - 6 for 7 Days

Passages booked to or from any part of the World.   Reduced fares to Australia and United States

Motor Coach Bookings to any part of the Country.
Seats Reserved Free   -   No Booking Fees

If you are considering a good holiday this year consult your local Agent

JOHN CRAIGS & CO., LTD.
Post Office Chambers, Ashington.

MIKE KIRKUP

Mike Kirkup left St. Aidan's School at fifteen to go down the Bothal Pit at Ashington Colliery. Beginning as a shaft-boy, he then worked with ponies as a timber leader and putter before graduating to filling on the coal face.

He left the pits after five years and after a number of jobs he passed his teacher training certificate at Newcastle College of Education in 1973.

He began to write musical plays while at Ashington High School. Together with Head of Music, Derek Hobbs, he wrote 'The Greatest Show on Earth' which has played at numerous venues over the last ten years.

For his script of the stage musical 'Wor Jackie', the Northumberland Theatre Company benefited from a major award from London Weekend Television.

His subsequent television documentary, 'JET', won for Tyne Tees the 1990 Royal Television Society's Rose Bowl for Best Regional Programme.

Since becoming chairman of the Friends of Woodhorn Museums, Mike has written a number of books on local history, among them 'The Pitmen's Derby', the history of the Northumberland Plate.

At the minute he is busy collating short stories by miners about mining which he hopes to publish soon.

Also written by Mike Kirkup:

Song of the Coal
The Greatest Show on Earth (*Rossleigh Music*)
Sticks 'n' Stones
JET, Tyne Tees TV tribute to Jackie Milburn
Jackie Milburn in Black & White (*Stanley Paul*)
The Pitmen's Derby (*MidNAG*)
Tide Lines (*Druridge Bay Campaign*)
Gallowa, story of a pit pony (*Woodhorn Press*)
Blood on the Coal (*performed by Northumberland Youth Theatre*)